THE QUESTION OF COMPETENCE IN THE EUROPEAN UNION

The Question of Competence in the European Union

Edited by
LOÏC AZOULAI

OXFORD
UNIVERSITY PRESS

OXFORD
UNIVERSITY PRESS

Great Clarendon Street, Oxford, OX2 6DP,
United Kingdom

Oxford University Press is a department of the University of Oxford.
It furthers the University's objective of excellence in research, scholarship,
and education by publishing worldwide. Oxford is a registered trade mark of
Oxford University Press in the UK and in certain other countries

First Edition published in 2014
Impression: 1

Published in the United States of America by Oxford University Press
198 Madison Avenue, New York, NY 10016, United States of America

British Library Cataloguing in Publication Data
Data available

Library of Congress Control Number: 2013950753

ISBN 978–0–19–870522–2

Printed and bound in Great Britain by
CPI Group (UK) Ltd, Croydon, CR0 4YY

Contents

II. THE ALLOCATION OF COMPETENCES IN EU PRACTICE

III. THE EUROPEAN COURT OF JUSTICE AND THE QUESTION OF COMPETENCE

IV. POLITICAL AND LEGAL LIMITS TO EU COMPETENCES

Table of Cases

EUROPEAN UNION CASES

Court of Justice

General Court

NATIONAL CASES

France (Constitutional Council)

Germany (Federal Constitutional Court)

Ireland (High Court)

Poland (Polish Constitutional Tribunal)

UK

US (US Supreme Court)

List of Abbreviations

AG	Advocate General
CCP	Common Commercial Policy
CFSP	Common Foreign Security Policy
DCT	Draft Constitutional Treaty
EC	European Community
ECB	European Central Bank
ECHR	European Convention on Human Rights
ECJ	European Court of Justice
ECR	European Court Reports
EEC	European Economic Community
EU	European Union
OJ	Official Journal
TEU	Treaty on European Union
TFEU	Treaty on the Functioning of the European Union

List of Contributors

Loïc Azoulai Professor of European Law, EUI

Olivier Beaud Professor of Public Law, Paris II Panthéon-Assas University

Roland Bieber Emeritus Professor of European Law, Lausanne University

Sanja Bogojević Associate Professor in Environmental Law, University of Lund

Lena Boucon Researcher in European Law, EUI

Marise Cremona Professor of European Law, EUI

Edouard Dubout Professor of Public Law, Paris-Est Créteil University

Xavier Groussot Professor of European Law, University of Lund

Hans-W. Micklitz Professor of Economic Law, EUI

François-Xavier Millet Associate Professor of Public Law, University of Toulouse-Capitole

Giorgio Monti Professor of Competition Law, EUI

Robert Schütze Professor of European Law, Durham University

Christiaan Timmermans Former Judge at the European Court of Justice

Guillaume Tusseau Professor of Public Law, Sciences-po Paris

Introduction: The Question of Competence

Loïc Azoulai

An understanding of the distribution of powers between the Union and its Member States and among the Union institutions is the mainstay of any study on European Union constitutional law. From its inception, the law of European integration has been said to deal mainly with 'the matter of defining spheres of competence and power relationships'.[1] It covers issues such as the delimitation of the areas of competence conferred on the Union (its jurisdiction; the nature of its competences whether exclusive or shared with the Member States) and the principles governing the exercise of these competences (the doctrine of pre-emption, the subsidiarity and proportionality principles). It also deals with matters such as the division of powers, both between Union institutions themselves and between the Union and national bodies in the implementation of Union acts. All these matters are regarded as issues of 'competence'. All refer to the problem of the coexistence of different political entities within a larger polity to which they are bound up and as such may readily be cast in 'federalist' terms.[2] And yet, two excellent authors have noted that '[u]ntil the end of the 1990s, there had been astonishingly little research on the system of the Communities' competences. Legal literature on competence issues had almost exclusively focused on Article 235 EEC Treaty'.[3] Isn't it a paradox

[1] P. Pescatore, *The Law of Integration. Emergence of a new phenomenon in international relations, based on the experience of the European Communities* (Leiden: Sijthoof, 1974), 26.

[2] On the comparison between Europe and US Federalism, see E. Stein, 'On Divided-Power Systems: Adventures in Comparative Law' (1983) 10 *Legal Issues of Economic Integration* 27; J. Temple Lang, 'European Community Constitutional Law: The Division of Powers between the Community and the Member States' (1988) 39(3) *Northern Ireland Legal Quarterly* 209; K. Nicolaidis and R. Howse (eds.), *The Federal Vision. Legitimacy and Levels of Governance in the United States and the European Union* (Oxford and New York: Oxford University Press, 2001). See more broadly B. Dubey, *La répartition des compétences au sein de l'Union européenne à la lumière du fédéralisme suisse: systèmes, enjeux et conséquences* (Geneva: Helbing & Lichtenhahn; Brussels: Bruylant; Paris: L.G.D.J., 2002); R. Schütze, *From Dual to Cooperative Federalism. The Changing Structure of European Law* (Oxford: Oxford University Press, 2009).

[3] A. von Bogdandy and J. Bast, 'The Federal Order of Competences', in A. von Bogdandy and J. Bast (eds.), *Principles of European Constitutional Law* (Oxford: Hart Publishing; Munich: Beck, 2011), 276. See, however, pointing to this effort of systematization, V. Constantinesco, *Compétences et pouvoirs dans les Communautés européennes. Contribution à l'étude de la nature juridique des Communautés* (Paris: Pichon & Durand-Auzias, 1974); K. Lenaerts, *Le juge et la Constitution aux*

that a matter central to the development of a legal system has not been explored further and properly systematized?

In the context of European integration, the question of competence has long been obscured. *Compétence/Kompetenz/Competenza/Competencia* is a traditional continental public law concept which has no proper translation in classical English but has become common in the language of European law through the English version of the European Treaties.[4] It was originally enshrined in Article 173 EEC Treaty, now 263 TFEU.[5] This broad concept refers both to the issue of jurisdiction (the scope of action) and to the issue of powers (the means and instruments for action). Occasionally, arguments articulated in terms of competence have clearly emerged in European law, especially in the external relations context in which the province of the Community/Union, originally ill-defined as in its other domains of action, had to be clarified in response to the demands of its partners (third countries and international organizations) and the concerns of its Member States. Nonetheless, the issue of the delimitation of competence was far from predominant. The sharing out of powers between the Community and its Member States was supposed to operate on a functional basis. As the European Community was for the most part set up to attain the broad objectives set out in the Treaties, it seemed natural that capacities and powers should generally be attributed to its institutions. As advocated by Pescatore, 'the vision of the objectives must be accompanied by a corresponding reality of powers'.[6] This has made possible a shift characteristic of the European legal argument where the issue of the delimitation of competence is much less central than in any other international organization or in a federal state.

It took a long period of time before arguments framed in terms of scope of competence were integrated into the Treaties.[7] The Lisbon Treaty revision has been essential in that regard. According to Article 1 TEU, the existence of the Union is based on the competences conferred upon it by its Member States. Article 5 TEU and Title I of Part One of the TFEU deal expressly with the limits and nature of the Union's competences. But, if the concept of competence features prominently in the new Treaties, the theory of competence enshrined therein, described by some as 'a federal order of competences', leads to notions that do not appear to be inherent in

Etats-Unis d'Amérique et dans l'ordre juridique européen (Brussels: Bruylant, 1988); J.H.H. Weiler, 'The Transformation of Europe' (1991) 100 *Yale Law Journal* 403; K. Boskovits, *Le juge communautaire et l'articulation des compétences normatives entre la Communauté européenne et ses Etats membres* (Athens: Sakkoulas; Brussels: Bruylant, 1999).

[4] For a recent account of the concept of competence in continental public law and international law, see AFDA, *La compétence* (Paris: Litec, 2008).

[5] Art 263(2) TFEU reads: '[the Court of justice of the European Union] shall (...) have jurisdiction in actions brought by a Member State, the European Parliament, the Council or the Commission on grounds of *lack of competence*, infringement of an essential procedural requirement, infringement of the Treaties or of any rule relating to their application, or misuse of powers.'

[6] Pescatore (n 1) 41.

[7] See, in relation to the Union's external competence, Art 216(1) TFEU and 3(2) TFEU. The rather problematic interaction between these provisions has been pointed out by M. Cremona, 'Defining Competence in EU External Relations: Lessons from the Treaty Reform Process' in M. Maresceau and A. Dashwood (eds.), *Law and Practice of EU External Relations*, (Cambridge and New York: Cambridge University Press, 2008), 34.

the practice of the European and national institutions. As shown in this book, important discrepancies exist between the formal allocation of powers provided in the Treaties and the actual legal practice. This gap between theory and practice points to the need for a more wide-ranging and deeper investigation.

In the first section of this introduction, I will offer a brief reconstruction of the problem of competence as it has been addressed in the original structure of European law. The second section will introduce the context in which the problem is now posed. It will critically examine the changes brought about by the Lisbon Treaty and present the structure of this book. However, the legal issue is only one aspect of the problem. There is also a political dimension to the competence problem and the last section accounts for it. In some ways the concept of competence has played the role that the unpronounceable 'F-word' was not able to assume in the European debate. This is undoubtedly due to the ambiguity and political sensitivity of the reference to federalism that may be deployed simultaneously as an argument against the expansion of the Union's competence and as an argument against the reluctance of Member States to confer more powers to the Union. As a matter of fact it did not take long for the initial draft of the first provision of the Treaty establishing a Constitution for Europe according to which '[t]he Constitution establishes a Union…which shall administer certain competences on a federal basis' to be replaced by a more neutral formula.[8] Absent a reference to federalism, as remarked by Franz Mayer, 'the competence issue has become a code word for the future of European integration as such. How much Europe do we want? What kind of Europe do we want?'[9] It is argued that the question of competence is all the more fundamental in today's Europe that it stands for a deep questioning of the contours of Member States' membership to the European Union.

I. The Structure of the European Legal Argument and the Competence Problem

A paradigmatic example of the way the question of competence has been treated in original EC law practice is the famous *ERTA* judgment of 31 March 1971.[10] The question was whether the power to negotiate the European Agreement concerning the work of crews of vehicles engaged in international road transport (ERTA) was vested in the Community or/and in the Member States. The response of the European Court of Justice was that the Community was entirely empowered to conclude this agreement with third countries thereby excluding the possibility of

[8] Art 1, first sentence TEU now reads: '[b]y this Treaty, the High Contracting parties establish among themselves a European Union…, on which the Member States confer competences to attain objectives they have in common.'

[9] F. Mayer, 'Competences—Reloaded? The vertical division of powers in the EU and the new European constitution' (2005) 3 *ICON* 512.

[10] Case 22/70 *Commission v Council (ERTA)* [1971] ECR 264.

concurrent powers on the part of Member States. To reach this conclusion, it relied on three main arguments. The first refers to the capacity of the Community to establish contractual links with third countries that derives from it enjoying legal personality. The second relates so to say to the 'commonality' of Community action. The existence of a common policy envisaged by the Treaty and the promulgation of common rules, driven by the idea of a common enterprise,[11] should lead the Member States to act within the framework of the common institutions. Once the Community's interest to perform a specific action is established Member States are compelled to use the institutional channels of the Community. This will ensure, as well as reflect, the independence of action of the Community in its external relations. There is a third argument. According to the Court, it lies in the necessity not to affect the *scope* of the EC rules. The Court refers even more broadly to the necessity to protect the 'whole sphere of application of the Community legal system'.[12] This is a striking argument. The Court sees EC law as a vast sphere composed of different areas whose integrity is to be protected. The first operation in determining the existence of a Community competence is therefore to define the area occupied by EC law.[13] In the *ERTA* case, the Court observed that the *sphere* of transport was covered by an EC Regulation and, as a consequence, ruled that the *powers* of the Community necessarily extend to relationships arising from international law within this area. Since the area concerned is occupied by EC law internally, so runs the argument, the Community should be granted the necessary means to act externally.[14] The grant of powers follows the scope of the Community's jurisdiction.

Piet Eeckhout aptly remarks that 'the Court could easily have adopted a different approach', one more traditionally based on the rule of primacy of EC rules over the international obligations of the Member States.[15] But, instead of approaching the dispute as a conflict of norms, the Court chose to frame it as an issue of competence. The problem then is one of scope and range of action. On this view, the relationship between the Community and its Member States is not dependent on any contradiction that may arise from the application of EU and national norms and on the hierarchy to be set between these norms. Rather the question is whether and to what extent the action of one overlaps with the action of the other. In *ERTA*, this approach allowed the Court to avoid the acknowledgement of a potential conflict between Member States' international commitments and EC rules. At the same time, however, it entailed far-reaching consequences by opening

[11] In its Opinion 1/76 [1977] ECR 754 para 14 the Court refers in French (the Court's working language) to the need to protect '*l'œuvre communautaire*'.

[12] *ERTA* (n 10) paras 18, 22, and 27.

[13] The Court refers to areas covered by EC rules or (if less frequently) to areas corresponding to the objectives of the Treaties: Opinion of the Court 2/91 [1993] ECR I-1061 paras 10 and 34. On the notion of 'area' in the context of external relations, see also Opinion 1/03 of the Court [2006] ECR I-1150 para 126.

[14] On the idea of 'necessity' involved in the argument of implied powers, see G. Tusseau, *Les normes d'habilitation* (Paris: Dalloz, 2006).

[15] P. Eeckhout, 'Bold Constitutionalism and Beyond', in M. Poiares Maduro and L. Azoulai (eds.), *The Past and Future of EU Law. The Classics of EU Law Revisited on the 50th Anniversary of the Rome Treaty* (Oxford and Portland: Hart Publishing, 2010), 218, at 219.

the door to a doctrine of complete pre-emption of national powers.[16] In *ERTA*, it eventually led to the 'absorption' of national powers into the broadened scope of the Community's area and to the recognition of its exclusive competence.[17] Ultimately the competence approach did away with the problem of the sharing of powers. It should be noted, however, that this implication has proved difficult to maintain. In later cases, the Court has accepted that exclusivity is the exception and the shared exercise of competence the rule.[18]

It is fair to say that this approach that derives the competence of the Community from the delineation of its fields of action has not been the most common approach in EC/EU law. The relationship between the Community and the Member States was primarily shaped as a transfer of decision-making capabilities and not so much as an allocation of specific subject matters. The 'transfers of competence' to which the Court referred as a '*permanent limitation of their sovereign rights*' by the Member States was intended as a transfer of state functions to the Community institutions, mainly legislative and adjudicative functions. Moreover, this functional understanding of the competence issue has been complemented by a structural conception of integration. Firmly rooted in the original conscience of the Court of Justice and the European Commission is the belief that 'at the origin of integration, of supranationality, is the acceptance by a group of states of values which are common to them and which therefore give them an objective and *an idea of order* to which the participants are ready to subordinate their national interests and their national hierarchy of values'.[19] Implicit in this statement is the argument that the Community forms a 'coherent whole' and that the Member States are committed to the 'common interests of the Community, within which the particular interests of the Member States must endeavour to adapt to each other'.[20] Moreover the common interests should preferably be expressed within the framework of the Community institutions. Such representation was dominant in the field of external relations, where there was a concern that the Community appeared as 'a unified system' to the outside world,[21] but could also be found in the internal legal domain, where it was justified by the necessity to ensure the effectiveness of the objectives of the Treaties. The rationale of the effectiveness of the Treaties and ultimately of the legal integration process has been essential in the approach to the competence problem in all areas and throughout different periods of integration. As a result, in most of the decisions handed down by the Court of Justice up to the mid-nineties, the balance was clearly tilted in favour of expanding the Community's competences.[22]

[16] See further on this point the chapter by Timmermans in this volume.

[17] The concept of absorption is borrowed from J.H.H. Weiler, *The Constitution of Europe. 'Do the New Clothes Have an Emperor?' And Other Essays on European Integration* (Cambridge: Cambridge University Press, 1999), 47.

[18] See Cremona's chapter in this volume.

[19] Pescatore (n 1) 50.

[20] Opinion of the Court 1/75 [1975] ECR 1355, at 1363–4.

[21] Opinion of AG Tesauro in Case C-53/96 *Hermès v FHT* [1998] ECR I-3606.

[22] See, however, for a balanced appreciation of the proper role of the Court in the competence debate in the European Communities, P. Craig, 'Competence and Member State Autonomy: Causality,

It is evident from this approach that despite some references, the Community legal context failed to address in a meaningful way an essential element of classic systems of competences: *the idea of limits*. In the law of international organizations, competences are always conferred as 'limits'.[23] Remarkably, the principle of conferral was not enshrined in the original treaties until the Maastricht Treaty (1992), which inserted it in conjunction with the subsidiarity principle when it was felt that the evolution and growth of Community competences bordered upon the complete absorption of national areas of competences. Article 5 TEU now reads: '[u]nder the principle of conferral, the Union shall act only within the *limits* of the competences conferred upon it by the Member States.' However, in the course of the legal integration process, two conceptions have coincided to obscure the sense of the limits to the Union's action.

The first is the traditional understanding of the European Union as a functional entity. From the outset, the European Community was said to operate on the basis of broad objectives provided by the Treaties. Community competences were derived from the list of objectives associated to each policy area. As a result, the way in which the objectives of the Treaty were construed dictated the reality of the allocation of powers between the Community and its Member States. This does not mean that there was no division of powers. However, from the dominant standpoint, the division was to be decided on the basis of the dynamics of the system. This led the central European players and the Court to adopt a broad interpretation of the Community's scope of action, especially regarding the cross-sectorial functional competence of establishing the internal market.[24] This approach became manifest at the Paris Summit in 1972 where the heads of the Member States' governments agreed to extend the scope of the activities and the powers of the Community. From then on, the former Article 100 of the EEC Treaty and later Article 100 A of the EC Treaty were interpreted so as to include both market and non-market activities within the ambit of the Community.[25] It also led to an intensive use of Article 235 EEC Treaty permitting the Council to take 'appropriate measures' if action by the Community should prove necessary to attain, in the course of the operation of the common market, one of the objectives of the Community where the Treaty had not provided the necessary powers.[26]

Consequence and Legitimacy', in H.-W. Micklitz and B. De Witte (eds.), *The European Court of Justice and the Autonomy of the Member States* (Antwerp: Intersentia, 2012), 11.

[23] As pointed out by the International Court of Justice, 'international organizations are subject of international law which do not, unlike States, possess a general competence. International organizations are governed by the "principle of speciality", that is to say, they are invested by the States which create them with powers, *the limits of which are a function of the common interests whose promotion those States entrust to them*' (Advisory Opinion of 8 July 1996, *Legality of the Use by a State of Nucelar Weapons in Armed Conflict*) ICJ Reports [1996] 66 para 19.

[24] On this point, see Schütze's chapter in this volume; also A. Somek, *Individualism. An Essay on the Authority of EU law* (Oxford University Press, 2008), notably ch. 7.

[25] B. De Witte, 'A Competence to Protect: The Pursuit of Non-Market Aims through Internal Market Legislation', in P. Syrpis (ed.), *The Judiciary, the Legislature and the EU Internal Market* (Cambridge, UK and New York: Cambridge University Press, 2011).

[26] On the growth of Community competences in general, see A. Tizzano, 'Quelques observations sur le développement des compétences communautaires' (1989) 48 *Pouvoirs* 81; P. Craig, 'Clarity,

Originally intended to give European institutions the means to act within the boundaries of the Community's competence, this clause has in effect been used as a way of expanding its scope.

For a long time it was simply taken for granted that the Community could act. The existence of a Community competence was not really disputed. The real question concerned the exercise of this competence. This was reflected in two particular contexts. Firstly, the debate focused on to whether the actual or potential exercise of its powers by the Community would pre-empt partially or in totality the exercise of national competences.[27] Most often the Court opted for a pragmatic doctrine of pre-emption leaving some leeway to the Member States.[28] As a result, the 'complex mixture' of Community and national powers was recognized.[29] However, whenever these powers entered into actual conflict, the Court would rely on the structural principle of primacy of EC/EU rules and objectives. Secondly, if the legal basis of Community/Union action really was an issue, and a recurrent one for many years in EC/EU law, it was posited in terms of the *exercise* rather than the *existence* of the competence. It concerned the appropriate legal instruments that may be used for the action contemplated and more importantly, the decision-making procedure to be followed. For these choices determined the relative importance of each European institution and indirectly the role of the Member States within the Community/Union's institutional system.[30] The functional view had shifted the centre of gravity of the legal debate from the question of the existence of Union's competence and the vertical distribution of powers between the Union and its Member States to the question of the exercise of Union's competence and the institutional balance within the Union.

A second conception clearly intertwined with the first has contributed to obscure the question of competence. It is traditionally captured by the expression: the 'constitutionalization of the Community legal order'.[31] It is often said to amount to the same form of 'competence creep' as the functional conception.[32] In truth, it leads to a phenomenon that we may more accurately call 'competence sweep'. As is well known, Treaty provisions, particularly the free movement

Conferral, Containment and Consideration' (2004) 29 *European Law Review* 323. From a political science point of view, M.A. Pollack, 'Creeping Competence: The Expanding Agenda of the European Community' (1994) 14 *Journal of Public Policy* 95.

[27] On the idea that a potential exercise of power, even if not actual, is to be preserved in external relations, see Opinion 1/76 [1977] ECR 754 para 14.

[28] See Timmermans' chapter in this volume and V. Michel, *Recherches sur les compétences de la Communauté européenne* (Paris: L'Harmattan, 2003), 382 *et seq.*

[29] C.W.A. Timmermans, 'Division of External Powers between Community and Member States in the field of harmonization of national law—A Case Study', in C.W.A. Timmermans and E.L.M. Völker (eds.), *Division of powers between the European Communities and their Member States in the field of external relations* (Deventer: Kluwer, 1981), 15, at 26.

[30] K. Lenaerts and P. Van Nuffel, *European Union Law*, 3rd edn (Sweet & Maxwell, 2011), 112 *et seq.*

[31] E. Stein, 'Lawyers, Judges and the Making of a Transnational Constitution' (1981) 75 *American Journal of Constitutional Law* 1; Weiler (n 3).

[32] See, however, S. Prechal, 'Competence Creep and General Principles of Law' (2010) 3 *European Administrative Law* 5.

provisions, the non-discrimination provision and the competition rules, have been construed in a similar fashion to constitutional provisions within the legal order of a state. Take for instance the free movement provisions. Imposing obligations on Member States, they were converted into rights directly conferred on individuals and immediately enforceable before national courts. Triggered by any cross-border situation that relates to the establishment of the internal market, these rights were granted a scope which is not restricted to specific matters.[33] Moreover, it is settled case law that the possibility to derogate from the free movement provisions does not 'reserve certain matters to the exclusive jurisdiction of the Member States'.[34] The Court has rejected the idea that state derogations from EU law enshrine 'reservations of sovereignty'. As a result, the invocation of EU free movement rights is largely indifferent to the division of powers between the Union and its Member States.[35] It works in and may intrude on any national policy field.[36] Monti shows that the same logic operates in the enforcement of EU competition rules. In the name of effectiveness, EU law permeates even the residual fields of national competence.[37]

In EU law, the language of individual rights has largely superseded questions relating to the delimitation of competences. As a result, Member States are affected by EU law well beyond the reach of the regulatory powers delegated to the Union. Their reserved or residual capacity to act is turned into a propensity to be affected. A first hint at this transformation has been the *Casagrande* decision issued in 1974.[38] This case concerned the refusal to award an educational grant for the child of an Italian worker who was resident in Germany. Article 12 of the EC Regulation on the free movement of workers provided that, in order to promote their integration, the children of migrant workers' families would be admitted to educational courses under the same conditions as the nationals of the host state. The German authorities argued that access to education is one thing, educational grant another; the latter is part of the general state education policy and within the exclusive competence of Member States. The Court retorted that although educational and training policy is not as such included in the spheres which the treaty has entrusted to the Community institutions, it does not follow that the fundamental rule of non-discrimination between national and migrant worker family members does not apply to an area of Community's interest such as measures intended to facilitate educational attendance. In other words, EC rights

[33] As pointed out by AG Kokott, the fundamental freedoms of the internal market and of European citizenship have 'a scope which is not restricted to specific matters' (Opinion in Case C-192/05 *Tas-Hagen and Tas* [2006] ECR I-10451 para 34).

[34] See e.g. Case 72/83 *Campus Oil* [1984] ECR 2727 para 32.

[35] See further L. Azoulai, 'The "Retained Powers" Formula in the Case Law of the European Court of Justice: EU Law as Total Law?' (2011) 4 *European Journal of Legal Studies* 193.

[36] For a clear example of free movement rights impinging on an alleged 'exclusive competence' of Member States as regards access of some categories of third country nationals to national territory, see Case C-127/08 *Metock* [2008] ECR I-6241, esp paras 65–68.

[37] See Monti's chapter in this volume.

[38] Case 9/74 *Casagrande* [1974] ECR 773 and see Weiler (n 3).

are legitimately applied to measures that lie outside the purview of the European legislator.

This was further developed in the *Bosman* ruling, even though this case concerned private law rules and not state measures. The private party involved being an organization regulating in a structural manner the sector in question, it was equated to a state authority subject to free movement law. On substance, the Court acknowledged that, even though sport is a special domain which was not included in the list of Community's areas of competence, it is subject to Community law in so far as it constitutes an economic activity within the meaning of the Treaties' objectives.[39] This argument has then been developed and codified in a recurring formula which applies any time the Court is confronted with a sensitive issue of applicability of EU constitutional law. The formula is striking and reads as follows:

> [w]hilst it is not in dispute that EU law does not detract from the powers of the Member States [recognized for instance in the areas of direct taxation, social protection, education, social rights, attribution of nationality, civil status of persons], the fact remains that, when exercising those powers, the Member States must comply with EU law.[40]

Literally this formula means that the scope of application of EU rights extends beyond the subject areas over which the Union has been given competence. It goes far beyond the limits of the legislative powers formally bestowed on EU institutions under the Treaties.[41] At this point, there seems to be no doubt that 'there simply is no nucleus of sovereignty that the Member States can invoke, as such, against the Community'.[42]

These words were written in 1990 and the context has since changed. There is a widespread perception of a competence problem in Europe. The penetration of EU law into all areas of Member States competence is seen as perhaps the most disturbing phenomenon in the last 10 years. This concern has been reflected since the creation of the European Union and the introduction of the principle of subsidiarity in the Treaties and has also found various expressions in the case law of the Court of Justice.[43] Yet, the application of EU law in sensitive areas of national policies is often associated in European public opinion with ideas of desocialization of individuals and the destructuring of political communities. At the same time, the idea that Member States are internal parts of a 'whole', a global system driven by a grand design towards

[39] Case C-415/93 *Bosman* [1995] ECR I-4921.

[40] See Boucon's chapter in this volume.

[41] An excellent example of how individual rights may trump the constitutional limits of EU legislative action is the recent EU directive on cross-border health care. Although the directive declares that it is 'fully respecting the responsibilities of the Member States for the definition of social security benefits relating to health and for the organisation and delivery of healthcare and medical care and social security benefits', it goes as far as to apply to the provision of health care to patients 'regardless of how it is organised, delivered and financed' thereby ignoring the limits of the Union's scope of action provided by the Treaties when it comes to the non-market aspects of human health (Directive 2011/24/EU of the European Parliament and of the Council of 9 March 2011 on the application of patients' rights in cross-border healthcare, OJ 2011 L 88/45 and art 2(5) and 168 TFEU).

[42] K. Lenaerts, 'Constitutionalism and the Many Faces of Federalism' (1990) 38 *American Journal of Comparative Law* 220.

[43] A. Dashwood, 'The Limits of European Community Powers' (1996) 21 *European Law Review* 113.

political unification, has been challenged, notably by the German Constitutional Court on solid democratic grounds.[44] In such a context, the idea of ever-increasing Union competence based on the effectiveness of the integration process is clearly insufficient as a justification. This rationale says nothing of the meaning and *finalité* of the whole project.

The Laeken Declaration on the future of Europe adopted by the European Council in December 2001 addressed the various concerns fuelling the debate over competences over the last decade stating that

> citizens often hold expectations of the European Union that are not always fulfilled. And vice versa, they sometimes have the impression that the Union takes on too much in areas where its involvement is not always essential. Thus the important thing is to clarify, simplify and adjust the division of competence between the Union and the Member States in the light of the new challenges facing the Union.

The ensuing dilemma was posed in these terms:

> there is the question of how to ensure that a redefined division of competence does not lead to a creeping expansion of the competence of the Union or to encroachment upon the exclusive areas of competence of the Member States and, where there is provision for this, regions. How are we to ensure at the same time that the European dynamic does not come to a halt?[45]

In the meantime the political and social context of distrust towards further integration and federalization of Europe has if anything increased.

II. The European Union as a Federal Order of Competences?

The overabundance of provisions limiting the Union's competences is one of the most obvious marks left by the Lisbon Treaty. The new Treaty on European Union makes clear that 'the Union shall act *only* within the limits of the competences conferred upon it by the Member States' (Article 5(2) TEU), it repeats that 'competences *not conferred* upon the Union in the Treaties remain with the Member States' (Articles 4(1) and 5(2) TEU), and it states that proposals for the amendment of the Treaties 'may serve either to increase or to *reduce* the competences conferred on the Union' (Article 48 (2) TEU). The cataloguing of Union's competences in

[44] If the Court acknowledges the existence of an autonomous EU legal order and accepts the tendency 'to effectively interpreting powers along the lines of the US doctrine of implied powers or the principle of *effet utile* under the law of international treaties', it maintains that 'autonomy can only be understood as an autonomy to rule which is independent but *derived, i.e. is granted by other legal entities*' which makes the sovereign state a sort of 'external partner' to the whole process of integration (German Constitutional Court, *Lisbon Treaty*, 30 June 2009 esp § 231–237).

[45] On the debate concerning the phenomenon of 'competence creep' between Laeken and the drafting of the Lisbon Treaty, see S. Weatherill, 'Competence Creep and Competence Control' (2004) 23 *Yearbook of European Law* 1. See also V. Constantinesco, 'Brève note sur la répartition des compétences comme clé de la future constitution européenne', in *Mélanges en hommage à Guy Isaac. 50 ans de droit communautaire*, Vol. I (Toulouse: Presses de l'Université des Sciences Sociales de Toulouse, 2004), 155.

the Treaties (Article 2 to 6 TFEU) and the clarification of their nature as exclusive, shared, coordinating, or supporting competences may be seen as an act of containment as much as an act of rationalization. The Member States were clearly concerned with setting boundaries to the Union's action. As regards the potential universalization of EU fundamental rights, Article 51(2) of the Charter of Fundamental Rights of the European Union clarifies that it '*does not extend* the field of application of Union law *beyond* the power of the Union'.[46] All of this comes down to one and the same message: EU competences have inherent limits and the scope of application of EU law should correspond to them.

The situation is certainly more nuanced than this simple statement. Opposing tendencies are also present. Article 114 TFEU conferring on the Union a broad legislative competence for harmonizing national laws was not affected by the amendment of the Treaties. This might come as a surprise given that the Laeken Declaration raised the possibility of reviewing the former Article 95 EC, a possibility that was expressly linked to the need 'to ensure that a redefined division of competence does not lead to a creeping expansion of the competence of the Union or to encroachment upon the exclusive areas of competence of the Member States'.[47] One may also notice the new Article 19 TEU which 'commandeers' the Member States to provide remedies sufficient to ensure effective legal protection in the fields covered by Union law.[48] This seems to run against the traditional doctrine of the procedural autonomy of Member States. However, this is in line with the case law of the Court which usually adopts a pre-emptive attitude as regards the judicial protection of EU rights.[49]

However, leaving these specific issues aside, there is no doubt that changes introduced by the Lisbon Treaty contain a direct challenge to the predominant functional and constitutional conceptions of the European legal order of the last 50 years. As for functionalism, the best evidence is the new Article 3(6) TEU which states that '[t]he Union shall pursue its objectives by appropriate means *commensurate with the competences which are conferred upon it in the Treaties*'. This clearly indicates a change of perspective. Objectives are no longer the main source for delimiting the powers and the legal instruments of the Union.[50] Instead, the

[46] See Dubout's chapter in this volume.

[47] See further S. Weatherill, 'The Limits of Legislative Harmonization Ten Years after *Tobacco Advertising*: How the Court's Case Law has become a "Drafting Guide"' (2011) 12 *German Law Journal* 827; D. Wyatt, 'Is the European Union an Organisation of Limited Powers?', in A. Arnull and others (eds.), *A Constitutional Order of States? Essays in EU Law in Honour of Alan Dashwood* (Oxford: Hart Publishing, 2011), 3.

[48] See in general D. Halberstam, 'Comparative Federalism and the Issue of Commandeering', in Nicolaidis and Howse (n 2) 213.

[49] In the *Unibet* case, the national court was required to interpret the rules governing its own jurisdiction 'in such a way as to enable those rules, wherever possible, to be implemented in such a manner as to contribute to the attainment of the objective... of ensuring effective judicial protection of an individual's rights under Community law' (Case C-432/05 *Unibet* [2007] ECR I-227 para 44; see also Case C-268/06 *Impact* [2008] ECR 2183 para 54). This practically results in directly empowering national courts by 'pre-empting' the grounds for action of national courts enshrined in domestic law.

[50] J. Larik, *Wordly Ambitions. Foreign policy objectives in European constitutional law*, PhD thesis (EUI, Florence, 2013), 201, 205.

objectives are made subject to the competences listed in the Treaties. This holds true for the 'internal market' which is referred to as a field of shared competence, implying that it too is intended to have inherent limits. As for the constitutionalization of EU individual rights, the challenge lies mainly in the new Article 4 TEU. Member States shall continue to observe their duty to facilitate the achievement of the Union's tasks. However, conversely, the Union shall respect the Member States' national identities, their fundamental structures, and their 'essential functions'. It is noteworthy that the state functions are not referred to as institutional functions (the functions to legislate, execute, or adjudicate) but as substantive ones, 'including ensuring the territorial integrity of the State, maintaining law and order and safeguarding national security'. The Treaty recognizes that Member States have a primordial competence in the organization of certain subject areas that are considered essential to social integration in Europe.[51] They are no longer reduced to powers that may potentially prejudice the establishment of the internal market and the protection of individuals. Instead they are recognized as legitimate political actors ensuring the cohesion of the society. This may lead to new legitimate restrictions on the operation of fundamental EU rules or may impose duties on categories of individuals traditionally treated as holders of rights under EU law.[52]

The introduction of the notion of the EU as a 'federal order of competences' can be considered as a response to this changing context and to the challenges associated with it. The term is historically rooted in Germany and refers back to the Constitution of the German federal state. Those who use it in the European context argue in favour of more clarity and transparency in the attribution and exercise of powers in the Union.[53] A typology of categories of competences may be needed so as to structure power relationships. This reference is also present in the Court's case law. When it examines the compatibility of international agreements with the Treaties, the Court repeatedly holds that 'the order of competences defined in the Treaties' must be safeguarded.[54] It then refers to the 'essential elements' of the Union's institutional system the core of which is constituted by the Court itself.

The reference to the Union as an order of competences is not entirely convincing. The European constitutional practice is essentially one of deep intertwining of EU and national powers in all the fields of EU action and at all the legislative,

[51] On this use of the term 'competence' as related to subject matters as opposed to legal functions, see Beaud's contribution in this volume.

[52] See further L. Azoulai and S. Coutts, 'Restricting Union citizens' residence on grounds of public security. Where Union citizenship and the AFSJ meet (Case C-348/09 *P.I.*)' (2013) 50 *Common Market Law Review* 553.

[53] von Bogdandy and Bast (n 3); R. Schütze, 'The European Community's Federal order of Competences—A Retrospective Analysis', in M. Dougan and S. Currie (eds.), *50 years of the European Treaties—Looking back and thinking forwards* (Oxford and Portland: Hart Publishing, 2009), 63.

[54] Our translation from the original French expression referring to '*l'ordre des compétences*'. See e.g. Joined Cases C-402/05 P and C-415/05 P *Kadi and Al Barakaat International Foundation v Council and Commission* [2008] ECR I-6351 para 282. The official translation reads: 'the allocation of responsibilities defined in the Treaties'.

executive, and judicial levels. There is little point therefore in using constitutional methods aimed at setting a clear-cut classification of the EU's enumerated powers. As a matter of fact, 'one would certainly [be] left bemused if one tried to rely on Articles 2–6 TFEU to understand the nature of the competences available in particular areas'.[55] Not only because, in many policy areas, there is a complex relationship between the space occupied by the Member States and the one occupied by the Union[56] but also, and primarily, because the scope of EU competence is itself a space of interaction of both EU and national powers. In reality we have, in the course of the exercise of an EU competence, what Boucon calls, in her contribution to this book, a kind of 'mutual adjustment resolution' whereby the boundaries of national and EU actions are constantly renegotiated.

The object of this book is to investigate this feature further. Reflections on the new provisions of the EU Treaties certainly provide some hint at the direction the Union is taking in the area of competences.[57] However, as shown throughout this book, discrepancies exist between the formal allocation of powers provided in the Treaties and the current practice of the European and national institutions. Moreover there is a mismatch between the division between the Union and the national competences at the legislative level and the imbrication of powers at the implementation level.[58] Furthermore, a gap, manifested in different ways, persists between the limited scope of competence of the Union and the far-reaching scope of application of EU law.[59] Added to this are various recent disturbing phenomena. On the one hand, we can observe the development of individual and joint Member States' actions outside the framework of the Treaties where, according to them, the Union is supposed to make use of its own powers. Flexibility is developing in a context of presumed centralization.[60] On the other hand, we see the Union interfering in areas where the Member States are supposed to act on their own behalf. Centralization, either voluntarily accepted or imposed, and heavy supranational intervention are taking place in areas of supposed national autonomy.[61] This may be observed in many fields of EU law but it is perhaps made more visible and acute in the field of economic policy and in the current context of Europe's

[55] S. Weatherill, 'The Constitutional Context of (Ever-Wider) Policy-Making', in E. Jones, A. Menon, and S. Weatherill (eds.), *The Oxford Handbook of the European Union* (Oxford: Oxford University Press, 2012), 572.

[56] S. Weatherill (n 55) 573, gives the example of social policy based on art 153 TFEU which consists of a collection of several fields where the boundaries between Union and state competence vary. See also the chapters by Tusseau and Cremona in this volume.

[57] As recalled by the Court in the recent Case C-414/11 *Daiichi Sankyo Co. Ltd.*, judgment of 18 July 2013, nyr., para 48: 'in view of that significant development of primary law, the question of the distribution of the competences of the European Union and the Member States must be examined on the basis of the Treaty now in force'.

[58] See some examples in external relational given by Cremona in her chapter. Cf. Monti's analysis in the field of competition law.

[59] See esp Monti's, Micklitz's, Boucon's, and Dubout's chapters.

[60] See the final considerations of Timmermans on the Fiscal Compact and the *Pringle* ruling of the ECJ on the Treaty on the European Stability Mechanism in his chapter in this volume. See also in the context of external relations Cremona's chapter in this volume.

[61] See esp the chapter by Bieber in this volume but also Cremona's and Micklitz's chapters.

economic crisis.[62] All of these developments point to a need to reconsider the question of competence from a fresh perspective.

Clearly the question posed by the Laeken Declaration more than 10 years ago of how to integrate a sense of limits into the EU legal order, while at the same time safeguarding the 'European dynamic' and without undermining the institutional balance developed over the last decades does not lend itself to a simple, generally applicable answer. To try and tackle the issue in most of its complexity this book proceeds as follows. In Part I, it invites the reader to step back and take a broad perspective on the problem of the allocation of competences as it is supposed to arise in a federation. As already noted, it is almost natural to consider the competence question in the European context from the perspective of federalism. However, the first two chapters suggest that the federal model fails to provide the adequate tools to analyse the division of powers in the European context. It is too broad a reference. Yet, some important conceptual clarifications on the notion of competence and the legal mechanisms of allocation of powers are put forward. Part II tackles the practical issues of concrete competences conferred on the Union and looks at the dynamic interactions of powers in these areas. The fields examined are selected with due consideration of the difficult problems of competence they are liable to raise. Of course others might have been included as equally relevant for the issue at stake. The specific studies confirm both the appeal and the difficulty of capturing the question of competence in the EU in federal terms and, in some cases, even more crudely, to capture the dynamic of EU law through the question of the division of powers. In Part III, the book looks at how the Court of Justice of the European Union struggles with issues of competence. Has the Court, as the main institutional actor dealing with this issue, developed a doctrine on the definition of EU competence? It does not seem so. The Court displays a lot of pragmatism in the handling of competence issues.[63] This does not exclude a principled commitment to safeguard the dynamic of EU law, of its objectives, and of its values. This results in a tension between the dynamic of EU law and the respect for national competences more particularly visible in sensitive contexts like the protection of fundamental rights or the area of the so-called 'retained powers' of the Member States. Finally, the question of the presumably new safeguards introduced by the Lisbon Treaty is addressed in Part IV. Whilst limits to the existence of Union's competence are traditionally deemed to fail, it is important to note that these safeguards concern the *exercise* of their powers by the Union and national institutions.[64] Potential limits lie in the implementation of the legislative competence to harmonize national laws, especially in areas perceived as sensitive areas in the

[62] See esp C. Joerges, 'Europe's Economic Constitution in Crisis', *ZenTra Working Paper in Transnational Studies No. 06/2012*, available at <http://www.zen-tra.de/publications/working-papers/en/?print=1>.

[63] See also in relation to external relations law, P. Eeckhout, 'Exclusive External Competences: Constructing the EU as an International Actor', in A. Rosas, E. Levits, and Y. Bot (eds.), *The Court of Justice and the Construction of Europe: Analyses and Perspectives on Sixty Years of Case*-Law (The Hague: Asser Press, Springer, 2013), 613.

[64] The point is thoroughly made by Millet in this volume.

national context, the enforcement of the new subsidiarity mechanism, and the application of the new reference to national identity. This part offers interesting new perspectives by looking at the question of the limits from a comparative perspective, taking US constitutional law as a privileged example.

III. Competence and Membership

Some of the great scholars of federalism have warned against the danger of reducing the thick federal question to a mere legal problem of competence and to technical mechanisms of sharing out of powers.[65] This risk also exists in the realm of the European legal studies. However, it should not be overestimated. In Europe, the legal question of competence has long been obscured. What we have been observing for many years is a process driven by 'immediate' and 'intermediate' objectives converted into functional means of action and interpretation.[66] Political union was seen both as a 'distant aim' and as the unquestionable assumption that underpinned the legal construction as a whole.[67] This was a way to remove from the legal debate questions of the essence and contours of the membership to the European Union. This resulted in a loss not only of the sense of limits but also of a sense of the finalities and values that structured the European space.

Returning now to the question of competence corresponds to a questioning of this assumption. This would mean a shift from defining integration on a purely functional basis as a transfer of powers to attain certain broad objectives to defining it as a fact of joint membership and participation in a larger polity. The sense of being bound together is stronger than ever, based on the high degree of interdependence of the Member States. At the same time, however, questions about the *finalités* of the European project are posed, conflicts of values emerge, mutual trust is not guaranteed, and central national actors may be tempted to exit from the Union's institutions and the legal competences framework.[68]

The Union is no longer in a position to operate as a traditional authority ensuring the prevalence of its provisions and the dominance of its interests. Confronted with real value conflicts and substantial solidarity issues, legal rules of conflict resolution like the pre-emption rule, the primacy rule, or the rules of competence laid down by the Treaties are of little use. Another approach is required. First of all, a sense of responsibility and ownership is needed. The various actors should fully

[65] See the chapter by Beaud in this volume.

[66] The terminology is borrowed from Pescatore (n 1) 19.

[67] Remember the reference to the very 'legal basis of the Community' in the *Costa v. ENEL* judgment: 'the law stemming from the treaty, an independent source of law, could not, because of its special and original nature, be overridden by domestic legal provisions, however framed, without being deprived of its character as Community law and *without the legal basis of the Community itself being called into question*' (Case 6-64 *Costa v ENEL* [1964] ECR 585). Arguably, the concept of the Community which is at the basis of the EU legal order is both an institutional reality and a political ambition.

[68] See L. van Middelaar, *The Passage to Europe. How a Continent became a Union* (New Haven and London: Yale University Press, 2013).

realize that the future of integration is in their hands. Theirs is the responsibility to decide which task they allocate to which level and for what specific reason in each single case.[69] For this sense of responsibility to emerge, mutual trust is essential. What this book begins to show is that the imagination of a true 'European community', beyond the institutional meaning of the term, requires more than a unique institutional structure and more than rigid rules essentializing the distribution of competences between the Union and its Member States. It requires more than a federal order of competences; it requires a set of conditions and principles capable of organizing and fostering mutual trust among the Member States and between the Member States and the European institutions. We see some of these principles timidly emerging in sensitive areas of application of EU law: the principle of loyalty, a duty of convergence as regards basic values, a due consideration of possible impact on others' sphere of autonomy and identity.[70] These are basic rules of conduct indispensable to address the question of competence properly. Yet, they do not seem to have been fully internalized by the main national and European players.

[69] See H.-W. Micklitz and S. Weatherill, 'Shaping responsibilities in the legal order of the European Community', in H.-W. Micklitz, T. Roethe, and S. Weatherill (eds.), *Federalism and Responsibility. A Study on Product Safety Law and Practice in the European Community* (London and Boston: Graham & Trotman/M. Nijhoff; Norwell, MA, USA: Kluwer Academic Publishers Group, 1994), 153.

[70] See esp Micklitz's and Groussot and Bogojević's chapters in this volume.

PART I

THE FEDERAL MODEL

1

The Allocation of Competences in a Federation—A General Introduction

Olivier Beaud

Introduction

In her essay *On Revolution* Hannah Arendt compares the genesis of the French and American Republics. About the founding fathers' task, she writes:

> [t]he chief problem of the founders was how to establish union out of thirteen 'sovereign', duly constituted republics; their task was the foundations of a 'confederate republic' which...would reconcile the advantages of monarchy in foreign affairs with those of republicanism in domestic policy. And in this task of the Constitution there was no longer any question of constitutionalism in the sense of civil rights...but of erecting a system of powers that would check and balance in such a way that the power neither of the union nor of its parts, the duly constituted States, would decrease or destroy one another.[1]

The problem raised by the German philosopher about the US experience is inherent to federation-making in general. How to conceive of a duality of powers (Federation and member states) on a single territory is the challenge that federal constitutions and theories of federation have had to take up. This problem has led the most radical philosopher of the state, Hobbes, to deny any viability to federal institutions, for an *imperium in imperio* is said to be inconceivable. However, jurists can study the history of federations, and set up a theory of those *respublica composita*, regardless of the opinions of philosophers on the possibility of a federation as a theoretical object.

In a *Théorie de la Fédération*,[2] I present the federation as a political form, or, more precisely, as a legal and political form, the distinctive feature of which is to stand 'on an equal footing' with the state, or even with the empire. This book is a theory of federalism for jurists. Its central argument has been perfectly summed up by Guy Carcassonne in his review of my book: 'the Federation is not a State; it is an autonomous political form to which the constitutive elements of the State, and

[1] H. Arendt, *On Revolution* (Harmondsworth: Penguin Books, 1973).

[2] O. Beaud, *Théorie de la Fédération*, 2nd edn (Paris: Presses Universitaires de France, coll. *Léviathan*, 2007).

notably sovereignty, are of no interest.'[3] In this book, the state and the Federation are opposed as ideal kinds of political form. The federation, as I describe it, is *a federal union of states, and not a federal state*. Here is the true novelty of this approach: while the dominant legal doctrine endeavours to expound the differences between the two federative forms (confederacy and federal state, or confederacy and federation), I try with the minority doctrine to underline their common features, thus supposing the existence of a 'federative law' (*droit commun fédératif*) instead of 'federal law', which includes only the law of federal states. This explains why I did not study some topical issues on federalism, such as the allocation of powers or competences, which is often described as a key problem of federalism. It is a major problem in the 'consolidated' federations, but not in emerging federalism. The present book forces me to confront the question of the allocation of competences that I did not deal with in my *Théorie*.

I would like to try to explain why the problem of the division of powers arises specifically in a federation. We know that in a unitary state there is also a problem of division of powers between the state and local governments,[4] as there may be in a federation—a problem of division of powers and municipalities.[5] However, it is in a federation that the problem of allocation of competences between the federation and its member states becomes acute. In any case, this is explained by Marcel Bridel (one of the best authors on federalism):

> [t]he tasks of the state are numerous and largely unpredictable. The Constitution does not list them all. As well, in unitary states, it need not indicate anything and leaves the task to the competent authorities as and when the need arises. But in a federative state [*Etat fédératif*], the situation is different. A special feature of this type of state (federal) consisting of a sharing of public activity between the federation and its components units, it is essential that the Constitution operates this division.[6]

The principal reason for asking this important question in a federation lies in the idea of the 'sharing of public activity', sharing 'state functions', which can be called both 'shared responsibilities of the state' and 'sharing public power'. Thus the fundamental difference between the state and the federation is illustrated, what I call the duality of the Federation and the unicity of the state.

One must note in passing a first conceptual difficulty: in this passage, which is contained in a chapter entitled 'The Sharing of Competences', Bridel does not have recourse to the word *competence*, but instead uses 'state functions', or the 'public activity', which must be performed by the various competent authorities, whether the federation or the member states.

[3] *Le Monde*, 29 February 2008.

[4] See the classic French thesis of J.-M. Pontier, *L'Etat et les collectivités locales. La répartition des compétences* (Paris: Librairie générale de droit et de jurisprudence, 1978).

[5] P. Dahinden 'The division of powers between the state and common laws of Switzerland' (D.Phil thesis, Lausanne University, 1979).

[6] M. Bridel, *Précis de droit constitutionnel et public suisse* (Lausanne: Payot, Vol. I, No. 66, 1965), 159.

It must be emphasized that the term 'compétence' raises problems. First, because the legal term most often used to describe what a French lawyer would call a *compétence*, a German jurist *Zuständigkeit*, or an Italian jurist *competenza* is the term 'jurisdiction'. Moreover—and most importantly—when reading the English language literature on federalism, it is rare to find the term 'allocation of competences'. Thus, in the classic book by Robert Bowie and Carl Friedrich, *Studies on Federalism*, we read, for example, the following in the chapter on Foreign Affairs: '[c]onstitutions of Federations usually contain both provisions allocating the power in the field of foreign relations to various organs of the federal government.'[7] Further, it is written that, 'in almost all Federations, there are areas in this field in which the component states have retained a certain *amount of jurisdiction*'.[8] The theme of the division of responsibilities between federal and federated competence is not, in itself, also studied in this book, but the phrase that describes it is '*allotment of responsibility*'.[9] As for Albert Dicey, he speaks of 'a division of powers under a common constitution between the nation on the one hand and the individual states on the other'.[10] It is thus the word 'powers' that is preferred over 'competences', and the majority of English lawyers and political scientists use this word. This is notably the case of Vicky Jackson in the recent outline she gave on federalism in the *International Treaty of Constitutional Law*.[11] For his part, William Riker speaks neither of 'division of powers', nor of 'distribution of powers', but of 'division of authority'.[12]

The proof of the scarce use of the word 'competence' is even easier to find: reading the provisions of federal constitutions. If one takes, for example, federal constitutions, and not the oft-cited example of the United States, one observes that they never use the term 'competences', but instead 'powers'. The 'British Act of North America' of 1867, establishing the Canadian Federation, contains a Title VI entitled 'Distribution of Legislative Powers', which notably contains an Article 91 in which the exclusive powers of the Federation of the Canadian Parliament are enumerated. Similarly, the Australian Constitution of 9 July 1900 contains a fifth part entitled 'Powers of the Parliament', which specifies (Articles 51 and 52) the subjects upon which the Australian Parliament is competent to legislate.

[7] R. Bowie and C. Friedrich (eds.), *Studies on Federalism* (Boston: Little Brown, 1954), 236.

[8] Bowie and Friedrich (n 7).

[9] Bowie and Friedrich (n 7) 173: '[t]he practice in all the federal systems studied has been to allot to the federal government exclusively the responsibility for the defence of the Federation.... This *allotment of responsibility* to the federal government has usually been made by express constitutional provision.'

[10] A. Dicey, *Introduction to the Study of Constitutional Law* (Indianapolis: Liberty Fund, 1982).

[11] 'On a "dual federalism" theory, each level of government is regarded as "supreme" or sovereign within its own sphere. On this model, there may be a tendency to *construe allocations of powers to the different levels exclusively*, and to rely heavily on categories to keep the allocations separate. But in any working federal system that lasts over time, powers are exercised in heavily interdependent ways, and in some modern federal constitutions, as we have seen, *many powers are designedly concurrent*'; V. Jackson, 'Fédéralisme. Normes et territoires', in D. Chagnollaud and M. Troper (eds.), *Traité international de droit constitutionnel* (Paris: Dalloz, Vol. II, 2012), 23.

[12] W.H. Riker, *The Development of American Federalism* (Boston, Dordrecht, Lancaster: Kluwer Academic Publishers, 1987).

This question of words is not merely semantic, as it involves a conceptual problem, one which I will return to later because it obviously determines how the subject should be understood: if competence is not a power, what then is competence?

I want to conclude with a brief discussion on the term 'federal order' referred to in the present book.[13] I suppose that this is a reference to what in German is defined as *Rechtsordnung*, that is the state law (legal order of the state) or the *federative* law (legal order of the Federation). However, I cannot fail to note that one of the best writers on federalism, Carl Friedrich, concluded his book on the topic with the following broad definition of a federal order:

> [a] federal order is a union of group selves united by one or more common objectives, a community of communities which retain their distinctive group being. It unites without destroying the selves as uniting and is meant to strengthen them in their group and communal relations.[14]

Friedrich's definition is very broad because it may include non-political federations such as trade unions and sports federations. However, in public law, the federal order is characterized by the fact that the entities or communities in question are political in nature. If this definition nonetheless interests us, it is because it allows us to include in the analysis of our subject both the confederacy and the federal state, i.e. all the forms of federation.[15]

To conclude this introduction, I will say a word about the method which has been used here to study this question. I have principally relied upon books that one can consider as 'classics of federalism', so to speak, and certain handbooks or treatises of constitutional law which describe federal mechanisms and the distribution of competences. The only point that merits attention is that with regard to the substantive law: I have preferred to examine federal constitutions rather than the innumerable judicial decisions on the issue of the allocation of competences. It is an approach that I borrowed from William Riker, an original author of political science who warned lawyers against their tropism, writing that:

> the obvious way to investigate the degree of centralization is according to the administrative theory of federalism, to look at the way in which the areas of action are in fact divided up. The traditional method is to examine the formal division in the Constitution and the gloss applied to it by judicial decision.... The fault in this method is that judicial decisions concern the boundaries of areas of action and do not in any way indicate their absolute size and importance. Most of the history and analysis of federalism has been written by constitutional lawyers using federalism as their raw material. As a consequence the tradition

[13] In this respect, see also A. von Bogdandy and J. Bast, 'The Federal Order of Competences', in A. von Bogdandy and J. Bast (eds.), *Principles of European Constitutional Law* (Oxford: Hart Publishing; Munich: Beck, 2011), 276, and R. Schütze, 'The European Community's Federal order of Competences—A Retrospective Analysis', in M. Dougan and S. Currie (eds.), *50 years of the European Treaties—Looking back and thinking forwards* (Oxford and Portland: Hart Publishing, 2009), 63.

[14] C. Friedrich, *Trends of Federalism in Theory and Practice* (London: Pall Mall Press, 1968), at 183.

[15] Friedrich explicitly states (n 14) that '[f]ederations of states and the federal state must be seen as particular applications of effective organized cooperation between groups'.

provides us with a highly distorted picture of the relationship between the nation and the states.[16]

I fully share this position of Riker on the exaggerated role played by the commentary of judicial decisions in the analysis of federalism and the allocation of competences between the federation and its member states. Although these are very scholarly analyses of the question of 'judicial federalism',[17] I do not take them into account here, for the main reason that the courts decisions reflect the pathology of law, and not law in action.

It is time to explain the way in which I attempt to treat the problem of the allocation of competences in a federation. The problem has been well described by Marcel Bridel, according to which we must consider that, in a federal system, the problem inherent in this term, in a federal system, is none other than 'mutual delimitation of federal and Member States' competences'.[18] To put it differently: what is the responsibility of the federation and what is the responsibility of the member states? Or, more simply, *who does what*? The difficult question is knowing what this 'what' is, that is to say, what is the 'subject' of the allocation? One thing is certain: it is abstract entities (federation or member states) that are competent, and not simply organs of the state. It is either a federal or federated competence (or both at the same time).[19]

I will try to present the problem by examining first the conventional understanding and then by suggesting a more inclusive analysis which is not reduced only to a federal state, with the objective of relativizing the importance of this issue. I am going to expound on and criticize the conventional view, which is linked to the state-oriented view of federalism, and I shall try to see if it is possible to open the way to an alternative way of thinking.

I. The Conventional Conception of the Allocation of Competences: a Technical and State-centred Conception

The allocation of competences between the federation and the member states is usually said to be federalism's principal issue. Jean-François Aubert, the master of Swiss constitutional law, considers this issue as being 'the big deal' of federalism.[20] Similar views are expressed on the other side of the Atlantic: in a famous Canadian

[16] Riker (n 12) at 51.

[17] There are at least two classic studies to be mentioned: first, Corwin's lectures on the interstate commerce clause; E.S. Corwin, *The Commerce Power versus States' Rights* (Princeton, NJ: Princeton University Press, 1936) and K. Lenaerts, *Le juge et la Constitution aux États-Unis d'Amérique et dans l'ordre juridique européen* (Brussels: Bruylant, 1988).

[18] Bridel (n 6) 170.

[19] We find the use of this term in C. de Malberg, *Contribution à la théorie générale de l'Etat* (Paris: CNRS, 1920) at 137–8 of Vol. I: '[i]n fact, it is certain that the Federal Constitution itself limitedly determines the objects reserved for federal competence, the remainder, that is, for all objects that are not reserved, it leaves the competence to the Confederate States.'

[20] J.-F. Aubert, *Traité de droit constitutionnel suisse* (Neuchâtel: Ides et Calendes, 1967).

textbook, a chapter devoted to federalism is entitled 'federalism, or the allocation of competences',[21] as if the two expressions were identical. Here, I will simply underline two of the main features of this doctrine. Indeed, by confusing the issues of federalism and of the allocation of competences, this doctrine relies upon two presupposed arguments: first, the federal state is conceived of as the only form of federalism; secondly, the issue of the allocation of competences is restricted to the technical aspects of the allocation of legislative competences.

1. A state-centred conception of the allocation of competences

In a recently issued thesis focused on the allocation of competences in both the European Union and the United States, the author underlines the 'direct and definite link which exists between federalism, its main features, and the question of the (vertical) allocation of competences, as it is made in federal constitutions'.[22] Then, on the one hand, the allocation of competences is said to be a 'vertical allocation' of competences and, on the other hand, the legal norm governing this allocation is the federal constitution itself. This is typical of a conception of the federation and the federal state as two similar concepts.

a) The conception of federalism as a vertical allocation of competences

To understand what the idea of a 'vertical' allocation of competences means, it is necessary to take as a starting point the popular idea that the 'superposition' of two legal orders is the central characteristic of a federation: these being the federal legal order, and the federated legal orders. Dating back to Georges Scelle, this idea takes for granted the '*superiority*' of one order over the other—the higher one being the federal order.[23] This reflects a state-centred vision of federalism, according to which the federation is, today, necessarily a state (i.e. a *federal state*), but a state characterized by two levels of organization. Then, when lawyers define 'from a legal point of view' the federalism as a '(vertical) allocation of competences',[24] they carry on the space-based metaphor of 'levels' or 'degrees', and the expression of a 'superposition' of legal orders expresses the idea of a federation conceptualized as a *hierarchical order*. It is a federal state to which the member states, the federated states,

[21] A. Tremblay, *Le droit constitutionnel. Principes*, 2nd edn (Montréal: Thémis, 2000), 191 *et seq*. Finally, R. Watts, 'Comparative Conclusions', in A. Majeed, R. Watts, and D. Brown (eds.), *Dialogues on Distribution of Powers and Responsibilities in Federal Countries* (Montréal: McGill-Queen's University Press, 2006), 322, comparing between federal constitutions, states that 'the distribution of authority, responsibilities and finances among the orders of government is a fundamental feature common to all these Federations'.

[22] B. Dubey, *La répartition des compétences au sein de l'Union européenne à la lumière du fédéralisme suisse: systèmes, enjeux et conséquences* (Geneva: Helbing et Lichtenhahn, and Brussels: Bruylant, 2002), 27.

[23] Dubey (n 22) speaks of 'superposition de niveaux étatiques'.

[24] C. Dominicé, 'Fédéralisme coopératif' (1969) 88 *Revue de droit suisse* 743, at 751: '[l]a Constitution de type fédéral opère une répartition des compétences entre les deux niveaux de l'organisation étatique, le niveau central ou supérieur, et le niveau local ou inférieur.'

are subordinated. Allocating the competences is then considered as a means to govern the distribution of powers—that is to say, to express this superiority.

Consequently, because the allocation of competences is seen as the way the federal state is organized, it is seen as not being a suitable model for a confederacy. This is the conclusion that was reached at the beginning of the twentieth century by a thesis summing up the doctrine: in this thesis, one can read that

> the constitutional allocation of competences between the central government and the individual States is the main and typical feature of the Federal State. Such a feature is absent from a conferation of states, which is not a genuine State, and into which the relation between the central government and the individual powers are not of a constitutional, but conventional, nature.[25]

And yet we will see below that issues arising from the allocation of powers also exist in emerging federations. Paradoxically enough, the federal state's superiority over the member state does not (or does not always) emanate from the nature of the competences allocated to the federation, or from their extent or volume, if compared with those of the member states. The federation is not said to be the higher authority, because it would have the most important (from the public power's point of view) or numerous competences. Indeed, this superiority has for its *raison d'être* the legal basis of this allocation of competences: the constitution.

b) The federal constitution as the allocation of competences' mandatory act

According to the conventional conception presented here, the fact that competences are allocated by a written text—the constitution—is the other main feature of the distribution of power in a federation. The constitution unilaterally rules the allocation of competences by distributing them either to the federation or to the member states. This idea must be understood as a polemical one: it means that the allocation of competences is governed neither by international law, nor by a straightforward contract.[26] To put it in another way, the allocation of competences is 'dictated' to both the federation and the member states by the constitution, which somehow stands for a third and higher collectivity.[27] What legitimates this 'constitutional', rather than conventional, mode of allocation of competences is the willingness to preclude member states from staying ahead of the allocation of competences' game, to preclude them from derogating from the constitutional allocation.[28]

[25] S. Wang, *De la Répartition des compétences dans les constitutions fédérales*, D.Phil thesis (Paris: Jouve, 1920), 6.

[26] See Aubert (n 20) no 603 *et seq* of Vol. I.

[27] Aubert (n 20) 229: '*Exclusion du mode conventionnel*—Le partage pourrait résulter soit d'une convention, soit d'une règle générale. Ou bien les collectivités qui exercent le pouvoir s'entendent entre elles sur la façon de le répartir. Ou bien cette répartition est dictée à l'une par l'autre, ou même à toutes les deux par une troisième collectivité qui lui est supérieure'.

[28] Aubert (n 20) 230, gives as examples the cantons of Zurich and Berne which would have liked to delegate their competences to the federal authorities relating to the military matter. But the Federal Council refused.

A French lawyer would say, then, that the allocation of competences is mandatory, and that no convention could derogate from it ('*d'ordre public*' in French). Conceived in this manner, the federal constitution is a *command*, that is to say, *statute law*, and not a contract.[29] The federal constitution is as much statute law as a unitary constitution. But, compared to the latter, the distinguishing feature of the former is its object, which is to allocate federal and federated competences.[30] American lawyers thus say about the Federal Constitution that, as Westel Willoughby wrote, it 'serves a double purpose. *It operates as an instrument to delimit the several spheres of Federal and State authority*, and to provide for the organization of the Federal Government'.[31]

This doctrine, which describes the federal constitution as a sort of sharer-out of competences, has another polemical aspect. Indeed, it contradicts the idea that, in a federation, a delegation of powers would occur from the member states to the federal authorities. The 'delegation thesis' can rely on constitutional provisions, such as the well-known Tenth Amendment to the US Constitution, which reads: '[t]he powers not delegated to the US by the Constitution, nor prohibited by it to the States, are reserved respectively to the States, or to the people.' But it is also true of another well-known article: indeed, according to Article 3 of the Swiss Constitution, the cantons 'shall exercise all rights that are not vested in the confederacy'. Some authors *object* that 'the idea of a "delegation" is confusing. The cantons do not delegate powers to the confederacy, it is the federal constituent who vests the power in the confederacy'.[32] Here, the federal state's superiority arises from the fact that the powers of the member states have their legal basis in the federal constitution. However, the very same authors maintain that such a constitution guarantees the federated entities' autonomy. Indeed, as Jean-François Aubert explains

> to get rid of the risk that the federal legislative power, by its laws, eradicates the federated States' legislative powers, the way competences are allocated has to be out of its reach. The powers then have to be allocated in a document which authority is higher than federal laws.[33]

This makes clear the federal (that is to say, the federal state) constitution's ambivalence. It is even clearer when one notices, once again with Jean-François Aubert, 'the allocation arises from federal law itself. The rules that govern the allocation

[29] See my explanations in my article 'La notion de pacte fédératif. Contribution à une théorie constitutionnelle de la Fédération', in H. Mohnhaupt and J.-F. Kervégan (eds.), *Liberté sociale et contrat dans l'histoire du droit et de la philosophie* (Frankfurt: Klostermann, coll. *Ius Commune*, 1997), 197.

[30] Bridel (n 6) 113: '[p]armi les attributions actuelles ou virtuelles de la puissance publique, la Constitution fédérale désigne celles qui compètent à la Confédération tandis que les autres sont cantonales'. H. Kelsen, 'La garantie juridictionnelle de la Constitution' (1928) *Revue du droit public* 258, writes for instance 'the allocation of powers is the fundamental part of the Constitution of the Federal State'.

[31] W.W. Willoughby, *Principles of the Constitutional Law of the United States*, 2nd edn (New York: Baker, Voorhis & co., 1930), 53.

[32] Aubert (n 20) no 611, at 232.

[33] J.-F. Aubert, 'Notion et fonctions de la Constitution', in D. Thürer, J.-F. Aubert, and J.-P. Müller (eds.), *Verfassungsrecht der Schweiz. Droit constitutionnel suisse* (Zürich: Schultheiss, 2001), no 14, at 7.

of competences between federal and member states authorities are federal rules'.[34] Such a conclusion leads to an obvious and important difficulty: if the allocation of competences between the federation and the member states is governed by the federation itself, and more precisely by the federal constitution, isn't the federation both judge and party? Such a danger has been taken into account by authors who plead for the conventional understanding of federalism, but they usually see in the member states' participation in the constitution's amendment process a sufficient guarantee.[35] Another proposal to avoid partial interpretations of the constitution is to set up an arbitral jurisdiction, composed of representatives from both parties, which would rule on jurisdictional disputes between the federation and the member states.

This remark leads us to underline the intrinsic link existing between the allocation of competences and its legal sanction.[36] Indeed, the allocated competences must be guaranteed. Ideally, this is the function of a jurisdictional organ, checking that neither the federal authority, nor the federated authorities cross the borders that the constitution draws between their competences. Kelsen explains this tiny link as follows:

> [t]he allocation of competences is the political cornerstone of the federalist idea. From a technical point of view, it means that federal constitutions govern the legislative process and set law-making's principles, as unitary States' ones, but also that they list the respective objects of federal and local laws. Any violation of those constitutional boundaries is a violation of the Federal State's fundamental law. The guarantee of the limit drawn by the constitution between confederacy and Member States' competences is a vital political issue, as proved by the passionate debates that often occur in the Federal State on jurisdictional issues. More than everywhere else is an impartial authority needed, to peacefully resolve the debates, a tribunal competent to rule on those disputes as legal disputes—that is to say, a constitutional tribunal'[37].

One of the federal constitution's aims would then be to allocate competences to the federal and federated authorities. Disputes arising from the allocation of competences issue in a federal state are egalitarian, which means that they concern both the federation and the member states. It is then quite difficult to conciliate the 'federative parity' principle with the idea of a superiority of the federal order vis-à-vis the orders of the member states.[38]

[34] Aubert (n 20) no 606, at 230. Bridel (n 6), no 20, adds too: 'A l'intérieur, la souveraineté fédérale se manifeste en ceci que la Confédération a le pouvoir de fixer elle-même sa propre compétence et de limiter du même coup celle des cantons.'

[35] Aubert (n 20), no 606, at 251: '[d]e prime abord, la formule est choquante. C'est un peu comme si les autorités centrales étaient à la fois juges et parties. Afin donc d'éviter que le partage ne soit inéquitable pour les Etats membres, il faut le faire dépendre de règles sur l'adoption desquelles ces Etats aient une influence. Or, en droit au moins, les Etats ont la plus grande influence sur l'adoption des règles *constitutionnelles*. C'est particulièrement clair aux Etats-Unis.... Même en Suisse, où la révision est aisée, une place est faite aux cantons, par le truchement du Conseil des Etats (qui peut au moins proposer un contre-projet) et par la manière dont les voix sont comptées dans le référendum final. Nous concluons de tout cela que le partage doit être fait de la Constitution fédérale.'

[36] It is the structure adopted by Aubert in his treatise.

[37] Kelsen (n 30), 254.

[38] See my article; 'De quelques particularités de la justice constitutionnelle dans un système fédéral', in C. Grewe and others (eds.), *La notion de justice constitutionnelle* (Paris: Dalloz, 2005), 49.

2. The narrow approach of the allocation of competences issue, or the focus on the allocation of the legislative competence

First of all, it is important to notice the doctrine's tendency to focus on the technical aspects of the subject, rather than on the jurisdictional issue in itself. Nowadays, there are fewer and fewer debates on the nature and extent of the principles governing the allocation of competences. Once upon a time, every discussion regarding the way to organize the allocation of competences would have begun with a debate about sovereignty.[39] This is where our hypothesis comes from: by focusing on technical issues, lawyers hope to avoid the jurisdictional issues' political dimension, which is, as mentioned above, explosive. Lawyers feel more comfortable with questions relating to the modes of allocating competences. The methods proposed by Jean-François Gaudreault DesBiens contradict this view: in his works, he

tries to go beyond the technical approach, which, too often, governs the legal understanding of this mode of government, and reduces its extent to the explicit constitutional allocation of competences. Indeed, the study should be reduced to the issue of the allocation of competences even though in Canada as in other federations this is seen as a mark of federalism. Federalism is a set of values and aspirations that makes it different from other models of government[40].

The second—and very striking—evolution is to be found in positive laws. It shows even more clearly how debates about federalism are trapped by the notion of federal state. Such an evolution is due to the ever-growing refinement of the legal techniques employed to allocate competences. Anglo-American and Euro-Continental federalisms are both concerned, and textbooks devoted to federal states are then full of ever-more complex technical rules.[41] There is no point in listing them all, but the main and usual distinctions can be mentioned: exclusive/concurrent (or shared) powers, enumerated or non-enumerated powers, implied (or inherent) or explicit powers, etc. Some authors say that a distinction must be drawn between, on the one hand, the 'techniques' governing the allocation of competences and, on the other hand, its different modes.[42] According to the three relevant techniques, the list of competences is the central issue. The point is thus

[39] See Louis Le Fur who 'imported' into France the German legal debate.

[40] J.-F. Gaudreault DesBiens, 'Le fédéralisme et le législateur fédéral' (2009) 2 *Journal of Parliamentary and Political Law Revue de droit parlementaire et politique* 427.

[41] See the illuminating example of the Swiss Confederacy. Four categories of competences are to be distinguished (cf. P. Lauvaux, *Les grandes démocraties occidentales contemporaines*, 3rd edn (Paris: P.U.F., 2004), no 109 bis): 'les compétences exclusives accordées à la Confédération, les compétences concurrentes "limitées aux principes"' ['qui sont des "matières qui peuvent être réglées dans leurs principes par les autorités fédérales, les cantons restant maîtres de fixer les détails. Appartiennent à cette catégorie l'aménagement du territoire, la chasse et la pêche, l'harmonisation fiscale formelle"', Lauvaux, at 405], 'les compétences concurrentes non limitées' [ce sont 'les matières dans lesquelles les cantons peuvent légiférer pleinement tant que la Fédération s'abstient de le faire. Lorsque celle-ci prend l'initiative d'agir, elle recouvre une plénitude de compétences. Il s'agit en principe du droit privé, du droit pénal, du droit du travail, mais aussi de la circulation routière et de la police du commerce', ibid.] et, enfin, les compétences 'admettant par leur nature des compétences cantonales *parallèles*'.

[42] M. Uyttendale, *Le fédéralisme inachevé, Réflexions sur le système institutionnel belge issu des réformes de 1988-1989* (Brussels: Bruylant, 1991), 151 *et seq.*

to know whether the list concerns federal, federated, or both competences.[43] The powers are then divided into the 'exclusively federal' ones, the 'exclusively federated' ones, and the concurrent ones. As to the mode of allocating competences, it raises the problem of 'mixed matters', that is to say, the possibility of allocating competences, for the same matter, to different authorities.[44] The system is said to be 'closed', or 'tight' if such a possibility does not exist, and 'open' if it exists. A time-based criterion can help to construe mixed matters: federated authorities remain competent as long as the federal authority did not act.[45] As we will see below, such a sophisticated technique mainly concerns the setting up of the legislator's competence.

Techniques to allocate competences are also of interest to the lawyers because they allow them to show how good they are at interpreting laws. As Bridel wrote, '[b]ecause a federal constitution cannot list all the competences that the State could have, it has to use a fiction: it does not enumerate all the competences, but it vests the general competence in the federal or federated entity, the other competences being inferred from it'.[46] By opposing a general competence to special competences, the lawyer is also led to use techniques of interpretation. One disputed issue is thus to know whether a special competence is to be strictly construed or not. Authors, of course, have diverse answers to this question. Another issue the lawyer must deal with is the nature of the concerned powers. In the US, for example, 'one continuing question is whether the powers delegated to the federal government are exclusive or concurrent..., but, by and large, whether a delegated power is exclusive or concurrent is often ambiguous, and it has been left to the US Supreme Court to decide the issue on a case-by-case basis'.[47]

However, rather than listing all those techniques of allocation and of judicial interpretation, what I would like to do is to underline the presupposed argument upon which they rely. The jurisprudence constantly identifies the allocation of competences issue with that of allocation of *legislative* competence. Thus, authors like Marc Uyttendale, who tried to make an 'allocation of competences theory',[48] only take into account the material aspect of the legislative power's jurisdiction.

[43] Uyttendale (n 42) 152: '[l]a première technique consiste en une énumération des compétences *respectives* de l'Etat central et des diverses entités qui le composent. Une deuxième technique consiste en l'énumération des compétences des Etats membres de telle sorte que les matières non visées expressément relèvent de la compétence de la Fédération. La troisième technique—de loin la plus usitée—consiste en l'énumération de l'ensemble des matières qui relève de la compétence centrale, étant bien entendu que, dans tous les autres domaines, les entités fédérées sont compétentes.'

[44] See C. Durand, 'L'Etat fédéral', in *Le Fédéralisme* (Paris: P.U.F., 1953), 185: '[e]n effet, cette répartition peut être parfaitement *étanche*, soit supposer l'existence de *matières mixtes* qui mettent en jeu la *coexistence de compétences*', emphasis added. See also Uyttendale (n 42) 152: '[i]l existe plusieurs manières d'insérer des matières mixtes dans un système de répartition des compétences'.

[45] Uyttendale (n 42) 152–3, describes all the possibilities which nowadays exist and which specify the contemporary federal states (peculiarly Germany and Switzerland).

[46] Bridel (n 6) 159.

[47] E. Katz, 'United States of America', in R. Blidenbacher and A.J. Ostien (eds.), *Dialogues on Distribution of Powers and Responsibilities in Federal Countries* (Montréal: McGill-Queen's Press, 2005), 301.

[48] Uyttendale (n 42) 405 *et seq.*

To put it another way, lawyers mainly ask themselves: what are the areas of the federal legislator's exclusive jurisdiction?[49]

The 'allocation of competences' issue thus seems to be restricted to the issue of the federal or federated legislative power's *rationae materiae* jurisdiction. Article 91 of the British North America Act demonstrates this perfectly well: 'it is hereby declared that (notwithstanding anything in this Act) the exclusive Legislative Authority of the Parliament of Canada extends to all Matters coming within the Classes of Subjects next hereinafter enumerated; that is to say...'. Contrary to the provisions of other federal constitutions (such as Article I, Section 8 of the US Constitution, or Article 51 of the Australian Constitution), Article 91 of the British North America Act clearly shows what it means to allocate legislative competences according to a material criterion. The Constitution defines the 'Matters coming within the Classes of Subjects', and allocates to the federal legislative power an exclusive jurisdiction in the said subjects. This is an express and constitutional competence, limited by the subjects enumerated in this long article. Most of the constitutions have such lists: the expansive list contained in the 1999 Swiss Constitution thus show the extent of the federal power's jurisdiction and its various modes of exercise. Indeed, there are nine sections devoted to the Confederacy's powers: 'Foreign Relations'; 'Security'; 'Culture'; 'Environment'; 'Transport'; 'Energy and Communication'; 'Economy'; 'Social Security'; and 'Foreigners'.

By limiting the 'allocation of competences' issue to the problem of the legislative power's jurisdiction, the doctrine raises a genuine question: what are the areas of the federal legislator's exclusive jurisdiction? And what are, by contrast, the areas falling within the federated legislator's jurisdiction? But it also greatly simplifies the federation's central problem, since the question of the allocation of 'powers' cannot be restricted to the issue of the distribution of areas of legislative jurisdiction to the federation and to the member states. According to us, this narrow perspective is the consequence of a confusion of the federation with the federal state, and of the federal compact with the constitution of a federal state (with the constitutional law of the federal state).

II. Another Way of Looking at the Allocation of Competences in a Federation

The usual way of talking of the allocation of competences in a federal structure appears as rather insufficient. One solution to solve this problem of dealing with the allocation of competences would be to broaden the meaning of federation and narrow the meaning of competence. The main idea is to disconnect the notion of competence from the notion of the State.

[49] This assimilation results from the following definition given by the Canadian Professor André Tremblay (n 21) 199: 'le fédéralisme n'est pas un mode de séparation des pouvoirs entre les organes d'un gouvernement souverain (législatif, exécutif, judiciaire), mais bien plutôt un partage de compétences législatives entre deux paliers de gouvernement égaux et coordonnés.'

1. An approach to the allocation of competences that is not centred on the state

Jurists describing the problem of allocation of competences in federalism start from the premise that it concerns only the federal government and that it 'distributes the power of government between the centre and the regions in such a way that each set of governmental institutions has a direct impact on the individual citizens and other legal persons within its area of competence'.[50] There is, however, a drawback to this approach: it prevents us from taking into account the birth of new federations, mostly described as confederacies, even though the crucial question of who does what also arises when new federations are born. If we insist on the need for taking emerging federations into account, and only consolidated federations, it is because they are an example of integrative federalism, like the European construction.

Is it possible to believe that the problem of allocation of competences (in the broad sense given to it) will not arise for these new federations? A mere reading of Article 2 of the Confederation of the United States suffices in order for us to understand that this issue is at the very heart of federal thinking: '[e]ach state retains its sovereignty, freedom, and independence, and every Power, Jurisdiction, and right, which is not by this confederacy expressly delegated to the United States, in Congress assembled.' The Philadelphia Constitution reiterated this idea in the Tenth Amendment and set forth the distribution of power in Article 1, Section VIII.

However, it is possible to go beyond the reading of federal compact provisions and to read the legal doctrine to demonstrate that the issue of allocation of competences has already arisen in emerging federations. Thus, Pellegrino Rossi's report on the revision of the Swiss Federal Compact (1832), which in our view represents the best commentary on European federalism in the nineteenth century,[51] mentions it directly. First of all, it describes the 'general attributions of the Federal Diet' (Article 50); then, the attributions 'in foreign affairs' (Article 51) and those 'in domestic matters' (Article 52) and on 'the military' (Article 53). Finally, he mentions those concerning the administration of federal finances (Article 54). Having decided to accord priority to cantonal sovereignty, Pellegrino Rossi, who was a Swiss deputy, considered that the application of this principle to the distribution of powers would result in the following picture:

> [t]he cantons will essentially remain their own legislators, administrators and judges. Sovereignty can be summed up in those three words. However, we ask them:
>
> Not to pass constitutional or other laws in contradiction with the Federal Compact, the basic principles of Swiss domestic public law and the friendly and fraternal relationships that must exist between the children of the same fatherland.

[50] G. Sawer, *Modern Federalism* (Melbourne: Watts, 1969), 1.

[51] P. Rossi, *Per la Patria Comune - Rapporto de la commissione della Dieta ai ventidue Cantoni sul progetto d'Atto federale da essa deliberato a Lucerna, il 15 dicembre 1832* (Manduria: P. Lacaita, 1997).

> Not to administer their finances and military such as to harm their confederates or to disrupt the federal organisation.
>
> Not to judge their own causes and not make justice an instrument that would cause prejudice to their confederates.
>
> Furthermore we ask them to leave to the Confederacy, either completely or partly, all legislation:
>
> On taxes on consumption and roads; on the postal services, coinage, weights and measures; on military organisation; on extradition of criminals; on banishment from one canton to another; on *heimatloses*.
>
> We ask them to leave to the Federal authorities the right of peace, war, and political and trade treaties, also the training of the army.
>
> Finally, we propose that they submit, in certain specific cases and in small numbers, to the judgements of the Federal courts.[52]

Not only does this recommend a certain sharing of power between the federation and the member states (the cantons), but it also lays down rights that are both authorized and prohibited in a typically federal manner, according to which the fact of granting certain rights to one side automatically entails the prohibition of their exercise by the other. Thus, emerging federations are clearly required to take account of the distribution of powers. While the term 'competence' is not used, that of 'attributions' replaces it, as does 'tasks' (*Aufgaben* in German) to describe the powers of the federal or federated authorities.[53] This question must also be raised in respect of so-called confederacies. Murray Forsyth, a more recent author than Pellegrino Rossi, has retrained the spotlight on the notion of confederacy. Quite logically, he acknowledges the necessity of a broad 'sphere of power'.[54] He warns against the commonly held idea that confederacies have few broad powers. The very fact that they monopolize foreign policy suffices to disprove it.[55] It is true that jurists have generally agreed that the breadth of power granted either to a federation or to member states was not a relevant criterion by which to distinguish between a federal government and a confederacy of states.

In sum, the tendency of the jurisprudence to limit the allocation of competences to the federal government alone is contradicted by an examination of the positive law in emerging federations.

The effect of the above is to change the view of federative law, and to question the frequent likening of distribution of power to a constitution (in the sense of a State's constitutional law). On this point, we may draw upon the recent, most

[52] Rossi (n 51) 122–4.

[53] See e.g. Dubey (n 22) 25. Marcel Bridel uses also this word whereas Aubert intends to distinguish between 'tâche' (which means the idea of goals of the state) and the notion of competence.

[54] '[t]he constituent treaty establishes institutions representing the union as such alongside the constituent units. These institutions are, once again, more than international agencies or organisations. They are authorised to act within a broad sphere of competence' ('Towards a new concept of Confederacy', *Report to the Venice Commission*, 1994).

[55] The way Kelsen describes the competences in a 'federal state' and a 'confederacy' in his American treatise ('Distribution of Competence in a Federal State and a Confederacy of States', in H. Kelsen, *General Theory of Law and* State, New York: Russell and Russell, 1961, 321) should deserve more details and critics.

innovative work of Nicholas Aroney. He questions the definition of federalism as a division of power in the following terms:

> [i]ndeed, to refer simply to a 'division of power' is tacitly to presuppose a particular view of the way the distribution has in fact been effected: that the 'power' in question was originally somehow a 'unity', which has subsequently been 'divided'. This presupposition of an original unity of power betrays the relationship between the idea of a division of powers and theories of sovereignty, understood as a unitary locus of supreme, unlimited governmental power.... However, to suggest that all federal systems must logically be understood in this way is to underplay the distinction between those cases in which previously independent political communities have been integrated into a federal system and those in which a formerly unitary-state has devolved governmental powers upon a number of regions within that state.[56]

The second remark is an obvious allusion to the opposition between integrative federalism (bottom-up) and disintegrative federalism (top-bottom), which is a commonly held tenet in the literature. Here, it is important to underline the fact that there is a link between the way a federation is formed historically and the way power is divided. As Aroney (rightly, in my view) suggests, '[i]ndeed,..., the way in which governmental competences are defined and structured (i.e. enumerated, residual, reserved, etc.) tends to reflect the process by which the federal system came into being (i.e. through a process of either integration or disintegration)'.[57] This idea has been confirmed many times. I will merely observe that Geoffrey Sawer already identified a link between emerging federalism and the priority given to the enumeration (and thus, the limitation) of power.[58] His analysis suggests that the way federations are formed has an incidence on the nature and form of the division of power. Thus, the fact that Canada and Australia were born from the unilateral act of the British Empire had an influence over the way the distribution of power was designed.

That being the case, in the case of integrative federalism, the usual way of describing the constitution as allocating power to federal and federated authorities does not really represent the constitutional reality. This is because the constitutions of emerging federations 'do not constitute the States or confer powers on the States, *since the States and their powers are presuppositions of the federal Constitution itself*'.[59] Legally speaking, the term 'federal compact' better describes the fundamental act of confederacy of *monad states* (*Etats monades*), prior to becoming member states of a federation,[60] in which they intend to keep power to themselves and only grant

[56] N. Aroney, 'Formation, Representation, Amendment, in Federal Constitutions' (2006) 54 *American Journal of Comparative Law* 277 (also available at: <http://papers.ssrn.com/sol3/cf_dev/AbsByAuth.cfm?per_id=89918>).

[57] Aroney (n 56) 6.

[58] *Allocation of defined powers to the Centre, leaving the undefined residue of powers to the Regions*. This was a natural approach, since a confederacy of independent states would normally cede only a few, carefully defined heads of powers to a common organ. See Sawer (n 50) 15–16.

[59] Aroney (n 56). He takes for instance the judicial decision *Sturges v Crowninnshield* 17 US [1819] (4 Wheat), 122, 193.

[60] See my *Théorie de la Fédération* (n 2) ch. 6.

certain powers to the federal government that they have agreed to create. Indeed, certain court decisions have held that the federal constitution could be interpreted as a federal compact and that this, historically, justified the existence of a 'comparatively decentralised pattern of interpretation'.[61]

Contrary to most of the literature, the fact of interpreting the constitution that created a federation as being in fact a federal compact does not give the member states the right to conventionally avoid the division of power. This method of interpretation ignores the particularity of the federal compact, which is an institutional compact, a mixed compact, 'contractual to start with and regulatory by its effects'. Once it has entered into force, the federal compact binds the contracting parties, and cannot be changed unilaterally or by convention like an ordinary contract under private law.

2. Clarifying the issue of the meaning of the term competence so that we can distinguish between 'subject matter line' and 'power line'

It is now that I would like to return to the ambiguity of the word 'competence', which I highlighted in my introduction. Its polysemia and ambivalence when applied to the sharing of power in a federation need to be discussed.

It is polysemic in that it is used increasingly today in a broad, perhaps even very broad, sense. We have already noted the use of 'competences' to describe the responsibilities of the state. However, it is frequently used also in federations to describe the 'attributions of the public power',[62] or again 'regalian rights' or even 'Powers and Responsibilities'. What should we think of these linguistic usages in the light of a theory of competence?[63] It would seem that these expressions betray a very extensive use of the word competence. It would be an abuse of language to say that 'the right to coin money' or 'the police' are 'competences' simply because they are the equivalent of 'marks of sovereignty' (Bodin) of 'regalian rights' or the means of the public power. The reason is easy to understand: 'competence is not an attribute of a State, while power is'.[64]

[61] Aroney (n 56) 27. He quotes the *Engineers* decision of the High Court of Australia of 1920 which gives an interpretation of the Constitution which was favourable to the federal power. See also Aroney's article 'The Ghost in the Machine: Exorcising Engineers', in J. Stone (ed.), *Upholding the Australian Constitution*, Vol. 14 (Sydney: Samuel Griffith Society, 2002, available at: <http://samuel griffith.org.au/papers/pdf/Vol14.pdf>).

[62] L. Le Fur, *Etat fédéral et confédération d'Etats* (Paris: Editions Panthéon-Assas, 2000), 597, writes that '[t]out ce qu'il est possible de faire, c'est d'indiquer les grandes lignes suivant lesquelles les diverses attributions de la puissance publique se trouvent ordinairement réparties entre l'État fédéral et ses membres'.

[63] We rely here on an earlier study: O. Beaud, 'Compétence et souveraineté', in Association française pour la Recherche en Droit administratif, *La compétence* (Paris: Litec, 2008), 5.

[64] J. Combacau, 'Conclusions générales', in *Les compétences de l'Etat en droit international: Colloque de Rennes* (Paris: Pédone, 2005), 308.

As for its ambivalence, this is plain in certain descriptions of the allocation of competences. It is clear when certain jurists try to think conceptually of the sharing of power. Thus, George Berman chose to assume

> that the allocation of power with which federalism is concerned, is essentially a subject matter rather than a functional allocation. This is a major assumption, since there are federal systems whose vertical allocations of power run along functional lines—for example, who legislates? who executes? who adjudicates? who taxes? who spends?—rather than subject matter lines. Focusing on subject matter allocations means essentially asking: Who gets to address what substantive issues? What general principles, if any, determine this allocation? What presumptions, if any, about the allocation may be at play? Do any particular rules of construction govern the exercise of power allocations? Are powers excluded allocated to one level, only, or are they shared? If powers are shared, what if any principles of sharing—for ex, subsidiarity—govern the sharing? Under what circumstances does the exercise of authority on a given subject at one level pre-empt the prior or subsequent exercise of power at another? And so on.[65]

This position in favour of a 'subject matter line' as opposed to a 'functional line' enables a fairly clear distinction between two conceptions of how power is shared, that vary depending on how the word 'competence' is construed: either it means a 'function' of the state in the sense of power in the functional sense, or it means the subject of the action of power (subject matter). It is clear that the classical conception of sharing power, which favours how to share out legislative matters, has chosen the subject matter line. However, it should be added that there is another legal doctrine which understands by the allocation of competence, the distribution or division of powers in the sense of legal functions. This is, for instance, what Marcel Bridel deducts from his analysis of the 'Methods of sharing duties between the Confederacy and the Cantons'.[66] Studying the provisions of the Swiss Constitution on federal power, he observes that they are dominated by a rational classification by subject, distinguishing the 'attributions of the Confederacy by their subject'.[67] However, a classification like this, he adds, disregards another problem: are these attributions according to subject accompanied by the power with which to exercise them? By powers, he means the *legal functions* of the state: the legislative, the executive, and the judiciary[68] which he has no hesitation in defining according to

[65] G. Berman, 'The Role of Law in the Functioning of Federal Systems', in K. Nicolaidis and R. Howse (eds.), *The Federal Vision: Legitimacy and Levels of Governance in the United States and the European Union* (Oxford and New York: Oxford University Press, 2001), 191–2.

[66] Bridel (n 6) 168 *et seq*, no 75 *et seq*.

[67] Bridel (n 6) 168, no 75, for instance: 'l'armée, les douanes (péages), l'assurance en cas d'accident, les P &T, la monnaie, les poids et mesure, le droit civil et le droit pénal, l'établissement et le séjour des étrangers'.

[68] Bridel (n 6) 168–9: '[u]n classement par matières serait relativement facile à établir si, en /169/ conférant diverses *attributions* à la Confédération, la Constitution lui avait toujours donné tous les *pouvoirs* nécessaires à l'exercice complet de ces attributions—plus précisément: si elle l'avait toujours chargée de légiférer, d'exécuter et de juger dans chacun des *domaines particuliers* qu'elle lui assignait. Ce fut parfois le cas; mais parfois aussi, la Confédération n'a été chargée que de faire la loi ou de poser des règles tout à fait générales dont l'application serait totalement ou partiellement confiée aux cantons. Il suit de là que les diverses attributions de la Confédération varient en étendue du point de vue des fonctions étatiques qu'elles mettent en œuvre.'

his classification as 'legislative competence, executive competence (administrative and governmental) and judicial competence'.[69] Here it is the second construction of the term competence which is used.

Without entering into too long an analysis of the word competence, we propose to consider that the most relevant construction of it in law is that which distinguishes competence from the notion of power (in the sense of a legal function of the state) and associates it with the English notion of jurisdiction. Here, we will merely repeat Jean Combacau's demonstration that competence designates the 'scope of application of power'[70] and not that power itself. In other words, competence is the 'scope of application of the rules',[71] since the role of competence would be to 'delineate the field in which these powers are recognized to it: what subjects it can decide, what people it can command, of what situations it can define the regulation, over which people it can deploy its material means of action, whatever the form of this power, therefore, whatever the limits it is subject to in substance'.[72] This definition, followed by an illustrative enumeration, corresponds to what Jules Basdevant said in his course given in the Hague when he described what the competence of a state is: 'to determine the competences of a State is to determine over whom that State may exercise its various functions, in respect of whom it may legislate, render justice, police, administer, provide diplomatic protection, and operate the various public services.'[73] That is why, as Jean Combacau said, it is legitimate in law to use expressions such as 'territorial competence' or 'personal competence'. There must therefore be a clear line between the concept of a state's power, its rights, and duties, and the competence or jurisdiction that limits the exercise of this power, determines the sphere in which it is exercised, and sets boundaries. Jurisdiction in this sense would be a kind of marker instrument if we were using a spatial metaphor. It should be distinguished from both power and empowerment.

> In the mechanism of empowerment, therefore, what the state is empowered to do is not to exercise a competence, a formula without meaning when referring to a subject that has no positive content, *but to exercise a power of which the competence, or jurisdiction, merely sets the boundaries*.[74]

Thus, it is perfectly possible to transpose this definition to the federal subject: competence or jurisdiction merely sets the boundaries and limits of action for the federal power and federal bodies. Like any jurisdiction, it supposes many people capable of exercising the same power and law intervenes to avoid conflicts of jurisdiction by attributing to each body involved a sphere of action that, should

[69] Bridel (n 6) 169. [70] Combacau (n 64) 314.

[71] Combacau (n 64) 316. Even more precisely, at 307: 'l'usage du mot compétence est ainsi réservé à la désignation du champ d'application légitime de ce que les pouvoirs permettent de faire du ressort spatial, de la sphère temporelle, du domaine matériel dans lesquels il peuvent légalement se déployer.'

[72] Combacau (n 64) 307.

[73] J. Basdevant, 'Règles générales du droit de la paix' (1936) IV 58 *Recueil des cours de l'Académie de la Haye* 471, at 591.

[74] Basdevant (n 73).

it be overstepped, would cause the constitution to be violated (in the case of a written constitution) or the jurisdiction to be violated (were it not expressly written into a constitution).

What is the practical ambit of this theoretical discussion of competence? It is that the question of drawing limits should not be reserved merely to legislation as the prevailing doctrine would have it (see above I.2). It is enough to quote the many questions posed by Berman: '*who legislates? who executes? who adjudicates? who taxes? who spends?*' to understand that limiting the scope of legislative action is only one of the issues of distribution of power that arise in a federation. We should also remember that associated questions on the right of member states to conclude interstate compacts, or again the recognition of the rights of man, can also have effects on the scope of power granted to federal and federated entities.[75]

The other effect of this remark on division of power, if viewed from the angle of the subject matter line, is its importance in respect of a theory of Federation. Having reduced the notion of competence (limited to the field of application of a power) we must relativize its importance in the theory of Federation. Thus, indirectly, we side with many eminent scholars on federalism. As Sawer said, '*the area of competence is not all that matters; the structure of governmental organisations can be equally important and is commonly dealt with in constitutions*'[76]. Structures will also need the adjunction of political arrangements, those 'political safeguards of federalism'[77] or again the values of federalism,[78] and finally the issue of political identity.[79]

Concluding Remark

It would be a serious mistake to reduce the federal question to what jurists would find the most 'legal'. They would do better to remember Nicholas Aroney's conclusion after studying the formation of the Federal Republic of Australia: 'federalism was centrally concerned with formative process, structures of federal

[75] Bridel (n 6) 169–70, warns us against a too literal interpretation of the allocation of powers: '[u]ne telle délimitation des pouvoirs découle aussi d'autres dispositions constitutionnelles qui—sans assigner en principe, une tâche à la Confédération—n'en restreignent pas moins la souveraineté cantonale. Tels sont notamment les articles qui énoncent des règles de droit intercantonal: ils limitent la "souveraineté" cantonale comme les règles du droit international public fixent des bornes à la souveraineté des Etats. Tels sont encore les articles qui proclament les droits de l'homme. Ils n'ont pas pour but ni pour effet d'enlever aux cantons le pouvoir de faire et d'exécuter leurs propres lois sur les objets qui ne rentrent pas dans la compétence législative fédérale. Mais, dans l'élaboration et l'application de ces lois—en bref, dans toute leur activité—les cantons sont tenus de respecter les libertés individuelles et d'une façon générale, tous les droits qu'on appelle en Suisse, "les droits constitutionnels des citoyens".'

[76] Sawer (n 50). [77] See the description by Jackson (n 11).

[78] J.-F. Gaudreault DesBiens, 'In Praise of Principles, or Beyond the Toolbox Approach to Federalism', Contribution in the 'Congrès international de droit constitutionnel', (Mexico, December 2010) (forthcoming in French in *Jus Politicum*).

[79] M. Feeley and E. Rubin, *Federalism. Political Identity and Tragic Compromise* (Ann Arbor: University of Michigan Press, 2008).

representation and amendment'[80] and concentrating on division of powers meant that they wrongly neglected the relationship between these three elements and the Australian Constitution. It would therefore be a bad mistake to believe that founding the European Union would merely entail sharing out powers. That is the rather paradoxical conclusion I have drawn from the general introduction to this book.

[80] N. Aroney, *The Constitution of a Federal Commonwealth: The Making and the Meaning of the Australian Constitution* (Cambridge and New York: Cambridge University Press, 2009), 369. On this book, see also our review in *Jus Politicum*, no 6, available at: <http://www.juspoliticum.com/Nicholas-Aroney-The-Constitution,399.html>.

2

Theoretical Deflation: The EU Order of Competences and Power-conferring Norms Theory

Guillaume Tusseau

I. A Metalinguistic Analysis of the Expression 'The EU as a Federal Order of Competences'

1. The conundrum of the EU's ipseity

Is the EU a 'federal order of competences'? We implicitly take for granted that there is an answer to this question that we can find by means of a scientific enquiry addressing the allocation of competences in the EU practice, the ECJ doctrines on competences, and the political and legal limits to EU competences. We assume that terms such as that of the 'federal order of competences' have a determined legal meaning. We consider that the construction of this concept will be able to provide for an intellectual ordering of legal phenomena.

My feeling is that this is not the case. First of all, one can very well wonder whether it is, in principle, apposite to envision transplanting and applying to the EU—and to the relationships between the EU legal order and the legal orders of the Member States—a concept that was devised in the context of the state itself. Is it not necessary to dismiss such an approach, which relies on concepts that deal with domestic legal orders and their internal subdivisions, in order to analyse a legal phenomenon that is obviously—and, to my knowledge, unanimously—regarded as not being a state? Would not such an approach conceptually imply at the outset the negation of the possible specificities of its object, and testify to legal scholars' incapacity to revise and adapt their conceptual frameworks when they face institutional cases that prove disturbing for their theories? Apparently, several authors have already answered 'yes' to the foregoing questions, when they decided that understanding the specificities of the EU legal phenomenon compelled them to resort to new concepts such as 'constitutional pluralism',[1] 'transnational

[1] M. Avbelj and J. Komárek (eds.), 'Four Visions of Constitutional Pluralism', *EUI Working Paper* 2008/21.

constitution[alism]',[2] 'countrapunctual law',[3] 'multilevel constitutionalism',[4] 'transconstitutionalism',[5] 'post-national constitutionalism',[6] or '*Verfassungsverbund*',[7] etc.

2. The defects of 'federalism-talk'

I purport here to focus on another set of difficulties, which I identify in using the vernacular of 'federation', 'federalism', 'federal order of competences', etc.—in a nutshell 'federalism-talk'.[8] These terms are part of what can be considered as 'grand narratives' or 'macro analysis'. They purport to convey a general idea of a complex bundle of interrelated and not always convergent phenomena. As a consequence, in spite of their undoubtedly suggestive and heuristic import prima facie, they can lack the analytical precision that is necessary in the daily work of legal scholars and legal practitioners. Therefore, using them is hardly sufficient to understand what they truly are talking about from a legal point of view. There are several forms of federalism in internal constitutional laws. No one would deny, for example, that Canadian federalism is very different from German, Russian, or South African federalisms or from federalism in the United States. This is evident from several elements that any legal scholar would regard as crucial to the analysis of the federal order of competences. In Canada, for example, the division of powers is embodied in sections 91 and 92 of the Constitutional Law of 1867, which establish two lists of powers, one for the federation and the other for the provinces, while granting residuary powers to the former. The Senate, which is supposed to represent the

[2] E. Stein, 'Lawyers, Judges and the Making of a Transnational Constitution' (1981) 75 *American Journal of International Law* 1.

[3] M. Poiares Maduro, 'Countrapunctual Law: Europe's Constitutional Pluralism in Action', in N. Walker (ed.), *Sovereignty in Transition* (Oxford: Hart, 2003), 501.

[4] I. Pernice, 'Multilevel Constitutionalism and the Treaty of Amsterdam: European Constitution-Making Revisited?' (1999) 36 *Common Market Law Review* 703; I. Pernice, 'Multilevel Constitutionalism in the European Union', *WHI Paper* 5/2002, available at: <www.whi-berlin.de/documents/whi-paper0502.pdf>.

[5] M. Neves, *Transconstitucionalismo* (São Paulo: WMF Martins Fontes, 2009).

[6] J. Shaw, 'The Emergence of Postnational Constitutionalism in the European Union', *Archive of European Integration*, available at: <http://aei.pitt.edu/2385/1/002528_1.pdf> (1999).

[7] I. Pernice, 'Bestandssicherung der Verfassungen: Verfassungsrechtliche Mechanismen zur Wahrung der Verfassungsordnung', in R. Bieber and P. Widmer (eds.), *L'espace constitutionnel européen—Der europäische Verfassungsraum—The European Constitutional Area* (Zürich: Schulthess, coll. 'Publications de l'Institut suisse de droit compare', Vol. 28, 1995), 225 *et seq.*

[8] See e.g. B.S. Frey and R. Eichenberger, *The New Democratic Federalism for Europe: Functional, Overlapping, and Competing Jurisdictions* (Cheltenham and Northampton, Mass.: Edward Elgar, 1999); M. Burgess, *Federalism and European Union. The Building of Europe 1950-2000* (London and New York: Routledge, 2000); B. Dubey, *La répartition des compétences au sein de l'Union européenne à la lumière du fédéralisme Suisse: systèmes, enjeux et consequences* (Geneva: Helbing & Lichtenhahn, Brussels: Bruylant, and Paris: LGDJ, 2002); S. Fabbrini (ed.), *Democracy and Federalism in the European Union and the United States. Exploring Post-national Governance* (London and New York: Routledge, 2005); A. Menon and M. Schain (eds.), *Comparative Federalism: The European Union and the United States in Comparative Perspective* (Oxford: Oxford University Press, 2006); T. Konstadinides, *Division of Powers in European Union Law. The Delimitation of Internal Competence between the EU and the Member States* (Austin: Wolters Kluwer Law & Business, and Alphen aan den Rijn: Kluwer Law International, 2009); A. Glencross and A.H. Trechsel (eds.), *EU Federalism and Constitutionalism. The Legacy of Altiero Spinelli* (Lanham, Md.: Lexington Books, 2010); E. Cloots, G. De Baere, and S. Sottiaux (eds.), *Federalism in the European Union* (Oxford and Portland: Hart Publishing, 2012).

provinces, is discretionarily appointed by the Governor General, provided that he respects a defined repartition of seats between the provinces (sections 21 to 36 CL of 1867). On the contrary, in the United States, the Union disposes of enumerated powers only. The Senate is elected on an egalitarian basis. German federalism is clearly based on the principle of federal primacy, according to which 'Bundesrecht bricht Landesrecht' (Article 31 of the Basic Law). On the contrary, Belgian federalism is exclusively based on the fact that each authority has an exclusive field of action, without any idea of a hierarchy between them.

The only information federalism-talk captures here is the fact that two levels of legislative power coexist. The fact that several authorities can simultaneously act with respect to a single set of subjects and a single set of individuals is undoubtedly the very core of the problem EU scholars are trying to grapple with. But this is hardly sufficient for any legal analysis.[9] In the end, one could very well contend that these concepts conceal more differences than they reveal common points.

Moreover, the terms that are employed in federalism-talk can hardly be regarded as neutral. A long time ago, one of the greatest analysts of legal discourse, Jeremy Bentham, established a threefold dictionary.[10] For the very same object, he opposed three ways to name it, which were at the same time three ways to talk about the object to which the term referred. Neutral terms convey the idea of the object without implying any disapproving or approving stance vis-à-vis it. Dyslogistic terms imply a negative stance vis-à-vis the object, whereas eulogistic terms imply a favorable stance. Bentham thus contrasted, the word 'hunger', which is neutral, with the word 'gluttony', which is dyslogistic, and with the expression 'love of the pleasures of good cheer', which is eulogistic. He insisted that, despite their dealing with the same empirical subject matter, the three expressions do not have the same impact upon the minds of the one who speaks or writes and the ones who hear or read. Their apprehension of the topic of the need for food can be mistaken by the way this phenomenon is talked about. From the point of view of legal analysis, one can very well fear that a similar problem appears with federalism-talk. These terms can prove detrimental to any clear apprehension of what is at stake. For example, during the French Revolution, 'federalism' was a political doctrine to be fought and eradicated, as it proved divisive and threatening from the point of view of the polity's unity and indivisibility. One of the originalities of the term 'federalism', as it appears for example in the Canadian constitutional debate, is that, depending on the context of its use, it can as well be a eulogistic as a dyslogistic term. A partisan of Quebec's increased autonomy can meaningfully contend to be a federalist, as he insists upon shared rule. But he can also meaningfully criticize his opponents as 'federalists', as they may be obsessed with constantly centralizing powers in Ottawa. In the European context, similar ambiguities are evident, so that the

[9] See e.g. A. Sagar, 'Les relations fédérales-fédérées. Etude comparative des rapports juridiques fondamentaux dans le contentieux des compétences', PhD thesis in Public Law (University of Rouen, 2013).

[10] J. Bentham, *Deontology Together with A Table of the Springs of Action and the Article on Utilitarianism* (edited by A. Goldworth, Oxford: Clarendon Press, 1983). See. G. Tusseau, *Jeremy Bentham. La guerre des mots* (Paris: Dalloz, coll. 'Les sens du droit. Essai', 2011).

federalism-talk, fraught with emotive language as it is, can appear as a dead end for legal analysis.

Finally, as the terms which structure federalism-talk are not unambiguous, it is highly probable that some precise definition of them will be given at the outset of a demonstration purporting to answer the question as to whether the EU is a 'federal order of competences'. But such an approach may be methodologically flawed if a purely ad hoc definition of 'federal' is adopted, which necessarily implies, according to the answer one wishes to give, either the idea that the EU is a 'federal order of competences' or the idea that it is not a federal order of competences. Such reasonings are strictly analytical, and only develop the premise from which they start, without adding any new knowledge. When they get involved with emotive terms, they can become all the more dishonest from an intellectual point of view.

Having said this, I cannot of course stop here. My suggestion is to go back to basics: what are legal scholars, provided they are engaged in a scientific activity, trying to grasp with the grand narrative concerning European federalism? What are, on the ground, the phenomena they are talking about?

II. A New Methodological Start

1. Methodological conventionalism

What a legal scholar wants to capture is what is operating at the legal level, i.e. the productions of legal institutions, be they, in the present context, EU institutions or Member States' institutions. Thus his conceptual tools must be appropriate to deal with these elements. This is not to deny that there also is a political, ideological, or justificative dimension in legal phenomena, nor to refuse to address it. But severing, in some sense, the legal product from the justificative or hostile discourses which accompany it is precisely a prerequisite in order to understand both the former and the latter. In the remainder of this chapter, I will only deal with 'the federal order of competences' in the first context. Accordingly, I will try to identify the meaning(s) that can be ascribed to this expression if one focuses on the EU as a legal order and tries to elucidate what can be, from the viewpoint of a concrete legal study of the basic elements of the EU legal order, the objects that the federalism-talk refers to. I will disregard the ways that federalism-talk can appear and operate in the respective discourses of the EU and the national institutions, be it to increase and fasten transfers of competences, to lower them, to change the way these competences are exercised, to alter the relationships between the various types of competences at the EU and at the state level, etc.

Trusting what the contemporary theory of knowledge has adopted as its main principle, I rely on the presupposition and adopt the framework of 'conceptual conventionalism'. The basic tenet of this approach is ontology's relativity.[11] Scientific

[11] W.V.O. Quine, *Ontological Relativity, and Other Essays* (New York: Columbia University Press, 1969).

theories no longer aim at offering real descriptions and definitely true explanations of the ultimate nature of the world. According to conventionalism, the world we inhabit has no natural, necessary, objective, a priori structure. It is shaped by the way*s* we conceive of it, i.e. the way*s* we cut in the magma of sensitive perceptions, impressions, feelings, and experiences, several units which prove meaningful and useful from a specific viewpoint. Several conceptual schemes can simultaneously apply to the same bundle of phenomena, and result in very different versions, all of which can be perfectly apposite for those who use them, in their respective perspectives. For example, a layman who wants the roof of his house to be repaired considers the phenomena he sees on top of the place where he lives as 'a roof', i.e. one object. On the contrary, the firm he will call to repair it cannot limit itself to such a primitive conceptual apparatus. For evident practical reasons, it has to resort to a more granular ontology,[12] distinguishing for example the tiles, the cement, the frame, the gutter, etc. Every specific field of knowledge comports its own vision of how the world is, i.e. how the flood has to be conceptually cut, which is comparatively the most useful for its purposes.

2. The choice of an ontology of law

As a consequence, in the legal context, there are several 'ways of legal worldmaking',[13] i.e. several ways to conceive of the basic legal formants of any legal phenomenon. This is the reason why some authors adopt a twofold vision of the basic elements of a legal phenomenon: Dworkin[14] thus opposes rules and principles. Manuel Atienza and Juan Ruiz Manero[15] distinguish between principles, rules, and values. Others conceive of the legal phenomenon as composed of norms or rules. But several options must be distinguished. Some consider that two types of rules must be distinguished: primary and secondary rules, as in Hart's terminology.[16] Others refuse to admit to their conceptual apparatus more than one type of legal norm. Such was Kelsen's option until 1962.[17] Others consider that legal phenomena should be analysed thanks to the identification of eight 'fundamental legal conceptions' corresponding to the situations of the legal subjects.[18]

I will adopt a normativist standpoint, considering not that the legal phenomena consist of norms but, more exactly, that jurists *can benefit from considering* the global

[12] P.R.S. Visser and T.J.M. Bench-Capon, 'A Comparison of Four Ontologies for the Design of Legal Knowledge Systems' (1998) 6 *Artificial Intelligence and Law* 27.

[13] N. Goodman, *Ways of Worldmaking* (Hassocks: Harvester Press, 1978).

[14] R.M. Dworkin, *Taking Rights Seriously*, 2nd edn with a new appendix (Cambridge, Mass.: Harvard University Press, 1978).

[15] M. Atienza and J. Ruiz Manero, *Las piezas del derecho. Teoría de los enunciados jurídicos* (Barcelona, Ariel, coll. 'Ariel Derecho', 1996).

[16] H.L.A. Hart, *The Concept of Law* (Oxford: Clarendon Press, 1961).

[17] Cf. H. Kelsen, *Reine Rechtslehre*, 2nd edn (Vienna: Franz Deuticke, 1960), on the one hand, with H. Kelsen, 'Derogation', in R.A. Newman (ed.), *Essays in Jurisprudence in Honor of Roscoe Pound* (Indianapolis and New York: The Bobb Merrill & Co., 1962), 339, and K. Ringhofer, H. Kelsen, and R. Walter (eds.), *Allgemeine Theorie der Normen* (Vienna: Manz, 1979), on the other hand.

[18] W.N. Hohfeld, *Fundamental Legal Conceptions as Applied in Judicial Reasoning*, edited by W.W. Cook and with a foreword by A.L. Corbin (Westport, Conn.: Greenwood Press, 1978).

bundle of phenomena which are *hic et nunc* called 'legal', *through the lens* of the concept of a legal norm. I will dispense with any other concept (principle, institution, value, policy, etc.) as not useful for my purposes. One of the advantages of the concept of a legal norm is that this concept is familiar to many legal scholars. Moreover, it is not linked to any specific legal context, domestic, national, statist, etc. and can, accordingly, be used as the concept of a general legal analysis, something that is especially useful when one purports to address problems such as that of EU federalism.

However, the normativist standpoint must be refined. Considering that legal phenomena are only composed of norms (or are preferably conceived of this way) is not the whole story. One must still make explicit whether there is only one sort of legal norm, so that a single concept would be used in the whole legal analysis, or whether a whole taxonomy of norms should preferably be used.

III. A Theory of Power-conferring Norms

1. The debate about power-conferring norms in legal theory

In the field of legal theory or jurisprudence, the literature on the concept of a legal power and on power-conferring norms has recently been burgeoning. Several learned and doctrinal proposals have been made by scholars, including Ota Weinberger,[19] Rafael Hernández Marín,[20] Torben Spaak,[21] Jordi Ferrer Beltrán,[22] Manuel Atienza, and Juan Ruiz Manero.[23] All of them intend to devise the conceptual tools which are best suited for the legal analysis of legal expressions which are prima facie related to the idea of a power to create norms (e.g. '[t]he Congress shall have Power To...' (Article I(8) United States Constitution), '[t]he General Court shall have jurisdiction to hear and determine at first instance actions or proceedings...' (Article 256(1) TFEU), etc.), and for legal reasonings which imply assessing the legal faculties of a legal actor (e.g. considering one's own range of possible actions, considering the possibility of appealing for the judicial review of the validity of legal norms, etc.).

I have participated in this debate in my PhD thesis, which was entitled 'Les normes d'habilitation'.[24] I would like to use the conceptual framework I sketched

[19] O. Weinberger, 'Normological Inferences and the Generation of Legal Norms' (1995) 8 *Ratio Juris* 261.

[20] R. Hernández Marín, *Introducción a la teoría de la norma jurídica* (Madrid and Barcelona: Marcial Pons, 1998).

[21] T. Spaak, *The Concept of Legal Competence. An Essay in Conceptual Analysis*, engl. trans. by R. Carroll (Aldershot: Dartmouth, 1994); T. Spaak, 'Explicating the Concept of Legal Competence', in J.C. Hage and D. von der Pfordten (eds.), *Concepts in Law* (Dordrecht, Heidelberg, London and New York: Springer, coll. 'Law and Philosophy Library', Vol. 88, 2009), 67.

[22] J. Ferrer Beltrán, *Las normas de competencia. Un aspecto de la dinámica jurídica*, prol. by R. Guastini, (Madrid: Centro de estudios políticos y constitucionales—Boletín oficial del Estado, col. 'El Derecho y la Justicia', 2000).

[23] Atienza and Ruiz Manero (n 15).

[24] G. Tusseau, *Les normes d'habilitation*, pref. by M. Troper (Paris: Dalloz, coll. 'Nouvelle bibliothèque de thèses', Vol. 60, 2006).

out in this book in order to address the problematic of the EU as a federal order of competences. In this study, I began by reviewing several individuations of the basic elements of legal phenomena, in order to assess their respective merits and demerits. I rejected as inappropriate to the activities of legal scholars and legal practitioners several theories that I considered reductionist. These theories refuse to use a concept of power-conferring norm, and prefer to embark on legal tasks by resorting only to the concept of prescriptive norm, i.e. the concept of a norm imposing a sanction in case a given behaviour is not adopted. According to such theories, all the raw legal material is to be reconstructed so as to fit into this conceptual pattern. I also rejected non-reductionist theories, which, contrary to the preceding ones, consider it more convenient to add other concepts of norms to that of prescriptive norm. According to my own position, for reasons that would be too long to give here, neither the addition of the concepts of permissive norm and constitutive norm can be regarded as sufficient.

I relied on a functional and on a structural analysis in order to advocate (once again: not the necessity but) the opportunity of using a concept of power-conferring norm in legal analysis. Studying a legal order's functions as a dynamic normative system in Merkl[25] and Kelsen's sense, and from the point of view of Hart's 'descriptive sociology'[26] invites one to devise a specific concept in order to account for the importance of power-conferring sentences in ordinary legal reasoning. Such is also the case when one focuses on the analysis of subjective legal positions and legal actors' practical reasonings when they are confronted with a power-conferring sentence. After examining thesis which, such as Ruiter's,[27] Weinberger's,[28] or Guastini's,[29] recommended individuating several types of norms on the production of norms, I sided with MacCormick[30] in proposing a unique and richer concept of power-conferring norm.

2. The proposed concept of power-conferring norm

I insist that this concept is adopted only as a matter of choice, of theoretical decision, which is revisable and must be tested against its utility for legal scholars' and legal

[25] A.J. Merkl, 'Prolegomena einer Theorie des rechtlichen Stufenbaues', in A. Verdross (ed.), *Gesellschaft, Staat und Recht. Untersuchungen zur reinen Rechtslehre. Festschrift Hans Kelsen zum 50. Geburtstag gewidmet* (Vienna: Springer, 1931), 252.

[26] Hart (n 16).

[27] D.W.P. Ruiter, *Institutional Legal Facts. Legal Powers and their Effects* (Dordrecht, Boston and London: Kluwer Academic Publishers, coll. 'Law and Philosophy Library', Vol. 18, 1993); D.W.P. Ruiter, 'Legal Powers', in S.L. Paulson and B. Litschewski Paulson (eds.), *Normativity and Norms. Critical Perspectives on Kelsenian Themes* (Oxford: Clarendon Press, 1998), 471.

[28] O. Weinberger, 'The Theory of Legal Dynamics Reconsidered' (1991) 4 *Ratio Juris* 18, at 22; O. Weinberger, 'Der Erlaubnisbegriff und der Aufbau der Normenlogik' (1973) 5 *Etudes de logique juridique* 113, at 124–5 (1973); O. Weinberger, *Normentheorie als Grundlage der Jurisprudenz und Ethik. Eine Auseinandersetzung mit Hans Kelsens Theorie der normen* (Berlin: Duncker & Humblot, 1981), 62.

[29] R. Guastini, 'Invalidity' (1994) 7 *Ratio Juris* 212.

[30] N. MacCormick, 'Powers and Power-Conferring Norms', in Paulson and Litschewski Paulson (n 27).

practitioners' tasks. The proposed concept includes four elements. The first is that of an actor being empowered to produce legal norms. The second is that of an action by means of which that actor can produce norms. The other two elements determine the norms that this actor is allowed to produce, provided he follows the procedure. The third element, called the 'range of application' of the power-conferring norm, refers to the area of reality, which is determined by territorial, temporal, material, and/or personal criteria, that an actor is empowered to govern. The fourth and final element is called the 'range of regulation'. It refers to the kinds of normative meanings that a power-conferring norm empowers to produce, i.e. both to the types of norms (according to the taxonomy I choose to adopt: prescriptive, permissive, derogating, and power-conferring) the legal actor can produce, and their levels in the normative hierarchy.

In a very Kelsenian tone, I then proposed the following concept of a power-conferring norm:

> if an actor *a* accomplishes the action—i.e. follows the procedure—*p* having the subjective meaning of a norm *n* relative to a range of application *ra* and included in the range of regulation *rr*, then its objective meaning ought to be.

Such a norm makes the behaviour of a given actor *a* the condition of production of a norm *n* bearing on the domain *ra* and having the normative meaning *rr*. Apart from a power-conferring norm, no one can produce any norm. No norm can result from a logical deduction. This power-conferring norm is the only condition to produce norms. My concept thus states the necessary and sufficient conditions for an actor to produce a legal norm.

How to substantiate these abstract reflections and make use of this theoretical suggestion with respect to the EU as a federal order of competences?

IV. Identifying Types of Power-conferring Norms in the EU Legal Order

1. A twofold theoretical construction

Specialists of EU law have proposed several taxonomies of the EU competences.[31] My ambition is not to substitute their proposals with mine. Within a perspective

[31] See e.g. V. Constantinesco, *Compétences et pouvoirs dans les Communautés européennes. Contribution à l'étude de la nature juridique des Communautés*, av.-prop. by P. Pescatore, pref. by R. Kovar (Paris: LGDJ, coll. 'Bibliothèque de droit international', Vol. 74, 1974); N.A. Neuwhal, 'Shared Powers of Combined Incompetence? More on Mixity' (1996) 33 *Common Market Law Review* 667; K. Boskovits, *Le juge communautaire et l'articulation des compétences normatives entre la Communauté européenne et ses Etats membres*, av.-prop. by N. Scandamis, pref. by D. Simon (Athens: N. Sakkoulas, and Brussels: Bruylant, 1999); A. Dashwood, 'The Relationship between the Member States and the European Union/European Community' (2004) 41 *Common Market Law Review* 355; A. von Bogdandy and J. Bast, 'The European Union's Vertical Order of Competences: The Current Law and Proposals for its Reform' (2002) 39 *Common Market Law Review* 227; V. Michel, *Recherches sur les compétences de la Communauté européenne* (Paris: L'Harmattan, 2003); A. Goucha Soares, 'The Division of Competences in the European Constitution' (2005) 11 *European Public Law* 603; R. Schütze, 'The

similar to that of these authors, and within the frame of the present discussion of a federal order of competences, I would like, in a very sketchy manner, to present and illustrate more precisely the specific methodological orientation I began to outline.

Following Charles Eisenmann,[32] I suggest that in order to design a useful conceptual tool, it is necessary at first to stay at a strictly theoretical level, and to map out abstractly all the theoretical possibilities. Classes of possibilities are identified, divided, and subdivided in an ordered way, so as to offer a complete map of what may (but need not) appear in practice. Classes must be elaborated so as to be both jointly exhaustive with regard to the field studied, and mutually exclusive of one another. Once these logical prerequisites for a sound intellectual framework are satisfied, an infinity of classifications is possible according to the criteria which are considered interesting.[33] In the present case, my purpose is to design a series of typologies of the classes of power-conferring norms that may appear concretely in the legal practice of EU law. Only after completing this first operation will it be appropriate to identify actual cases that fit in one of the theoretical hypotheses previously identified. I am not the best qualified to identify, in the daily operations of EU institutions, the concrete examples—if any—of the various types of competences I have purported to individuate at the abstract, theoretical, level. I will nevertheless try to provide clear illustrations of the conceptual tools that I offer. This legal casuistry is the second step. It allows the ordering of the several power-conferring norms which can be identified in EU law, according to the four components of the concept of a power-conferring norm that I have suggested. Of this methodology, I only want to give a limited outline, resorting to examples which may be among the most evident and the most relevant for the study and practice of EU law. Among the infinity of possible classifications which each element of the power-conferring norm admits, I briefly mention and illustrate the following ones, with the following important qualification: I only rely on the text of the Treaties, and do not use the case law of the ECJ, which would, of course, be necessary in a more thorough enterprise than mine.[34]

European Community's Federal Order of Competences—A Retrospective Analysis', in M. Dougan and S. Currie (eds.), *50 Years of the European Treaties. Looking Back and Thinking Forward* (Oxford and Portland, Or.: Hart, 2009), 63; L.S. Rossi 'Does the Lisbon Treaty Provide a Clearer Separation of Competences between EU and Member States?', in A. Biondi, P. Eeckhout, and S. Ripley (eds.), *EU Law After Lisbon* (Oxford and New York: Oxford University Press, 2012), 85.

[32] C. Eisenmann, *Centralisation et décentralisation. Esquisse d'une théorie générale* (Paris: LGDJ, 1948); C. Eisenmann, 'Quelques problèmes de méthodologie des définitions et des classifications en science juridique' (1966) 11 *Archives de philosophie du droit* 25.

[33] G. Tusseau, 'Classificazioni', in L. Pegoraro (ed.), *Glossario di Diritto pubblico comparator* (Rome: Carocci, 2009), 41–2.

[34] This may, however, be debated: e.g., C.Timmermans, in his contribution in this book, contends that the Court has not developed a real doctrine on the division of competences between the EU and its Member States.

2. Outline of a typology of power-conferring norms in the EU legal order

a) *The actor*

First, with respect to the actor, one can oppose power-conferring norms that are attributed to a whole organization, such as 'the Member States' or 'the EU' in general, and those which are attributed to specific organs of such an organization. Although talking about the respective competences of the states or the EU in general is not the most precise way to discuss the respective responsibilities of legal actors, similar formulations may nevertheless be useful in specific legal contexts. Such is precisely the case in the discussion about the EU as a federal order of competences, which crucially focuses on the global picture that emerges from the relationships between the two levels of decision-making. As a consequence, the proposed taxonomy must account for them.

More precisely, one can oppose power-conferring norms the addressee of which is a single individual and those the addressee of which is a whole institution consisting of several individuals. As an example of the former situation, Article 17(6) TEU empowers a single-seated institution, namely the President of the Commission, to

> (a) lay down guidelines within which the Commission is to work; [to] (b) decide on the internal organisation of the Commission, ensuring that it acts consistently, efficiently and as a collegiate body; [and to] (c) appoint Vice-Presidents, other than the High Representative of the Union for Foreign Affairs and Security Policy, from among the members of the Commission.

In the latter case, one can moreover distinguish between power-conferring norms the addressee of which is a single institution—for example the Commission, the European Court of Justice, etc.—and those the addressees of which are several institutions. In this last situation, the empowered actor is in fact a set of co-authors, whose converging consent is necessary for the production of a norm. Among many examples where several institutions have to cooperate, each having a veto power—be it in the form of an initiative, a proposal, or the consent to a proposed norm—in order for a norm to be adopted, Article 215(1) TFEU reads:

> [w]here a decision, adopted in accordance with Chapter 2 of Title V of the Treaty on European Union, provides for the interruption or reduction, in part or completely, of economic and financial relations with one or more third countries, the Council, acting by a qualified majority on a joint proposal from the High Representative of the Union for Foreign Affairs and Security Policy and the Commission, shall adopt the necessary measures. It shall inform the European Parliament thereof.

Similarly, several actors must cooperate, and are as a consequence jointly empowered as a complex actor, according to Article 81(3) TFEU, which reads:

> [n]otwithstanding paragraph 2, measures concerning family law with cross-border implications shall be established by the Council, acting in accordance with a special legislative procedure. The Council shall act unanimously after consulting the European Parliament.

The Council, on a proposal from the Commission, may adopt a decision determining those aspects of family law with cross-border implications which may be the subject of acts adopted by the ordinary legislative procedure. The Council shall act unanimously after consulting the European Parliament.

The proposal referred to in the second subparagraph shall be notified to the national Parliaments. If a national Parliament makes known its opposition within six months of the date of such notification, the decision shall not be adopted. In the absence of opposition, the Council may adopt the decision.

In this case, the complex empowered actor consists of (1) the Council, (2) the Commission, (2') but *not* the Parliament, because as it is only consulted and does not decide, it is only part of the procedure, as distinguished from the empowered actor itself, (3) the 28 national parliaments.

b) The action or procedure

Secondly, with respect to the action or procedure, one can oppose EU power-conferring norms which impose resorting to one specific action and those which allow for several actions to result in the production of a new norm. For example, by providing that

[t]he [Economic and Social Committee] may be consulted by [the European Parliament, the Council or the Commission] in all cases in which they consider it appropriate,

Article 304 TFEU introduces some kind of indifference as to the legal procedure which is to be used in order to establish a norm. It appears that, for every power-conferring norm in the Treaties, the empowered actors have a choice between following a procedure where they do not consult the Economic and Social Committee, and one where they *proprio motu* decide to ask for its advice. On the contrary, most of the power-conferring norms which are present in the EU Treaties prove more constraining as to the procedure which must be followed. Very detailed rules on voting and consultation are frequently established. They frequently impose several consultations. Consultations as such do not amount to a sharing of the normative power. As a consequence, they do not affect the identity of the empowered legal actor, but only the way he makes his decisions and produces norms. Such is, for example, the case of Article 43(2) TFEU, which reads:

[t]he European Parliament and the Council, acting in accordance with the ordinary legislative procedure and after consulting the Economic and Social Committee, shall establish the common organisation of agricultural markets provided for in Article 40(1) and the other provisions necessary for the pursuit of the objectives of the common agricultural policy and the common fisheries policy.

Similarly, Article 66(1) TFEU reads:

[w]here, in exceptional circumstances, movements of capital to or from third countries cause, or threaten to cause, serious difficulties for the operation of economic and monetary union, the Council, on a proposal from the Commission and after consulting the European

Central Bank, may take safeguard measures with regard to third countries for a period not exceeding six months if such measures are strictly necessary.

A double consultation is imposed by Article 91 TFEU, which reads:

> [f]or the purpose of implementing Article 90, and taking into account the distinctive features of transport, the European Parliament and the Council shall, acting in accordance with the ordinary legislative procedure and after consulting the Economic and Social Committee and the Committee of the Regions, lay down:
>
> (a) common rules applicable to international transport to or from the territory of a Member State or passing across the territory of one or more Member States;
> (b) the conditions under which non-resident carriers may operate transport services within a Member State;
> (c) measures to improve transport safety;
> (d) any other appropriate provisions.

A further subdivision is possible among the power-conferring norms that impose a specified procedure. One can contrast power-conferring norms that impose a unanimous decision and those that do not. For example, Article 22(1) TFEU imposes unanimity in the Council:

> [e]very citizen of the Union residing in a Member State of which he is not a national shall have the right to vote and to stand as a candidate at municipal elections in the Member State in which he resides, under the same conditions as nationals of that State. This right shall be exercised subject to detailed arrangements adopted by the Council, acting unanimously in accordance with a special legislative procedure and after consulting the European Parliament; these arrangements may provide for derogations where warranted by problems specific to a Member State.

Among those that do not, one can oppose those which ask for a simple majority and those which ask for a qualified majority. For example, Article 150 TFEU reads:

> [t]he Council, acting by a simple majority after consulting the European Parliament, shall establish an Employment Committee with advisory status to promote coordination between Member States on employment and labour market policies.

On the contrary, according to Article 236 TFEU, a qualified majority is necessary for the European Council to adopt

> (a) a decision establishing the list of Council configurations, other than those of the General Affairs Council and of the Foreign Affairs Council, in accordance with Article 16(6) of the Treaty on European Union; (b) a decision on the Presidency of Council configurations, other than that of Foreign Affairs, in accordance with Article 16(9) of the Treaty on European Union.

c) The range of application

Thirdly, with respect to the range of application, one can oppose power-conferring norms according to the criterion or the combination of criteria that are used to define the subject matter the regulation of which is entrusted to the empowered legal actor. For example, Article 59(2) TFEU uses a material criterion to define the Parliament and the Council's power-conferring norm in order to achieve the liberalization of specific services, as it stipulates that

> priority shall as a general rule be given to those services which directly affect production costs or the liberalisation of which helps to promote trade in goods.

On the contrary, Article 66 TFEU defines the range of application of the power-conferring norm using a temporal and a territorial criterion when it states that

> [w]here, in exceptional circumstances, movements of capital to or from third countries cause, or threaten to cause, serious difficulties for the operation of economic and monetary union, the Council, on a proposal from the Commission and after consulting the European Central Bank, may take safeguard measures with regard to third countries for a period not exceeding six months if such measures are strictly necessary.

Another classification can oppose power-conferring norms that are dedicated to only one object to those which enjoy a wider scope. For example, Article 308 TFEU is only relevant to one strictly defined object, namely the Statute of the European Investment Bank. Thus this power-conferring norm can be deemed 'special'. On the contrary, Article 24(1) TEU considers a far broader empowerment by providing that:

> [t]he Union's competence in matters of common foreign and security policy shall cover all areas of foreign policy and all questions relating to the Union's security, including the progressive framing of a common defence policy that might lead to a common defence.

Thus, this is a 'generic' power-conferring norm.

d) The range of regulation

Fourthly, with respect to the range or regulation, one may oppose power-conferring norms that confer a broad discretion to the empowered actor as to the types of norms he may produce, and power-conferring norms that only confer the power, if one chooses to exercise it, to produce a single, totally predetermined norm.

For example, Article 18 TFEU establishes a wide range of regulation in order to 'prohibit discriminations'. It reads:

> [t]he European Parliament and the Council, acting in accordance with the ordinary legislative procedure, may adopt rules ['*toute* réglementation', in the French version] designed to prohibit such discrimination.

On the contrary, Article 14(3) TEU predetermines the range of possible norms the European Council and Parliament can adopt regarding the composition of the Parliament:

> 1. The European Parliament shall, jointly with the Council, exercise legislative and budgetary functions. It shall exercise functions of political control and consultation as laid down in the Treaties. It shall elect the President of the Commission.

2. The European Parliament shall be composed of representatives of the Union's citizens. They shall not exceed seven hundred and fifty in number, plus the President. Representation of citizens shall be degressively proportional, with a minimum threshold of six members per Member State. No Member State shall be allocated more than ninety-six seats.
3. The European Council shall adopt by unanimity, on the initiative of the European Parliament and with its consent, a decision establishing the composition of the European Parliament, respecting the principles referred to in the first subparagraph.

Using another nomographic device, Article 24(1) TEU excludes the adoption of 'legislative acts', as defined by Article 289 TFEU, from the range of regulation of the power-conferring norm of the European Council and the Council regarding the range of action of the common foreign and security policy. Only other types of norms or acts can be adopted by the empowered complex legal actor. Even more strictly, Article 98 TFEU only empowers the Council, acting on a proposal from the Commission, to adopt one (derogation) norm:

[t]he provisions of this Title shall not form an obstacle to the application of measures taken in the Federal Republic of Germany to the extent that such measures are required in order to compensate for the economic disadvantages caused by the division of Germany to the economy of certain areas of the Federal Republic affected by that division. Five years after the entry into force of the Treaty of Lisbon, the Council, acting on a proposal from the Commission, may adopt a decision repealing this Article.

In EU law, as is evident from the examples provided and from the litigation of the legal basis of EU acts, one can notice that it is not exceptional for some ranges of application to be strictly associated by the power-conferring norms to a specific actor, to a specific procedure, and to a specific range of regulation (especially a specific legal act). But this is only dependent upon the choices of positive law, and this is by no means a conceptual necessity. For example, Article 308 TFEU establishes a power-conferring norm which simultaneously empowers two different complex legal actors—the Council and the European Investment Bank, on the one hand, the Council and the Commission, on the other hand—to act:

[t]he Statute of the European Investment Bank is laid down in a Protocol annexed to the Treaties. The Council acting unanimously in accordance with a special legislative procedure, at the request of the European Investment Bank and after consulting the European Parliament and the Commission, or on a proposal from the Commission and after consulting the European Parliament and the European Investment Bank, may amend the Statute of the Bank.

As a consequence, it remains useful to distinguish as I have proposed, so as to obtain the general mapping outlined in Figure 2.1.

Thus far, EU law power-conferring norms have been considered in isolation. However, when one ponders over the '*federal* order of competences', he or she obviously has in mind the way several power-conferring norms, which empower the EU and the states considered globally, or more precisely, power-conferring norms which empower EU institutions and power-conferring norms which empower national institutions, interlock with one another, how an empowerment

Figure 2.1 Types of power-conferring norms

Actor				Procedure				Range of application						Range of regulation			
General reference to the Member States or the EU	Specified			Imposed			Undetermined	Criteria for definition				Scope		Degree of flexibility		Type of legislative act	Type of legal norm
	Single individual	Collective body or bodies		Unanimous vote	Not unanimous vote			Territorial	Temporal	Material	Personal	Special	Generic	Discretion	Predetermination		
		Single institution	Co-authors		Simple majority	Qualified majority											

at one level impacts upon the legal situation at the other level, and how the ensuing normative productions themselves interact.

V. Identifying Types of Relationships between Power-conferring Norms in the EU Legal Order

1. Coordination and hierarchization of power-conferring norms

One of the advantages of the theoretically-anchored approach I suggest is, at least provisionally, to ignore the traditional terms which are used by scholars and practitioners. This allows for the avoiding of the emotive—positive or negative—connotations these terms inevitably convey. By focusing on the power-conferring norms and their relationships, it also allows one to escape from the ambiguities of terminologies which, though traditional, are more or less metaphorical and are not always understood in the same ways by several authors, such as 'concurrent', 'parallel', 'shared', 'complementary', 'coordinate', 'joint', etc. powers.

Two major modes of relationship between norms are usually distinguished in the Italian theory of legal sources.[35] The 'principle of hierarchy' imposes upon some actors the need to respect and to conform to the normative production of other actors. When norms conflict, the superior one prevails and the other is invalid. The power of the actor whose norms are called 'inferior' is limited to the production of norms that respect the norms produced by the actor whose norms are called 'superior'. On the contrary, the 'principle of competence' does not operate on a vertical scale, but on a horizontal one. Its function is to specialize sources of law. Any source can only produce norms that bear on a specific subject matter. No other source can operate in this field. The relationship is not of superiority and inferiority, but of exclusion. I propose to restate these two principles of normative ordering in my theory of power-conferring norms. The principle of hierarchy operates between the normative qualifications that can be produced thanks to several power-conferring norms. The relationship between power-conferring norms is thus situated at the level of their respective ranges of regulation. There is a hierarchy between two power-conferring norms when the normative productions that the range of regulation of the inferior one authorizes cannot violate the normative productions that the range or regulation of the superior one authorizes. The principle of competence, which I rename 'coordination of power-conferring norms' distinguishes power-conferring norms not according to the normative meanings they authorize, but according to the matters, objects, persons, territories, etc. about which they authorize the production of norms. In other words, the relation

[35] A. Ruggeri, *Gerarchia, competenza e qualità nel sistema costituzionale delle fonti normative* (Milan: Giuffrè, coll. 'Pubblicazioni dell'Istituto di scienze giuridiche, economiche, politiche e sociali della Università di Messina', Vol. 103, 1977); R. Guastini, *Teoria e dogmatica delle fonti* (Milan: Giuffrè, 1998). See also the contribution by C. Timmermans in this book, opposing 'rules of competence' and 'rules of conflict'.

of power-conferring norms is thus situated at the level of their respective ranges of application.

Starting with this basic bifurcation, one can offer a more detailed analysis of several types of coordination and hierarchization.

2. Outline of a typology of relationships between power-conferring norms in the EU legal order

a) *Forms of coordination*

Several techniques can result in the establishment of a relationship of coordination between two power-conferring norms. A first one can be identified, which I call 'parcelling competences'. An activity, a territory, a time span, or a group of human beings is divided into fragments. Thus the coordinated power-conferring norms are 'special', for they only authorize the production of norms about that range of application. The various actors between whom the range is divided have an identical power-conferring norm. Such is for example the case of all the national central banks, which are empowered by Articles 282 *et seq*. TFEU, and amongst which the conduction of the monetary policy of the Union is equally divided from a material point of view, according to the territorial jurisdiction of each.

A second way to create a coordination of power-conferring norms is to distinguish between what French doctrine calls '*compétence de principe*' and '*compétence d'attribution*'. A global range of application is divided into two parts, only one of which is precisely defined. The other one is defined as 'all that remains'. Thus the coordination is between a 'special' and a 'generic' power-conferring norm. For example, this operation of coordination is present in Article 4(1) TEU, which reads:

> [i]n accordance with Article 5, competences not conferred upon the Union in the Treaties remain with the Member States.

Article 5(2) TEU similarly reads:

> [u]nder the principle of conferral, the Union shall act only within the limits of the competences conferred upon it by the Member States in the Treaties to attain the objectives set out therein. Competences not conferred upon the Union in the Treaties remain with the Member States.

When power-conferring norms are coordinated, they seem to establish what is traditionally called 'exclusive competences' vis-à-vis each other.[36] But one relation of coordination between two power-conferring norms does not necessarily imply that the two power-conferring norms in question are in a situation of coordination vis-à-vis every other power-conferring norm the legal order might contain, which is generally understood as a necessary condition for a situation of exclusive competence to arise. It is perfectly possible that one of the two power-conferring norms

[36] On the idea of 'retained powers', see the contribution by L. Boucon in this book.

considered to be in a relation of hierarchization vis-à-vis a third power-conferring competence. As a consequence, situations of coordination cannot automatically be said to establish an exclusive competence in the traditional sense. On the contrary, an exclusive competence can be identified for example in Article 128(1) TFEU, which reads:

> [t]he European Central Bank shall have the exclusive right to authorise the issue of euro banknotes within the Union. The European Central Bank and the national central banks may issue such notes. The banknotes issued by the European Central Bank and the national central banks shall be the only such notes to have the status of legal tender within the Union.

The empowerment of the ECB is coordinated with every other power-conferring norm the EU legal order may contain, for this institution alone can deal with the specified range of application.

b) Forms of hierarchization

Relations of hierarchization can take two broad forms. In a relation of 'delegation', a superior power-conferring norm limits itself to empowering an actor to produce norms which deal with the totality or part of its own range of application. Such is, for example, what is envisioned in Article 290(1) TFEU, which stipulates:

> [a] legislative act may delegate to the Commission the power to adopt non-legislative acts of general application to supplement or amend certain non-essential elements of the legislative act.
>
> The objectives, content, scope and duration of the delegation of power shall be explicitly defined in the legislative acts. The essential elements of an area shall be reserved for the legislative act and accordingly shall not be the subject of a delegation of power.

This power-conferring norm, the range of regulation of which is limited by the specifications of the article itself, empowers an actor to empower another actor to produce norms. Similarly concerning the relationships between the Member States and the EU, one can identify a relation of delegation in the schemes of enhanced cooperation. Article 20(1)TEU reads:

> Member States which wish to establish enhanced cooperation between themselves within the framework of the Union's non-exclusive competences may make use of its institutions and exercise those competences by applying the relevant provisions of the Treaties, subject to the limits and in accordance with the detailed arrangements laid down in this Article and in Articles 326 to 334 [TFEU].

It accordingly gives the Member States the faculty to empower EU institutions, i.e. to delegate to them increased powers which until then were their own.

As distinguished from the relation of delegation, the relation of 'primacy' limits the normative productions that are possible thanks to an inferior power-conferring norm. The study of relations of primacy among power-conferring norms must be twofold. 'Typical' (i.e. relatively intuitively perceived and known) relations of primacy are of two types, between which the difference is more of degree than of nature.[37] The first is the relation of 'conformity', i.e. a strict correspondence between the normative productions that the inferior power-conferring norm authorizes and those that the superior power-conferring norm authorizes. The second typical relation of primacy is that of 'compatibility'. It is looser than the previous one. A simple absence of conflict between normative productions is sufficient for the inferior norm's validity. Both are related to the way a superior norm is applied or executed by an inferior norm.

Article 75 TFEU seems, on the face of it, to characterize a relation of conformity among several EU institutions, as it empowers the Commission and the Council to execute the norms laid down by the Parliament and the Council concerning terrorism:

> [w]here necessary to achieve the objectives set out in Article 67, as regards preventing and combating terrorism and related activities, the European Parliament and the Council, acting by means of regulations in accordance with the ordinary legislative procedure, shall define a framework for administrative measures with regard to capital movements and payments, such as the freezing of funds, financial assets or economic gains belonging to, or owned or held by, natural or legal persons, groups or non-State entities.
>
> The Council, on a proposal from the Commission, shall adopt measures to implement the framework referred to in the first paragraph.
>
> The acts referred to in this Article shall include necessary provisions on legal safeguards.

A relation of conformity also subsists between the respective power-conferring norms of the Member States and the EU institutions according to Article 14(3) of the Statute of the European System of Central Banks and of the European Central Bank. This text reads:

> [t]he national central banks are an integral part of the ESCB and shall act in accordance with the guidelines and instructions of the ECB. The Governing Council shall take the necessary steps to ensure compliance with the guidelines and instructions of the ECB, and shall require that any necessary information be given to it.

Because of its range of regulation, the inferior power-conferring norm can only authorize the production of norms which strictly respect what has been decided when the superior power-conferring norm was employed. A similar situation appears in Article 13 TFEU, according to which:

> [i]n formulating and implementing the Union's agriculture, fisheries, transport, internal market, research and technological development and space policies, the Union and the Member States shall, since animals are sentient beings, pay full regard to the welfare requirements of animals, while respecting the legislative or administrative provisions and customs of the Member States relating in particular to religious rites, cultural traditions and regional heritage.

A double relationship of strict hierarchization is thus established. First, the EU and the states implement what has been enacted by the EU institutions with regard to

[37] C. Eisenmann, 'Le droit administratif et le principe de légalité', in *Etudes et documents du Conseil d'Etat* (1957), 25.

the specified ranges of application. Secondly, in so doing, these actors must moreover comply with the normative productions that result from the use of domestic power-conferring norms.

Article 146(1) TFEU seems closer to a relation of compatibility, as it appears to leave more space for the states' autonomous decisions:

> Member States, through their employment policies, shall contribute to the achievement of the objectives referred to in Article 145 in a way consistent with the broad guidelines of the economic policies of the Member States and of the Union adopted pursuant to Article 121(2).

In contrast to typical ones, two types of 'non-typical' relations of primacy can be identified. In the first case, the range of regulation of the superior norm is itself limited. As a consequence, the empowered actor is not left free to produce any norm he wants, and to limit accordingly the ambit of the inferior power-conferring norm, which empowers other actors (or the same actor) to execute the first norms. While he uses its own, superior, power-conferring norm, the actor must leave enough leeway for the inferior power-conferring norms. Such is the situation, which seems to be implied by the principle of proportionality,[38] created by Articles 82 and 83 TFEU. In the field of judicial cooperation in criminal matters, and

> [t]o the extent necessary to facilitate mutual recognition of judgments and judicial decisions and police and judicial cooperation in criminal matters having a cross-border dimension, the European Parliament and the Council may, by means of directives adopted in accordance with the ordinary legislative procedure, establish minimum rules.

The same Article 82(2) TFEU insists that

> [a]doption of the minimum rules referred to in this paragraph shall not prevent Member States from maintaining or introducing a higher level of protection for individuals.

As a consequence, the whole regulation of the range of application in discussion cannot be dealt with in totality by the EU institutions. Whatever the norms they are empowered to produce, they must be limited, so as to guarantee some autonomous legal action at the national level.

The second type of non-typical relations of primacy, I propose to call 'relations of intensification'. In this case, the inferior normative productions do not strictly implement—within the framework of strict conformity or looser compatibility—the superior ones. They can only increase the effect of the superior norms. Such is the case, for example, in Article 193 TFEU, which reads:

> [t]he protective measures adopted pursuant to Article 192 shall not prevent any Member State from maintaining or introducing more stringent protective measures. Such measures must be compatible with the Treaties. They shall be notified to the Commission.

Both the States and the European institutions are empowered to produce norms regarding the range of application of the protection of environment (Article 191

[38] See e.g. E. Ellis (ed.), *The Principle of Proportionality in the Laws of Europe* (Oxford: Oxford University Press, 1999).

TFEU). However, the inferior normative productions, which in this case are the national ones, must not only respect what the superior normative productions have established. They can only pursue the continuation of the normative dynamics in one sense.

Power-conferring norms in the field of social policy are good illustrations of atypical hierarchizations. Article 153(2)(b) TFEU only empowers the European Parliament and the Council to enact minimal norms. In other words: the range of regulation of their power-conferring norms is limited, so that they cannot totally predetermine the ranges of regulation of the states' power-conferring norms. According to this provision,

> [t]o this end, the European Parliament and the Council:
> (a) may adopt measures designed to encourage cooperation between Member States through initiatives aimed at improving knowledge, developing exchanges of information and best practices, promoting innovative approaches and evaluating experiences, excluding any harmonisation of the laws and regulations of the Member States;
> (b) may adopt, in the fields referred to in paragraph 1(a) to (i) [(a) improvement in particular of the working environment to protect workers' health and safety; (b) working conditions; (c) social security and social protection of workers; (d) protection of workers where their employment contract is terminated; (e) the information and consultation of workers; (f) representation and collective defence of the interests of workers and employers, including codetermination, subject to paragraph 5; (g) conditions of employment for third-country nationals legally residing in Union territory; (h) the integration of persons excluded from the labour market, without prejudice to Article 166; (i) equality between men and women with regard to labour market opportunities and treatment at work], by means of directives, minimum requirements for gradual implementation, having regard to the conditions and technical rules obtaining in each of the Member States. Such directives shall avoid imposing administrative, financial and legal constraints in a way which would hold back the creation and development of small and medium-sized undertakings.

Article 153(4) TFEU insists that the range of regulation that is left undetermined to the benefit of national power-conferring norms is not to be interpreted as authorizing any normative production. Only those which pretend to better fulfil the goals of social policy are allowed:

> [t]he provisions adopted pursuant to this Article [by the EU institutions]:
> — shall not affect the right of Member States to define the fundamental principles of their social security systems and must not significantly affect the financial equilibrium thereof,
> — shall not prevent any Member State from maintaining or introducing more stringent protective measures compatible with the Treaties.

Eventually, the general picture that emerges from this analysis is presented in Figure 2.2.

As a last element, one should notice that chronological elements, i.e. the fact that some power-conferring norms are used or not and the way they are used may result in major changes in the relationships between them. When two power-conferring

Figure 2.2 Types of relationships between power-conferring norms

<table>
<tr><th colspan="2">Coordination</th><th colspan="5">Hierarchization</th></tr>
<tr><td>Parcelling competence</td><td>Special v. generic power-conferring norm</td><td>Delegation</td><td colspan="4">Primacy</td></tr>
<tr><td colspan="3" rowspan="2"></td><td colspan="2">Typical</td><td colspan="2">Non-typical</td></tr>
<tr><td>Compatibility</td><td>Conformity</td><td>Limitation of the inferior range or regulation</td><td>Intensification</td></tr>
</table>

norms are not coordinated in the preceding sense, both share the same range of application and can only be related to one another with respect to their range of regulation. Such is for example the case in Articles 151 *et seq*. TFEU, which insist that the range of application of 'social policy' is and must remain common to EU power-conferring norms and national power-conferring norms. Article 151 TFEU explicitly reads:

The Union and the Member States, having in mind fundamental social rights such as those set out in the European Social Charter signed at Turin on 18 October 1961 and in the 1989 Community Charter of the Fundamental Social Rights of Workers, shall have as their objectives the promotion of employment, improved living and working conditions, so as to make possible their harmonization while the improvement is being maintained, proper social protection, dialogue between management and labour, the development of human resources with a view to lasting high employment and the combating of exclusion.

To this end the Union and the Member States shall implement measures which take account of the diverse forms of national practices, in particular in the field of contractual relations, and the need to maintain the competitiveness of the Union economy.

They believe that such a development will ensue not only from the functioning of the internal market, which will favour the harmonisation of social systems, but also from the procedures provided for in the Treaties and from the approximation of provisions laid down by law, regulation or administrative action.

Nevertheless, in this respect, one has to distinguish between two possibilities. In the first case, a given range of application constantly remains common to the power-conferring norms of several actors, which is the case according to the foregoing Article, and illustrates a situation of hierarchization. Several actors can simultaneously legislate vis-à-vis this range of application. In the second case, the range of application is only common to both power-conferring norms on a conditional basis, i.e. provided none of the actors which are empowered to produce norms regarding it uses its power. When one of them uses its power, he becomes the only actor entitled to produce norms related to this range of application. This is for example the case with Article 71(1) of the German Basic Law (BL), which reads:

[o]n matters within the concurrent legislative power, the Länder shall have power to legislate so long as and to the extent that the Federation has not exercised its legislative power by enacting a law.

The range of application, which is defined by Article 74 BL, is only temporarily common to federal and local actors. Once the federation acts, only the Bund is empowered to produce norms regarding these subject matters.

Article 2(2) TFEU provides a device which may be compared with the foregoing one. This text reads:

> [w]hen the Treaties confer on the Union a competence shared with the Member States in a specific area, the Union and the Member States may legislate and adopt legally binding acts in that area. The Member States shall exercise their competence to the extent that the Union has not exercised its competence. The Member States shall again exercise their competence to the extent that the Union has decided to cease exercising its competence.

Accordingly, the range of application of their respective power-conferring norms is only temporarily common to EU and Member States institutions, and only on a potential basis. Once the Union acts, it monopolizes the normative production vis-à-vis the considered area in the limits set by Protocol No. 25, and states can act only provided that the Union refrains from legislating. A situation of coordination thus follows. The analysis of power-conferring norms thus has to take into account a chronological dimension in order to identify precisely which kind of normative situation subsists between the EU and the Member States.

Concluding Remarks

After making such a long theoretical detour, it could seem legitimate, eventually, to try and confront this book's fundamental interrogation. To the question 'Is the EU order federal?', I would give the following answer*s*: yes if you want; no if you do not. In either case, what you say is devoid of any precise legal meaning. Nonetheless, despite resulting in a somewhat disappointing answer, having refrained from locating the enquiry within the framework of federalism-talk, the suggested approach may be quite revealing of the doctrinal dynamics this viewpoint participates in.

Using the vernacular of federalism could be regarded as a kind of compensatory attitude in front of the disruption of established habits of thinking and their inappropriateness to confront current phenomena, as exemplified in the EU legal order, but which are more general (the disaggregation of the post-Westphalian order, the end of former hierarchies, the empowerment of new transnational actors, the heterarchical relationships between autonomous legal spheres, the fragmentation of international law into a multiplicity of specialized regimes,[39] societal constitutionalism, global constitutionalism, global administrative law, etc.). To understand the tensions that this situation raises in the legal mentality, Jerome

[39] International Law Commission, *Report on the Fragmentation of International Law: Difficulties Arising from the Diversification and Expansion of International Law*, UN Doc. A/CN/4/L.682, 13 April 2006.

Frank's realism[40] suggests regarding resorting to the federal paradigm as a way for legal scholars and practitioners to relieve themselves from the anguish of hardly being able to face what is changing. Using the federal mindset would be a minimal way to come to grips with a reality which makes one feel both theoretically and practically uncomfortable. As a simple extension of pre-existing, familiar, securing concepts, federalism-talk would amount to a psychoanalytic version of what Anne Peters calls 'compensatory constitutionalism'.[41] As Martti Koskenniemi puts it,

> [m]uch 20th century debate about Western modernity may be depicted as a succession of perceptions about breakdown, explosion, dispersal, fragmentation, normative collisions, followed by reassuring counter-narratives that explain the apparent chaos as mere complexity, healthy pluralism, dynamism, freedom.[42]

In this respect, instead of using this opportunity to renew the intellectual framework of legal scholarship, using the federal lens to address the EU phenomenon would only be an avatar of 'rationalizing legal analysis'.[43]

We are still waiting for a fully convincing grand narrative able to account for the originalities of the EU as a legal phenomenon (and maybe of other global phenomena), what Pedro Cruz Villalón calls the 'unprecedented constitutionalism' of EU law.[44] While I openly reckon I am totally unfit for such a job, my recommendation in the meantime would be to resort safely to a strong normativist theory in daily legal analysis and practice, such as the one I have put forward here or, preferably, a more useful one, as the metatheoretical framework I advocate invites one to conceive of.

[40] J. Frank, *Law and the Modern Mind*, 6th edn (London: Stevens & Sons, 1949).

[41] A. Peters, 'Compensatory Constitutionalism: The Function and Potential of Fundamental International Norms and Structures' (2006) 19 *Leiden Journal of International Law* 579.

[42] M. Koskenniemi 'Global Legal Pluralism: Multiple Regimes and Multiple Modes of Thought', available at: <http://www.helsinki.fi/eci/Publications/Koskenniemi/MKPluralism-Harvard-05d[1].pdf>, 3.

[43] R.M. Unger, *What Should Legal Analysis Become?* (London: Verso, 1996).

[44] P. Cruz Villalón, *La constitución inedita. Estudios ante la constitucionalización de Europa* (Madrid: Trotta, 2004).

PART II

THE ALLOCATION OF COMPETENCES IN EU PRACTICE

3

EU External Relations: Unity and Conferral of Powers

Marise Cremona

Introduction

The legal personality of the European Union indicates its legal capacity as an international organization to enter into international obligations.[1] However, this leaves open the question of the extent and nature of the EU's external competence in specific fields, which is derived directly and indirectly from the Treaties.[2] If we consider allocation of competence in EU practice in the external relations field, there are two dimensions to consider. First is the issue common to all policy fields: that of the relation between EU competence and Member State competence, the extent to which and the circumstances under which one might displace or constrain the other. In our external relations context this common theme is complicated both by the involvement of third countries and the fact that the Member States retain their sovereignty and international capacity alongside the EU's international legal personality and its attributed (and therefore limited) external powers.

The second dimension, which is peculiar to external relations, and which is also faced by federal states, is the relationship between internal and external powers. To what extent is the external power of the EU dependent on possessing—or exercising—internal competence? Can the EU enter into international obligations which must then be implemented by the Member States? To what extent are external powers tied to the achievement of internal Union objectives? Is the division of competence between the EU and its Member States to act internally mirrored in the division of competence to act externally? This last expression of the question makes clear the link between the two dimensions we are considering here.

[1] Art 47 TEU.

[2] See e.g. R. Schütze, *European Constitutional Law* (Cambridge and New York: Cambridge University Press, 2012), 187–222; P. Eeckhout, *EU External Relations Law*, 2nd edn (Oxford and New York: Oxford University Press, 2011), 70–164; G. De Baere, *Constitutional Principles of EU External Relations* (Oxford and New York: Oxford University Press, 2008), 9–32; M. Cremona, 'Defining Competence In EU External Relations: Lessons from the Treaty Reform Process', in A. Dashwood and M. Maresceau (eds.), *Law and Practice of EU External Relations: Salient Features of a Changing Landscape* (Cambridge and New York: Cambridge University Press, 2008), 34.

Let us start by recalling two rather different perspectives on these questions.

First, that of Joseph Weiler in his article on 'Mixity and the Federal Principle: external legal relations of non-unitary actors', re-published in his essay collection *The Constitution of Europe* in 1999,[3] but first published in 1983 in Henry Schermers and David O'Keeffe's edited book on mixed agreements.[4] Weiler distinguishes between internal legislative competence and external treaty-making powers, and adds to these the question of international capacity (defined as acceptance by the international legal order of the polity's capacity to act). He addresses the nature of the EU as an external actor—as neither a federal state nor a classic international organization—in fields of activity where competence is shared between the EU and its Member States. He argues that whereas federal *states* generally adopt a principle based on unity in external action, in the sense of only one actor, this is not an inevitable result for other types of federal (non-unitary) system. In fact, the mixed agreement should be seen not as a necessary (and perhaps temporary) evil but as an inventive and creative way of dealing with this problem: a true 'federal principle', allowing the EU to participate in fields where it does not yet act internally, and even where it may not have competence internally.

Secondly, we may consider Robert Post's analysis of the *AETR* and *Open Skies* cases in Loïc Azoulai and Miguel Poiares Maduro's *The Past and Future of EU Law*, published in 2010.[5] Post writes of the difference between internal and external politics from the perspective of the needs of a polity. He defines internal politics as the creation of a political space that allows for the emergence of common commitments through the engagement of a plurality of actors in a process founded on trust and reciprocity. External politics in contrast is based on the expression of collective unity enabling the polity to act in an outside world that (may) lack trust and reciprocity. He argues that there is a need to safeguard internal political discourse with its reliance on mutual trust (the 'internal agora') through unified external action. In *AETR* the Court appreciated this need for external unity in order to safeguard the internal legislative process, the Court basing exclusive external competence on the existence of internal rules and their pre-emptive effect.[6] Thus 'unity of international representation' is linked, in this view, with internal

[3] J.H.H. Weiler, *The Constitution of Europe* (Cambridge: Cambridge University Press, 1999).

[4] H.G. Schermers and D. O'Keeffe (eds.), *Mixed Agreements* (Deventer and Boston: Kluwer Law and Taxation, 1983). So-called mixed agreements are those international agreements to which both the EU and its Member States are party; see more recently C. Hillion and P. Koutrakos (eds.), *Mixed Agreements Revisited: The EU and its Member States in the World* (Oxford: Hart Publishing, 2010).

[5] R. Post, 'Constructing the European Polity: *ERTA* and the *Open Skies* Judgments', in M. Poiares Maduro and L. Azoulai (eds.), *The Past and Future of EU Law* (Oxford and Portland: Hart Publishing, 2010), 234.

[6] Case 22/70 *Commission v Council* (*AETR/ERTA*) [1971] ECR 263. 'The bringing into force, on 25 March 1969, of Regulation 543/69... necessarily vested in the Community power to enter into any agreements with third countries relating to the subject-matter governed by that Regulation' (para 28). 'These Community powers exclude the possibility of concurrent powers on the part of Member States, since any steps taken outside the framework of the Community institutions would be incompatible with the unity of the common market and the uniform application of Community law' (para 31). 'Wherever a matter forms the subject of a common policy, the Member States are bound in every case to act jointly in defence of the interests of the Community' (para 77).

action and debate; on the one hand external unity safeguards the internal policy space, on the other hand the trust and reciprocity that emerge in the formation of a specific internal policy provide the basis for the transfer of powers (pre-emption) necessary to achieve external unity.

These approaches seem rather different both in their approach to unity and in the way they regard the relation between internal and the external powers in the perspective of the principle of conferral. In Weiler's perspective, if we accept that the EU may be a non-unitary external actor, the scope of its internal and external powers need not necessarily be coterminous. For Post, the operation of internal politics both calls for and facilitates external unity. But both reject a simple parallelism between internal and external powers in determining the division of competence between the EU and its Member States, and both can help us understand different aspects of the EU's approach to mixed external competences.

I. An Evolution in Thinking about EU External Competence

It is possible to see an evolution in thinking—including the thinking of the Court of Justice—about EC/EU external competence, an evolution which is not so much a matter of moving from one conception of competence to another but rather of adding new perceptions to the two dimensions we are considering here: that of unity and the EU/Member State relation; and that of conferral and the internal/external relation.

The original Treaty of Rome contained only two express external competences: the Common Commercial Policy (CCP), which the Court of Justice held to be exclusive in Opinion 1/75,[7] and the power to conclude Association Agreements. The exclusivity of the Common Commercial Policy is not dependent on any act of the EU;[8] it was—and still is—an a priori or constitutional exclusivity based on the need for unity and the effective defence of the common interest.[9] Association Agreements, the Court held in *Demirel*, could cover the whole field of application of the Treaty despite the fact that in some fields internal competence had not been exercised;[10] an Association Agreement concluded by the Community may in part be implemented by its Member States. Thus, in the case of these original express external powers, both the requirement of unity and the scope of external competence were dissociated from the existence of internal rules.

[7] Opinion 1/75/EEC (*Local cost standard*) [1975] ECR 1355.

[8] Case 41-76 *Suzanne Criel, née Donckerwolcke and Henri Schou v Procureur de la République au tribunal de grande instance de Lille and Director General of Customs* [1976] ECR 1921 para 32. According to the Court in Opinion 1/75 the Common Commercial Policy 'is in fact made up by the combination and interaction of internal and external measures, without priority being taken by one over the others'.

[9] Opinion 1/75/EEC (n 7). See R. Schütze, 'Dual federalism constitutionalized: the emergence of exclusive competences in the EC legal order' (2007) 32 *European Law Review* 3. The Common Commercial Policy is now expressly characterized as exclusive in the Treaties: art 3(1)(e) TFEU.

[10] Case 12/86 *Demirel* [1987] ECR 3719.

The doctrine of implied external powers developed in the *AETR* line of cases[11] dealt creatively and constructively with the dilemma of reconciling the principle of conferred powers with the need to provide a dynamic organization with the necessary tools to match its internal development with a growing international presence (the dilemma still remains, presenting itself in different ways).[12] This doctrine was based on a different logic: the existence of internal powers for identified EU objectives implies the possibility of unified external action by the Union where needed to achieve those objectives. Thus, implied external competence is closely linked to internal powers and internal objectives. Nonetheless, the approach to both express and implied competence was based on conceptions of effectiveness and unity, and in the initial cases the Court assumes that unity requires a transfer of competence and therefore exclusivity. In its reasoning on the exclusivity of implied powers the Court in *AETR* used the arguments that it was to use a few years later in Opinion 1/75 in the context of the CCP: the defence of the common interest of the EU and the need to protect the internal *acquis*, including free movement and undistorted competition. It was therefore in this phase that the conceptions of a priori exclusivity (as for the CCP) and pre-emption (as in *AETR*) were worked out: the conditions under which the Member States no longer have the power (under EU law) to act externally.

In this initial phase, external competence was perceived as a zero-sum game in which either the EU or the Member States are competent. Internal powers might justify the use of external instruments even where not expressly foreseen in the Treaty if the development of an internal *acquis* demands an external unity. Shared external powers were seen as a temporary measure, applying only until the EU had legislated.[13] However, over the years between the 1970s and the Lisbon Treaty exclusivity came to be seen as the exception rather than the rule for external relations.[14] Only one other type of a priori exclusive competence (not dependent on legislative pre-emption) was discovered by the Court, in 1981: fisheries conservation in the context of the common fisheries policy.[15] A number of factors both expanded the scope for shared competences and altered the perception of shared competence as a temporary expedient. From the Single European Act onwards, new express external powers were included in the Treaty, covering new explicit fields of EU competence such as environmental policy and development cooperation; these new external competences have almost always

[11] Cases 3, 4 & 6/76 *Kramer* [1976] ECR 1279; Opinion 2/91 [1993] ECR I-1061; Opinion 1/94 [1994] ECR I-5267; Case C-476/98 *Commission v Germany* [2002] ECR I-9855.

[12] A. Dashwood and J. Heliskoski, 'The Classic Authorities Revisited', in A. Dashwood and C. Hillion (eds.), *The General Law of EC External Relations* (London: Sweet & Maxwell, 2000), 6.

[13] *Kramer* (n 11).

[14] See AG Kokott, Case C-13/07 *Commission v Council*, 26 March 2009 (case withdrawn, Opinion available at: <http://curia.europa.eu/jcms/jcms/j_6/>): 'exclusive Community competence is the exception and, as a rule, the Community shares its areas of competence with the Member States because only in that way is it possible to ensure that the principle of subsidiarity, a fundamental stipulation of the Treaties which applies only to non-exclusive competence..., has appropriate scope for application.'

[15] Case 804/79 *Commission v UK* [1981] ECR 1045. See now art 3(1)(d) TFEU.

been explicitly shared.[16] And different types of shared competence came to be accepted: although shared competence in general is subject to pre-emption, some of the new shared external competences do not pre-empt Member State action, in particular powers in the fields of development cooperation and humanitarian assistance,[17] as well as the Common Foreign and Security Policy (CFSP).[18] These are 'parallel' competences in the sense that EU action does not prevent the Member States from acting and both the EU and the Member States may act alone.[19] Then the Nice Treaty revision of the Common Commercial Policy introduced in Article 133(6) EC the idea of a shared competence where the EU is *obliged* to act together with the Member States.[20] The growth of shared competences, while expanding the EU's external powers, demonstrates an acceptance that external solidarity and the principle of unity of international representation does not necessarily require exclusivity but can be consistent with shared competence operating subject to the duty of sincere cooperation.[21] Indeed, we see the Court working out the implications of this duty in the context of external relations, especially—but not only—in the framework of mixed agreements, where the EU and the Member States act side-by-side.[22]

What of the relationship between internal action and external competences? As we have seen, *AETR* established the concept of pre-emption: it is the *exercise* of EU competence which precludes the Member States from continuing to exercise their competence (sometimes referred to as the '*AETR*-effect'). The Member States—subject to the substantive and procedural obligations flowing from the primacy of EU law and the duty of sincere cooperation—may act as long as the EU has not done so. The exercise of competence by the EU which triggers pre-emption

[16] The only new express exclusive external competence created since the Treaty of Rome has been in the field of monetary policy for the euro-zone Member States (see now arts 3(1)(c) and 219 TFEU). Competition policy (art 3(1)(b) TFEU), which is also declared to be an exclusive competence, is not given an express external dimension in the Treaties, although external powers have been implied.

[17] Art 4(4) TFEU.

[18] Art 2(4) TFEU and Declarations 13 and 14 attached to the Treaties.

[19] In the field of development cooperation, see Case C-316/91 *European Parliament v Council* [1994] ECR I-625; Case C-268/94 *Portugal v Council* [1996] ECR I-6177.

[20] It was not entirely clear whether in such a case the Member States were also prevented from acting alone. Art 133(6) EC, second subparagraph: '[a]greements relating to trade in cultural and audio-visual services, educational services, and social and human health services, shall fall within the shared competence of the Community and its Member States. Consequently, in addition to a Community decision taken in accordance with the relevant provisions of Article 300, the negotiation of such agreements shall require the common accord of the Member States. Agreements thus negotiated shall be concluded jointly by the Community and the Member States.' While it lasted this was the only explicit provision for mixed agreements. For an interpretation see Opinion 1/08/EC [2009] ECR I-11129; M. Cremona, 'Balancing Union and Member State interests: Opinion 1/2008, choice of legal base and the common commercial policy under the Treaty of Lisbon' (2010) 35 *European Law Review* 678. This specific type of shared competence no longer exists, having been replaced in the Lisbon Treaty by an alternative mechanism for ensuring that the views of Member States are taken into account: that of unanimous decision-making: art 207(4) TFEU.

[21] Art 4(3) TEU.

[22] Opinion 1/94 (n 11); Case C-25/94 *Commission v Council* [1996] ECR I-1469; Case C-239/03 *Commission v France* [2004] ECR I-9325; Case C-266/03 *Commission v Luxembourg* [2005] ECR I-4805; Case C-433/03 *Commission v Germany* [2005] ECR I-6985; Case C-246/07 *Commission v Sweden* [2010] ECR I-3317.

is generally *legislative*, i.e. based on the adoption of internal legislation, but pre-emption may also occur, even in the absence of internal legislation, by a decision on the part of the EU to exercise its competence to act externally, for example by concluding an international agreement. This is much less common.[23] Indeed, the Member States, as drafters of the Treaties, have been concerned to limit the possibility of what has been termed a 'reverse-*AETR* effect': the possibility of an external agreement operating pre-emptively to turn a previously shared *internal* competence exclusive.[24] Advocate General Kokott argued for the possibility of pre-emption via external action in her interpretation of the EU's competence under Article 133(5) EC, which related to agreements on trade in services and the commercial aspects of intellectual property.[25] In her view, although the wording of the provision excluded the application of a priori exclusivity to such agreements,[26] the Union's shared competence was concurrent (that is, subject to pre-emption) in the sense that, once the EU had decided to exercise its competence in relation to a specific agreement, the Member States were precluded from doing so: such agreements, in contrast to those concluded under Article 133(6) EC, should not be mixed. She argued this on grounds of effectiveness, as well as on the need to ensure the protection of the Union interest in international fora.[27] It remains the case however that pre-emption is normally linked to the existence of internal legislation.

The rationale of effectiveness as the basis of pre-emption in the context of EU external relations was summarized in 2003 by the Court of Justice: 'it is essential to ensure a uniform and consistent application of the Community rules and the proper functioning of the system which they establish in order to preserve the full effectiveness of Community law.'[28] However, by 2003 it had become accepted

[23] For a rare example see Opinion 1/76/EEC [1977] ECR 741, explained thus in Opinion 1/03/EC [2006] ECR I-1145 para 115: '[a]s regards exclusive competence, the Court has held that the situation envisaged in Opinion 1/76 is that in which internal competence may be effectively exercised only at the same time as external competence…, the conclusion of the international agreement being thus necessary in order to attain objectives of the Treaty that cannot be attained by establishing autonomous rules…'

[24] E.g. in art 207(6) TFEU, '[t]he exercise of the competences conferred by this Article in the field of the common commercial policy shall not affect the delimitation of competences between the Union and the Member States, and shall not lead to harmonisation of legislative or regulatory provisions of the Member States in so far as the Treaties exclude such harmonisation'.

[25] AG Kokott, Case C-13/07 *Commission v Council* (case withdrawn).

[26] AG Kokott (n 25) 54–59. As provided by the fourth subparagraph of art 133(5) EC, '[t]his paragraph shall not affect the right of the Member States to maintain and conclude agreements with third countries or international organisations'. Note that under the Lisbon Treaty competence in the field of the Common Commercial Policy, including trade in services and the commercial aspects of intellectual property, is now an a priori exclusive competence, although subject to unanimous voting: arts 3(1) and 207(4) TFEU.

[27] 'Bearing in mind the objective of representation of Community interests at international level which should be as effective as possible, the Member States cannot be allowed, without restriction, to maintain or conclude agreements with non-member countries or international organisations in the fields of trade in services and the commercial aspects of intellectual property, but may do so only in so far as the Community itself does not act': AG Kokott (n 25) para 77. See also the Court's judgment in *AETR/ERTA* (n 6) para 31.

[28] Opinion 1/03/EC (n 23) para 128.

that it is not enough simply to identify the existence of Union rules in a particular field to trigger the operation of pre-emption; the nature as well as the operation of those rules and even their possible future development will be relevant in order to ascertain whether individual Member State action would affect 'the proper functioning of the system' and the effectiveness of Union law. Thus, on the one hand whereas in *AETR* the Court refers to common rules adopted in the implementation of a common policy, later cases accepted that common rules may exist outside the framework of a common policy,[29] and also that pre-emption may apply to a field covered not completely but 'to a large extent' by common rules.[30] On the other hand, the evolution in internal legislation towards minimum harmonization which followed the Single European Act put into question earlier assumptions that *any* Community legislation could pre-empt Member State activity: '[i]n certain cases, analysis and comparison of the areas covered both by the Community rules and by the agreement envisaged suffice to rule out any effect on the former', and thus remove the necessity of excluding the Member States from the latter.[31] Hence the need for the Court to engage in a sometimes detailed examination of both an agreement and the internal EU *acquis* before deciding whether or not pre-emption applies.

How do the *post*-Lisbon Treaties reflect this evolution of thinking about external competence? We should say first that external policy is much more visible in the revised Treaties. They contain specific provisions on external action, Title V of the TEU and Part V of the TFEU which identify specifically external policies and powers, such as the CFSP, the Common Commercial Policy, and Development Cooperation, as well as general and procedural provisions. A set of specific external objectives is gathered together. Second, although the provisions on external action might be among those where a comparatively large number of revisions were made, these are intended to incorporate and consolidate past practice and to codify the case law of the Court. The general enumeration of exclusive, shared, and complementary competences in the TFEU includes external powers and we can find examples of each type among the external policy powers, following the categorization developed in the former Treaties and by the Court.[32] The result is, in a number of instances, a historical path-dependency rather than a wholesale rationalization.[33]

This tendency is visible in the treatment of exclusive external competence, as it is defined in Article 2(1) TFEU. The original context in which this type of exclusivity was developed has been explained by Robert Schütze in terms of conflict avoidance

[29] Opinion 2/91 (n 11) paras 10–11.

[30] Opinion 2/91 (n 11) para 25; Case C-476/98 *Commission v Germany* [2002] ECR I-9855 para 108; Opinion 1/03/EC (n 23) para 126.

[31] Opinion 1/03/EC (n 23) para 125; see also Opinion 2/91 (n 11).

[32] The CFSP is a special case, being given a separate paragraph in art 2 TFEU, the implication being that it is somehow outside the categories of competence defined in the other paragraphs.

[33] A couple of examples: the express mention of the external treaty-making powers in relation to some 'internal' policies, such as environmental policy (art 191(4) TFEU) but not others, such as culture or civil justice; and the explicit exclusion of transport services from the extension of the Common Commercial Policy to trade in services, in art 207(5) TFEU.

and primacy: exclusivity is necessary where there is no clear rule of hierarchy; conflict (which would require a rule of hierarchy to resolve) is prevented by the separation of exclusive spheres of competence.[34] The Court developed the notion of exclusive external competence in the 1970s at a time when the primacy of EU law with respect to the Member States' international agreements was uncertain, at least with regard to agreements with third countries.[35] Now that the primacy of EU law over the Member State's international agreements—subject to Article 351 TFEU which is read restrictively—[36]is established as a matter of EU law,[37] the doctrines of shared competence, compliance, pre-emption, and sincere cooperation in the Union interest deal with the risks of conflict.[38] Certainly the Lisbon Treaty in Article 3(1) TFEU reproduces the limited instances of exclusivity already determined by the Court's case law,[39] the implied rationale being the need in these policy instances for a single set of rules established at the Union level.

But the seemingly clear distinction between types of competence, with a limited role for exclusive competence, and shared competence being the 'default' subject to pre-emption,[40] is complicated by one of the more ambiguous provisions introduced by the Lisbon Treaty: Article 3(2) TFEU.[41] At first sight this provision appears simply to codify earlier case law on external competence, including the so-called '*AETR*-effect'. However its relationship to Article 2(2) TFEU is far from clear. How does pre-emption operating within shared competence under Article 2(2) TFEU interact with the exclusive competence derived from Article 3(2) TFEU

[34] Schütze (n 9): 'the demarcation of mutually exclusive spheres—in which either the Community or the Member States were "sovereign"—elegantly avoided the question of the normative hierarchy of the Community over the Member States being even posed *in the context of international relations*', emphasis in original. See also P. Eeckhout, 'Bold Constitutionalism and Beyond', in Poiares Maduro and Azoulai (n 5).

[35] Earlier cases had already established the primacy of Community law over both prior (Case 10/61 *Commission v Italy* [1962] ECR 1) and later (Case 26/62 *Van Gend en Loos* [1963] ECR 1) international agreements of the Member States *inter se*. For a more recent example see Case C-301/08 *Bogiatzi v Deutscher Luftpool and Others* [2009] ECR I-10185.

[36] Case C-170/98 *Commission v Belgium* [1999] ECR I-5493; Case C-62/98 *Commission v Portugal* [2000] ECR I-5171; Case C-84/98 *Commission v Portugal* [2000] ECR I-5215.

[37] See e.g. Case C-307/97 *Saint-Gobain ZN* [1999] ECR I-6161 on double tax treaties; Case C-55/00 *Gottardo v INPS* [2002] ECR I-413, holding that a bilateral social security convention concluded by a Member State with a third country must be implemented in such a way as to comply with the principle of non-discrimination; Case C-476/98 *Commission v Germany* [2002] ECR I-9855, holding that a Member State infringed EU law rules on rights of establishment and non-discrimination between EU nationals by concluding a non-compliant bilateral *Open Skies* agreement.

[38] M. Cremona, 'Defending the Community Interest: the Duties of Cooperation and Compliance', in M. Cremona and B. de Witte, *EU Foreign Relations Law: Constitutional Fundamentals* (Oxford and Portland: Hart Publishing, 2008), 145.

[39] E.g. the conservation of marine biological resources under the common fisheries policy, declared to be exclusive in Case 804/79 *Commission v UK* [1981] ECR 1045.

[40] Art 2(2) TFEU provides that in the case of shared competences '[t]he Member States shall exercise their competence to the extent that the Union has not exercised its competence'.

[41] Art 3(2) TFEU follows the enumeration of exclusive competences in Art 3(1) and provides that '[t]he Union shall also have exclusive competence for the conclusion of an international agreement when its conclusion is provided for in a legislative act of the Union or is necessary to enable the Union to exercise its internal competence, or in so far as its conclusion may affect common rules or alter their scope'.

where an international agreement 'may affect common rules or alter their scope'? And how do both these provisions relate to Article 216(1) TFEU according to which the Union possesses treaty-making powers where an international agreement 'is likely to affect common rules or alter their scope'? The Treaties here certainly do not maintain a clear conceptual distinction between the *existence* of external competence (Article 216(1) TFEU), the *exclusivity* of that competence (Article 3(2) TFEU), and the operation of legislative pre-emption (Article 2(2) TFEU).[42] The almost—but not quite—identical language of Article 216(1) and Article 3(2) TFEU invites a potentially large expansion of exclusive external competence. In any event the attempt to codify the Court's case law on exclusivity, which is still evolving, has not led to greater clarity. The general statement on pre-emption in relation to shared competence found in Article 2(2) TFEU, together with the principle of sincere cooperation, would have provided a sufficiently clear Treaty basis for delimiting the exercise of competence.

We might say that Article 216(1) TFEU renders explicit the doctrine of implied powers. Alongside the specific external policies of the Union, it provides a clear legal basis for what is elsewhere referred to as the 'external dimension of its other policies'[43] such as competition policy, transport, energy, or social policy. It provides a general treaty-making competence 'where the conclusion of an agreement is necessary in order to achieve, within the framework of the Union's policies, one of the objectives referred to in the Treaties, or is provided for in a legally binding Union act or is likely to affect common rules or alter their scope'. The dangers of insufficient differentiation between this provision and Article 3(2) TFEU have already been pointed out; we would be very far from seeing exclusive competence as the exception were we to find that in fields ranging from energy policy to criminal cooperation the Union either has exclusive competence or no external competence at all. The formulation of Article 216(1) TFEU also impinges on the relationship between internal and external powers. The doctrine of implied powers was linked to the possession by the Union of internal powers designed to achieve a specific objective. Article 216(1) TFEU refers to Union acts in its second and third grounds of competence, but in its first and broadest, it breaks this link. No longer is there a need for the agreement to be necessary to achieve an objective for which internal powers have been provided (and which is therefore likely though not inevitably to be internal in orientation); all that is needed is for the objective to be referred to in the Treaties, which would include the very widely drawn general external objectives of Article 21 TEU, and for the action to take place 'within the framework of the Union's policies'. Thus, external action in the context of the Area of Freedom, Security and Justice (AFSJ), including migration policy, could be deemed necessary not only for AFSJ objectives but also in order to safeguard the security of the Union or to 'assist populations, countries and regions confronting

[42] For a critique of art 3(2) TFEU, see A. Dashwood, 'The Draft EU Constitution—First Impressions' (2002-3) 5 *Cambridge Yearbook of European Legal Studies* 395; see also M. Cremona, 'Defining Competence in EU External Relations: Lessons from the Treaty Reform Process', in A. Dashwood and M. Maresceau (n 2).

[43] Art 21(3) TEU.

natural or man-made disasters'.[44] Article 216(1) TFEU might be interpreted more restrictively, to require a closer link between the objective and the policy field within which action is taken,[45] but this is not required by the text.[46]

II. Give and Take in EU Practice

In the last decade we can identify two somewhat opposing tendencies. On the one hand, as we have just seen, the Lisbon Treaty attempts to clarify competences, to codify the Court of Justice case law. As a result, types of competences and their implications *should* be clearer and more distinct. On the other hand, as a counterpoint to the attempt to clarify competences in the Treaties (and as we have already seen, the codification in itself is full of ambiguity), institutional practice—and also decisions of the Court—have tended to undermine rigid distinctions between exclusive and shared competence in the interest of pragmatic solutions. This 'blurring' tends to occur in the context of the *exercise* of competence, as opposed to its existence, but this should not surprise us: where competence is shared, decisions about its exercise (whether, when, how) become important since the exercise by one party (EU or Member State) of its competence may affect the ability of the other to exercise theirs.

What is interesting about this practice is, first, that the flexibility concerns exclusive as well as shared competences, and, secondly, that it operates in both directions, i.e. both as reticence in insisting on the exercise of EU powers even where they are exclusive, and as willingness on the part of Member States to see the EU exercise external powers alone even where competence is shared.

1. Finding ways to allow Member States to act alongside the EU even where there is (partial) exclusivity

On several occasions in the last decade, the Council has adopted a procedural framework within which the Member States are authorized to continue to exercise a competence which has become exclusive. The first followed the *Open Skies* cases in which the Court had held that certain aspects of the air services agreements being concluded with third countries by individual Member States fell within exclusive competence.[47] In addition the Court found that the ownership and control clauses in the bilateral agreements infringed Article 43 EC (now Article 49 TFEU) and there was therefore a need to renegotiate a large number of them. Since

[44] Art 21(2)(a) and (g) TEU.

[45] For a recent discussion of the relationship between art 216(1) TFEU, internal powers and explicit external powers such as the CCP, see the Opinion of AG Kokott of 27 June 2013 in Case C-137/12 *Commission v Council*, pending, para 44.

[46] It is also worth noting in this context that the residual powers provision (Art 352 TFEU) also reflects this choice of wording, having removed the requirement of a connection with the common market formerly in art 308 EC.

[47] See e.g. Case C-476/98 *Commission v Germany* [2002] ECR I-9855.

the EU was not able or willing to enter immediately into negotiations for replacement agreements, it was decided to authorize Member States, under certain conditions, to maintain existing and even conclude new agreements.[48]

The preamble to the resulting Regulation refers to the duty of cooperation and confirms that the cooperation procedure established by the Regulation is 'without prejudice to the division of competences between the Community and Member States'.[49] The Regulation imposes two main types of obligation on the Member States, procedural and substantive. As far as procedural obligations are concerned, the Member States are to notify the Commission about the start, process, and conclusion of national negotiations, and the conclusion of the agreement is subject to authorization. Substantively, Member States are to include in their agreements relevant standard clauses developed jointly by the Commission and the Member States, and there are several obligations requiring equal treatment of all Union carriers. The Commission will notify the Member States both if it sees a likely incompatibility and if it takes the view that the negotiations 'are likely to undermine the objectives of Community negotiations underway with the third country concerned'. Even further, where the standard clauses are not incorporated into the agreement, authorization of its conclusion will depend on the terms of the agreement being found not to harm the object and purpose of EU transport policy. Alongside this Regulation, the Member States also agreed that the Union should negotiate, effectively on their behalf, amendments to some of their existing bilateral air transport agreements with third countries so as to bring them into compatibility with the EU *acquis* (so-called horizontal agreements), while also negotiating new EU agreements with strategic countries.[50]

As a consequence of Opinion 1/2003,[51] in which the Court had held that conclusion of the Lugano Convention on jurisdiction and the recognition and enforcement of judgments in civil and commercial matters was within the exclusive

[48] Reg 847/2004/EC on the Negotiation and Implementation of Air Service Agreements between Member States and Third Countries [2004] OJ L/157/7; recital 6 of the preamble states: '[a]ll existing bilateral agreements between Member States and third countries that contain provisions contrary to Community law should be amended or replaced by new agreements that are wholly compatible with Community law.'

[49] Reg 847/2004/EC, recital 4: '[w]here it is apparent that the subject-matter of an agreement falls partly within the competence of the Community and partly within that of its Member States, it is essential to ensure close cooperation between the Member States and the Community institutions, both in the process of negotiation and conclusion and in the fulfilment of the commitments entered into. That obligation to cooperate flows from the requirement of unity in the international representation of the Community. The Community institutions and the Member States should take all necessary steps to ensure the best possible cooperation in that regard.'

[50] According to the Commission, '[t]he joint effort of the Commission and Member States has already made possible to bring into conformity more than 900 bilateral agreements with 107 countries. Among them, the European Commission negotiated 45 Horizontal Agreements which have amended all the bilateral agreements between a given third country and all EU Member States with which that country has bilateral agreements.' See: <http://ec.europa.eu/transport/modes/air/international_aviation/external_aviation_policy/index_en.htm>. For an example of such a horizontal agreement, see the Agreement between the European Community and Ukraine on certain aspects of air services, OJ 2006 L 211/24. EU agreements have been negotiated with the USA, Canada, and Brazil and are under negotiation with Australia and New Zealand.

[51] Opinion 1/03/EC (n 23).

competence of the Community, two Regulations were adopted in 2009, one on the law applicable to contractual and non-contractual obligations,[52] and one on the jurisdiction and recognition of judgments in matrimonial matters.[53] In both cases their scope of application is linked to specific internal EU legislation on the same subject matter, and thus to areas of competence where an '*AETR*-effect' and therefore pre-emption—or now Article 3(2) TFEU—applies.[54] These Regulations follow a similar procedural pattern of notification and authorization of Member State bilateral agreements, the Commission having the option to propose negotiating guidelines or to request the inclusion of specific clauses. The authorized agreements must also contain a clause providing either for the full or partial denunciation of the agreement in the case of a future agreement between the EU and the third country on the same subject matter, or direct replacement of the relevant clauses by those of a subsequent EU agreement.

The third example—that of bilateral investment agreements (BITs)—is striking since it arises in the context not of pre-emption but within the exclusivity of the CCP. The Lisbon Treaty both confirmed that the CCP is a matter of exclusive competence and brought foreign direct investment within its scope.[55] Bearing in mind the 1200 existing Member State BITs, a Regulation was adopted which authorizes the Member States, under certain conditions, to maintain in force and amend their existing BITs and to conclude new BITs while requiring them to eliminate incompatibilities between bilateral BITs and EU law.[56] As the preamble to the Regulation recognizes, it was important in the interests of legal certainty for both Member States and investors to confirm the continued existence of these Member State BITs unless and until they can be replaced by Union agreements. There is a requirement to notify all existing BITs to the Commission and such notified agreements may enter into or remain in force until replaced by a Union agreement. The Member States are under a duty—referred to as a duty of cooperation—to take appropriate measures to ensure that the provisions of the notified BITs do

[52] Reg 662/2009/EC establishing a procedure for the negotiation and conclusion of agreements between Member States and third countries on particular matters concerning the law applicable to contractual and non-contractual obligations, OJ 2009 L 200/25.

[53] Reg 664/2009/EC establishing a procedure for the negotiation and conclusion of agreements between Member States and third countries concerning jurisdiction, recognition and enforcement of judgments and decisions in matrimonial matters, matters of parental responsibility and matters relating to maintenance obligations, and the law applicable to matters relating to maintenance obligations, OJ 2009 L 200/46.

[54] Reg 662/2009 is linked to the scope of application of Reg 593/2008/EC on the law applicable to contractual obligation (Rome I), OJ 2008 L 177/87, and Reg 864/2007 on the law applicable to non-contractual obligations (Rome II), OJ 2007 L 177/40; Reg 664/2009/EC is linked to the scope of Reg 2201/2003/EC, concerning jurisdiction, recognition and enforcement of judgments and decisions in matrimonial matters, matters of parental responsibility, OJ 2003 L 338/1, and of Reg 4/2009/EC, on jurisdiction, applicable law, recognition and enforcement of decisions and cooperation in matters relating to maintenance obligations, OJ 2009 L 7/1.

[55] Arts 3(1) and 207(1) TFEU.

[56] Reg 1219/2012/EU, establishing transitional arrangements for bilateral investment agreements between Member States and third countries OJ 2012 L 351/40. For an example of incompatibility between a Member State BIT and EU law see Case C-118/07 *Commission v Finland* [2009] ECR I-10889.

not constitute an obstacle to the negotiation or conclusion by the Union of BITs with third countries. The negotiation and conclusion of new BITs are subject to notification and authorization by the Commission, which may refuse authorization where the Union has decided to conclude a BIT with that third country, or on grounds of incompatibility with EU law, or inconsistency with the Union's principles and objectives for external action as set out in the TEU.[57]

These initiatives have been agreed between the Member States and the institutions within the legislative process, and they have not yet come under the Court's scrutiny. There may be some question as to the extent to which the institutions should be able to re-authorize the Member States to act where competence is exclusive. Advocate General Kokott has, in a different context, outlined a potential limit:

> [c]ontrary to the Council's view, it cannot voluntarily waive some or all of its powers under Article 133(5) EC in favour of the Member States, but must take account of the Community interest in the most effective and coherent representation at international level as is possible and must make full use of its powers to that end. The Council must not allow the powers of the Community and its institutions, as formulated in the EC Treaty, to be distorted.[58]

The Air Services Regulation is designed, with other measures such as the horizontal agreements mentioned earlier, to manage a transitional phase. Both the Air Services Regulation and the Regulations related to civil justice (private international law) address a situation where one aspect of EU competence which has become exclusive via pre-emption impinges on legislative fields where the Union's *acquis* is currently limited and international agreements are likely to contain provisions falling within both exclusive and shared competence. The BITs Regulation touches upon a competence which is exclusive independently of the existence of the EU *acquis*, and might thereby be distinguished from the other two examples, but it is clearly presented as a transitional measure. The formal requirements of exclusivity may have been preserved, but the result is a highly pragmatic solution which allows both the Union and Member States to play their part while preserving an overall unity and common interest.

2. Maintaining mixed agreements

Despite the widening extent of EU external powers, covering now also the broader aspects of foreign policy in the CFSP, mixed agreements remain widely used. This is true of the wide-ranging modern partnership and Association Agreements with a political dimension but also of multilateral sectoral agreements, such as environmental agreements, where competence is shared. There are cases—particularly where agreements are politically important, where they represent an element in a broader policy framework towards a third country, or are seen as a significant part of the global governance of important issues—where the unity of the European

[57] An important instance of the legal effect of these principles and objectives: see art 21 TEU.
[58] AG Kokott in Case C-13/07 *Commission v Council* (n 14) para 83.

Union is served not by the participation of the EU alone (even where this would be possible) but rather by the joint participation of the EU and all its Member States, with the powerful signal of concerted action that this sends.

It is noticeable that the Lisbon Treaty says nothing about this very central aspect of EU external relations practice, either in the provision dealing with the negotiation and conclusion of agreements (Article 218 TFEU), or in any other provision. The fact that a proportion of the most important external agreements are mixed is simply ignored. Although it is true that the principles underlying the Union law obligations of the Member States and the institutions in the context of mixed agreements are derived from general principles which appear in the Treaties, in particular the principle of sincere cooperation in Article 4(3) TEU, some recognition of the phenomenon, especially at the procedural level, would have assisted transparency. However it must be said that one of the attractions of mixed agreements for the Union and the Member States is that it may not be necessary to identify the precise delimitation of competence between Union and Member States, and that changes in the distribution of competence do not call the agreement into question.[59]

3. The EU acts alone

The previous examples of practice have focused on maintaining a role for the Member States even where it might not be strictly necessary in legal terms, or even where EU competence is exclusive. However, we can also find examples of cases where the Member States are happy to let the EU act alone, although competence is shared. Somewhat paradoxically perhaps, this seems particularly to be the case in those former second and third pillars, the CFSP and the AFSJ, where the Member States are ostensibly most protective of their prerogatives. Despite the clearly non-exclusive nature of CFSP competence[60] all international agreements concluded under CFSP powers have been concluded by the EU alone.[61] Mixed agreements are rare in the AFSJ field, and even agreements on sensitive issues such as migration, for example readmission agreements,[62] and agreements involving criminal justice,[63] are concluded by the EU alone.

[59] Even the so-called declarations of competence which are sometimes required as the price of joint EU/Member States participation do not really illuminate the distribution of competence; they mainly serve to put the other parties on notice that competence is shared. See A. Delgado Casteleiro, 'EU Declarations of Competence to Multilateral Agreements: A Useful Reference Base?' (2012) 17 *European Foreign Affairs Review* 491.

[60] As will be recalled, CFSP competence is not defined in art 2(4) TFEU as exclusive, shared, or complementary. The provisions on the CFSP emphasize the role of the Member States; see e.g. arts 24, 32, and 42(1) TEU.

[61] Admittedly these agreements have been relatively limited in character: status of forces agreements, agreements with third states participating in EU crisis management missions, and on the exchange and protection of classified information. Where more general political or foreign policy issues are covered in broader agreements, these as we have seen tend to be mixed.

[62] An explicit competence to conclude readmission agreements is found in art 79(3) TFEU.

[63] E.g.: the Agreement between the EU and Australia on the processing and transfer of EU-sourced passenger name record (PNR) data by air carriers to the Australian customs service, OJ 2008

One specific aspect of agreements such as these requires comment. The conclusion of the agreement by the EU alone does not necessarily imply that it will be implemented only or even at all by the EU. It will not infrequently be the case that competence to implement the agreement lies substantially with the Member States. Weiler, in the paper referred to at the start of this chapter,[64] puts forward the possibility of what he calls 'vertical mixity', by which he means an agreement concluded by the Union alone, but which (1) may exceed *internal* Union competence; (2) will not have the effect of extending internal Union competence, and therefore (3) it may be implemented by the Member States; and (4) will not pre-empt Member State competence. We can in fact see examples of this in practice:

- Agreements on extradition and mutual legal assistance are EU agreements designed to be implemented by the Member States. In the case of the extradition and mutual legal assistance agreements with the US, a complex relationship with pre-existing bilateral agreements with the Member States was constructed and the United Stated insisted on an Exchange of Letters with each Member State acknowledging this before the agreement was concluded.[65] The agreement on mutual legal assistance in criminal matters between the EU and Japan defines itself as designed to establish more effective cooperation between the EU Member States and Japan and refers throughout to action to be taken by the states.[66]
- Development cooperation is a shared competence but agreements with third countries on development cooperation may be concluded by the EU alone, and may then be implemented—as far as matters within Member State competence were concerned—by the Member States.[67]
- Even though CCP powers are exclusive and have been extended to cover trade in services, commercial aspects of intellectual property, and foreign direct investment, Article 207(6) TFEU provides that '[t]he exercise of the competences conferred by this Article in the field of the common commercial policy shall not affect the delimitation of competences between the Union and the Member States…'. Thus the EU may include services and intellectual property rights in a trade agreement even in the absence of internal legislation; however, in such a case the shared competence of the Member States to act in these fields internally will not be affected, nor will internal EU powers be extended.

L 213/49; Agreement between the EU and the United States of America on the processing and transfer of Financial Messaging Data from the EU to the United States for the purposes of the Terrorist Finance Tracking Program, OJ 2010 L 195/5.

[64] Weiler (n 3) 178.

[65] Agreement on extradition between the European Union and the United States of America, OJ 2003 L 181/27; Agreement on mutual legal assistance between the European Union and the United States of America, OJ 2003 L 181/34; specific clauses of the EU-US agreements will in some cases replace, in other cases be additional to, and in other cases apply only in the absence of, the equivalent clause in the existing bilateral agreements.

[66] Agreement between the EU and Japan on mutual legal assistance in criminal matters, OJ 2010 L 39/20.

[67] Case C-268/94 *Portugal v Council* [1996] ECR I-6177.

What do these examples of practice tell us about the concept of unity in EU external relations (section III) and the relationship between internal and external competences (section IV)?

III. Unity and the Scope of Application of EU Law

The Court refers, in a case involving a mixed agreement, to 'the principle of unity in the international representation of the Union and its Member States'.[68] Unity, as practice shows, does not depend on—nor is it guaranteed by—exclusivity, a single actor or a single voice. Shared competence is not per se inimical to unity, which is compatible not only with shared possession of competence but with the shared exercise of competence. As Weiler argued, mixed agreements can strengthen the framework for the conduct of external relations, the ability of the Union and its Member States to operate effectively at an international level, and not merely the centre at the expense of the periphery.[69] In such a context, choices over when and how to exercise competence become very important. The focus shifts from defining the exclusionary effects of competence to defining the scope of application of EU law, i.e. the space within which EU law constrains the Member States *in the exercise of their competences.* These constraints include both obligations of compliance with substantive EU law rules such as non-discrimination or freedom of establishment, and procedural obligations; both are required to manage overlapping and shared competences and both are ultimately based on the duty of sincere cooperation (Article 4(3) TEU). It is important that the duty to cooperate, as interpreted by the Court, ensures that the Union interest is protected even where competence is not exclusive. The Union interest comes into play even in the absence of the exercise of an internal legislative competence, or the launching of an international negotiation, but it does require the formation of a 'common strategy' or decision to act in a particular way.[70] As Christophe Hillion says, '[t]his cooperation jurisprudence suggests a growing [acceptance by the Court] of the plurality that characterises the EU system of external relations'.[71] However the key role played by the duty of sincere cooperation in managing the exercise of competence creates its own difficulties. It is used as a legal basis for the primacy of EU law, for exclusivity, for pre-emption, and to define the parameters within which the Member States may exercise their competence to act. The precise nature of the duty in these different situations is not always clear and this leads to the distinction between them being blurred.[72]

[68] Case C-246/07 *Commission v Sweden* [2010] ECR I-3317.

[69] Weiler (n 3) 186.

[70] Case C-266/03 *Commission v Luxembourg* [2005] ECR I-4805; Case C-433/03 *Commission v Germany* [2005] ECR I-6985; Case C-246/07 *Commission v Sweden* [2010] ECR I-3317.

[71] Hillion and Koutrakos (n 4) 232.

[72] A. Delgado Casteleiro and J. Larik, 'The Duty to Remain Silent: Limitless Loyalty in EU External Relations' (2011) 36 *European Law Review* 524. Nevertheless the difference is still contested: see e.g. Case C-137/12 *Commission v Council*, pending.

One aspect of the duty of cooperation concerns the management of ongoing joint participation in multilateral agreements (and organizations) where the EU and Member States continue to act side-by-side as parties or members. The duty of cooperation is the applicable principle, but how should we define the nature of this duty so that it is effective in furthering the Union interest, and still ensure that both EU and Member State powers are respected? A logic based on the duty of cooperation underpins the judgment in the *PFOS* case.[73] The Court here argued on the basis that pre-emption had not occurred, that competence was still shared and that the issue concerned rather *how that competence is exercised*. Once the EU has decided how to act, the Member States cannot depart from this even where no legislative pre-emption has taken place. In *PFOS* the Court said that for a Member State to act unilaterally, dissociating itself 'from a concerted common strategy within the Council... is likely to compromise the principle of unity in the international representation of the Union and its Member States and weaken their negotiating power with regard to the other parties to the Convention concerned'; this was a breach of Article 10 EC (now Article 4(3) TEU).[74] Does the Court here introduce a de facto exclusivity under another name? The *PFOS* case shows the difficulties that arise where there are no clear rules, especially in deciding at what point the Member States become 'free' to act alone because there is no EU position, and the difficulty of deciding whether the situation is one of 'no decision' or a 'decision not to act'.[75] Under what circumstances must the Member States refrain from acting except through, or in accordance with, positions adopted by the Union, as opposed to seeking as far as possible to achieve a common position?[76] And under what circumstances is it necessary for a Union objective—to which Member State loyalty is owed under Article 4(3) TEU—to be formulated through a formal act adopted on an identified legal basis?[77]

There is also the problem of finding a way to present a common position of the EU and Member States, and especially the collective position of the Member States, exacerbated by the removal by the Lisbon Treaty of a formal role for the rotating Presidency in foreign affairs. An attempt at simplification of the international representation of the Union has instead created more difficulty. The Council has arrived at an agreement on the representation of EU positions in multilateral organizations,[78] which makes it clear that the EU can only present a position where it is competent, and there is an agreed position, and also that arrangements for coordination and representation do not affect competences.

[73] Case C-246/07 *Commission v Sweden* [2010] ECR I-3317.

[74] *Commission v Sweden* (n 73) para 104.

[75] See further M. Cremona, 'Case C-246/07 *Commission v Sweden*, judgment 20 April 2010 (Grand Chamber)' (2011) 48 *Common Market Law Review* 1639.

[76] Cf. Case C-246/07 *Commission v Sweden* [2010] ECR I-3317 (shared competence) with Case C-45/07 *Commission v Greece* [2009] ECR I-701 (exclusive competence).

[77] For a case contesting the substantive legal basis of a Council decision on the position to be taken by the EU in the framework of an international agreement, see Case C-431/11 *UK v Council*, judgment of 26 September 2013.

[78] General Arrangements for EU Statements in multilateral organisations, Council doc. 15901/11, 24 October 2011.

The document refers to 'EU Actors', and explains that '[t]he term EU actor is used to denote those actors competent to represent the Union as provided in the Treaties, i.e. the President of the European Council, the Commission, the High Representative and EU Delegations.' Member States will decide case-by-case how to coordinate and who will represent them: this could be an 'EU Actor' or a Member State ('notably the Member State holding the rotating Presidency of the Council'). The Member States undertake to ensure and promote possibilities for the 'EU Actors' to deliver statements on behalf of the EU. One may hope that, as a result, issues of representation do not get submerged in discussion of competence allocation, but it might also mean that, in practice, in order to decide who will speak (the Presidency, the Commission, or the High Representative/Vice-President), decisions need to be taken over whether an issue is (1) Member State competence, (2) EU competence but not CFSP, or (3) EU CFSP competence. The duty of cooperation may facilitate plurality but does not mean that questions of competence have become irrelevant.

IV. Internal and External Policies and the Union Interest

Each of the three alternative conditions for exclusivity set out in Article 3(2) TFEU is linked to internal powers: power-conferral by internal legislation; the external agreement is necessary in order to exercise an internal competence; the agreement may affect common rules or alter their scope. In both the *Open Skies* cases[79] and Opinion 1/94[80] the Court argued that the EU could achieve the objectives of the internal market by adopting *internal* legislation, and that there was therefore no legal necessity for EU *external* action. These cases suggest an essential dependence of external action on the (prior) development of internal policy in the tradition of *AETR*. We can also see that the Union interest that is to be protected in cases of exclusivity or legislative pre-emption is essentially an internal one: it is free movement and undistorted competition within the internal market (Opinion 1/75), or more generally 'the unity of the common market and the uniform application of Community law' and 'the full effectiveness of Community law' (Opinion 1/03). There is a need to protect not only an existing internal *acquis*, but also the development of policy in the future: as the Court put it in Opinion 1/03, '[i]t is also necessary to take into account not only the current state of Community law in the area in question but also its future development, insofar as that is foreseeable at the time of that analysis'.[81] Where Member States are authorized to act in situations of exclusive EU competence, they need to take future policy plans into account.[82]

[79] E.g. Case C-476/98 *Commission v Germany* [2002] ECR I-9855.

[80] Opinion 1/94 (n 11).

[81] Opinion 1/03/EC (n 23) para 126.

[82] E.g., the Regulation on Air Services Agreements (n 48): '[i]t is essential to ensure that a Member State conducting negotiations takes account of Community law, broader Community interests and ongoing Community negotiations.' The Regulation on bilateral investment treaties (n 56) requires the Member States to promote the replacement of the Member State BITs by EU agreements.

And both the BITs cases[83] and the *PFOS* case[84] illustrate in different ways that the duty of cooperation operating in a context of shared competence requires the Member States to preserve the possibility of future EU action.

As we have seen, the duty of cooperation in the service of the Union interest is presented as a guiding principle for Union and Member States, but how is the Union interest to be defined? It becomes easier to do so if a common position has already been adopted in the context of internal policy debate. Furthermore, in pragmatic terms, and especially in cases of shared competence, if there is an agreed policy internally then it is easier to present a united position externally, even if through several actors/voices. These are reflections of Post's argument that links external unity with the need to safeguard the results of deliberation in the 'internal agora'. The *PFOS* case is a good example: the Council was clear that it did not want to move ahead externally (to ban PFOS) more quickly than it was moving at an internal level. The Court enforced this decision by the Council through the duty of cooperation, insisting that it bound the Member States in loyalty. The negotiation of the Anti-Counterfeiting Trade Agreement (ACTA) is another example. Although the powers existed for the EU to conclude the agreement as a whole, it was agreed that the EU would not choose to exercise its powers as regards the part of the agreement dealing with criminal enforcement of intellectual property rights, since there is as yet no internal EU legislation on this; as a result the agreement would have been mixed.[85] Here there was a choice not to exercise potential external powers because there was no internal legislation. Again this is not a point about the existence of competence, but rather about the practice, i.e. the choice of whether to exercise competence or not in a particular case.

Thus, despite more explicit external powers in the Treaties, and despite the loosening of the ties between internal and external powers that we find in Article 216(1) TFEU, the need for formation of policy at the internal level is still important. Is external action then merely a means to achieve internal objectives? Where does this leave the specifically external objectives of Article 21(2) TEU and the development of an external competence which is somehow autonomous of internal policy-making? And does this mean that external action will always 'lag behind' internal policy-making? We need to nuance the picture in several ways.

[83] Case C-205/06 *Commission v Austria* [2009] ECR I-1301; Case C-249/06 *Commission v Sweden* [2009] ECR I-1335; Case C-118/07 *Commission v Finland* [2009] ECR I-10889.

[84] See n 73.

[85] COM (2011) 380 final, para 6 of the Explanatory Memorandum: 'ACTA contains a number of provisions on criminal enforcement that fall within the scope of Article 83(2) TFEU.... [T]he Commission has opted not to propose that the European Union exercise its potential competence in the area of criminal enforcement pursuant to Article 83(2) TFEU. The Commission considers this appropriate because it has never been the intention, as regards the negotiation of ACTA to modify the EU *acquis* or to harmonise EU legislation as regards criminal enforcement of intellectual property rights. For this reason, the Commission proposes that ACTA be signed and concluded both by the EU and by all the Member States.' In the event, following a negative vote in the European Parliament, it seems very unlikely that the ACTA will ever be concluded by the EU: European Parliament legislative resolution of 4 July 2012 on the draft Council decision on the conclusion of the Anti-Counterfeiting Trade Agreement, 12195/2011–C7-0027/2012–2011/0167(NLE) P7_TA-PROV(2012)0287.

First, the broad external powers granted under Articles 207 (CCP), 208 and 212 (development and economic cooperation), 217 (Association Agreements) TFEU and the CFSP, leave room for the development of a distinctive external identity for the EU, with its own agenda and policy-formation structures and explicit external objectives.

Secondly, as we have seen, the EU may wish to negotiate a position externally without having yet enacted internal legislation, leaving open the question of implementation and allowing a dynamic development of EU policy (and external competence). For example, it is clear from the *Mox Plant* case[86] that the scope of Union law (which formed the basis for the scope of the Court's exclusive jurisdiction) had developed considerably in the field of environmental protection after the signing of the UN Convention on the Law of the Sea. The use of mixity allows that development to be reflected in the operation of an ongoing international agreement; thus, the ability of the Union to act externally is not 'frozen' at the moment when the agreement was concluded.

Thirdly, where an international agreement does break new ground for the EU, it may prove a trigger for the development of new internal legislation. The Passenger Name Record (PNR) agreements with the USA and Australia are an example here;[87] following the conclusion of the international agreements the Commission has proposed a new PNR Directive to establish an equivalent internal PNR regime.[88]

Concluding Remarks

How federal is all this? There is no single federal model for the conduct of external relations. Nevertheless, as Weiler points out, it is not uncommon for federal systems to limit the exercise of external powers to the federal entity, and to accept that it has external powers which go beyond the federal internal legislative competence. We have seen that the EU shows signs of this phenomenon too: the development (initially by the Court, later enshrined in the Treaties) of exclusivity; the fact that conclusion of an agreement by the EU does not necessarily imply that it will implement it internally: that may be a matter for Member State competence. But there are several ways in which the EU does not conform to this particular federal model.

[86] Case C-459/03 *Commission v Ireland* [2006] ECR I-4635.

[87] Agreement between the EU and the United States of America on the processing and transfer of Passenger Name Record (PNR) data by air carriers to the United States Department of Homeland Security, OJ 2007 L 204/18; Agreement between the EU and Australia on the processing and transfer of EU-sourced passenger name record (PNR) data by air carriers to the Australian customs service, OJ 2008 L 213/49.

[88] COM (2011) 32, Proposal for a Directive on the use of Passenger Name Record data for the prevention, detection, investigation and prosecution of terrorist offences and serious crime; see also COM (2010) 492, Commission Communication on the global approach to transfers of Passenger Name Record (PNR) data to third countries.

First, certainly, external competence as a whole has not been definitively transferred to the Union; its external competence is still limited by the principle of conferral. Still, if we look at the broad scope of its specifically external competences—including the CFSP which may cover 'all areas of foreign policy'—together with the potentiality of Article 216(1) TFEU, it is difficult to establish real limits to Union competence. However, there is less evidence, especially in practice, of a real exclusionary effect on the competence of the Member States. It is increasingly difficult to identify distinct and limited fields of competence occupied by the Union and Member States respectively; instead these competences overlap. Even where EU competence is formally exclusive the Union may decide to re-authorize the Member States to act, subject to procedural and substantive constraints to ensure protection of the Union interest. Shared external competence has become the norm and ways are being found to ensure, within the scope of Union action, unity, loyalty, and defence of the Union interest. The focus is on constraining the exercise of competence rather than its existence, although the constraints may be severe.

Secondly, the link between internal and external competence is still strong. The Union is directed to pursue its general external objectives when developing and implementing the external dimension of its internal policies. External instruments are used to serve objectives that have an essentially internal focus. Pre-emption and exclusivity under Article 3(2) TFEU are based on the adoption of legislation, requiring external unity to safeguard this internal *acquis*. As a matter of practice rather than doctrine, the Union is more likely to choose to exercise its competence externally, and is perhaps more likely to be able to formulate a common external position, where a policy has already been formulated internally.

It is in the interaction between formal rules and practice that innovative solutions are found for the very specific type of federal system that is the EU as an international actor. This chapter has illustrated some of this practice, including some creative responses but also demonstrating some of the tensions inherent between the Union and the Member States, each with the capacity to undertake international obligations: the Member States willing to see the Union engage effectively internationally but also wary of the impact of that action on their own internal and external autonomy; the Union's institutions defending its hard-won internal and external *acquis* and its sense of a common interest, as well as their own prerogatives and place in the institutional system. It is to be hoped that the attempt in the revised Treaties to redact 40 years of legal development and practice into definitive rules governing competence will not inhibit the continuing search for a pragmatic balance between the different actors and institutions that play their parts in the competence space of the European Union's external relations system.

4

The Allocation of Economic Policy Competences in the European Union

Roland Bieber

Introduction

The practice (and problems) as regards the allocation of competences in the area of economic policy in the European Union turn on two statements, one in the Treaty on European Union (TEU), the other in the Treaty on the Functioning of the European Union (TFEU):

- '*The Union* shall establish an economic and monetary union whose currency is the euro' (Article 3(4) TEU); and
- '*Member States* shall conduct their economic policies with a view to contributing to the achievement of the objectives of the Union' (Article 120 TFEU).[1]

Those statements reflect fundamental and enduring controversies over the distribution of economic policy competences between the Member States and the Union which go beyond the normal tensions between the centre and periphery within a federation. When the relevant provisions of the Maastricht Treaty were being drafted, there were already considerable differences of opinion among the various governments as to the degree of power to be attributed to the Union in the area of economic governance.[2] As a result, the corresponding provisions of the EU Treaties were worded obscurely, which favoured inconsistent implementation. Since 2009, it has become apparent that the wording and management of the system put in place for economic governance within the Union has failed to lead to the development of a coherent economic 'union' or to provide adequate tools to control the financial crisis in several Member States.[3] Recent efforts of EU Member States which are intended to create new modes of economic governance by way of international agreements have been brought to national courts

[1] Emphasis added.

[2] See J-V. Louis, *L'Union européenne et sa monnaie* (Brussels: Éditions de l'Université de Bruxelles, IEE Institut d'études européennes, 2009), 9.

[3] Cf. P. de Grauwe, *Economics of monetary union*, 9th edn (Oxford: Oxford University Press, 2009), 222.

and to the ECJ. In *Pringle* the ECJ has found those agreements compatible with the present distribution of competences in economic and monetary affairs.[4] The German Bundesverfassungsgericht has rejected applications for temporary injunctions to prevent the ratification by Germany of the European Council Decision amending Article 136 TFEU, the European Stability Mechanism (ESM) Treaty, and the so-called 'Fiscal Compact' Treaty.[5] This chapter addresses the question as to whether the existing provisions in the EU Treaties on economic and monetary union, in combination with the new instruments, are capable of bringing about a stable allocation of competences and the necessary reforms without damaging the project of an economic union within 'an ever closer union among the peoples of Europe' (Article 1 TEU).

I. General Economic Policy: an Allocation of Competences *sui generis*

In accordance with its traditional definition, the term 'economic policy' is used here in the sense of comprising all measures adopted by public authorities that are aimed at the allocation, stabilization, and redistribution of resources (Article 120 TFEU).

Within the area of economic policy in the European Union, two groups of competences should be distinguished. According to Article 3(3) and (4) TEU, the Union exercises competences for specific economic policies (e.g. transport, agriculture, etc.) and for general economic policy (e.g. fiscal policy). Whilst the legal nature of the former ('exclusive' or 'shared' competence according to the definition given in Article 2 TFEU) results explicitly from Articles 3 and 4 TFEU, general (macro) economic policy is not so precisely defined. This chapter is limited to a discussion of the specific problems arising from this lacuna in the latter area.

Although in European law different legal regimes apply to economic policy, on the one hand, and to monetary policy, on the other, both areas are closely interconnected. For example, the pivotal institution for monetary policy, the European System of Central Banks (ESCB), should, amongst other tasks, 'support *the general economic policies* in the Union' (Articles 127(1) and 282(2) TFEU).[6]

In a formal sense, the interconnection becomes apparent in Title VIII TFEU, which reads 'Economic *and* Monetary Policy'. The relationship between the competences in the two areas is discussed in section II.

1. A system of multiple competences

Article 119 TFEU states: '[t]he activities of the Member States *and* the Union shall include, as provided in the Treaties, the adoption of an economic policy which is

[4] Case C-370/12 *Pringle v Government of Ireland*, judgment of 27 November 2012, nyr.

[5] Bundesverfassungsgericht, 12.09.2012, 2BvR 1390/12 and others. The principal proceeding is still pending.

[6] Emphasis added.

based on the close coordination of Member States' economic policies, on the internal market and on the definition of common objectives'. Implementing provisions are laid down in Articles 120 to 144 TFEU and Protocols Nos. 12, 13, and 14.

The Treaty thus establishes a system of *overlapping competences*, consisting primarily of measures adopted by the Member States.

This assignment of competences has brought into being a *unique and not yet stable mix of actors, competences, and* powers, hence a unique form of federalism:

- *actors* include, to varying degrees, the EU and its Member States. In certain areas, the Member States enjoy a differentiated legal status (e.g. resulting from their participation in the Monetary Union or from specific situations);
- *competences* oscillate between a 'virtually complete assignment to the EU level for some functions or policy domains to the strict preservation of national autonomy in others'.[7] According to their subject matter they are *exclusive, shared, supplementary*, or *sui generis*;
- equally, the *powers* of the EU institutions vary considerably, according to subject matter.[8] Six groups, each of which has a different impact on national competence, must be distinguished:

  a) the EU Council may adopt (by way of non-binding recommendations) the 'broad guidelines' of the economic policies of the Member States and the Union;
  b) the Council and the Commission are also competent *to monitor the consistency* of economic policies with the broad guidelines ('Multilateral Surveillance Procedure', Article 121(3) TFEU);
  c) furthermore, the European Parliament and the Council may exercise *legislative powers*
     - to adopt detailed rules for the multilateral surveillance procedure (Article 121(6) TFEU);
     - for the definition of the prohibitions mentioned in Articles 123 to 125 TFEU (e.g. overdraft facilities) (Article 125(2) TFEU);
     - for the definition of implementing rules for Protocol No. 12 on the excessive deficit procedure (Article 126(14) TFEU);
  d) the Council may adopt *specific measures* aimed at reducing excessive government deficits (Article 126(9) TFEU);
  e) the Council may, under exceptional circumstances, *grant assistance* to a Member State and may lay down *conditions* for this assistance;
  f) finally the Council may impose *sanctions* on Member States which fail to comply with the provisions on excessive deficit.

[7] I. Begg, 'Lisbon as economic governance: Fusion by dif-fusion?', in U. Diedrichs and others (eds.), *Europe Reloaded* (Baden-Baden: Nomos, 2011), 331.

[8] On the difference between 'competences' and 'powers' see V. Constantinesco, *Compétences et pouvoirs dans les Communautés européennes* (Paris: Pichon & Durand-Auzias, 1974), 82.

This arrangement of competences, institutions, and powers does not match the *traditional* definition[9] of federalism as a vertical allocation of competences. The way in which competences for economic policies within the European Union are allocated in practice reveals instead—at least in part—a *pluralist concept* in respect of the exercise of public authority, whereby all actors are supposed to achieve *a common objective* by way of a mix of overlapping voluntary and mandatory activities.

The overlap is illustrated by the legislative practice for the implementation of Articles 121 and 126 TFEU. Those provisions concern the mechanisms for the coordination of national economic policies and for avoiding excessive government deficits. In neither area may Union action replace national action. Hence, the pre-emptive effect of 'shared competences' (Article 2(2) TFEU) does not apply. Nevertheless, the Union may adopt procedural rules and sanctions, both of which are intended to stimulate the Member States to act in a certain manner through binding norms within the scope of their competences. As a result, the manner in which they may use their competence becomes subject to (EU) conditions. Recent legislative activities of the Union (the 'six-pack' measures of November 2011 and measures adopted with regard to certain Member States with an excessive government deficit) indicate a trend towards using the competences of the Union, which are limited to the adoption of procedural provisions (Article 121(6) TFEU) and implementing rules (Article 126(14) TFEU), for far-reaching restrictions of national competences.

This practice reveals a paradox: in an area of particularly extensive national autonomy and seemingly weak competences of the Union, hence a non-hierarchical structure, we observe potential for particularly strong intervention by the Union.

Under those circumstances, it is not surprising that the Treaty fails to list general economic policy among the three categories ('shared', 'exclusive' and competence to 'support, coordinate, supplement' (Article 2(1), (2), and (5) TFEU)). It establishes instead, in Article 5(1) TFEU, an undefined special category. Article 2(3) and (5), first subparagraph, TFEU appears to imply that the EU possesses a competence falling outside the category of 'shared' competences, but does not provide any indication of the consequences of this special treatment. It is only indirectly that one may infer from the totality of the Treaty's provisions that exercise by the EU of such a competence in the economic policy field does not have the effect of pre-empting Member States' power to act.

Certain measures (e.g. sanctions) can be used, however, only by the Union; they may therefore be regarded as *exclusive. Other measures* that are authorized by the Treaty in order to impose specific conduct upon Member States or to establish definitions of Treaty provisions (e.g. Article 121(6) and Article 125(2) TFEU) produce a transfer of competence to the Union to the extent of their use (similar to shared competences, see Article 2(2) TFEU). A *third* category, namely that of

[9] See e.g. B. Dubey, *La répartition des compétences au sein de l'Union européenne à la lumière du fédéralisme Suisse: système, enjeux et consequences* (Geneva: Helbing and Lichtenhahn, and Brussels: Bruylant, 2002), 19 *et seq.*

measures adopted by the Union on economic policy pursuant to Article 121(1) TFEU ('guidelines'), has no *direct* effect on the allocation of competences.

It has been suggested that the Union's competences in the area of economic policy should be grouped among the *supplementary competences* listed in Article 6 TFEU.[10] This classification is, however, inconsistent with the powers of the Council to adopt implementing legislation and to control and sanction excessive public deficits (Article 126 TFEU).[11] On the other hand, it is not fully 'shared' either.[12] It is therefore preferable not to apply the ordinary categories mentioned in Article 2 TFEU but to consider instead the competence for general economic policy to be a competence *sui generis*.

2. The flexibility of competences or the significance of 'practice'

Inasmuch as economic policy competences of the European Union include powers to adopt measures that are binding on Member States, they enjoy the ordinary flexibility recognized in the field of shared competences (cf. Article 2(2) TFEU). Hence, the Union legislature determines the extent to which the Member States' corresponding competence is reduced.[13] In addition, the system of competences in the area of general economic policy *varies according to several external factors.*

First, EU competence on economic policy varies in its degree of intervention in Member State competences. Whilst, under 'normal' circumstances, the most important acts of the Union are non-binding recommendations, an excessive deficit in a Member State triggers a shift of competence from that state to the Union and enables the latter to adopt far-reaching compulsory measures.

Secondly, the Union has different competences in respect of Member States within or outside the euro-area. Hence, the 'broad economic policy guidelines' (Article 121 TFEU) distinguish between euro-area Member States and Member States 'with a derogation' (Articles 136(1)(b) and 139(2)(a) TFEU). Equally, coercive means of remedying excessive deficits (Article 126(9) and (11) TFEU) cannot be imposed on non-euro-area Member States. Any accession to the Monetary Union therefore implies a shift of economic policy competences to the Union (see Article 139(2)(a) and (b) and Article 136 TFEU).

Thirdly, the tensions between centralized monetary policy and decentralized economic policies generate pressure for harmonization of the different competences by creating a new balance within the system or parts of it. Those tensions recently brought about an amendment to Article 136 TFEU which authorizes the

[10] See J-P. Jacqué, *Droit institutionnel de l'Union européenne*, 6th edn (Paris: Dalloz, 2010), 159.

[11] J. Dutheil de la Rochère, 'Fédéralisation de l'Europe? Le Problème de la clarification des compétences entre l'Union et les Etats', in O. Béaud and others (eds.), *L'Europe en voie de constitution* (Brussels: Bruylant, 2004), 317, at 329.

[12] D. Wyatt and A. Dashwood consider it as 'variants(s) within the more general category of shared competence': *Wyatt and Dashwood's European Union Law* (Oxford: Hart, 2011), 105; similarly: J-C. Piris, *The Lisbon Treaty: a legal and political analysis* (Cambridge and New York: Cambridge University Press, 2010), 77 ('Shared competence').

[13] On the limits to flexibility in the excessive deficit procedure, see Case C-27/04 *Commission v Council* [2004] ECR I-6649.

establishment of a stability mechanism, aimed at granting financial assistance to Member States[14] and several extra-EU Treaty arrangements of a legally binding character:

- the *European Financial Stability Facility* (EFSF); established subsequent to an agreement between the Member States of the euro-area of 10 May 2010;
- the *European Stability Mechanism* (ESM), a treaty between the euro-area Member States, signed on 1 February 2012, which is intended to replace the EFSF;
- the *Treaty on stability, coordination and governance in the Economic and Monetary Union* ('Fiscal Compact'), signed by 25 Member States on 2 March 2012.

None of those texts operates an additional transfer of competences to the European Union. Both, the EFSF and the ESM are entirely controlled by the euro-area Member States. The 'Fiscal Compact' aims 'to strengthen the economic pillar of the economic and monetary union' (Article 1). To that end the Member States to which the Treaty applies subscribe to certain obligations in matters of economic policy that are already in the realm of EU competence. The Treaty furthermore entrusts certain supervisory powers to the Council, the Commission, and the Court of Justice (Articles 3, 5, 8). Although the procedure of Article 329 TFEU was not followed, this Treaty represents a special case of enhanced cooperation.

Answering to a request for a preliminary ruling, the ECJ has examined the European Council Decision amending Article 136 TFEU and the ESM. With regard to the amendment of Article 136 TFEU, the Court held that the amendment does not create a legal basis for the Union to be able to undertake any action which was not possible before the entry into force of that amendment.[15] Therefore the amendment does not confer any new competence on the Union.

Equally it found that neither Article 122(2) TFEU nor any other provision of the EU and FEU Treaties confers a specific power on the Union to establish a permanent stability mechanism such as the ESM. Therefore the Member States are entitled, in light of Articles 4(1) TEU and 5(2) TEU, to act in this area. Hence the ESM does not infringe the provisions of the FEU Treaty relating to economic and monetary policy.[16]

3. Practice

a) Acts applicable to all Member States

All Member States are addressed by Regulations, which lay down detailed rules for the 'multilateral surveillance procedure' as regards national economic policy.

[14] European Council Decision 2011/199/EU amending Article 136 TFEU with regard to a stability mechanism for Member States whose currency is the euro [2011] OJ L 91/1.

[15] *Pringle* (n 4) para 73.

[16] *Pringle* (n 4) para 105.

For example, Regulation 1466/97,[17] as most recently amended by Regulation 1175/2011,[18] introduces obligations for the Member States to provide information to the EU and to accept 'guidance' from the Council. The recent Regulation 1176/2011 on the prevention and correction of macroeconomic imbalances establishes definitions of such economic situations and lays down rules for 'corrective action'. It is also necessary to mention Directive 2011/85 on requirements for budgetary frameworks, adopted pursuant to Article 126 TFEU. The common denominator of those acts is a *reduction* of Member States' competence in matters of general economic policy and a resulting transfer to the Union.

Hence, by way of a broad interpretation of a procedural power, the Union has activated a 'dormant' substantive competence.

The *broad guidelines* for the economic policies of the Member States provided for in Article 121(2) TFEU are adopted on an annual basis. Until 2009, they comprised a country-by-country recommendation.[19] Since 2010, the Council has adopted 'integrated guidelines' which are drafted in more general terms.[20] They form the basis for country-specific recommendations, which may be adopted by the Council.[21]

As such, the Recommendations do not operate a shift in the allocation of competences. Any non-compliance by Member States may, however, trigger a power of the Council to intervene. Therefore, the autonomy of the Member States in this area exists only to the extent that the criteria established by the Union are met.

b) Acts applicable to some Member States only ('Euro-group')

Article 136(1) TFEU authorizes the Council to adopt measures specific to the Member States whose currency is the euro in order

- to strengthen the coordination and surveillance of their budgetary discipline;
- to set out economic policy guidelines for them. Those guidelines must be compatible with those adopted for the whole of the Union and are kept under surveillance.

[17] Council Reg (EC) 1466/97 on the strengthening of the surveillance of budgetary positions and the surveillance and coordination of economic policies [1997] OJ L 209/1. For a detailed analysis of Regulations 1466/97 and 1467/97 see K. Hentschelmann, 'Der Stabilitäts–und Wachstumspakt', *Discussion Paper 1/10*, Europa-Kolleg Hamburg, Institute for European Integration, available at <www.wirtschaftsdienst.eu/downloads/getfile.php?id=2333>.

[18] Reg (EU) 1175/2011 amending Council Regulation (EC) 1466/97 [2011] OJ L 306/12.

[19] See Council Recommendation (EC) 2009/531 on the 2009 update of the broad guidelines for the economic policies of the Member States and the Community and on the implementation of Member States' employment policies [2009] OJ L 183/1, annex.

[20] See Council Recommendation (EU) 2010/410 on broad guidelines for the economic policies of the Member States and of the Union [2010] OJ L 191/28.

[21] E.g. Council Recommendation addressed to Belgium on 12 July 2011, on the National Reform Programme 2011 of Belgium and delivering a Council Opinion on the updated Stability Programme of Belgium 2011-2014 [2011] OJ C 209/1.

An important restriction applies to specific measures on budgetary discipline. Article 136(1) provides that those measures must be adopted 'in accordance with the relevant provisions of the Treaties'. Since Protocol No. 12 on the excessive deficit procedure is part of the Treaties (Article 126(2) TFEU), any measure envisaged on the basis of Article 136 TFEU must observe the reference values prescribed by the Protocol. No measures other than those provided for in Articles 121 and 126 TFEU can therefore be adopted on the basis of Article 136 TFEU.[22] Recent practice reveals, however, that the power entrusted by Article 121(6) TFEU to the EU legislature 'to adopt detailed rules for the multilateral surveillance procedure' has been interpreted broadly, thus operating a shift of substantive economic competences from the euro-area Member States to the Union itself.[23]

The possibility of setting out separate 'economic policy guidelines' (Article 136(1)(b) TFEU) has been used by the Council since 2003.[24]

An amendment to Article 136 TFEU, which is in the process of ratification,[25] introduces a competence of euro-area Member States to establish a 'stability mechanism'.

Article 139(2)(a), (2)(b), and (4) TFEU require a distinction to be drawn between the euro-area and the remaining Member States with regard to the broad guidelines of economic policy to be formulated under Article 121(2) TFEU. Likewise, the coercive measures for the reduction of an excessive deficit (Article 126(9) and (11) TFEU) are applicable only within the euro-area. Protocol No. 15 to the TEU furnishes further special arrangements for the United Kingdom.

In this respect a more far-reaching shift of competences has been effected by Regulation 1174/2011 on enforcement measures to correct excessive macroeconomic imbalances in the euro-area.[26] This provides, *inter alia*, for interest-bearing deposits and fines in the case of such an imbalance.

Equally, Regulation 1173/2011 provides for sanctions and fines if a Member State has not complied with economic policy recommendations, or if it is shown to have manipulated statistics. Since 2003, the Recommendations concerning the broad guidelines for the economic policy of the Member States and of the Union[27] (based on Article 121(2) TFEU) contain a specific part devoted to the euro Member States. According to Article 139(2)(a) TFEU, this part does not apply to non-euro countries. Therefore the Union does not have competence to issue coercive measures in the case of non-compliance by the 10 non-euro Member States.

[22] See Louis (n 2), 122–4; U. Häde, 'Die Wirtschafts—und Währungsunion im Vertrag von Lissabon' (2009) *Europarecht* 200, at 205; M. Rodi, 'Artikel III–194', in C. Vedder and W. Heintschel von Heinegg (eds.), *Europäischer Verfassungsvertrag, Kommentar* (Baden-Baden: Nomos, 2007), 558.

[23] See nn 26 and 27.

[24] See Recommendation 2010/410 (n 20) Annex, Guideline No. 3; Recommendation 2009/531 (n 19) Annex, part 2; Council Recommendation (EC) 2008/390 on the broad economic policy guidelines for the Member States and the Community 2008-2010 [2008] OJ L 137/13, part A.2.

[25] European Council Decision 2011/199/EU (n 14).

[26] Reg (EU) 1174/2011 of the European Parliament and the Council on enforcement measures to correct excessive macroeconomic imbalances in the euro area [2011] OJ L 306/8.

[27] See the Recommendations quoted in n 24.

The Regulation on the surveillance of budgetary positions, adopted pursuant to Article 121(6) TFEU, contains special provisions on convergence programmes which apply *only* to Member States with a derogation (Articles 7 to 10).[28] Regulation 1467/97 on the excessive deficit procedure is applicable to non-euro states only in respect of Articles 1 to 4 thereof.[29]

c) Acts addressing exceptional situations in individual Member States

Under certain exceptional conditions, the Council may adopt binding decisions with regard to individual Member States. To this end, the TFEU, in Articles 122 and 126, establishes unspecified, albeit far-reaching, competences, which can be regarded as *federal elements* of the Union's economic policy. Both provisions were used during the financial crisis of 2010/2011.

aa) Assistance to individual Member States (Article 122 TFEU)

If severe difficulties arise in the supply of certain products, then undefined 'measures appropriate to the economic situation' (including, therefore, binding legislation) can be adopted (Article 122 TFEU). This competence was used by the Council for the first time in 2010, when it adopted Regulation 407/2010 establishing a *European financial stabilisation mechanism*.[30] The Regulation authorizes the grant of EU financial assistance to *any Member State* (including, therefore, those Member States which have introduced the euro) which is in difficulties, or is seriously threatened with severe difficulties caused by exceptional occurrences beyond its control (Article 1).

In respect of the allocation of competences for economic policy, the Regulation effects a considerable *shift from the national level to that of the Union*. It provides in Article 3(3):

> The decision to grant a loan (i.e. to a Member State) shall contain:
> a) . . . ;
> b) the general economic policy *conditions* which are attached to the Union financial assistance.

Hence, Article 122 TFEU provides for the Union to have competence to adopt binding substantive economic policy decisions for individual Member States if they receive assistance from the Union.

Such measures were adopted in 2010 vis-à-vis Ireland[31] and in 2011 vis-à-vis Portugal.[32]

[28] Reg 1466/97 (n 17), as last amended by Reg 1174/2011 (n 26), 1.

[29] Council Reg (EC) 1467/97 on speeding up and clarifying the implementation of the excessive deficit procedure [1997] OJ L 209/6, as last amended by Reg 1174/2011 (n 26) 33.

[30] Council Reg (EU) 407/2010 establishing a European financial stabilization mechanism [2010] OJ L 118/1.

[31] Council Implementing Decision (EU) on granting Union financial assistance to Ireland [2011] OJ L 30/34, as amended by Council Implementing Decision (EU) 2011/827 [2011] OJ L 329/7.

[32] Council Implementing Decision (EU) 2011/344 on granting Union financial assistance to Portugal [2011] OJ L 159/88, as amended by Council Implementing Decision (EU) 2011/683 [2011] OJ L 269/32.

Article 136 TFEU, in the amended version, provides an explicit, albeit indirect, legal basis for the competence to establish conditions as far as euro-area Member States are concerned. It stipulates that the granting of any required financial assistance under the mechanism 'will be made subject to *strict conditionality*'.[33] Since the mechanism is to be established by the euro-area Member States outside the framework of the EU Treaty, the effect of the planned Treaty amendment will be a shift of competences from the Union back to Member States.

For Member States outside the euro-area, a further mechanism for granting assistance is provided for via Article 143(2) TFEU. This provision also authorizes the Council to adopt directives or decisions laying down 'conditions' and details of such assistance.[34] Assistance on the basis of Article 143 has been granted, for example, to Romania.[35]

bb) Excessive deficit (Article 126 TFEU)

If a Member State with an *excessive deficit* fails to put recommendations of the Council intended to bring to an end that deficit into practice, such a failure triggers *two* ad hoc *competences* for the Union to adopt coercive means. Those competences can only be used in respect of Member States that have joined the euro-area (Article 139(2)(b) TFEU).

The Treaty contains particulars of such EU provisions only with regard to *sanctions* (Article 126(11) TFEU) whilst in respect of 'measures' pursuant to Article 126(9) TFEU, no details as to their nature or how comprehensive they might be are prescribed. It therefore leaves a large discretion to the Council (adoption of '*measures* for the deficit reduction which . . . are . . . judged necessary by the Council in order to remedy the situation').

The Council's Decision of 10 May 2010, giving notice to Greece to take measures for deficit reduction, established a controversial precedent for the interpretation of the scope of this provision.[36] It was adopted on the assumption that there was an existing competence on the part of the EU to establish far-reaching obligations for the adoption of internal legislative and other measures by a specific Member State. The Decision was based on Articles 126(9) and 136 TFEU.

It required Greece to 'put an end to the present excessive deficit situation', and to 'adopt the following measures', *inter alia*, to:

- reduce pensions (Article 2(1)(e));
- reduce Easter, summer and Christmas bonuses and allowances (Article 2(1)(f));

[33] Emphasis added.

[34] Cf. Council Reg (EC) 332/2002 establishing a facility providing medium-term financial assistance for Member States' balances of payments [2002] OJ L 53/1.

[35] Council Decision (EC) 2009/459 providing Community medium-term financial assistance for Romania [2009] OJ L 150/8.

[36] Council Decision (EU) 2010/320 of 10 May 2010 addressed to Greece with a view to reinforcing and deepening fiscal surveillance and giving notice to Greece to take measures for the deficit reduction judged necessary to remedy the situation of excessive deficit [2010] OJ L 145/6, as amended by Council Decisions (EU) 2011/734 [2011] OJ L 296/38 and 2012/211 [2012] OJ L 113/8.

- collect revenue from the licensing of gaming (Article 2(2)(a));
- replace only 20 per cent of retiring public sector employees (Article 2(2)(a)); etc.

The dramatic shift in the allocation of competences with regard to such countries is highlighted by a comparison with the last annual 'Stability Programme', which was adopted before 2010. In respect of pensions, the programme did not require any specific action to be taken, but invited Member States 'to reform age-related public expenditure such as pensions'.[37]

If a Member State fails to comply with a decision taken in accordance with Article 126(9) TFEU, Article 126(11) establishes a competence of the Union to adopt specific *sanctions* vis-à-vis that Member State. This competence of the Union has, to date, never been exercised.

II. Monetary Policy: an Exclusive albeit Divided Competence

1. The initial concept: a common and exclusive competence, provisionally divided

According to Articles 119(2) and 127 TFEU the Union is competent for the definition and implementation of monetary policy. Monetary policy of the European Union is to aim at price stability and to comprise the conduct of foreign exchange operations, the holding and the management of the official foreign reserves of the Member States, and the promotion of the smooth operation of payment systems. It furthermore comprises the competence to authorize the issuing of euro banknotes (Article 128 TFEU).

This competence is, however, divided horizontally. It is exclusive only in respect of 'the Member States whose currency is the euro' (Article 3(1)(c) TFEU). The remaining Member States are free to pursue an autonomous monetary policy. The division between 'ins' and 'outs' was meant to be provisional only. It is, however, likely to remain a permanent feature of the common monetary policy. The coexistence of multiple authorities responsible for monetary policy alone renders the system unnecessarily complex. The complexity and the corresponding reduction in efficiency is, however, amplified by its combination with the autonomy of the Member States in respect of their economic policy.[38]

Only to a limited extent can Treaty provisions absorb the tensions resulting from the combined effects of exclusivity, horizontal division, and the difference between the EU competences in economic and in monetary affairs.

[37] See Recommendation 2009/531 (n 19).

[38] See section I of this chapter.

2. Qualifications to exclusivity and division

The exclusive nature of the EU competence in monetary affairs requires qualification in respect of its differentiated application to (1) euro-area Member States and other Member States and (2) its quality as an entirely common policy.

i) Article 141(2) TFEU establishes various powers of the European Central Bank (ECB) in respect of those 'Member States with a derogation' (e.g. strengthening cooperation between the national central banks, strengthening coordination of the monetary policies of the Member States with the aim of ensuring price stability, monitoring the functioning of the exchange-rate mechanism, etc.). Moreover the use of the autonomy of Member States which have not yet introduced the euro is restricted by the duty of 'sincere cooperation' with the Union (Article 4(5) TEU), more specifically by the requirement, set out in Article 131 TFEU and Article 14 of the ESCB Statute, which applies to *all* Member States. According to those provisions the structure of the national central banks must be compatible with the TEU, the TFEU, and the ESCB Statute. National central banks are to act in accordance with the guidelines and instructions of the ECB (Article 14(3) ESCB Statute). They may perform functions other than those specified at EU level, as long as they do not interfere with the objectives and tasks of the ESCB.

Finally the *scope* of the EU competence can be extended, by way of a special legislative procedure, to include tasks concerning the prudential supervision of credit institutions, etc. (Article 127(6) TFEU). On this basis, an extension of exclusive competence was decided upon in 2010 in order to confer specific tasks upon the ECB concerning the functioning of the *European Systemic Risk Board*.[39] This new task of the ECB applies to *all Member States* (see Article 129(2)(c) TFEU and Article 9 of Regulation No 1096/2010).

ii) Although the EU Council, the Euro-area Council, the Commission, and the ECB are involved,[40] monetary policy is conducted and implemented by the 'Euro System' (Article 282(1) TFEU). To that end it is represented by the *Governing Council of the European Central Bank*, which comprises the members of the Executive Board of the ECB *and* the Governors of the national banks of the Member States whose currency is the euro (Article 283(1) TFEU). This unique institution is not part of the 'institutional framework' (Article 13 TEU) of the Union. It is not, however, an instrument of the Member States either, although the representatives of the (independent) national Central Banks constitute a majority (17, as

[39] Council Regulation (EU) 1096/2010 of 17 November 2010 conferring specific tasks upon the European Central Bank concerning the functioning of the European Systemic Risk Board [2010] OJ L 331/162.

[40] See arts 127, 136(2), and 138 TFEU.

compared to 6 members of the ECB Executive Board). This unique setting can be described as a 'federal institution with a decentralized structure'.[41]

3. Practice

Exclusive competences for monetary policy have been fully used, in particular for the adoption of legislation for the introduction of the euro, current policy management (e.g. the fixing of key interest rates, see Article 12 ESCB Statute), and interventions in the financial market.[42]

Since several Member States have not yet introduced the euro, the derogations provided for in Articles 139 and 141 and in Protocols Nos. 15, 16, and 17 apply.

As a result, the Union's competence in monetary affairs is implemented in a differentiated manner.

Insofar as competences exist, the ECB has interpreted Article 127(2) TFEU in a broad sense. For example, the programme for the carrying out of interventions in the euro-area public and private debt securities' market of 10 May 2010[43] was criticized as being in contradiction with the aim of the prohibition in Article 123 TFEU against the purchasing of debt instruments directly from Member States.

An unorthodox view of the role and powers of the Central Banks was expressed in a letter from ECB President Trichet to the Prime Minister of Italy, dated 5 August 2011.[44] The President of the European Central Bank asked the Government of Italy to adopt specific and far-reaching economic reforms, *inter alia*, to carry out a thorough review of rules regulating the hiring and dismissal of employees... together with the establishment of an unemployment insurance system and a set of active labour market policies. A constitutional reform tightening fiscal rules was also indicated as being appropriate.

This initiative can be understood as 'supporting' the general economic policies in the Union and therefore founded on Article 127(1) TFEU. It should, however, be noted that the measures recommended by the Council or the European Council on the basis of Article 121 TFEU in respect of Italy have never been as explicit as the aforementioned letter.[45] One may therefore ask whether the letter remained within the confines of a supporting measure.

It has been argued, that the conclusion of the ESM Treaty and the 'Fiscal Compact' would violate the exclusive competence of the Union for monetary policy. In *Pringle* the ECJ rejected this interpretation.[46] According to the Court it is not the purpose of the ESM to maintain price stability, but rather to meet the

[41] T. Padoa Schioppa, 'Economic Federalism and the European Union', in K. Knop and others (eds.), *Rethinking Federalism: citizens, markets and governments in a changing world* (Vancouver: UBC Press, 1995), 154, at 162.

[42] See Decision ECB/2011/17 on a bond purchase program [2011] OJ L 297/70.

[43] OJ 2010 L 124, p. 8.

[44] The letter was published in its original English version by the Italian newspaper *Corriere della Sera* of 29 September 2011.

[45] See e.g. Council Recommendations 2009/531 and 2010/410 (nn 19 and 20).

[46] See *Pringle* (n 4).

financing requirements of ESM Members. To that end, the ESM is not entitled either to set the key interest rates for the euro-area or to issue euro currency.

Conclusion

The separation of competences is considered in traditional academic writing to constitute the central feature of federalism.[47] Competence for general economic policy in most federations is allocated to the central authority (e.g. Article 74(1) No. 11 German *Grundgesetz*; Article 100 of the Constitution of Switzerland).[48] As a consequence, federal law in this area prevails over the law of the composing entities.

The *simultaneous* allocation of competences for general economic policy to the composing entities *and* to the joint (or central) authority without a precise demarcation line is singular and has no parallel in federal states. Combined with an exclusive but divided central competence for monetary policy such a system bears a high risk of inefficiency or even failure. Nevertheless, from the point of view of a Swiss author, the foundations of the EU economic policy competence share many features of the economic constitutions of federal states.[49]

Conceptually, the allocation of competences in this area covered by the EU Treaty is not based on hierarchy and is neither a hierarchy resulting from pre-emption nor a hierarchy resulting from specialization.

This 'vague', 'unstable' allocation of competences would not necessarily be a sign of immaturity if it were rooted in a solid foundation of legitimacy, deriving from, for instance, the participation of the directly elected European Parliament in the decision-making process. Such a system has considerable federal potential, since it obliges all participating authorities to participate in a transparent endeavour to achieve an appropriate allocation. Hence, allocation would result from procedure rather than from fixed attribution. The resulting flexibility would be more open to adaptation and would offer greater protection in respect of the identity of the participating entities.

In theory, and under normal circumstances, the pluralist approach may present many advantages, not the least of which is a wider democratic legitimacy. Sanctions are *not suitable* in such a horizontally structured system, and are therefore unlikely to be used effectively. On the other hand, it requires close and sincere cooperation among the actors. In the absence of willingness to offer such cooperation, no coherent policy can be achieved.

[47] See Dubey (n 9).

[48] For a discussion including the US, see T. Heller and J. Pelkmans, 'The Federal Economy: Law and Economic Integration and the Positive State–The U.S.A. and Europe Compared in an Economic Perspective', in M. Cappelletti, M. Seccombe, and J.H.H. Weiler (eds.), *Integration through Law*, Vol. I, Book 1 (Berlin and New York: Walter de Gruyter, 1986), 245.

[49] R. Rhinow, G. Schmid, and G. Biaggini, *Öffentliches Wirtschaftsrecht* (Basel: Helbing Lichtenhahn Verlag, 1998), 203.

We have also learned that such a system is very vulnerable in stressful situations. The rather unexpected, recent legislative technique of the Union, whereby non-binding rules are given binding effect by way of sanctions and fines in the case of non-compliance, seems to indicate a shift from heterarchy to hierarchy in the relationship between the law of the Union and national law.

Urgently required measures do, it is true, more easily lead to an overdose of hierarchical intervention, which, under normal conditions, would be excluded. Since Member States have not respected their commitment to a converging economic policy, one may have doubts as to the efficiency of a pluralist constitutional arrangement based on voluntary coordination.

It is, however, too early to consider the pluralist model a failure. It seems clear that the potential for sincere cooperation between the Member States and the Union with a view to achieving the common aims has not yet been exploited to the full.

In any event, the allocation of competences in the field of general economic policy between the European Union and its Member States not only provides an interesting paradigm for *federalism without hierarchy* or, as is preferred here, *pluralist governance*, but deserves closer examination regarding its capacity to reconcile economic efficiency with respect for national identity and democracy.

This comes close to a definition of federalism proposed by Carl Friedrich as early as 1955, according to which federalism is 'the process by which a number of separate political organizations, be they states or any other kind of associations, enter into arrangements for making joint decisions on joint problems'.[50]

[50] See C. Friedrich, 'Federal Constitutional Theory and Emergent Proposals', in A.W. MacMahon (ed.), *Federalism: Mature and Emergent* (Garden City, N.Y.: Doubleday, 1955), 510.

5

Legislative and Executive Competences in Competition Law

*Giorgio Monti**

Introduction

Competition lawyers seldom reflect on issues pertaining to competences, and discussions of constitutional questions in this field are found infrequently.[1] This might be because such matters are not really problematic: competence allocation may be found in Article 3(1)(b) TFEU and in Regulation 1/2003 on the implementation of the rules on competition laid down in Articles 81 and 82 of the EC Treaty (now Articles 101 and 102 TFEU),[2] but any critiques one might make of these legislative choices have more to do with the economic logic of such allocation, or the implications for fundamental rights protection, than about the constitutional problems it generates. In litigation, competence arguments are raised infrequently and unsuccessfully.[3]

In this essay, we try to discern what kinds of competence exist in this field as a way of understanding the nature of the EU's 'federal' order. It is beyond the scope of this essay to address the question of how far the EU is properly a federal system.[4] That said, this essay shows that if we speak of 'federal' competition law in the EU context, the development over the years has been towards 'more power to Brussels'.[5]

* With thanks to Loïc Azoulai and Basje Bender for their comments. Any errors remain my responsibility.

[1] For two notable exceptions, see J. Drexl, 'Competition Law as Part of the European Constitution', in A. von Bogdandy and J. Bast (eds.), *Principles of European Constitutional Law*, 2nd edn (Oxford: Hart Publishing and Munich: Verlag CH Beck oHG, 2010) (although this focuses on the link between the Constitution and substantive competition law), and F. Cengiz, *Antitrust federalism in the EU and the US* (Abingdon: Routledge, 2012), esp ch. 3, suggesting that both jurisdictions referred to in the title display a model of cooperative federalism.

[2] [2003] OJ L 1/1.

[3] E.g. Case C-550/07 P *Akzo Nobel and others v Commission* [2010] ECR I-8301 paras 116–119.

[4] This question has divided many scholars. E.g. W. Van Gerven, *The European Union: A Polity of States and Peoples* (Oxford: Hart Publishing, 2005), 268, suggests that the EU has de facto a federal structure, while for J. Habermas, *Questa Europa è in crisi* (Bari: Laterza, 2012), 67 *et seq*, it remains an 'unaccomplished federal republic'.

[5] As recently noted, federalism in the US means more power to states, while in the EU context it usually means more power to the EU institutions: cf. D. Halberstam, 'Federalism: A Critical

It is helpful to distinguish between legislative and executive competence.[6] Legislative competence gives rise to two issues: what kind of competence has been conferred upon the EU in the field of competition law, and what is the legal impact of a finding that there is insufficient competition in a defined market on the EU's competence under Article 114 TFEU. We focus on the first issue here in section II.[7] The puzzle we try to unravel is that, in spite of the evidence pointing to shared competences, the TFEU declares that the competence is exclusive. Executive competence relates to the enforcement of competition law and raises questions about the coordination of national and supranational competition law enforcement. We discuss these matters in section III, and suggest that national enforcement of *EU* competition law is, in large part, subject to the Commission's wishes: the competence is not parallel but rather shared, while when it comes to the enforcement of *national* competition law, competences may be exercised in parallel with the EU's competences, even though there are limits to the applicability of national law.

In section IV, we ask whether there is any sign of rebellion against the developments charted in sections II and III. This might be expected in light of the displacement of national law. The evidence suggests that, insofar as the enforcement of Articles 101 and 102 TFEU and the application of the EU merger rules are concerned, there is little sign of resistance. However, when the Commission exercised its legislative and executive powers in certain sensitive fields challenging firms that had been granted certain privileges by the Member States (e.g. those in telecommunications and energy markets), Member States have at times raised objections based on competences to slow down the Commission's drive towards liberalization, with partial success. Likewise the delays in securing an EU-wide merger regime also point to Member States resisting EU competition law in those fields of competition law which are more closely associated with national industrial policy. An alternative to resistance could be that national competition authorities (NCAs) have the flexibility to experiment, so they participate in the shaping of EU competition law. However, I suggest that at present competition law enforcement is not a site where we witness experimentalist governance.

Before we explore the dimensions of legislative and executive competence however, it may be helpful to set out some background about EU competition law enforcement before and after Regulation 1/2003, a significant turning point for the allocation of legislative and executive competences.[8] This is provided in section I below.

Guide' (2011) *University of Michigan Law School Public Law and Legal Theory Working Paper Series*, No. 251, 3.

[6] For present purposes I define these terms in a conventional way; for a close analysis of these notions, see the essay by O. Beaud in this volume.

[7] The second is discussed in the essay by R. Schütze in this volume.

[8] This summary draws on G. Monti, *EC Competition Law* (Cambridge: Cambridge University Press, 2007), ch. 11. See also R.D. Kelemen, *Eurolegalism* (Cambridge, MA: Harvard University Press, 2011), ch. 5.

I. The Enforcement of Competition Law in the EU

In the beginning, competition law was enforced almost exclusively by the Commission; most Member States had no credible competition laws, and the notification/exemption provisions in Regulation 17/62 (the First Regulation implementing Articles 85 and 86 of the [EEC] Treaty)[9] shifted the burden of supervision upon the Commission, rendering decentralized enforcement of EU competition law difficult except in clear-cut cases. Member States had not foreseen that empowering the Commission would have any major consequences, but this expectation was confounded by an activist DG Competition and Commission, supported by the ECJ's case law. Beginning in the mid-1980s, and aided by the presence of two charismatic Commissioners for competition (Peter Sutherland and Leon Brittan), competition law enforcement by the Commission increased in scale and scope and was so successful that it was hailed as the EC's first supranational policy by the mid-1990s.[10]

The success of EC competition law led to three responses and developments. First, subjects of the law sought greater controls over the Commission. This was successful: the Commission's procedures were kept in check by reference to fundamental rights and by a watchful Court of First Instance; and its substantive norms were evolving to embrace the teachings of mainstream economics, to sustain some degree of output legitimacy. Secondly, DG Competition looked for ways of streamlining its enforcement and experimented with a number of formal and informal practices (e.g. comfort letters, settlements, and Block Exemption regulations). By the late 1990s, the Commission was coming close to eliminating its backlog of cases, though the EU's enlargement would likely have created a new wave of notifications. Thirdly, and of more relevance for the theme of this volume, beginning in the 1980s a number of Member States enacted their first competition laws (or redrafted their laws) and these national laws in large part reproduced the text of Articles 101 and 102 TFEU, the major antitrust provisions. Moreover, in some jurisdictions the interpretative principles of the ECJ were made binding upon national authorities interpreting national laws, and many national authorities were empowered to apply EU competition law.[11] For existing Member States this was done absent any legal requirement from the EU; for accession states, drafting competition laws was a requirement for joining the EU, but these states also preferred to align national laws to EU standards even if this was not required expressly.

As a result of these developments, by 1999 (the year when the 'White Paper on the Modernisation of the rules implementing Articles 85 and 86 of the EC Treaty'

[9] [1962] OJ Spec Ed 87.

[10] L. McGowan and S. Wilks 'The First Supranational Policy in the European Union: Competition Policy' (1995) 28 *European Journal of Political Research* 141.

[11] E.g. Italy, Ireland, France. See generally H. Vedder, 'Spontaneous Harmonisation of National Competition Laws in the Wake of the Modernization of EC competition law' (2004) 1 *Competition Law Review* 5.

was released),[12] the conditions were right for taking further steps to decentralize the enforcement of competition law: national agencies could be trusted to apply the law dispassionately, and tasking them with enforcing EU law anticipated similar calls for decentralization in the Commission's White Paper on Governance on European Governance of 2001.[13] Also anticipating the White Paper on Governance is the view that DG Competition could use this reform as a means of refocusing its enforcement efforts on cases of major European significance, so as 'to add value to national policies and address people's concerns more effectively at European and global level.'[14]

In this perspective, Regulation 1/2003 is not a radical break with the past, but rather an incremental reform that builds upon the developments noted earlier and adds the following features: first, it empowers national courts and agencies to apply the exemption of Article 101(3) TFEU (absent this the only times national agencies and courts could pronounce on the application of this provision was when an agreement fell within the scope of a Block Exemption Regulation); secondly it abolishes the system of notification (and moves competition law towards a crime-tort model of enforcement and away from a regulatory model);[15] and thirdly, and most relevant for present purposes, it requires national agencies and courts to apply Articles 101 and 102 and to avoid conflicts between these provisions and national competition laws.[16]

Regulation 1/2003 has been adjudged to be a huge success, at least numeric ally: NCAs have been active, initiating over a thousand investigations (but completing a far smaller number); and NCAs have not rocked the boat: only a few minor difficulties have arisen with the operation of the new scheme, and these have been resolved without fuss.[17] From the perspective of this essay, we have witnessed a shift from a system where the Commission operated supranational antitrust enforcement, with some national laws also enforced by Member States, towards a system where NCAs are involved in executing EU competition law together with the Commission. In this new system, what space is left for national competition law?

II. Legislative Competence

Of the many variations of legislative competence found in EU law,[18] there are only two realistic options in the field of competition law: competence is exclusively conferred to the EU, so that a single set of rules is applicable across the EU, and

[12] COM (99) 101 final. [13] COM (2001) 428, 'European Governance: A White Paper'.

[14] COM (2001) 428, 'European Governance: A White Paper', 9.

[15] The terminology is from D. Crane, *The Institutional Structure of Antitrust Enforcement* (Oxford, Oxford University Press, 2011).

[16] These three moves are achieved by arts 1 and 3 of Council Reg 1/2003 (n 2). (This takes a leaf out of the approach in Italian law where, for infringements that affect interstate trade, the competition authority must only apply EU competition law.)

[17] COM (2009) 206 final, Communication from the Commission to the European Parliament and the Council, 'Report on the Functioning of Regulation 1/2003', paras 24–8.

[18] For a thorough classification, see R. Schütze 'The European Community's Federal Order of Competences–A Retrospective Analysis', in M. Dougan and S. Currie (eds.), *Fifty Years of the European*

Member States surrender what legislative competence they have, or competence is shared; that is to say, the EU legislator leaves space for national competition legislation, provided that the latter does not conflict with the former.

1. From shared to exclusive?

Let us begin to consider the competence question by resorting to concrete examples. There are two that will help to shape our discussion: (1) a proposed merger between two firms operating in Spain is likely to have an effect on trade between Member States and to have adverse effects on competition in the EU because there will be higher prices in France, Italy, and Germany. However, the merger lacks an EU dimension, Spanish law applies, and the merger is authorized;[19] (2) a pricing practice operated by a dominant firm is perfectly lawful under Article 102 TFEU (prohibiting abuse of dominance), but the French competition authority applies a stricter competition rule and declares it unlawful.[20]

Take the first example: the Merger Regulation[21] does not apply even though there is harm to the EU economy. The formal reason for the incomplete coverage of the Merger Regulation is that the legislator respected the principle of subsidiarity, which is a strong indication that competences are shared as subsidiarity analysis is not required when the EU legislator acts in a field where its competence is exclusive.[22] However, the formalism of this response hides the reality behind the enforcement of merger law: first it is fairly clear from legislative history that the reason for the limited application of the Merger Regulation has almost nothing to do with subsidiarity and is the result of Member States wanting to retain the capacity to regulate mergers in the national interest; the Commission's requests for the scope of the Merger Regulation to be extended have regularly been rejected.[23] Secondly, it is worthwhile noting how the principle of subsidiarity is invoked in the preambles to the Merger Regulation to justify the limited scope of the Regulation on the one hand, *and* the possibility provided for in the Regulation for some mergers that do not fall within the relevant thresholds to be referred to the Commission

Treaties (Oxford: Hart, 2009); A. Von Bogdandy and J. Bast 'The Federal Order of Competences', in von Bogdandy and Bast (n 1).

19 This example is based on Case COMP/M.3986, *Gas Natural/Endesa* (15 November 2005) where the Commission did not have jurisdiction and the merger was said to have advanced Spain's industrial policy objectives at the expense of the EU's interests in developing an internal market for energy. See A. Nourry and N. Jung, 'EU State Measures against Foreign Takeovers: "Economic Patriotism" in All But Name' (2006) 2 *Competition Policy International* 99.

20 This is inspired by the French laws that were addressed in Joined Cases C-267/91 and C-268/91 *Keck and Mithouard* [1993] ECR 6097.

21 Council Reg 139/2004 on the control of concentrations between undertakings [2004] OJ L 24/1.

22 See art 5(3) TEU.

23 There is copious literature on the legislative history: for a summary, see D. Chalmers, G. Davis, and G. Monti, *European Union Law: Text and Materials* (Cambridge: Cambridge University Press, 2006), ch. 24.

for decision under the Regulation anyway.[24] This is either a sign that the turnover thresholds are an imprecise proxy for subsidiarity, or that, since the thresholds are significantly higher than the thresholds for applying Articles 101 and 102 TFEU, they are not based on considerations of subsidiarity at all, but rather on a political compromise. This also indicates that there is a good reason why Member States would have been loath to confer on the Union exclusive competence in the sphere of competition law.

In the second example, stricter national law continues to apply, which is an illustration of the application of Article 3(2) of Regulation 1/2003, which provides that certain aspects of national law may coexist with EU competition law. It is probable that the application of stricter national law would contribute to create a more competitive EU market. And again, competences here appear to be shared, for the rule in Article 3(2) could be rescinded, removing the national legislative competence. Furthermore, as with the Merger Regulation, it is worth noting that subsidiarity played a role in the Commission's analysis for reforming the procedural rules, and it is also mentioned in Regulation 1/2003, where it is invoked to justify the extent of the Commission's enforcement powers in the enforcement of competition law.[25]

These examples allow us to make two points: first, that the two major pieces of secondary legislation in the field of competition law are implemented respecting subsidiarity, and second, that if we consider the economic impact of national law in the two examples, we find that the national legislator has been left free to apply different standards to activities that do not fall within the scope of the EU's rules, but that this competence may be reduced if the secondary legislation is amended.[26] The competences seem shared.

If we now turn to Article 3(1)(b) TFEU, this provides as follows: '[t]he Union shall have exclusive competence in…the establishing of the competition rules necessary for the functioning of the internal market.' This text is like that found in Article 3(f) EEC (renumbered as Article 3(1)(g) EC), although in the earlier Treaties, the matter was not spelled out in terms of competences, but in terms of the *activities* of the Community.[27]

Now, one of the mandates set by the Laeken Declaration was to clarify and simplify the division of competences between the Union and its Member States.[28] That said, it would be inaccurate to say that Article 3(1)(b) TFEU is a codification of this competence: as has been seen, the available evidence points towards

[24] Council Reg 139/2004 (n 21), recitals 8 and 11.

[25] Council Reg 1/2003 (n 2), recital 34.

[26] Both Regulations make express provision for regular review and possible revision, see Council Reg 1/2004, art 44, and Council Reg 139/2004, art 1(4) and (5), and art 4(6), providing that the thresholds for the application of EU merger control are regularly reviewed.

[27] 'the activities of the Community shall include…a system ensuring that competition in the internal market is not distorted.'

[28] The *Laeken Declaration on the Future of the European Union* (available at: <http://european-convention.eu.int/pdf/lknen.pdf>), 3–4 suggested a review of all competences based on three themes: namely clarification, simplification, and adjustment, all read in the light of the challenges facing the Union at the time.

competences being shared.[29] The first suggestions that competition should be the EU's exclusive competence appear to have been made in a 1992 Communication on subsidiarity.[30] The default rule is that competences are shared unless otherwise stated, so it would appear that the TFEU turns a shared competence into an exclusive one.[31]

It is worth looking at Article 3(1)(b) TFEU in closer detail to verify this. First, when compared with other exclusive competences listed in this Article it stands out as the only one with a detailed phrasing of its remit. In particular, it is the only head of exclusive competence that identifies this competence in a narrow manner: the competence is limited to 'establishing... rules'. The other competences are phrased in terms of terms of policy fields. This suggests that competence is exclusive only in terms of legislative, but not executive competence. Secondly, the word 'necessary' is, as intimated earlier, probably redundant, insofar as the proportionality test is only applied in fields of shared competence. Third, if we review the legal bases upon which competition legislation may be drafted (recall that Article 3 TFEU merely confers competences, it does not, of itself, provide a legal basis), then not all of these point to the competence being exclusive. The principal legal basis is Article 103 TFEU, which empowers the legislator to set out 'appropriate regulations or directives to give effect to the principles set out in Articles 101 and 102 [TFEU]'. These may include provisions for fines, definitions of the scope of application of the competition rules, and definitions regarding the relationship between EU and national competition law.[32] The vast majority of the legislation enacted under Article 103 TFEU can really only be enacted at EU level, since it regulates how the Commission, in its capacity as a competition authority, should act. It makes no sense for this competence to be shared. However, insofar as Regulation 1/2003 regulates the relationship between national and EU competition law, this indicates that competences are shared, in that the way this relationship is managed may change over time, so that the scope of national law may diminish further. Furthermore, another possible legal basis for competition law is Article 83(2) TFEU, a new provision on the basis of which criminal penalties may be prescribed for competition law infringements. However, certain Member States have already imposed criminal sanctions for certain forms of anti-competitive conduct. Finally, the Merger Regulation (which was adopted on the basis of both Articles 83 and 352 TFEU) represents an example of shared competences.

29 M. Dougan, 'The Convention's Draft Constitutional Treaty: Bringing Europe Closer to its Lawyers?' (2003) 28 *European Law Review* 763, at 770.

30 SEC (92) 1990, Communication from the Commission to the Council and the European Parliament, 'The Principle of Subsidiarity', Final Annex, p. 7.

31 See also Cengiz (n 1) 79–81, noting that the current law and practice of competence allocation points to shared competences. L.S. Rossi, 'Does the Lisbon Treaty Provide a Clearer Separation of Competences between EU and Member States?', in A. Biondi, P. Eeckhout, and S. Ripley (eds.), *EU Law After Lisbon* (Oxford: Oxford University Press, 2012), 99, suggests that the draftsman might have been thinking of state aid law. The author also notices that it is unusual that legislation in a field of exclusive competence could be based on art 352 TFEU as surely an exclusive competence would find an explicit legal base.

32 Art 103(2) TFEU.

The implications of switching from a shared to an exclusive competence could be profound: it would mean that national competition law cannot any longer be enforced, for an exclusive competence does not allow Member States to legislate unless authorized by the EU to do so. It could also mean that NCAs would be unable to enforce EU competition law, because national laws (including rules of procedure necessary to enforce EU competition law) would be inapplicable, again unless the EU were to allow Member States to so legislate or the EU itself were to provide relevant legislation to empower NCAs. However, neither of these profound changes has taken place. In fact were this to be the case, it would have undermined the Commission's policy of enhancing the role of NCAs. Granted, Regulation 1/2003 empowers NCAs in some ways, but not in such a complete manner. For example, procedures are largely left for national legislation, as matters currently stand.[33] The EU and Member States have acted as if the TFEU made no change to competence allocation.

Were competences then always exclusive? According to Alan Dashwood, the answer is in the affirmative. In his view, the new Treaty provision on competition law competences (at the time of writing he was commenting on the one that appeared in the Constitutional Treaty, but it is worded identically) was 'technically inept' for two reasons: (1) we know that competence is exclusive because Member States simply have no power to establish competition rules that are *applicable throughout the internal market*; (2) national rules on competition cannot interfere with the uniform application of the Community rules as a result of the principle of loyal cooperation.[34] This second point is more relevant to the issue of executive competence, but the first point he makes is plausible, because the jurisdiction of an NCA when applying national competition law is usually limited to penalizing acts that affect its territory (though it may secure such evidence abroad).[35] Two responses might be made: first, a legal response is found in the writings of Robert Schütze: in his view, it is an 'ontological fallacy' to assert exclusive competence by reference to the functioning of the internal market, because this confuses the basis on which the Union may legislate with the field itself: just as in the internal market, legislative competences are shared, competences are also shared in the field of competition.[36] Second, from an economic perspective, one cannot deny that enforcing national competition law can help the EU's economic interests: deterring cartels under national law also serves to help deter cartels that might fall under EU competition law, and addressing abusive conduct can open up opportunities

[33] For a clear illustration see the points noted by AG Kokott in Case *Akzo Nobel* (n 3) paras 127–129, when discussing the laws applicable to inspections.

[34] A. Dashwood, 'The Relationship Between the Member States and the European Union/European Community' (2004) 41 *Common Market Law Review* 355, 371–2. *Contra*: G. Monti, 'New Directions in EC Competition Law', in T. Tridimas and P. Nebbia (eds.), *European Union Law for the Twenty-First Century* (Oxford: Hart, 2004), notably 178–9.

[35] This is now changing because some Member States, when applying EU competition law, may wish to impose a penalty for the effects of the practice in other Member States; however, the matter is delicate.

[36] R. Schütze, 'Dual federalism constitutionalised: the emergence of exclusive competences in the EC legal order' (2007) 32 *European Law Review* 3, 21–2.

to trade. It would be hard to deny the fact that the enforcement of national competition law helps the development of the internal market. Two concrete examples among many may be offered. German law penalizes bid rigging with criminal sanctions and the relevant provisions have been applied frequently: opening up the German procurement market must serve to enhance competition across the EU, as foreign participants are more likely to compete.[37] Second, many of the market investigations carried out by the Competition Commission in the UK are likely to have had pro-competitive effects across the EU.[38] Accordingly, insofar as the application of national competition law has EU-wide pro-competitive effects, this suggests that competences are shared, even if the national rules are not applicable throughout the internal market.

One way of supporting Alan Dashwood's claim is to refer back to the seminal *Walt Wilhelm* judgment.[39] Even though this is more relevant for executive competences, there is also a passage that may be used to explain why legislative competences are exclusive. The ECJ said:

> Community and national law on cartels consider cartels from different points of view. Whereas [Article 101 TFEU] regards them in the light of obstacles which may result for trade between Member States, each body of national legislation proceeds on the basis of the considerations peculiar to it and considers cartels only in that context.[40]

This passage can be read in such a way as to show that Article 3(1), lit (b) TFEU merely codifies matters because, according to the Court, only EU competition law looks at internal market considerations. However, this passage from the Court's judgment may be criticized from a number of perspectives. First, if it is intended to say that Article 101 TFEU is infringed only when the activity in question harms trade between Member States, then this is an inaccurate portrayal of how Article 101 TFEU has been enforced: while it is true that in some cases the division of markets has been the basis for a finding of an infringement, this is not a necessary condition. Secondly, if it is intended to say that Article 101 TFEU only applies when there is a harmful effect on trade between Member States, then, again, this is misleading because the effect need not be a negative one for Article 101 TFEU to apply, and national law may also apply if there are positive effects on trade. Thirdly, it is sometimes true that national competition law may have different objectives to EU competition law, but this is the exception now, and not the norm. As noted in section I, the evolution of EU and national competition law has been towards greater similarity in the approaches taken. Therefore, this passage cannot be read in such a way as to say that the EU has exclusive competence because the Treaty competition articles somehow deliver different economic results; in most cases,

[37] F. Wagner von Papp, 'What if all bid riggers went to prison and nobody noticed? Criminal antitrust law enforcement in Germany', in A. Ezrachi and C. Beaton-Wells (eds.), *Criminalising Cartels: A critical interdisciplinary study of an international regulatory movement* (Oxford: Hart, 2011).

[38] See e.g. the structural remedies imposed in the *BAA Airports Market Investigation* (2009) (available at <http://www.competition-commission.org.uk>).

[39] Case 14/68 *Walt Wilhelm v Bundeskartellamt* [1969] ECR 1.

[40] *Walt Wilhelm v Bundeskartellamt* (n 39) para 3.

both EU and national rules serve to deter unlawful conduct and to improve consumer welfare.

Another indication that competences have always been exclusive is found in the *Akzo* judgment. The dispute focused on whether communications between an in-house lawyer and her client were privileged. The Court had earlier held they were not and the parties were asking the ECJ to reconsider. One argument was that the EU had not been conferred the powers to make this determination. The Court gave this short shrift, saying that the rules of procedure set out first in Regulation 17/62 and then in Regulation 1/2003 were 'part of the provisions necessary for the functioning of the internal market whose adoption is part of the exclusive competence conferred on the Union by virtue of Article 3(1), lit (b) TFEU'.[41] So the Court appeared to think that the TFEU had merely codified the law relating to competences. For a possible explanation of why this is so we can turn to AG Kokott's Opinion. In one passage, she states that the EU's exclusive competence relates to laying down 'the competition rules necessary for the functioning of the internal market and the substance and limits of the powers of investigation available to the Commission as European competition authority'.[42]

Therefore, insofar as procedural rules to empower the Commission to apply the Treaty provisions on competition are concerned, competences are exclusively held by the EU.[43] As noted above, this appears to make sense because to allow Member States to legislate in this context would render the uniform and effective application of EU competition law by the Commission impossible: different procedures would regulate how it may conduct its investigations depending on the Member State in question. However, in the exercise of this exclusive competence, the EU legislator has been sensitive to certain national considerations. This is best exemplified by reference to Article 20 of Regulation 1/2003. This gives the Commission significant powers to inspect premises, but a concession is made for those Member States under whose rules of procedure a judicial warrant is required before such investigations are carried out. This means that in some instances the Commission will have to abide by different national procedural requirements. Strictly speaking this concession need not have been made if a competence is exclusive, but it is likely that the legislator preferred to avoid a controversial displacement of national procedures in this context, even if this may risk hampering its enforcement powers somewhat.

Accordingly, *Akzo* helps explain that the EU has exclusive competence in the field of the procedures that empower the Commission to act. We still need to explain the nature of the EU's legislative competence when it comes to substantive rules.

A possible answer is that the competence is exclusive, but the EU grants some of the competences back to the Member States. This approach is provided for in Article 2(2) TFEU, where the final sentence provides that, in an area where the

[41] *Akzo Nobel* (n 3) para 116. [42] *Akzo Nobel* (n 3) para 182.

[43] At times this competence will be exercised by the Council, and at times the Council may delegate it to the Commission. For discussion, see Case 41/69 *ACF Chemiefarma NV v Commission* [1970] ECR 661 paras 60–70.

Union has exclusive competence, Member States shall exercise their competence 'to the extent that the Union has ceased exercising its competence'. This text is far from clear, but in the competition law context we have a particularly visible illustration in Article 3 of Regulation 1/2003:

- Article 3(1) provides that, in cases where Articles 101 or 102 apply, then national authorities/courts must apply EU law as well as national competition law, and Article 3(2)'s first sentence (plus the seminal judgment in *Walt Wilhelm*) provides that, in applying national competition law, they must not reach a result contrary to that under EU law. In economic terms, this means that, if there is no harm to the EU market (and so the agreement is lawful under the EU laws), you cannot prohibit this under national law; conversely, if the acts harm the EU markets (and the agreement is thereby contrary to EU law), you cannot authorize it using national laws. In effect, Member States have no competence to apply national competition law.
- Article 3(2) allows stricter national competition laws, which proscribe unilateral conduct. A clear example of this is found in the facts of the *Keck* judgment.[44] Here French legislation banned below cost sales so as to protect small retailers, and this certainly affected the trading conditions of market players outside France in a number of ways. Here, competence is granted back to Member States, as Article 2(2) TFEU intimates.
- Article 3(3) clarifies that national merger control rules are not affected by this Regulation, which may also be read as another grant-back to the Member States, because Articles 101 and 102 TFEU could apply to some mergers.

However, this interpretation would fly in the face of the desire to clarify competences, which was one of the factors motivating the new Treaties. Moreover, the notion of shared competence fits best because the grant-backs in Article 3 are not permanent; the EU for example is under some pressure from businesses to remove the exemption in Article 3(2), who complain that this stifles EU-wide investments.[45] Nor is the grant-back argument compelling when we look at the Merger Regulation, where the reality is the opposite: Member States resisted the Union's full exercise of its exclusive competence.

So then, competence is certainly shared, at least when viewed from an economic perspective, because many cases where national law is invoked will have positive effects on the market as a whole and so contribute to the EU's goals. This view is also reflected in a sweeping statement by the ECJ in a recent judgment (*Tele2*): 'it is only where European Union law does not lay down a specific rule that an NCA may apply its national rules.'[46]

[44] *Keck and Mithouard* (n 20). [45] COM (2009) 206 (final) (n 17) para 27.
[46] Case C-375/09 *Prezes Urzędu Ochrony Konku rencji i Konsumentów v Tele2 Polska sp. z o.o., devenue Netia SA.* [2011] ECR I-3055 para 33.

2. How much competence?

As suggested above, the nature of the EU's competence in competition law is unclear, but perhaps a more relevant question is: what is the scope of the EU's competences? For, while the current rules may be necessary for the functioning of the internal market, they are certainly not sufficient, in two respects.

a) Legislative gaps in EU competition law

First, the legislator could do a lot more to expand the scope of application of EU competition law, for example in the sphere of merger control. In addition, more secondary legislation in terms of procedures would make competition law enforcement function even better; for example if the EU clarified questions about access to leniency documents for plaintiffs seeking damages, as revealed by the litigation in *Pfleiderer*,[47] there would be more effective enforcement through increased deterrence. Similarly many procedural rules could be harmonized (e.g. the extension of legal and professional privilege to communications between investigated undertakings and in-house lawyers) and the EU is potentially competent to do so.[48] The Commission is aware of this and has recently proposed a modest draft directive to harmonize certain rules governing actions for damages for competition law infringements.[49]

The major implication of these legislative gaps for the purposes of this essay is that they mean that the Court of Justice is increasingly called upon to place limits upon the exercise of national legislative competences when this might hamper the effective enforcement of EU competition law by NCAs or national courts. One important example is the ruling in *Courage v Crehan* where the Court ruled that the scope of the illegality defence in UK private law was too wide and would put at risk 'the full effectiveness of Article 101 [TFEU]'.[50] A particularly striking indication of the infinity inherent in the concept of effectiveness is found in *VEBIC*.[51] Belgian legislation prevented NCAs from being parties to an appeal against their own decision (the Belgian NCA is divided into a section that prosecutes and a section that adjudicates, so understandably the legislator had provided that, on appeal from the decision of the NCA's adjudicatory panel, the NCA should have no right to appear before the court). The ECJ held that such a procedure would undermine (1) *effective* compliance with Articles 101 and 102 TFEU; (2) *effective* application of those Articles (thrice); (3) the *effet utile* (in the French version) or the *effectiveness* (in the English version) of those provisions.[52] Thus, to ask where the EU's competence ends is not fruitful because with the principle of

[47] Case C-360/09 *Pfleiderer* [2011] ECR I-5161.

[48] AG Kokott, *Akzo Nobel* (n 3) para 134.

[49] COM (2013) 404 final, Proposal for a Directive of the European Parliament and of the Council on certain rules governing actions for damages under national law for infringements of the competition law provisions of the Member States and of the European Union.

[50] Case C-453/99 *Courage v Crehan* [2001] ECR I-6297 para 26.

[51] Case C-439/08 *VEBIC* [2010] ECR I-12471.

[52] *VEBIC* (n 51), respectively at paras 56, 57, 59, 60, and 61.

effectiveness, one can challenge many national procedural rules that have been put into place to enforce EU competition law. For instance, in a recent judgment concerning the application of Austria's leniency programme the Court held that an NCA can only decide not to impose a fine in cases where this would 'not undermine the requirement of effective and uniform application of Article 101 TFEU'.[53] This strand of case law delimits the legislative and executive competences held at Member State level, and confers greater competences on the Union. Whether any limits may be found by reference, for example, to the protection of fundamental rights remains to be seen.

b) Anti-competitive state laws

Secondly, EU law lacks a comprehensive mechanism to tackle national legislation that has anti-competitive effects. This even extends to national competition law that might have anti-competitive effects. Suppose national merger law allows for anti-competitive effects: the EU might seize jurisdiction under Articles 101 or 102 TFEU if these are applicable, or the EU might challenge the authorization of an anti-competitive merger on the basis of the internal market rules.[54] The sole general principle that exists that could serve as a basis for challenging anti-competitive state law is the duty that states have to disapply anti-competitive legislation because they have a duty not to enforce laws that dent the *effet utile* of Articles 101 and 102, on the basis of Article 4(3) TEU.[55] Having said this, what is clear from the case law of the Court is that there is no systematic legal basis that allows one to challenge every aspect of national competition law that has anti-competitive effects EU-wide: in a set of judgments in the early 1990s, the Court refused to establish a general rule to allow a party to challenge any national law that has anti-competitive effects. The rule is only applicable when national law allows or requires an anti-competitive action by the dominant firm, which serves to limit the rule considerably.[56]

In sum, whatever the nature of the EU's legislative competence, it appears that more of it could be exercised to create a truly competitive internal market. Having said that, it is also important to recall that the absence of competition in a market may also be a basis for implementing legislation under Article 114 TFEU. In this context the Court has held that, insofar as a legal measure has a beneficial effect on competition, this is not sufficient ground to state that the measure is one that the Union has exclusive competence to implement; for instance rules creating a unified system of patent protection among 25 Member States under the procedures

[53] Case C-681/11 *Bundeswettbewerbsbehörde e Bundeskartellanwalt v Schenker & Co. AG and others* [2013] nyr. para 47.

[54] An example of this is Case C-196/07 *Commission v Spain* [2008] ECR I-41, where national law imposed further hurdles on a merger already authorized by the Commission, thus infringing the Merger Regulation.

[55] Case C-198/01 *Consorzio Industrie Fiammiferi v AGCM* [2003] ECR I-8055.

[56] The key ruling delimiting the application of art 4(3) TEU in the sphere of competition law is Case C-2/91 *Meng* [1993] ECR 5791 (see especially AG Tesauro's Opinion).

for enhanced cooperation will affect competition, but the ECJ has said that the patent rules are not therefore competition rules for the purposes of Article 3(1)(b) TFEU, they are rules regulating the internal market, for which competences are shared.[57] Competences are thus exclusive only with respect to Articles 101 to 109 TFEU.[58] The upshot of this approach is a formalistic and economically irrational notion of competences when it comes to regulating markets: some competences are expressly shared, some are expressly exclusive, but some of the exclusive competences have been granted back to Member States. This legal complexity should have been avoided given the importance that the EU has always placed on the economic aspect of integration.

III. Executive Competence

We now turn to the enforcement of EU competition law. Regulation 1/2003 states that there is a 'system of parallel powers'.[59] This means that 'the Commission and the Member States' competition authorities can apply [Articles 101 and 102 TFEU]'.[60] However, there is a second parallelism, which the Court had already noted in the seminal *Walt Wilhelm* judgment in 1969: that national competition law may apply in parallel to EU competition law. We consider both sets of claims in this section, and suggest that the claim that executive competences are parallel is exaggerated.

1. Shared competences in the application of EU competition law

Suppose an NCA wishes to commence an infringement proceeding for breach of Article 101 TFEU, is it free to do so? An affirmative answer would be called for if the competence in question were truly parallel, because such powers may be exercised by Member States alongside the EU. However, a degree of cooperation and control is exercised over the exercise of this executive power that calls into question the parallel nature of this competence.

The first step for a NCA is to inform the Commission of its intention to apply Article 101 TFEU.[61] In practice, this information is also transmitted to the other NCAs, which collectively constitute the European Competition Network (ECN). This is a network which, among other things, decides on which authority is best placed to appraise a suspected infringement. In reality, the Commission and/or the ECN operate reactively: a case is not allocated *ab initio* but it is reallocated once one authority has notified this fact. Provided no other NCA argues that the case at hand should be reallocated to it, then the NCA may continue. (In principle it

[57] Joined Cases 274/11 and 295/11 *Spain and Italy v Commission* [2013] nyr. para 22.

[58] *Spain and Italy v Commission* (n 57) para 24.

[59] Council Reg 1/2003 (n 2), recital 22.

[60] Commission Notice on cooperation within the Network of Competition Authorities [2004] OJ C101/43 para 1.

[61] Council Reg 1/2003 (n 2), art 11(3).

is free to continue even if another NCA wishes to pursue parallel proceedings, but the Commission prefers that this scenario is avoided for reasons we discuss later.) Matters differ if the Commission considers that it is best placed to handle the case. In these situations the national authority is relieved of the competence to apply Articles 101 and 102 TFEU.[62]

The second step, if the authority wishes to proceed to an infringement decision or any other type of decision (e.g. commitment decisions, or decisions withdrawing the benefit of a Block Exemption Regulation), then it must inform the Commission, which may vet the decision, seek further information, and ultimately veto the proposed decision by choosing to take over the handling of the dispute, thereby relieving the national authority of its powers.[63] So far, this scenario has not happened, but it is probable that the Commission has used the threat of vetoes to 'steer' NCAs to reach a result that is consistent with the Commission's interpretation of the law. Indeed, it would not be the first time that the Commission uses these powers. On at least two occasions it has applied competition law to 'correct' the decision of national regulatory authorities.[64]

The ECJ has yet to pronounce upon the operation of this system directly, but in its judgments it has given strong indications that the Commission enjoys extensive powers over NCAs. In the first dispute that reached it, the undertaking had earlier been fined by the Commission and there were continuing complaints about its practices. The matter was being investigated by the French NCA when the Commission requested to inspect the parties' premises. The undertaking questioned the Commission's decision to inspect when the NCA was already active and asked whether 'the Commission infringed the division of powers or the duty to cooperate in good faith with the national competition authorities arising under the principle of subsidiarity'.[65] The Court of First Instance did not hesitate to reject this complaint, noting that Regulation 1/2003 left the Commission free to initiate proceedings even when this would remove the case from the NCA, although, on the facts, an inspection by the Commission did not mean the NCA's competence had yet been lost.[66] It is perhaps unfortunate that the applicants did not press the CFI to consider more fully the nature of the discussions that had taken place between the NCA and the Commission, in order to uncover whether the Commission's own investigations were perceived to yield better evidence. Indeed, the parties might have fared better had they tested the proportionality of the Commission's investigation, for it appears wasteful to duplicate the efforts of the NCA. However the tenor of the CFI's judgment is such that any inspection,

[62] Council Reg 1/2003 (n 2), art 11(6).

[63] Art 11(4) provides for information duties, art 11(6) empowers the Commission to take over the case.

[64] Case C-280/08 P *Deutsche Telekom v Commission* [2010] ECR 9555; Case T-398/07 *Spain v Commission* [2012] nyr. See also *Commission Staff Working Paper accompanying the Report on the functioning of Regulation 1/2003* SEC(2009) 574 final paras 250–9, noting that the Commission has so far preferred to advise NCAs under art 11(4) and it would thus appear that NCA compliance has meant there was no need to engage the powers in art 11(6).

[65] Case T-339/04 *France Telecom v Commission* [2007] ECR II-526 para 78.

[66] *France Telecom v Commission* (n 65) paras 77–90.

as it is only a preliminary step, is by definition proportionate, a somewhat narrow approach.[67] Perhaps this judgment merely shows how difficult it will be to find a good basis for challenging the reallocation of cases from one competition authority to another, given the Commission's leading role.

The Court has also clarified that the power of an NCA is restored once the Commission has concluded its investigation.[68] This is inherent in the wording of Article 16(2) of Regulation 1/2003, which authorizes NCAs to rule on issues that have been the subject of a Commission decision, subject to the NCA not being able to issue a decision that 'runs counter' to that of the Commission. Furthermore, this power must be read subject to the principle of *non bis in idem*, which would prevent a second prosecution of the same issue.[69] This means that, in practice, there will be few instances when power can be effectively restored to the NCA: one instance could be when the NCA prosecutes the undertaking for harm caused that was not identified by the Commission, or possibly when the NCA seeks to apply stricter national competition law.

A third issue the Court has managed to address is that if the NCA wishes to declare that there is no infringement, the Court has held that it cannot say so. It should merely drop the case. This is based on the following rationales. The first is a literal reading of Article 5 of Regulation 1/2003: this enumerates the powers of NCAs and there is nothing in that list allowing an NCA to declare that there has been no breach of competition law. Moreover, Article 10 of Regulation 1/2003 provides that only the Commission may make such a ruling and then only 'when the community public interest so requires'.

The policy rationale for this judgment is well worth quoting:

> Empowerment of national competition authorities to take decisions stating that there has been no breach of Article 102 TFEU would call into question the system of cooperation established by the Regulation and would undermine the power of the Commission.
>
> Such a 'negative' decision on the merits would risk undermining the uniform application of Articles 101 TFEU and 102 TFEU, which is one of the objectives of the Regulation highlighted by recital 1 in its preamble, since such a decision might prevent the Commission from finding subsequently that the practice in question amounts to a breach of those provisions of European Union law.[70]

Note that the harm is to the Commission's powers, but what about other NCAs? Moreover, the guarantor of uniform application is the Commission. Cooperation indeed! Then there is the more telling point that finding no infringement is somehow a bad thing, because there might well have been an infringement that the national authority missed. In this situation, the *non bis in idem* principle may prevent a second prosecution of the same offence by another competition authority in the European Union. This might provide a legally sound basis for the ruling,

[67] *France Telecom v Commission* (n 65) paras 89–90. Note that the proportionality analysis is very limited.

[68] Case C-17/10 *Toshiba Corporation and Others v Úřad pro ochranu hospodářské soutěže* [2012] nyr. para 80.

[69] This is discussed at length in *Toshiba* (n 68).

[70] *Tele2* (n 46) paras 27 and 28.

however if the principle of *non bis in idem* protects individuals from a second investigation, then this applies even if the NCA does not reach a decision but merely drops a case after some investigation. This is because one of the rationales of *non bis in idem* is that individuals should be spared the burdens of successive investigations. From a different perspective, we know that authorities might get it wrong, either when condemning an infringement, or when finding that there is no infringement, so why should it be of concern if one authority's decision leads to some under-enforcement when the risk of over-enforcement is not really addressed?

Enforcement of competition law in the national courts is similarly constrained. Insofar as the Commission has not acted, then national courts remain competent, but such competence is severely limited once the Commission takes action: courts are bound by Commission decisions insofar as they may not issue judgments that would conflict with an actual or contemplated Commission decision. It means that judges should stay proceedings pending a Commission decision.[71] That said, national courts have no duty to have their judgments reviewed by the Commission; the sole way for the Commission to make its position heard is to exercise its power to make written or oral submissions to the Court.[72] So there is some scope for divergence in the way competition law develops, though many national courts, when uncertain, will refer matters to the ECJ.

Based on this analysis, it is clear that the competence to apply EU competition law is not parallel, because in many instances the NCAs or national courts lose the powers to apply the law. In reality, the competence is *concurrent*: the NCA has the power to apply EU competition law only up to the point when the Commission decides to exercise its powers. At that moment the Member States' executive competence is suspended.[73]

It is worth explaining why competences are concurrent: the main thrust of Regulation 1/2003 is to decentralize the enforcement of EU competition law, thereby multiplying the number of bodies able to apply the law and affording a better-regulated internal market. Key to this is that all NCAs and courts should interpret the law in the same way, thereby avoiding forum shopping whereby parties would wish their practices to be reviewed by a lenient authority, while complainants would seek action from a more activist authority. The solution provided for in Regulation 1/2003 is to monitor the performance of competition authorities, which serves to induce uniformity through two related channels: formally, as we saw above, the Commission can take steps to avoid 'bad' decisions by de-seizing NCAs, and informally the ECN serves as a site which encourages the various authorities to coordinate and harmonize their performance. This is why some commentators have suggested that, far from decentralizing competition

[71] Council Reg 1/2003 (n 2), art 16. This codifies the case law of the ECJ in Case C-234/89 *Delimitis v Henninger Bräu* [1991] ECR I-935, and Case C-344/98 *Masterfoods Ltd v HB Ice Cream Ltd* [2000] ECR I-11369.

[72] Council Reg 1/2003 (n 2), art 15(3).

[73] On parallel competences generally see von Bogdandy and Bast (n 1) 290–1.

enforcement, Regulation 1/2003 serves to centralize it further, leaving little autonomy for national authorities.[74]

In response, it may be stated that national authorities still retain prosecutorial discretion, and may determine how to prioritize enforcement, so that some might prefer to focus on hard-core cartels, others on distribution agreements, and still others on access to essential infrastructure in newly liberalized markets. However even here, the NCA's interpretations of the substantive provisions of EU competition law fall under the watchful eye of the Commission. Moreover, when an issue arises that is of general interest for the development of an EU-wide market, or raises novel legal issues, then it is likely that the Commission will wish to consider the matter. This was the result of the sole publicly available instance where a case (e-Book sales) was moved on the basis of Article 11(6) of the Regulation from an NCA (in this case the UK's Office of Fair Trading) to the Commission in view of its significance.[75] Accordingly, not only are competences concurrent, but the criteria by which the cases shift from the national to the EU level have to do with the relative importance of the case. In constitutional law language, this may well be said to be the application of subsidiarity, but in competition law terms, this has been viewed as the usurpation of the independence of NCAs to take the intellectual lead on new kinds of practices. Granted, the Commission will consult NCAs, but this is not the same as NCAs handling the case.[76] Thus, all national competition authorities are equal, but one is more equal than others, a point that even the General Court acknowledged: '[t]he Commission thus retains a leading role in the investigation of infringements.'[77]

2. Limited parallel competences in the application of national competition law

As noted above, in *Walt Wilhelm* the Court specified that national competition law may continue to apply notwithstanding the application of EU competition law. However the Member States' executive competences were limited: the national court or competition authority could not reach a decision that conflicted with that reached under EU law. For many years, this was the source of uncertainty: what kinds of decisions by the Commission would create such conflict and thereby render the application of national competition law impossible? It was clear that, if a practice was declared restrictive of competition by the Commission, the national authorities could not declare it lawful, but it was less certain how far stricter national laws could apply once the Commission had

[74] S. Wilks, 'Agency Escape: Decentralization or Dominance of the European Commission in the Modernization of Competition Policy?' (2005) 1 *Governance* 431.

[75] While the Commission's Press release IP/11/1509 of 6 December 2011 notes that the powers in art 11(6) of Council Reg 1/2003 were used to de-seize the OFT, it also notes that the OFT had dropped the case on grounds of administrative priority.

[76] This also leads to the 'functional disappearance of national competition law': see Cengiz (n 1) 101.

[77] *France Telecom v Commission* (n 65) para 79.

declared a practice lawful or had granted an exemption. This uncertainty has been resolved by Article 3 of Regulation 1/2003. This was summarized earlier, and it will be recalled that this limits the ability to apply stricter national competition law when a practice is lawful under Articles 101 and 102 TFEU (meaning therefore that there is a limit to when competences may be parallel). Moreover, even in the residual fields where competences remain parallel (as identified in Article 3(2) and (3) of the Regulation), this is limited by the general principles of EU law, which means that if the stricter national competition rules somehow have an adverse effect on the EU market, then they may be challenged as infringing internal market law. To take a concrete example, if a takeover is blocked on the basis of national laws when this would stifle say the free movement of capital, then EU law prevents the application of national merger policy; conversely, if an NCA authorizes a merger that has anti-competitive effects, it is possible for the Commission to utilize its residual powers under Articles 101 and 102 TFEU to challenge the transaction.[78]

It follows that, while there is a system of parallel competences,[79] the space for national law is constrained in two ways: first by the duty not to contradict EU competition law; secondly, in those exceptional cases where national competition law may be stricter than EU law, the national rules might well be subjected to challenge for infringing the EU's internal market rules.

IV. National Reactions

1. Resistance

NCAs appear to be 'docile bodies'.[80] They have generally applied EU competition law in line with the preferences of the Commission. The success of Regulation 1/2003 is measured by uniformity of conduct and this has largely been achieved. However, this might not be through discipline, but rather because of self-interest. According to Stephen Wilks, agencies will comply with the current scheme through a mix of agency solidarity (NCAs all feel part of the same club) and a unifying competition law discourse. However, there are also risks that this settlement might break down: agencies have different capacities and differences may arise when sensitive cases are allocated.[81] Similarly, there is no example that I am aware of where a national court has applied competition law in a manner radically divergent from the way the rules were interpreted by the Commission, although several examples exist of

[78] E.g. Case C-171/08 *Commission v Portuguese Republic* (*Golden shares*) [2010] ECR I-6817; see also AG Kokott, Case C-174/04 *Commission v Italy* [2005] ECR I-4933 para 45, noting the application of arts 101 and 102 TFEU to mergers falling outside the Merger Regulation.

[79] Reaching the same conclusion, Schütze (n 18) 84 and note 83.

[80] The phrase is from M. Foucault, *Discipline and Punish: The Birth of The Prison* (London: Allen Lane, 1977).

[81] S. Wilks 'Agencies, Networks, Discourse and the Trajectory of European Competition Enforcement' (2007) 3 *European Competition Journal* 437.

some divergences.[82] It may be that the right dispute to trigger a rebellion has not yet occurred. Or it may be that the Member States are content with enforcing a supranational policy at national level for the economic gains this yields.

On the other hand, we find some evidence of resistance when the EU purports to exercise its legislative and executive competences in more sensitive domains. The story of Member State resistance to the Merger Regulation has been told enough times to show how national approaches to merger control differed because of diverging visions regarding which policy was most likely to benefit local industry, and how these differences made states reluctant to agree a Regulation until strong diplomatic efforts were undertaken in the late 1980s. Another well-known story is the apparent resistance Member States put forward when faced with the Commission using competition law to open up the telecommunications and energy markets.[83] For present purposes, it is worth recalling that some Member States did question the EU's competence exercised under Article 106(3) TFEU, but the Court affirmed that this provision could be used in lieu of Article 114 TFEU.[84] It is also worth noting, however, that while the liberalization of telecoms took place in part unilaterally through the use of antitrust law and Article 106(3) TFEU, the Commission was careful to avoid using the same approach in energy markets where the legal basis for the liberalization directives has been Article 114 TFEU, which gives more of a say to Member States.

2. Experimentation

An interesting response to the disempowerment of national competition law and NCAs is found in the literature discussing experimentalist governance.[85] Experimentalism forms part of the fabric of federalism in the US, where states are said to have 'constitutional leeway to experiment'.[86] Does the EU's order of competences allow for this, in spite of all the controls identified above?

Charles F. Sabel and Jonathan Zeitlin suggest that one should look for a four-stage process to identify the possibility for experimentation in a governance scheme: (1) broad goals are set; (2) local units are given a broad discretion

[82] A non-exhaustive list includes *Inntrepreneur Pub Company and others v Crehan* [2006] UKHL 38 where, according to some, the House of Lords was less than deferential, and *Island Ferries Teoranta v Minister for Communications, Marine and Natural Resources & Ors* [2011] IEHC 388 para 73, where the interpretation of the EU rules might be more restrictive than that provided by the European Courts.

[83] See, generally, M. Thatcher, 'The Commission and national governments as partners: EC regulatory expansion in telecommunications 1979-2000' (2001) 8 *Journal of European Public Policy* 558. This analysis is useful for present purposes for it shows that beneath the surface of the constitutional debates in the case law, Member States were not unwilling to open markets to competition.

[84] Case C-202/88 *France v Commission* (*Telecommunications Terminal Equipment*) [1991] ECR I-1223.

[85] C.F. Sabel and J. Zeitlin, 'Experimentalist Governance', in D. Levi-Faur (ed.), *The Oxford Handbook of Governance* (Oxford: Oxford University Press, 2011) is an accessible starting point.

[86] S. Breyer, *The Supreme Court: Making Democracy Work* (Oxford: Oxford University Press, 2010), 123.

to pursue these goals; (3) the local units report regularly and participate in peer review; (4) the broad goals are reviewed in light of (2) and (3).

In my view, there are several difficulties with applying this framework to EU competition law.[87] First, it is not particularly certain who identifies the broad goals for the Union: the Commission has a mandate and a work plan for itself, and so does each NCA, so there is no centralized framing of the objectives. Secondly, national authorities may have some discretion (e.g. in how they appreciate complex facts) but not as much as one might think: as we saw above each decision is reviewed by the Commission. Thirdly, there is no peer review as such (although it is possible that within the ECN there is some informal peer review); the sole review is by the Commission, which can judge how well a given authority is proceeding and de-seize it of its executive competences. Fourthly, since there was no original agreement on the general goals, it is not easy to see how any overall review could lead to any outcome and anyway each discrete determination of NCAs is already closely watched. It might be said that the broad goals were agreed when Regulation 1/2003 came into force, and then one could point to the 2009 review of the new enforcement system. However, this focused on the network generating effective enforcement measured by the number of cases and the absence of divergences in the approaches of each Member State. Therefore, looking at the structure of the system in place, if the goals are heavy enforcement in a uniform manner, then this prevents the diversity that is at the root of experimentalist governance.

This theoretical objection is strengthened by considering what the ECN actually does. To begin with, we should note that its mandate is quite limited: to reallocate cases and to assist with information sharing among members. However, neither of these tasks can be linked to experimentation. As a matter of fact, it appears that the ECN has not had much to do with respect to these two tasks: there have been very few contested case allocations and few requests for information to be shared. What the ECN has done instead is not always clear, as it mostly operates in secrecy, but two tangible outputs have emerged: the first is a model leniency programme; the second is a series of best practices in merger cases. We consider the leniency programme here.

The leniency programme is a document that encourages every Member State to enact a leniency policy that is as close as possible to the model drafted by the ECN, so as to help leniency applicants. 'The ECN members commit to using their best efforts, within the limits of their competence, to align their respective

[87] More particularly, there appears to be a tension when Sabel and Zeitlin (n 85) refer to the right to challenge the approach of an NCA (by the Commission or another NCA) to an individual case as a 'destabilisation mechanism' to unblock an impasse in framework rule-making and revision. In my view, this right undermines the possibility for experimentation because, as indicated in the text, the Commission may withdraw the case from a deviant NCA. The point of experimentation in the field of competition law means, in my view, that one NCA is allowed to try a new theory of harm and to see how well that approach resolves a competition problem. A more promising application of this theory to competition law is found in Y. Svetiev, 'Networked Competition Governance in the EU: Delegation, Decentralisation or Experimentalist Architecture?', in C.F. Sabel and J. Zeitlin (eds.), *Experimentalist Governance in the European Union* (Oxford: Oxford University Press, 2010), 79, esp at 103–4.

programmes with the ECN Model Programme.'[88] It is hard to see this output as a result of experimentalist governance. Furthermore, if one compares the model with the Commission's own leniency policy, there are striking similarities in content, suggesting that the Commission model is effectively the basis from which the best practices were generated.[89] The only margins for divergence are set out in the explanatory notes to the model, and these at times related to differences in national procedural laws. In 2009, the ECN released a study on the effects of the model leniency programme. Its subtitle is telling: 'Report on Assessment of State of Convergence'.[90] The report recalls that the aim of the ECN here is to remove discrepancies between leniency programmes and facilitate procedures for would-be applicants, and the political commitment made by the NCAs to align leniency programmes based on the model.[91] There is some space for experimentation, as Member States may opt to be more generous than the model programme, so the ECN model may be seen as a quest for minimum harmonization. However, to date, no assessment has been carried out to evaluate whether any such experiment is worth replicating on a wider scale. Instead, the report focuses on the remaining divergences, identifying which Member States have yet to achieve complete convergence. Moreover, as discussed earlier, such experimentation is limited by the ECJ's ruling in *Schenker* that forbids experiments that threaten effective enforcement of EU competition law. Accordingly, the most successful of the ECN outputs to date is not an example of experimentalist governance.

Furthermore, it should be noted that the ECN's efforts in the field of leniency are a second best solution anyway: the best would be for there to be a single leniency procedure across the EU; absent the legislative will to proceed in this direction, the ECN has crafted a solution that places pressure on NCAs to align each other's leniency policies. This is hardly an outcome consistent with experimentation.[92]

It might be the case that the ECN is doing a lot more which gives NCAs a real voice in shaping the direction of EU competition law, but it is not clear what evidence there is to support this claim. The ECN publishes briefs on how NCAs address certain issues (e.g. cases on 'food and retail'). However, these are no more than a compilation of cases, and there are competing providers that can give us information about national cases. It may well be the case that the real engines of cooperation are the discussions held among ECN members about how cases are resolved, or discussions within the advisory committee when reviewing draft Commission decisions. In other words, experimentalism is found in the day-to-day working processes of the network, rather than in its formal output. This assumption requires further investigation.

[88] ECN Model Leniency Programme (2006), available at: <http://ec.europa.eu/competition/ecn/index_en.html>: para 3.

[89] Commission Notice on Immunity from fines and reduction of fines in cartel cases [2006] OJ C298/17, notably parts I and II, dealing with immunity.

[90] ECN Model Leniency Programme—Report on Assessment of State of Convergence (2009), available at: <http://ec.europa.eu/competition/ecn/index_en.html>.

[91] Report on Assessment of State of Convergence (n 90) 2.

[92] For a contrary view, see Svetiev (n 87).

Conclusion

The main finding of this essay is that the way competences are labelled in primary and secondary law appears inaccurate: insofar as legislative competences are concerned, these seem to be shared, not exclusive; executive competences are not always parallel, they are often shared when it comes to national enforcement of EU competition law, and parallel only in a limited sphere when it comes to the enforcement of national competition law. However, while competence is the key word for this volume, it nevertheless seems not to open any doors in the field of competition law: neither Member States nor the Commission appear unduly troubled by how competences are described.

However, a focus on competences reveals two issues: first, the gap in the exercise of the EU's legislative competences. More could be done in two respects. As the 2010 report by Mario Monti reminded us, further steps are needed to enhance competition in the internal market.[93] At present, the existing internal market rules, plus the duty of cooperation in Article 4(3) TEU, are applied in the absence of direct legislative intervention, but as indicated here, these cannot apply systematically to every action that has anti-competitive effects in the internal market. Secondly, the incomplete codification of a range of procedural issues means that the principle of effectiveness is invoked to quash national laws that stifle the application of competition law. It might be preferable, rather than to continue to use these tools of negative integration, for there to be greater use of the Union's competence to establish clear procedural rules for public and private enforcement.

Secondly, and on a related point, while the Member States resist the incursion of competition in certain spheres, the reason for shrinking national competences in the field of Articles 101 and 102 TFEU, the concomitant shrinkage in the scope of application of national antitrust law, and the pre-eminence of the Commission over NCAs are somewhat puzzling, and require explanation. We offer two such explanations below.

An intergovernmental explanation is that it was in the economic interests of states to marginalize national competition law: national firms have increasing European strategies, so measures that lower the costs of doing business within the EU are welcomed. On the other hand, Regulation 1/2003 built a system that created a credible reciprocal commitment. Now no Member State could misuse competition law to their advantage: the Commission's supranational scrutiny of national decisions and the ECN's ability to identify deviations serve to prevent defection.[94] Note moreover, that the countries who had the most developed national competition laws (Germany and France) also had the most to gain from

[93] M. Monti, *A New Strategy for the Single Market–Report to the President of the European Commission* (9 May 2010).

[94] This hypothesis draws on A. Moravcsik, *The Choice For Europe* (Ithaca, NY: Cornell University Press, 1998) where these two considerations are used to explain major turning points in the EC's development.

the marginalization of other countries' national competition laws: their traders would benefit from reliable antitrust enforcement Europe-wide. On a cost-benefit analysis, the marginal cost of reducing the role of their national competition laws is less than the marginal benefit of ensuring a better economic climate for their firms exporting abroad.

Looking at this question from a supranational perspective, and absent much evidence of experimentalist governance, it seems that the EU's 'federal order' shows the EU's preference for limiting divergence. This might be explained by the wish to avoid results like those that sometimes emerge in the United States when state and federal antitrust laws apply in parallel. Two examples suffice. In actions for damages, claims are launched by the same set of plaintiffs at both state and federal levels, because not all defendants can be sued at federal level. This leads to an inefficient use of judicial resources. Even US commentators agree that this is a poor model.[95] Second, absent certain aberrant cases (e.g. the *Microsoft* litigation in the late 1990s) state and federal enforcement are broadly consistent, but this is against the background of a more settled understanding of antitrust principles.[96] In a European Union where several Member States have only recently made the transition towards a market economy, it seems appropriate that federalism principles work in the opposite direction, with the centre controlling the way states apply competition law.

[95] R.H. Lande, 'Why Antitrust Damage Levels Should Be Raised' (2004) 16 *Loyola Consumer Law Review* 329, at 330.

[96] Antitrust Modernization Commission, *Report and Recommendations* (2007), 192–6.

6

The EU as a Federal Order of Competences and the Private Law

*Hans-W. Micklitz**

Prologue or Why Private Law

There is no such thing as a born European private lawyer. Legal education is still national. Private lawyers are trained in their national legal and cultural environment. This is true for continental lawyers and for lawyers from common law countries. When it comes to European law—not European private law—legal training broadens the scholarly perspective. Gradually but steadily, the private lawyer trained in his or her national private law system is confronted with the public law character of EU law, first and foremost what might be called administrative law, and, to an ever-increasing degree with EU constitutional law, via its two strains, namely institutions and rights, both of which are familiar from the national educational context. What I would suggest and what I have experienced in my academic life is a shift in focus from national private law to EU law, which implies studying EU public, administrative and constitutional law.

* This chapter is the direct result of my research project on European regulatory private law funded by the ERC authorities. The project is documented in H.-W. Micklitz and Y. Svetiev (eds.), 'Self-sufficient European Private Law—A Viable Concept?' *EUI Working Paper*, 2012. It rests on previous research: (1) on my understanding of European private law: 'The Visible Hand of European Private Law' (2009) 28 *Yearbook of European Law* 3; (2) on the interplay between European private legal order building and European constitution building: 'Failure or Ideological Preconceptions? Thoughts on Two Grand Projects: the European Constitution and the European Civil Code', in K. Tuori and S. Sankari (eds.), *The Many Constitutions of Europe* (Farnham: Ashgate, 2010), 109; (3) on the relationship between Europe as a market state and European private law building: with D. Patterson, 'From the Nation State to the Market: The Evolution of EU Private Law', *EUI Working Paper* 2012/15, also published in B. van Vooren, S. Blockmans, and J. Wouters (eds.), *The EU's Role in Global Governance: The Legal Dimension* (Oxford: Oxford University Press, 2013), 59; (4) on subsidiarity: 'The Maastricht Treaty, the Principle of Subsidiarity and the Theory of Integration' (1993) 4 *LAKIMIES Special Issue on European Integration* (periodical of the Association of Finnish lawyers) 508; and (5) on the many faces of social justice: *The Many Concepts of Social Justice in European Private Law* (Cheltenham: Edward Elgar, 2011). I would like to thank my colleague Loïc Azoulai for his comments which pushed me deeper and deeper into the question of whether private law bears a special character or not. I have not been able to answer this question satisfactorily in this chapter, but I keep on working on tentative solutions. The usual disclaimer applies.

Five years ago I started working as a professor of economic law at the European University Institute. The composition of the law department reflects the way in which EU law has developed. 75 per cent of my colleagues are working in—what I would call from my German educational background—the field of public law, EU constitutional law, comparative constitutional law, international public law, human rights law and so on. This is paradigmatic of the way in which academic discourse in and around European law has developed over the decades in academic fora, conferences, and law journals. To put it bluntly, academic European legal discourse is first and foremost a public law discourse. So, to slightly twist the language of Mattias Kumm,[1] 'total constitutionalism' in the EU is already in action, at least in form of the claim of 'intellectual hegemony' of constitutional law over private law.

But is it really correct to speak about the public character of EU law? Is there something special about private law that should make the EU reluctant or at least hesitant to intervene when it comes to private law relationships? One might suggest that EU lawyers ask: does the EU have competence to regulate private law, be it related to public or private law within the national legal order? The way the Union's competences are presented in the Treaty substantiates this point: competences relate to subject matter, not to administration, constitutional bodies, or private relationships. If this point is accepted, the burden of proof is reversed and the question is: what is so special about the 'private legal order' that calls for a specific approach in terms of competences? Private lawyers might be tempted to refer to the *ius commune*, which dates back to Roman law,[2] or they may refer to the idea of a '*Privatrechtsgesellschaft*',[3] the existence of a private law society—the German term cannot accurately be translated—which needs constitutional protection but for the reason of maintaining and guaranteeing the freedom of private parties to shape their self-government. For the purpose of this chapter it might suffice to draw the attention to the ever-growing body of European private law which is developed and elaborated in the absence of a clear competence for the EU in matters of private law, a European private law which is different from national private law, a European private law which challenges well-established categories in the Member States of what private law is all about, a European private law in which private autonomy and freedom of contract is transformed in regulated autonomy and regulated freedom of contract.[4] Re-translated into the category of competences, the question then is whether the shaky competence of the EU allows for such a deep change in what some private lawyers would indeed call 'the special character' of the private legal order (not law alone) for the building of a European society.

Prior to the new millennium, it was first and foremost consumer law that made strides within European law. It took, however, the adoption of two directives,

[1] M. Kumm, 'Who is Afraid of Total Constitution? Constitutional Rights as Principles and the Constitutionalisation of Private Law' (2004) 7 *German Law Journal* 341.

[2] R. Zimmermann, 'Savigny's Legacy: Legal History, Comparative Law, and the Emergence of a European Science' (1996) *Law Quarterly Review* 576.

[3] F. Böhm, 'Privatrechtsgesellschaft und Marktwirtschaft' (1966) 17 *ORDO* 75.

[4] This will be developed under IV.2.

namely Directive 93/13/EEC on unfair terms in consumer contracts[5] and, more prominently, Directive 99/44/EC on consumer sales[6] before the *national* private law community started to realize that private law matters had reached the level of EU law. The big breakthrough came with the publication of the 'Communication from the Commission to the Council and the European Parliament on European Contract Law' in 2001.[7] European private law is now high on, if not at the top of, the academic agenda in the Member States of the European Union and not only there. The discussion revolves around the relationship between national private legal orders and the feasibility and the desirability of a coherent body of what has been downgraded from much more ambitious projects of a European civil code to a European sales law (CESL).[8] Every other day, an article if not a new book is published dealing with conceptual or doctrinal issues concerning the much-debated Draft Common Frame of Reference (DCFR) and CESL project, in a truly European environment. Private law research is no longer national and has turned into a European debate, mainly led in English with all the well-known although under-discussed implications.[9] It seems that private lawyers in the EU are engaged in a learning process, bringing private law and European public law debates nearer to one another.

It seems so but it is not the case. This is the reason why I am writing the paper and why I am grateful to the Editor who recognizes that private law is part of the 'federal order of competences'. Somewhat overstatedly, I argue that private law discourse is 'Europeanized'—it has even reached the curricula of law schools all over Europe—but it remains more or less disconnected from the European public—administrative and constitutional—legal discourse. There is no counterpart to Mattias Kumm, no private lawyer has so far claimed the need and the legitimacy of 'total private law' (I have to admit that I have difficulties in using the word 'total'). Today, we are close to an academic discourse where EU public lawyers discuss European constitutionalism in their 'circles' and where EU private lawyers discuss European private law codification in their 'circles'. On the surface, there is no harm organizing academic discourse in circles, but it has far-reaching implications for the way in which the discourse is framed and develops.

By and large, EU public lawyers discuss constitutionalism without private law and EU private lawyers discuss codification of European private law without EU constitutionalism. Whenever EU public lawyers engage in a discourse on EU competences and federalism, they do not conceive of private law as a relevant field; or maybe—I do not know it for sure— they simply begin from the premise that private law has no place in EU law, and remains a matter of nation state competence; at least quite often it seems so. Private lawyers involved in the European codification project discuss concepts, scope, and, with verve, the tricky doctrinal details of

[5] Council Directive 93/13/EEC on unfair terms in consumer contracts, [1993] OJ L 95/29.

[6] Directive 1999/44/EC of the European Parliament and of the Council on certain aspects of the sale of consumer goods and associated guarantees, [1999] OJ L 171/12.

[7] COM (2001) 398 final. [8] COM (2011) 635 final.

[9] But now R. Sefton-Green, 'How far can we go when using the English language for private law in the EU?' (2012) 8 *European Review of Contract Law* 30.

contract law-making and the like, but they do not discuss whether the EU has the competence to adopt the rules in the development of which they have invested so much time of their academic life. To be sure, there are exceptions to the rule, on both sides. From the public law side, I would like to mention Oliver Gerstenberg[10] and Stephen Weatherill.[11] On the private law side—which I am better acquainted with—Jurgen Basedow,[12] Norbert Reich,[13] Wulf-Henning Roth,[14] and, more recently, Kathleen Gutman[15] and Martijn Willem Hesselink[16] always had an eye on the deeper constitutional implications of private law-making at the EU level.

Wer zu spät kommt, den bestraft das Leben: 'He who comes too late is punished by life', one might feel tempted to exclaim in light of the bursting fiction that the EU has competence to adopt the CESL. Whatever the outcome of CESL will be, whether it will be adopted or not and in what form, the European landscape of competences has tremendously changed. EU competence in private law is on the legal and the political agenda now and will not vanish easily. Neither European and national politics nor the European public and private law academy were prepared when the issue arose and when Member States claimed that the EU has no competence to adopt the CESL. In the light of this deficit, the self-imposed task is to bridge the gap between public and private law discourse with regard to competences, and to embark on the search for long-term solutions on the competence dilemma.

I will deliberately rely on the questions that Loïc Azoulai has raised in his opening speech to the conference which stands behind this book,[17] which I quote from the written version. The point at stake is 'to approach European integration through the mechanisms of allocation of competences'. Three questions are on the table: (1) 'the scope of the competence'—'not to be conflated with the scope of application of the rules produced on the basis of existing competences', (2) 'the limits of competence'—'the relation and the balance between the capacity to act

[10] O. Gerstenberg, 'Private Law and the New Constitutional Settlement' (2004) 10 *European Law Journal* 766.

[11] S. Weatherill, 'European Private Law and the Constitutional Dimension', in F. Cafaggi (ed.), *The Institutional Framework of European Private Law* (Oxford and New York: Oxford University Press, 2006), 81; S. Vogenauer and S. Weatherill, *The Harmonisation of European Contract Law: Implications for European Private Laws, Business and Legal Practice* (Oxford and Portland, Or.: Hart, 2006), and, more recently, S. Weatherill, 'The Consumer Rights Directive: how and why a quest for "coherence" has (largely) failed' (2012) 49 *Common Market Law Review* 1279.

[12] J. Basedow, 'Grundlagen des Europäischen Privatrechts' (2004) *JuS* 89; and earlier: 'A common contract law for the common market' (1996) 33 *Common Market Law Review* 1169.

[13] N. Reich, 'Der Common Frame of Reference und Sonderprivatrechte im Europäischen Vertragsrecht' (1997) *Zeitschrift für Europäisches Privatrecht* 161.

[14] See the references in W-H. Roth, 'Rechtsetzungskompetenz für das Privatrecht in der Europäischen Union' (2008) *Zeitschrift für Europäisches Wirtschafts- und Steuerrecht* 401.

[15] K. Gutman, *The Constitutional Foundations of European Contract Law: A comparative Analysis* (Oxford: Oxford University Press, forthcoming).

[16] M. Hesselink, C. Mak, and J.W. Rutgers, 'Constitutional Aspects of European Private Law: Freedoms, Rights and Social Justice in the Draft Common Frame of Reference', *Centre for the Study of European Contract Law Working Paper Series*, No. 05/2009 (opinion commissioned by the European Parliament, report for the CoPECL project, available at: <http://ssrn.com/abstract=1413089>).

[17] 'The EU as a Federal Order of Competences—What's in a competence?' Spring 2012 manuscript on file with the author.

and the capacity to be affected'; and (3) the relation of competence to task and function—'the Member States shall facilitate the achievement of the Union's task', 'the Union shall respect "the Member States identities, their fundamental structures and the essential functions"'.

I will focus on these three *conceptual* issues, taking them for granted without discussing whether a particular concept of the state lurks behind the three categories.[18] The first and the third category allow for a rather conventional understanding of the state as the nation state, the second is indeed more open via the category of 'affectedness'. I will not embark on the *normative* issues, in my context the constitutionalization of private law via the 'rights rhetoric' of the EU. Much has already been written on this issue. I will leave my contribution to the forthcoming publication of the summer school of the European Academy of Law, which deals exactly with this question, though not from the point of view of competences.[19]

The hypothesis I would like to develop runs like this: the EU as a competence order favours and enables the elaboration of a genuine European private legal order, which is market-bound and market-related. I use the term private legal order, which I understand to be distinct from the private law system and private law, whenever the deeper philosophical relationship between national and European private law is at stake. Private law and European private law refer to the body of rules, which are enshrined in the national and European private law system. This is where the focus of the chapter lies.[20]

The European private legal order and European private law, so runs the argument, are different from national private orders; it is regulatory in substance and comes into an ever-stronger conflict with traditional national private law, whether codified or enshrined in the common law on contract and tort. European regulatory private law shifts the focus from the national to the European level; it tends to disconnect itself from traditional national private law patterns, thereby establishing a new legal regime standing side-by-side with, though not unrelated to, national private law regimes.

After having highlighted what I understand by regulatory private law in general and European regulatory private law in particular, I will use the three parameters of 'scope', 'limits', and 'intensity' to examine the relationship between the two legal orders as it stands today with the possible impact of the Lisbon Treaty on the competence order. Under the heading of 'scope' I will analyse if and how the new competence structure after Lisbon requires a rethinking of the divide between market-driven European regulatory private law and traditional national private

[18] P. Bobbitt, *The Shield of Achilles: War, Peace and the Course of History* (New York: Knopf, 2002); S. Sassen, *Territory, Authority, Rights: From Medieval to Global Assemblages* (Princeton, N.J.: Princetown University Press, 2006); D. Patterson and A. Afilalio (eds.), *The New Global Trading Order* (Cambridge and New York: Cambridge University Press, 2008).

[19] H.-W. Micklitz (ed.), *Constitutionalisation of European Private Law* (Oxford University Press, forthcoming) with contributions by M. Bell, O. Cherednychenko, A. Ciacchi, H. Collins, G. Commandé, C. Godt, and C. Mak.

[20] This is not really the place to discuss in depth the differences between private law, the private law system, and the private legal order; for more details on the debate, see under IV.1.

law. I will then embark on the 'limits' of competence, and will demonstrate how the European regulatory private law *affects* the capacity of the Member States to act. This kind of stock-taking relates to a rough comparison of the substance of European regulatory private law in relation to national traditional private law. In the search for a re-balancing of the capacity to act and the capacity to be affected I will revitalize the subsidiarity principle, understood here not as a defence against intrusion from the EU, but as imposing responsibilities on Member States and as re-organizing their inner architecture. My last point concerns the issue of 'intensity'. Approaching European integration via competences is more than a formal division of responsibilities in a federal order of range and limits. The overall assumption is that the EU has not only extended its scope and thereby narrowed its limits; it has first and foremost intensified its grip on national law by shifting the focus from minimum to maximum harmonization. Referring to earlier research,[21] I will discuss whether the maximum harmonization of private law matters affects 'essential state functions' and infringes the Member States' 'national identities'. It is my hope that this chapter might contribute to enhancing the dialogue between EU public/constitutional law and EU private law academia, and perhaps also dialogue with political science.

I. European Regulatory Private Law and Traditional National Private Law: some Clarifications

Private law is understood as economic law,[22] covering not only contract and tort or, systematically speaking, the continental codifications, but also public and private regulation of the economy. The broad concept of private law is crucial for the development of a deeper understanding of the ongoing transformation process of private law in the European Union in its interaction with the national private law systems. Traditional national private legal orders, with their focus upon contract and tort have emerged and are deeply rooted in nation state building processes of the 18th and 19th century in continental Europe. The starting point is private autonomy, freedom of contract, *l'autonomie de la volonté*. The actors are private individuals, private economic actors originally and largely operating within the territorial boundaries of the state. The states claim the authority to adopt private legal rules in their territory. The grand codifications of the early-19th and late-19th century led to an enormous gain in economic efficiency and legal coherence.

Not a state, the European Union was never concerned with the underpinnings of establishing private law as a national legal order, based on private autonomy or freedom of contract. The overall project of the European integration process was

[21] H.-W. Micklitz, 'German Constitutional Court (Bundesverfassungsgericht BVerfG) 2 BvE 2/08, 30.6.2009—Organstreit proceedings between members of the German Parliament and the Federal Government' (2011) 7 *European Review of Contract Law* 528.

[22] H.D. Assmann, G. Brüggemeier, D. Hart, and C. Joerges, *Zivilrecht als Teil des Wirtschaftsrechts* (Königstein: Athenäum,1980).

first the common market, later the internal market, and only gradually the building of a legal order that reached beyond mere economic transactions, the shaping of a *social order*, a citizens' order or even a constitution. Private law—aside from family law—may by and large be associated with economic transactions with a social outlook, as enshrined in consumer law and anti-discrimination law. In European private law, the internal market rhetoric sets the tone. Here, the European Union appears as a *regulator*, be it through the ECJ, which challenges national economic rules that hinder free trade of products, services, capital, or persons, or be it via the EU legislator, which adopts horizontal or vertical market-related rules on private transactions, often by way of new modes of governance.[23] Regulatory private law, in its negative variant through the impact of the four freedoms on private law and in its positive variant through the bulk of EU rules that have been adopted in the aftermath of the Single European Act outside consumer and anti-discrimination law, deserves the utmost attention. This is the *European regulatory private law* that I am interested in. This private law is different from national private legal orders based on private autonomy and free will. This private law's form, procedure, and content are instrumentalized for building and shaping markets,[24] and it yields its own pattern of justice. Its regulatory framework is developed through EU institutions, the EU-driven building of new market surveillance authorities, the fine-tuning of the rules through intermediary forms of cooperation between EU and Member States institutions—via comitology, Lamfalussy, or open method of coordination—,the development of new substantive legal mechanisms that reach beyond traditional private law rules, and, last but not least, the enforcement of the self-standing rules through sectoral regulatory agencies and through new forms of alternative dispute settlement mechanisms.

There is an obvious argument against the distinction between traditional nation state private law and modern European regulatory private law. Regulation in private law is a matter that has been discussed for more than one hundred years. Otto von Gierke belongs to those who, already in the late-19th century, defended the need for a distinction between private law and private law regulation; although, at that time, with a clear, highly political message.[25] In comparison to the beginning of the 21st century, there are, however, major differences, both in terms of substance and in terms of institutions, which justify the maintenance of the equations: nation states = the traditional concept of private law (contract and tort law (common law and/or codifications)) and the EU = the modern concept of private law (European regulatory private law).

[23] F. Cafaggi and H. Muir Watt (eds.), *Making European Private Law: Governance Design* (Cheltenham, UK, and Northampton, MA: Edward Elgar, 2008); by the same authors, see also 'The Regulatory Functions of European Private Law' (Cheltenham, UK, and Northampton, MA: Edward Elgar, 2009).

[24] In the German understanding of private law as economic law, see Assmann, Brüggemeier, Hart, and Joerges (n 22); for Europe see C. Schmid, *Die Instrumentalisierung des Europäischen Privatrechts durch die Europäische Union* (Baden-Baden: Nomos, 2010).

[25] O. von Gierke, *Die Soziale Aufgabe des Privatrechts* (Berlin: Julius Springer, 1889), 13.

Regulatory law in the late-19th century was mainly labour and social law which was kept outside the Bürgerliches Gesetzbuch (BGB). The German BGB provided only for a basic set of rules on the contract for services, the so-called *Dienstverträge*, setting aside all the social concerns of labour lawyers who were fighting for better protection of the legal position of dependent workers. This is what Otto von Gierke was referring to. Today's regulatory private law cuts across all sectors of the economy and across policies. It lies at the heart of, in particular, service contracts: financial services, telecommunications, energy (electricity, gas), (the increasingly privatized) health care services, more and more educational services, and, last but not least, transport. Services amount for 70 per cent of the gross income in the EU. The driving force behind all these rules that aim mainly at opening up markets, at establishing competition, at liberalizing former public services, at promoting privatization in former areas of public services, is undoubtedly the EU, or more precisely, the European Commission. Private law issues form only part of other more 'important aspects' of the appropriate market design. This private law is regulatory law, but regulation should not be equated with rules that restrict private autonomy and freedom of contract. Its instrumental character shields it against easy classification. Regulatory private law contains both elements, establishing market freedoms, therefore increasing private autonomy, whilst at the same time providing for rules that set boundaries to the newly created competitive market autonomy. The 'White Paper on the Completion of the Internal Market'[26] provided the European Commission with the necessary legal mandate and legitimation to initiate legislative measures which aimed mainly at establishing markets, which *inter alia*, however, contain a whole series of private law rules, provided private law is understood as economic law.

II. Scope of Competence in Private Law: from Market Bound to Justice Bound?

I will first offer an account of the competence order as it stood and had been applied for more than 30 years in the field of private law and shall then look into possible changes resulting from the Lisbon Treaty.

1. The market-bound competence order

There is agreement between EU lawyers that, strictly speaking, the EU has no competence to regulate private law. Private law does not show up in the fields where the EU has exclusive powers or where the EU has to share powers with the Member States. Whether or not the EU should gain competence in the traditional field of private law was not even on the agenda during the preparatory work on the then envisaged European Constitution.

[26] COM (1985) 310 final.

In continental Europe, nation state building goes hand in hand with the elaboration of a constitution and a coherent civil code. This is not only true for the past but also for the present, as developments in Middle-Eastern and South-Eastern Europe so amply demonstrate. The discussion on the role and function of a European Civil Code, even during the heady days of the discussion on the 'European Constitution', documents a bias which allows for two different interpretations: either the members were not aware of the importance of a civil code for the EU, or they were aware but were wise enough not to raise the sensitive question of code building. Either way, the preparatory work on the European Constitution had obviously started from the premise that transforming the European Community into the European Union, and providing it with what has misleadingly been termed a 'constitution', could be achieved without European rules on private law relationships. Under the German Constitution, the Federal Government enjoys the exclusive power to deal with matters of private law.[27] The non-discussion of private law matters is amazing. One need not be an ordo-liberal to recognize the link between private law building and civil society building which is so blatantly neglected in Europe.[28]

Therefore, the basic structure of the Federal Order of Competence in private law has remained largely the same over the last 65 years. Private law was left to the Member States. Only two amendments are noteworthy, the introduction of Article 100a EC, which later became Article 95 EC before it was renumbered in the Treaty of Lisbon into Article 114 TFEU, and EU powers granted to regulate international private law issues, now Article 81 TFEU. However, the EU does not possess any explicit conferred powers. It must combine conferred powers in particular policy fields to private law issues, be it as large as the internal market or merely cross-border issues. The powers granted are all *shared* powers, within in the meaning of Article 4 TFEU.

Metaphorically, we could imagine EU competences forming a ring that surrounds a national private law core. The core is the codified private law in continental Europe or contract and tort law in common law countries. Details and differences between the orders are of no importance.[29] What matters is the deep link between the national private legal order and the respective nation states, as a kind of 'institutional' band. The policy-related conferred powers may be grouped around five different categories, from left to right (see Figure 6.1): (1) the internal market competence; (2) sector-related polices (transport and since Lisbon, energy); (3) horizontal policies (environmental protection, health and safety, economic and social cohesion); (4) status-related policy (with regard to companies,

[27] According to art 74(1) of the German Basic Law, civil law belongs to the concurrent competences. This means that the German *Lander* are entitled to take action only if action has not yet been taken at the federal level. The German Civil Code dates from 1900, the German Basic law from 1949. This means that the allocation of competences in art 74(1) (concurrent competences) is rather symbolic. It was and it remains for the federal level to amend the German Civil Code.

[28] Which brings together Böhm (n 3), E.-J. Mestmäcker *Wirtschaft und Verfassung in der Europäischen Union, Beiträge zu Recht, Theorie und Politik der Europäischen Integration* (Baden-Baden: Nomos, 2003), and H. Collins, *The European Civil Code—The Way Forward* (Cambridge and New York: Cambridge University Press, 2008).

[29] What really counts here is the link to the nation state.

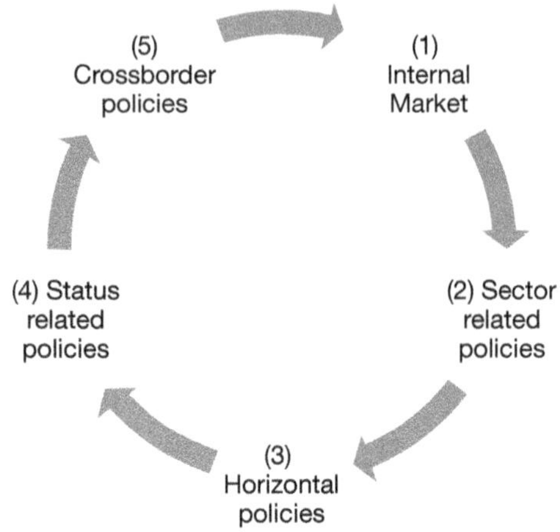

Figure 6.1 European regulatory law (the ring) and traditional national private law (the core)

workers, and consumers); (5) cross-border transactions (jurisdiction, applicable law, enforcement).

The functional market-driven logic of the order of competence is inbuilt into the Treaty.[30] All that the European Commission and, pursuant to its proposals, the European Parliament and the Council had to do was to implement that which was 'constitutionally' pre-determined. The outcome was as predictable as it is now subject to critique. The EU tied private law issues in a pick-and-pack procedure: (1) to the internal market competence, mainly with regard to a private law for consumers, (2) to the shaping and building of regulated markets in the field of telecommunications, energy, transport, post services and financial services, services of general economic interest, mainly via integrating private law issues into market access and market surveillance mechanisms, (3) to tying environmental protection, health and safety, economic and social cohesion to regulating liability or to establishing a safety net; (4) to breaking down the universal subject of private law—the natural person—into the consumer, the worker, entrepreneur, and even deeper into men and women, heterosexual and same sex persons, children and disabled persons, not to forget legal entities such as companies as addressees of EU legislation; and (5) to developing a dense network of rules on jurisdiction, on the applicable law in contract and non-contractual relations, on the mutual trans-border enforcement of judgments. Only the fifth category is fully accepted in private law academia, as the cross-border dimension involves international private lawyers.

All this is well-known, though it is still not given the attention it deserves. If anything, consumer law has made certain inroads into the hard core of private law, contract and tort, suspiciously observed by the vast majority of private lawyers,

[30] For an early analysis on the consequences, see E. Steindorff, *EG-Vertrag und Privatrecht* (Baden-Baden: Nomos, 1996).

notwithstanding their origin and nationality. The 'rest'—in particular the broad set of rules dealing with services of all kinds—are set by the wayside or overlooked, even today.[31] The implications are far-reaching. The private law dimension of this kind of regulatory private law fell into a vacuum, thereby providing leeway for the European Commission, the European Parliament, and the ECJ to enhance and to promote the functional market-driven logic of European integration.

The ECJ has taken a sympathetic attitude in approving the applicability of Article 114 TFEU to all sorts of regulatory private law legislative activities. The much-debated *Tobacco* judgment did not lead to long-lasting changes in the Court's reasoning. When already purported cross-border implications backed up by so-called impact assessments on which the Court uncritically relies suffice to open up the scope of Article 114, the *Tobacco* judgment seems, de facto, to be overruled.[32] What remains as a last barrier against the nearly unlimited scope of Article 114 TFEU is the ECJ judgment on the annulment of Regulation (EC) No 1435/2003 (European Cooperative Society (SCE)),[33] due to the choice of the wrong legal basis, namely Article 95 EC (now Article 114 TFEU) instead of Article 308 EC (now Article 352 TFEU),[34] the potential impact of which on the CESL has led to a controversy in legal academia.[35]

The market-driven logic of EU law reaches beyond the scope of competence. Outside *Viking*[36] and *Laval*,[37] there are no cases in European private law that have reached the same level of political and academic attention. This does not mean that there are no cases and that national private is shielded against the scope of EU law. The contrary is true. Two sets of cases have to be kept distinct. In *Alsthom Atlantique*[38] and *CMC Motorradcenter*[39] the ECJ exempted private law from the scope of application of the four freedoms. This is what the critics of *Viking* advocate. It means that basic concepts of national private law (such as the *action directe* in French law) in non-harmonized fields, such as the concept of liability, have been protected against the grip of EU law. In the harmonized

[31] Paradigmatic, the Study Group by M. Barendrecht, C. Jansen, M. Loos, A. Pinna, R. Cascao, and S. v. Gulijk, *Service Contracts (PEL SC)* (Munich: Sellier, 2007).

[32] See K. Gutman, 'The Commission Green Paper on European Contract law: Reflections on Union Competence in Light of the Proposed Options' (2012) 20 *European Review of Contract Law* 151, at 155, Weatherill (n 11), under 6 'Legal base'. The bottom line of a rather lenient approach of the ECJ is Case C-58/08 *Vodafone* [2010] ECR I-4999.

[33] Council Reg (EC) No 1435/2003 on the Statute for a European Cooperative Society (SCE), [2003] OJ L 207/1.

[34] Case C-436/03 *Parliament v Council* [2006] ECR I-3733.

[35] Pro in extensively discussing the judgment the German Bar Association, Ausschuss Europäisches Vertragsrecht des deutschen Anwaltsvereins, 'Art. 14 AEUV als Rechtsgrundlage für das Gemeinsame Europäische Kaufrecht' (2012) *ZIP* 809; against Weatherill (n 11), fn 120; reluctant but not against, Gutman (n 32) 160–1. For our position, scope yes, but not in compliance with the proportionality principle, H.-W. Micklitz and N. Reich, 'The Commission Proposal for a "Regulation on a Common European Sales Law (CESL)"—Too Broad or Not Broad Enough', *EUI Working Paper* 2012/4.

[36] Case C-438/05 *The International Transport Workers' Federation and The Finnish Seamen's Union* (*Viking*) [2007] ECR I-10779.

[37] Case C-341/05 *Laval and Partneri* [2007] ECR I-11767.

[38] Case C-339/89 *Alsthom Atlantique* [1993] ECR I-107.

[39] Case C-93/92 *CMC Motorradcenter* [1993] ECR I-5009.

field of European private law, potential conflicts turn on the reach of EU law. In *Gysbrecht*,[40] the ECJ was ready to submit national private law rules reaching beyond the minimum harmonized level to the proportionality test. In *Gonzales Sanchez*,[41] the ECJ held that the product liability directive aims at full harmonization, though no such reference can be found in the text of the directive. Within the scope of the directive, Member States can only maintain negligence-based liability rules. Quite prominent conflicts have arisen as to whether, and to what extent, Directive 2005/29/EC,[42] which aims at the full harmonization of commercial practices, covers sales promotion measures. In a whole series of cases, the ECJ took a tight grip on national laws and regulations, thereby promoting a liberalizing market logic in the regulation of unfair commercial practices.[43]

2. Markets and values in the Lisbon Treaty

The Lisbon Treaty is said to have led to a change in the functional logic of market-driven EU private law. The following questions arise. Is there a link to be built between Article 2 TEU laying down the values (all of them non-market related), Article 3(1) TEU making the values one of the three aims of the EU (the other two being the peace and well-being of people), Article 3(3) TEU establishing 'a highly competitive social market economy', and Article 3(6) TEU requesting that 'the Union shall pursue its objectives by appropriate means commensurate with the competences which are conferred upon it in the Treaties'?

Beyond the TEU, does the Charter of Fundamental Rights affect the order of competences? Article 6(1) TEU recognizes the legally binding value of the Charter of Fundamental Rights. Article 6(1), subparagraph 2, TEU however, states that 'the Charter shall not extend in any way the competences of the Union as defined in the Treaties'. This begs the question whether the 'values' laid down in Article 2 TEU allow for the use of the Charter as a means to give a clearer shape to the values, which would render it, via Article 3(6) TEU, an integral part of the conferred competences. Read this way, a potential conflict between the UK and Poland and the reservations laid down in Protocol 30 could be the consequence.[44] Do Articles 2, 3(1), (3), (6), 6(1) TEU, combined with the Charter of Fundamental Rights, imply a new reading of Article 114 TFEU 'which have as their objective the establishment and functioning of the internal market'?

[40] Case C-205/08 *Gysbrecht* [2008] ECR I-9947.

[41] Case C-183/00 *Gonzales Sanchez* [2002] ECR I-3901.

[42] Directive 2005/29/EC of the European Parliament and of the Council concerning unfair business-to-consumer commercial practices in the internal market and amending Council Directive 84/450/EEC, Directives 97/7/EC, 98/27/EC and 2002/65/EC of the European Parliament and of the Council and Regulation (EC) No 2006/2004 of the European Parliament and of the Council ('Unfair Commercial Practices Directive'), [2005] OJ L 149/22.

[43] See for a discussion of the differences between product liability *(Sanchez)* and unfair commercial practices V. Mak, 'Full Harmonization in European Private Law: A Two-Track Concept' (2012) 20 *European Review of Private Law* 213.

[44] The ECJ has given some indication on the limited effect of the Protocol in Case C-411/10 *N.S. v Secretary of State*, judgment of 21 December 2011, nyr., paras 116 *et seq*.

Strictly speaking all three issues do not concern the scope of the federal order of competences in private law, insofar as they do not reshape the balance of powers laid down in Articles 4–6 TEU. If at all, they influence the *content* of the conferred powers, provided that the values reach beyond the functional market logic *and* provided that the new values have to be taken into account in the exercise of the conferred powers.

I will first discuss the 'new' values. From a private law perspective, three highly relevant issues focusing on the interplay between Articles 2, 3 TEU, Article 114 TFEU, and the Charter have been discussed: (1) values in private law, (2) the new social design of the European Economic Constitution, and (3) private law and fundamental rights. A new outlook of European private law would affect the order of competences only indirectly. If EU private law would become 'more social' or more 'value laden' and less market functional, it would impact upon the relationship between the European regulatory private law and national private law in two directions. Member States with a 'more' social private legal order would welcome the new design, whereas member states with a 'less' social private legal order would fear an intrusion of the new European values into their national private laws.

(1) I have argued elsewhere[45] that European private law is yielding its own pattern of justice, what I have termed access justice (*Zugangsgerechtigkeit*). In brief, European access justice lies somewhere in between social distributive and libertarian allocative justice. It goes together with an understanding of the European Union as an institution enabling economic freedoms, but tying economic freedoms to social values. Owing to the non-statutory character of the EU, access justice does not emanate from a central power as a political project, but is bound to the European integration process which is market driven and bound to a market integration logic. This is said to explain the piecemeal character of the EU rules that enshrine access justice.

There is a tension between the European model of justice and the different concepts of social justice in the Member States. The social justice deficit of the private law *acquis* has indirectly been recognized, when the European Parliament mandated M. Hesselink to evaluate the level of social justice in the then DCFR.[46] Article 2(2) TEU enumerates 'justice' without defining more clearly what kind of justice is meant, *ius distributiva* or *ius commutativa*. As a stand-alone mechanism, it does not reach much beyond the obligation in Article 114(3) TFEU to take as a basis in health, safety, environmental, and consumer protection a 'high level of protection', which serves as the legal base that is most often employed. However, Article 2(2) TEU establishes justice as a general parameter. Therefore 'justice' has to be respected in all four other variations of competence where no ruling similar to Article 114 (3) TFEU exists, such as, for example, Article 90

[45] See asterisked footnote.

[46] M.W. Hesselink, *CFR & Social Justice: a short study for the European Parliament on the values underlying the draft Common Frame of Reference for European private law: what roles for fairness and social justice?* (Munich: Sellier, 2008).

TFEU (transport) and Article 190 YFEU (energy). On paper, it seems to make a difference; in practice the level of social protection in the field of regulated markets does not differ too much. It is hard to argue that the degree of, for example, consumer protection in the so-called consumer contract law directives is higher than in those which only indirectly cover the consumer, such as, for example, transport, energy, or telecommunications. This might be due to the so-called horizontal clause (*Querschnittsklausel*) in Article 169(2) TFEU.[47]

(2) At first glance, the introduction of the social market economy in Article 2(3) TEU seems more promising. It replaced the famous formula of Article 3 lit. (g) of the Rome Treaty on the guarantee of undistorted competition which was moved to Protocol No. 27:

> [t]he High Contracting Parties considering that the internal market as set out in Article 3 of the Treaty on European Union includes a system ensuring that competition is not distorted, have agreed that to this end the Union, shall, if necessary take action under the provision of the Treaties, including under Article 352 of the Treaty on the Functioning of the European Union.

Since the change of paradigm, a conflict has emerged on the positioning of the new formula, in particular on the role and importance of the outlook of the so-called European Economic Constitution.[48] To simplify, one might distinguish two camps: on the one hand are those who argue that the transfer of the objective of undistorted competition from the Treaty to the Protocol has left the competition-based economic constitution unaffected; whereas on the other side of the spectrum are those who champion the need to reconsider the outlook and concept of the European Economic Constitution in the light of changed values amply introduced in Article 2 TEU. The conflict goes back to the early days of the European Economic Community as it then was. Strong voices in German academia defended the idea that the European Economic Community had introduced a competitive market economy as a *Gesamtentscheidung* (a fundamental and overall comprehensive decision)[49] in line with ordo-liberal thinking, though this position remained under attack from all sides, but in particular from France, where the statutory influence on the economy was regarded as legitimate and where social rights and human rights were upheld against a mere economic construction of Europe. The new design of the Lisbon Treaty could be interpreted as an attempt to reconcile the two positions... or not!

Enshrined into the debate is a conflict on what the word 'social' in the context of market economy means. The social market economy is regarded as key to understanding the German '*Wirtschaftswunder*'. Thus, the question arose as to

[47] A.M. Weidemann, *Die Bedeutung der Querschnittsklauseln für die Kompetenzen innerhalb der Europäischen Gemeinschaft* (Peter Lang, Frankfurt a. M. 2009).

[48] Cahiers À Thème, 'La Constitution Économique Européenne Revisitée' (2011) 4 *Revue Internationale du Droit Economique* 411–600, with contributions of J. Drexl, J. Stuyck, R.M. Hilty, M. Pallemaerts, L. Azoulai, and K. Tuori.

[49] E.-J. Mestmäcker, ,'Macht—Recht—Wirtschaftsverfassung' (1973) *Zeitschrift für das Gesamte Handels- und Wirtschaftsrecht* (*ZHR*) 9.

whether and to what extent the European Union is, in an ever-stronger manner, advocating a social constitution, for the development of a genuine European social model.[50] Among French scholars and beyond, the new formula in the Lisbon Treaty was understood as bringing an end to post-war German ordo-liberalism. German scholars agree on the limited importance of the 'social' element in the TEU, although from totally different perspectives. Whereas Drexl[51] downplays the transfer of undistorted competition to the protocol, Joerges[52] locates the end of ordo-liberalism in the EU Treaty to the Treaty of Maastricht, thereby rejecting the idea of drawing a parallel between the German *Wirtschaftswunder* and the new formula in the Lisbon Treaty. In *Glaxo Smith*[53] the ECJ confirmed Drexl's understanding of the role and function of undistorted competition in the European market economy. There is thus far no judicial statement that would justify a more social reading of the Treaty or of a similar conceptual stance.

(3) At the conceptual—though not at the normative—level[54] the Charter of Fundamental Rights might have a strong impact on European private law, though not for the UK and for Poland. Constitutionalization of private law contains the undertone that reference to fundamental and human rights will lead to a more just and more social private law.[55] Here we are back to Kumm and his question of 'who is afraid of total constitution'. Conceptually, the point is whether constitutional law (here fundamental and human rights) and private law should remain self-standing, though interlinked, legal orders, or whether constitutional law should superimpose upon private law and set benchmarks against which private law rules are to be measured.[56]

The dominant understandings of German and English law are on the same footing, and strive for an independent private legal order. In my understanding of private law as economic law (*Privatrecht als Wirtschaftsrechts*), which is certainly a minoritarian position, the two legal orders are more permeable than in an orthodox ordo-liberal (German) or liberal (UK) understanding. The *Bürgschaftsurteil*[57] is famous because the German Constitutional Court (the GCC) reminded the highest civil court in the country, the *Bundesgerichtshof*, that private autonomy is

[50] D. Damjanovic and B. de Witte, 'Welfare Integration through EU Law: The Overall Picture in the Light of the Lisbon Treaty', in U. Neergard, R. Nielsen, and L.M. Roseberry (eds.), *Integrating Welfare Functions into EU Law—From Rome to Lisbon* (Copenhagen: DJØF, 2009), 53.

[51] J. Drexl, 'La Constitution économique européenne—L'actualité du modèle ordolibéral' (2011) *Revue internationale de droit économique* 419.

[52] C. Joerges, 'A Renaissance of the European Economic Constitution', in Neergard, Nielsen, and Roseberry (n 50) 42

[53] Case C-501/06 P *GlaxoSmithKline Services Unlimited v Commission* [2009] ECR I-9291 para 63.

[54] As I made clear in the beginning, I will not discuss the role and function of constitutional rights in private law.

[55] See, on the ambiguity of such an approach, H. Collins, 'The Constitutionalisation of European Private Law as a Path to Social Justice', in H.-W. Micklitz (ed.), *The Many Concepts of Social Justice in European Private Law* (Cheltenham: Edward Elgar, 2011), 133.

[56] For a critical account see also Lord Hoffmann, 'The Universality of Human Rights Judicial Studies Board', Annual Lecture of 19 March 2009, available at: <http://www.judiciary.gov.uk/media/speeches/2009/speech-lord-hoffman-19032009>.

[57] Bundesverfassungsgericht, 19 October 1993, BVerfGE 89, 214.

not unrestricted and that there are *constitutional* limits to its exercise. The decision was taken in 1994, nearly 20 years ago. Since then, no comparable issue in private law-setting—labour and anti-discrimination issues aside—has reached the GCC. This means that a constitutional intervention is the exception to the rule. This is exactly the reason why the *Bürgschaftsurteil* carries such importance. The House of Lords, now the Supreme Court, rejected the opportunity to take a similar stance and uphold private autonomy against judicial intervention on two occasions when the Office of Fair Trading sought to make financial transactions more social.[58] However, this is not the whole story. In the aftermath of the two judgments, the Office of Fair Trading renegotiated the contract terms in issue with the banking sector, and reached an agreement in the bank charges case, which reduced the costs imposed on vulnerable consumers by 50 per cent.[59] Therefore, in the UK, in contrast to Germany, the supervisory agency is taking over the compensatory task of 'adjusting' the governing rules of the banking sector. This seemingly simple—though in fact highly complicated—example demonstrates that constitutionalization is not the only manner in which to give private law relations a more social outlook.[60]

At the European level, no comparable conflicts of such a conceptual dimension have been decided thus far or are pending before the ECJ, perhaps with the exception of *Mohammed Aziz* where, however, the constitutional dimension remains hidden.[61] However, the so-called *ex officio* case law of the ECJ is about to gain a similar strategic importance.[62] The ECJ tends to impose a duty on national judges to investigate whether mandatory EU rights meant to protect the weaker party have been respected by the supplier in b2c relations. The difficulty remains that not all private law disputes bear a constitutional dimension. What remains to be clarified is how to distinguish conceptual issues—which should be left to the Constitution (at least in my understanding)—and what kind of issues should remain at the level of civil courts. The European debate is just at the beginning, although the reference in Article 5 TEU to the Charter of Fundamental Rights opens up new avenues to reconsider the relationship between the functional market-driven logic of European private law and a more value-laden approach.

All in all, there is a potential to rethink the content of the competences in light of the Lisbon Treaty; however, all reflections have to have regard to one crucial *caveat*: is there a formal link between the social re-orientation of private law and the conferral of power? 'The Union shall pursue its objectives by appropriate means

[58] Judgment of the House of Lords of 25 October 2001, *The General of Fair Trading v First National Bank plc* [2001] UKHL 52; Judgment of 25 November 2009, *Office of Fair Trading (Respondents) v Abbey National plc & Others (Appellants)* [2009] UKSC 6, on appeal from [2009] EWCA Civ 116.

[59] See in this context G. Comparato, 'Europe's steps towards a financially inclusive private law', unpublished MS 2012, on file with author. To be published as an EUI Working Paper within the ERC project on European Regulatory Private Law.

[60] Personal information of the Financial Ombudsman at the UK Financial Supervisory Authority.

[61] Case C-415/11 *Mohammed Aziz*, judgment of 14 March 2013, nyr.

[62] Case C-240/98 *Océano Grupo Editorial SA* [2000] ECR I-4941; Case C-168/05 *Mostaza Claro* [2006] ECR I-10421; Case C-40/08 *Asturcom Telecomunicaciones SL/Christina Rodriguez Nogueira* [2009] ECR I-9579; Case C-243/08 *Pannon GSM Zrt* [2009] ECR I-4713.

commensurate with the competences which are conferred upon it in the Treaties'. 'Commensurate' is translated into German with '*entsprechend*', into French '*en fonction*', and into Italian '*in ragione*'. The English version provides for a much stronger link between the objectives and the conferred powers. 'Commensurate' comes close to 'pursuing in parallel', whereas the other three versions are more functional, although they underpin the overall idea that the EU in making use of its conferred powers has to do so in compliance with the objectives of the Treaty, which include, *inter alia*, to strive for 'justice', for a 'social' market economy, and 'for the recognition of' the Charter of Fundamental Rights.

III. Limits of Competence: the Uncoupling of European Private Law from National Private Law and Possible Counter-reactions

The European Union 'shall act within the limits of the competences conferred upon it by the Member States', per Article 5 TEU. I will try to show how the existing body of secondary community law affects the capacity of the Member States to act. In essence, my argument is that European private law covers all economically relevant issues, thereby downgrading national private law to a kind of a second order. The Lisbon Treaty allows for a new reading of the subsidiarity principle as a means of sharing responsibilities and of reconceptualizing the inner architecture of the order of competences. I would like to demonstrate how the Member States could take a more active stand against the European intrusion, if they were so inclined.

1. The substance of regulatory private law and what remains for the national private law

Over the last few decades, the European Union has developed a dense set of rules, covering a broad field of economic activities. The following account is taken from earlier writings, though in a shortened form, and without references:

(1) Anti-discrimination. The European Community modernized and extended antidiscrimination law by way of a whole series of directives (2000/43/EC, 2000/78/EC, 2002/73/EC, 2004/113/EC and 2006/54/EC)[63] to private law, i.e. beyond labour law. Anti-discrimination law introduces new values into the private law system (these values are not bound to particular areas of the visible private law).

[63] Respectively, Council Directive 2000/43/EC implementing the principle of equal treatment between persons irrespective of racial or ethnic origin, [2000] OJ L 180/22; Council Directive 2000/78/EC establishing a general framework for equal treatment in employment and occupation, [2000] OJ L 303/16; Directive 2002/73/EC of the European Parliament and of the Council amending Council Directive 76/207/EEC on the implementation of the principle of equal treatment for men and women as regards access to employment, vocational training and promotion, and working

(2) Regulated markets. The privatization (liberalization) of former state monopolies in the sectors of telecommunications, energy, and transport has raised the importance of contract law. The regulatory role of contract law as a device within regulated markets to serve the overall purpose of liberalization and privatization is nearly neglected. The network law develops within the boundaries of universal services concepts devices whose reach has to be tested with regard to its potential for generalization beyond the narrow subject matter.

(3) Insurance law (which is usually regarded as a subject of its own) and capital market law (investor protection law). EC Directive 2004/39/EC on Markets in Financial Instruments (the so-called MIFID)[64] lays down a broad framework within level 1 of the Lamfalussy approach, completed by two level 2 pieces of regulation, Directive 2006/73/EC on organizational requirements and operating conditions for investment firms and the implementing Regulation 2006/1287/EC.[65] They establish a dense network of rules, which contain strong links to the contractual relations, where a professional or a private investor engages with his or her investment firm.

(4) Commercial practices. The most important instruments are Directive 2005/29/EC on unfair commercial practices dealing with b2c relations,[66] and Directive 2006/114/EC on misleading and comparative advertising in b2b relations.[67] The e-commerce Directive 2000/31/EC has to be taken into account as well.[68] Directive 99/44/EC on consumer sales links contract law and advertising together such that third party advertising may affect contractual duties.[69] EC commercial practices law affects the modalities under which the contract is concluded.

(5) Intellectual property rights. The EC policy is meant to extend the existing intellectual property rights law and give it a European outlook coupled with appropriate legal redress mechanisms to sanction violations of property

conditions, [2002] OJ L 269/15; Council Directive 2004/113/EC implementing the principle of equal treatment between men and women in the access to and supply of goods and services, [2004] OJ L 373/37; Directive 2006/54/EC of the European Parliament and of the Council on the implementation of the principle of equal opportunities and equal treatment of men and women in matters of employment and occupation, [2006] OJ L 204/23.

[64] Directive 2004/39/EC of the European Parliament and of the Council on markets in financial instruments amending Council Directives 85/611/EEC and 93/6/EEC and Directive 2000/12/EC of the European Parliament and of the Council and repealing Council Directive 93/22/EEC, [2004] OJ L 145/1.

[65] Commission Directive 2006/73/EC implementing Directive 2004/39/EC of the European Parliament and of the Council as regards requirements and operating conditions for investment firms and defined terms for the purposes of that Directive, [2006] OJ L 241/26.

[66] See n 42.

[67] Directive 2006/114/EC of the European Parliament and of the Council concerning misleading and comparative advertising, [2006] OJ L 376/21.

[68] Directive 2000/31/EC of the European Parliament and of the Council on certain legal aspects of information society services, in particular electronic commerce, in the Internal Market ('Directive on electronic commerce'), [2000] OJ L 178/1.

[69] Directive 1999/44/EC of the European Parliament and of the Council on certain aspects of the sale of consumer goods and associated guarantees, [1999] OJ 171/12.

rights (Directive 2004/48/EC).[70] The heavy expansion of intellectual property rights restricts at the same time the users' rights. These restrictions are often found in standard terms which form part of the licence contract which the consumer concludes often via the internet.

(6) Private competition law (*Kartellprivatrecht*). The diverse regulations on exclusive and selective distribution, the umbrella Regulation 2790/1999,[71] Regulation 1400/2002 on the car sector,[72] and Regulation 772/2004 on technology transfer, intervene indirectly into contract-making.[73] The content of the rights and duties in vertical agreements is determined to a large extent by block exemptions. The parties will often copy the articles in the block exemptions into their contracts to avoid discrepancies between the EU rules and the contractual rights.

The new economic approach on state aids has led to the adoption of the *de minimis* Regulation 1998/2006.[74] European state aid law may be divided into a substantive and a procedural part. Illegal state aids, that is to say, the question of repayment of unlawful state aids and the possible remedies of third parties are key questions in private law. Similar effects can be reported from Directive 2009/81/EC amending Directive 2004/17/EC dealing with procurement procedures dealing with entities operating in the water, energy, transport, and postal services and Directive 2004/18/EC on the coordination for the procurement procedure on public works contracts, public supply contracts, and public services contracts.[75] Whilst the purpose of these directives is to enhance competition and strengthen the market freedoms, they shape at the same time contractual relations. This is particularly true with regard to appropriate remedies.

(7) Product safety and food safety law. In Directive 2001/95/EC on product safety[76] there are new devices that enhance the role of contract law as a means to shape contractual relations. Liability rules may be found in the Feed Hygiene Regulation 183/2005,[77] the Food Hygiene Regulation

[70] Directive 2004/48/EC of the European Parliament and of the Council on the enforcement of intellectual property rights, [2004] OJ L 157/45.

[71] Commission Reg (EC) No 2790/1999 on the application of Article 81(3) of the Treaty to categories of vertical agreements and concerted practices, [1999] OJ L 336/21.

[72] Commission Reg (EC) No 1400/2002 on the application of Article 81(3) of the Treaty to categories of vertical agreements and concerted practices in the motor vehicle sector, [2002] OJ L 203/30.

[73] Commission Reg (EC) No 772/2004 on the application of Article 81(3) of the Treaty to categories of technology transfer agreements, [2004] OJ L 123/11.

[74] Commission Reg (EC) No 1998/2006 on the application of Articles 87 and 88 of the Treaty to de minimis aid, [2006] OJ L 379/5.

[75] Directive 2009/81/EC of the European Parliament and of the Council on the coordination of procedures for the award of certain works contracts, supply contracts and service contracts by contracting authorities or entities in the fields of defence and security, and amending Directives 2004/17/EC and 2004/18/EC, [2009] OJ L 216/76.

[76] Directive 2001/95/EC of the European Parliament and of the Council on general product safety, [2002] OJ 11/4 now under revision.

[77] Reg (EC) No 183/2005 of the European Parliament and of the Council laying down requirements for feed hygiene [2005] OJ 35/1.

852/2004,[78] the Regulation on Official Feed and Food Controls 882/2004,[79] and Regulation 178/2002 on Food Law.[80]

The so-called Services Directive 2006/123/EC enhances the elaboration of 'technical standards' by the European standard bodies CEN/CENELEC as well as by National Standards Bodies that come near to some sort of standard contract conditions,[81] which might be subject to control under Directive 93/13/EEC on unfair contract terms.[82]

In order to describe the 'scope' of the competences, I have used the metaphor of a ring or a circle, which surrounds the core of traditional national private law. When it comes to 'limits', another metaphor might be more telling. Let us imagine traditional private law as a cake. What European private law is doing is to cut out of national private law the economically most important and most relevant—in other words, the fattest—slices. A prominent example is the Europeanization of contracts for services. Continental codes as well as the common law on contract do not provide much guidance for modern services, enshrined for example, in regulated markets or digital services. National laws still rely on the old distinction first introduced in the French Code Civil between *obligation de moyen* and *obligation de résultat*. Modern contract law on services reaches far beyond these basic rules and establishes sector-related rules, which are no longer connected to the old distinction. A second example is the rules on the conclusion of the contract. In a number of contract-relevant directives and regulations, we may find a recital stating that this and that directive or regulation in no way affects the national rules on the conclusion of contracts (e.g. Article 3(2) Directive 2005/29/EC on unfair commercial practices). This is, at the very least, misleading.[83] What the EU regulator is doing is harmonizing the initial state of affairs prior to the conclusion of a contract and the consequences after the conclusion of a contract, thereby downplaying the importance of offer and acceptance.

My major argument is the following: there is a clash between national ideologies on the maintenance of the sovereign national private legal orders in academia and politics, and the practical realities whereby almost every relevant field of private law understood as economic law is affected by European private law rules.[84] To be

[78] Reg (EC) No 852/2004 of the European Parliament and of the Council on the hygiene of foodstuffs, [2004] OJ L 139/1.

[79] Reg (EC) No 882/2004 of the European Parliament and of the Council on official controls performed to ensure the verification of compliance with feed and food law, animal health and animal welfare rules, [2004] OJ L 165/1.

[80] Reg (EC) No 178/2002 of the European Parliament and of the Council laying down the general principles and requirements of food law, establishing the European Food Safety Authority and laying down procedures in matters of food safety, [2002] OJ L 31/1.

[81] Directive 2006/123/EC of the European Parliament and of the Council on services in the internal market, [2006] OJ L 376/36.

[82] Council Directive 93/13/EEC on unfair terms in consumer contracts, [1993] OJ L 95/29.

[83] S. Whittaker, 'The Relationship of the Unfair Commercial Practices Directive to European and National Contract Law', in S. Weatherill and U. Bernitz (eds.), *The Regulation of Unfair Commercial Practices under EC Directive 2005/29/EC—New Rules and New Techniques* (Oxford: Hart, 2007), 139.

[84] A perfect example is the collection of European directives and regulations in the field of private law, R. Schulze and R. Zimmermann (eds.), *Basistexte zum Europäischen Privatrecht: Textsammnlung*

'affected' can take different forms and can range from weak to strong effects. The still-dominating view is that European private law covers only remote areas and does not go to the heart of national private legal orders. So, the perception is one of a rather loose relationship between the two, which leaves the national private law intact; in fact the economic and practical reality is different. More visible and more concrete are cases in which the two legal orders clash, for example *Putz/Weber*,[85] where European regulatory private law does not correspond to the system of German warranty law (*Gewährleistungsrechts*), since it abolishes negligence as a prerequisite for a claim of compensation.

The examples are endless, but the common perception still seems to be to take the cases and the directives behind them as pointillistic, whereas in reality the pointillistic islands of European private law are about to merge into a new mainland, the one of a largely self-standing European private law, which is not coherent, which is fragmented, sector- and field bound, but which is gradually replacing national private law rules.[86] The true question today is 'what remains for national private law', not in terms of a well-built ideological edifice, but in the daily reality of contract and tort. 'Affectedness' cannot be more drastic than that: it is the whole system of national private law and its role in the nation state legal order which is at stake. This is not the place to give normative shape to the potential relationship between the different legal orders, as this would imply embarking upon a journey dealing with the different legal tools and with the methodology of European private law, with a focus in particular on the role and function of the much debated 'common principles of private law', as invented by the ECJ.[87]

2. Subsidiarity from without and subsidiarity from within

The Treaty of Lisbon states in Article 5(1) TEU: '[t]he limits of Union competences are governed by the principle of conferral. The use of the Union competence is governed by the principles of subsidiarity and proportionality.' The subsidiarity principle has a long history in the EU treaties. John Major[88] claimed, as early as 1992, after the signing of the Maastricht Treaty, that the subsidiarity principle should be used as a powerful weapon of the Member States to defend 'their powers'

(Baden-Baden: Nomos, 2000), which contain consumer law and anti-discrimination law, but not all the other areas of European private law enlisted in this chapter.

85 Joined Cases C-65/09 and C-87/09 *Jürgen Wittmer and Ingrid Putz* [2011] ECR I-5257.

86 R. Michaels, 'Of Islands and the Ocean: The Two Rationalities of European Private Law', in R. Brownsword and others (eds.), *The Foundations of European Private Law* (Oxford: Hart, 2011), 139.

87 Case C-412/06 *Hamilton* [2008] ECR I-2383 para 42; AG Trstenjak, Case C-489/07 *Messner* [2009] ECR I-7305 paras 91 and 108, and para 29 of the judgment; Case C-101/08 *Audiolux* [2009] ECR I-9823; in the literature, see J. Basedow, '*Mangold, Audiolux* und die allgemeinen Grundsätze des europäischen Privatrechts', in S. Grundmann and others (eds.), *Festschrift für Klaus J. Hopt* (Berlin and New York: De Gruyter, 2010), 27; S. Weatherill, 'The "principles of civil law" as a basis for interpreting the legislative *acquis*' (2010) 6 *European Review of Contract Law* 74; A. Hartkamp, 'The General Principles of EU Law and Private Law' (2011) *RabelsZ* 241.

88 See the telling cartoon in *The Independent* of 6 July 1992, 20, showing Major as the superman telling the European Union what to do.

against the 'conferred powers'. This expectation turned out to be completely unrealistic. The subsidiarity principle has not played any role in the development of European regulatory private law. The directives and regulations were adopted with the consent of the vast majority of Member States.

The Treaty of Lisbon, however, has upgraded the subsidiarity principle, in particular with regard to the field of shared competence which dominates the field of private law. Article 6(3) TEU inserts into the Treaty what was well-established before: 'the Union shall act only if and in so far as the objectives of the proposed action cannot be sufficiently achieved by the Member States, either at a central level or at a regional and local level, but can rather, by reason of the scale of effects of the proposed action, be better achieved at the Union level.' Protocol No. 2 then specifies the conditions under which a non-compliance claim can be raised, and by whom. The first time the subsidiarity principle played a crucial rule in private law-making, is in the discussion on a legal base for CESL, when four Member States, Austria, Belgium, Germany, and the UK,[89] raised the newly introduced subsidiarity claim, but did not achieve the quorum set out in Article 7 of Protocol No. 2. In light of the substantial increase of EU directives and regulations in the field of regulatory private law, one might wonder what exactly the Member States are defending.[90]

The role and function of the subsidiarity principle calls for re-invigoration due to its embeddedness in the 'objectives' under Article 3(1) TEU, as concretized in Articles 2(1), 3(3) TEU, and 6 TEU, in combination with the Charter of Fundamental Rights.[91] My argument is that the values enshrined in the objectives of the Treaty materialize the subsidiarity principle.

In 1993, I attributed[92] to the subsidiarity principle a twofold momentum: (1) traditionally it has to do with power sharing, with defining and delimiting competences (subsidiarity here may be called 'subsidiarity from without'), but (2) subsidiarity is also linked to the inner organizational structure of a community, insofar as it contains, at least implicitly, a conception of what should be done at what level ('subsidiarity from within'). The first momentum turns the classical reading of the subsidiarity principle as a means to reallocate powers—subsidiarity from without—upside down and raises the question whether it could become *a means to generate responsibilities* instead of merely defending competences. The second momentum aims at the inner architecture of the community legal order; it advocates an order of competence. Such a reading of the subsidiarity principle could render the Community legal order more flexible and invalidate the Community's encroachment upon the Member States' powers. Both contain an element of 'competition' bottom-up, of 'interbrand' competition[93] and they allow for a comprehensive view of subsidiarity (from without and from within).

[89] On file with the author, not all are publicly available, but see for the UK Council Doc. 18547/11 of 14 December 2011, for Germany BT-Drucksache 17/800, for Austria 8609 der Beilagen zu den stenographischen Protokollen des Bundesrates. Another three Member States have provided critical statements.

[90] See under III. [91] See in more detail under I.1. [92] See asterisked footnote.

[93] N. Reich, 'Competition, Competition between Legal Orders: A New Paradigm of EC Law?' (1992) 28 *Common Market Law Review* 861, at 899 and 895: '[t]he more competences the Community

'Subsidiarity from without' cannot be used as a mere weapon of Member States to curtail Community activities. Inherent in the principle of subsidiarity is a positive constructive element, which implies that the Member States have to support the Community in the development of adequate rules to achieve the objectives of the Community. Subsidiarity does not aim at the shaping of competence structures alone which bring together or divide Member States and the Community, it encourages *the allocation of competences on the basis of efficiency rather than nationality.*[94] Already in the 1980s the Court of Justice started to oblige national courts and national administrations to enforce Community law.[95]

The order of competence established in the Lisbon Treaty allows for a much more nuanced and powerful reading of the reach of Member States' responsibilities. What was already enshrined in the case law of Article 36 TFEU can now be turned into a rule. The Lisbon Treaty imposed obligations and responsibilities on the Member States to look after the social dimension not only of the internal market project but of European integration per se. This is the true potential enshrined in the combination of the objectives of the Lisbon Treaty with the values, in particular justice, 'social market economy', and fundamental rights. Through such an understanding 'subsidiarity from without' requires much more from the Member States than simply delegating private law-making to the EU within the limits of the conferred powers. It bears a genuine European responsibility to bring the social dimension to life.

How can this be achieved? Here the subsidiarity 'from within' comes to bear. The leading idea is to seek the solution in the allocation of competences on the basis of efficiency and not in the fruitless differentiation between internal market-related measures and pure non-market-related private law measures. Efficiency means deciding what can be done best at what level. This has been pinned down in Article 5(3) of the Lisbon Treaty. If one accepts that the Union cannot survive as an internal market alone, but that it must meet the social challenge and transform the near-to completed internal market into a social European space, which appears to be the purpose of the Lisbon Treaty, then it is necessary to enable the Union to take action at the European level and to prevent the subsidiarity principle from becoming just another hurdle to overcome in the transformation of Europe.[96]

Such a concept could work only if the distinction between *minimum* harmonization and *maximum* harmonization, which is so crucial and equally so sensitive in European private law, is used in a positive and forward-looking way. When the

is acquiring, the less exclusive will be its jurisdiction and the more "interbrand" competition between legal orders will take place.'

[94] S. Weatherill, 'Shaping Responsibilities in the Legal Order of the European Community', in H.-W. Micklitz, T. Roethe, and S. Weatherill, *Federalism and Responsibility: a Study on Product Safety and Practice in the European Community* (London and Boston: Graham & Trotman/M. Nijhoff, and Norwel, MA, USA: Kluwer Academic Publishers Group, 1994), 153.

[95] See Case 103/88 *Fratelli Costanzo SpA v Comune di Milano* [1989] ECR 1839 and Case 14/83 *Sabine von Colson and Elisabeth Kamann v Land Nordrhein-Westfalen* [1984] ECR 1891.

[96] How can efficiency be reconciled with the social dimension of life? The answer lies in the concept of access justice (asterisked footnote).

European Union started to get involved in the harmonization of private law matters, minimum harmonization was the means of establishing a common platform of rules, thereby leaving higher levels of protection and legal experiments to the Member State level. The turning point in this EU history was the so-called Lisbon declaration in 2000, certainly inspired by the forthcoming establishment of the Euro-zone.[97] From this moment on, the European Commission started to combine the building of 'the most competitive market in the world' (EU speak) with the principle of full harmonization. The European Commission has been more or less successful, depending on the field of European private law. The peak of the debate and maybe the turning point came with the Consumer Rights Directive 2011/83/EC,[98] where the European Commission initially planned to merge eight consumer contract law directives into one, by a policy of full harmonization. In the end, the European Commission failed, at least with regard to the more important areas of sales law and standard contract terms.[99] It is plain that this failure will have long-lasting effects even if Commissioner Reding does not seem ready to accept this change.[100]

Subsidiarity read this way would make minimum harmonization a constitutional rule in the field of shared competences and maximum harmonization the exception to the rule, utilized only in exceptional circumstances. Such a new interpretation of the subsidiarity principle would guarantee a platform of social protection for all EU citizens, which must be jointly realized by the EU and the Member States under the shared competences available in private law. This would leave room for Member States to go beyond the EU minimum level, if they so wish. There is, however, no EU obligation beyond the guarantee of the minimum level of protection. Translated into the different concepts of justice it would mean that the EU has to provide for access justice as a minimum standard, whereas Member States could go beyond and use private law to realize social distributive justice.

IV. Intensity: the Relationship with Task and Function

The notion of intensity and the relationship with task and function raises questions which should be investigated separately, first the link between intensity and Article 4 TEU, and secondly the importance of the tool that is used in the exercise of conferred powers.

97 <http://www.europarl.europa.eu/summits/lis1_de.htm>, continued in COM (2010) 2020 final, EUROPE 2020 A strategy for smart, sustainable and inclusive growth.

98 Directive 2011/83/EU of the European Parliament and of the Council on consumer rights, amending Council Directive 93/13/EEC and Directive 1999/44/EC and repealing Council Directive 85/577/EEC and Directive 97/7/EC, [2011] OJ l 304/64.

99 For a full account of the history of the Consumer Rights Directive, see Weatherill (n 11) 49. I would understand his conclusion so as to support my interpretation of the minimum harmonization rule.

100 Speech in Warsaw, 10 November 2011, available at: <http://europa.eu/rapid/pressReleasesAction.do?reference=SPEECH/11/742&type=HTML>.

1. National identity and essential state functions

The Treaty of Lisbon has introduced a new constitutional barrier against which EU law-making must be measured. Article 4(2) TEU states:

> [t]he Union shall respect the equality of Member States before the Treaties as well as their national identities, inherent in their fundamental structures, political and constitutional, inclusive of regional and local self-government. It shall respect their essential state functions, including ensuring the territorial integrity of the state, maintaining law and order and safeguarding national security. In particular national security remains the sole responsibility of the Member States.

The Lisbon Judgment of the German Constitutional Court is the first decision of a national supreme court which discusses the meaning of 'essential state functions' and to some extent 'national identity', which stand side-by-side in the Treaty, though obviously in a different context.[101] The judgment of the GCC on the constitutionality of the measures taken at the EU level to rescue the Euro will certainly not put much flesh on the bones.[102] By now the ECJ has referred to Article 4(2) TEU on three occasions. In *Sayn-Wittgenstein* the ECJ accepted that the status of a republic, enshrined in the Austrian law on the abolition of the nobility, forms part of the national identities of Member States, whereas in *Runevič-Vardyn* and *Anton Las* the Court considered that the national identity of the Member States includes the protection of the official language or languages of those states.[103]

So far it is not clear whether and to what extent the national private legal order being codified or not belongs to the 'essential state functions' and/or to 'the national identity'. As long as we are thinking and operating within the category of a nation state, we have to accept that the national private legal order constitutes one of the basic pillars on which a nation state is built, outside the constitution or the equivalent rules in the UK. In light of the two judgments of the GCC and the ECJ, I tend to understand the private legal order as a part of the national identity, in all its particularities and differences that have engaged private lawyers for the last centuries—at least since the Westphalian Peace—and equally as an essential state function, as no state can organize its market economy without the power of regulating private law relationships.

There are follow-up questions and they are linked to the deeper relation between the private legal *order* and the European competence order. The first set of questions turns around the particular character of private law. The *ius commune* scholarship postulates the existence of a private law community which cuts across national boundaries and which provides a common ground for the different national legal orders. Such an understanding questions the existence of a

[101] Micklitz (n 21) 528.

[102] See the press release of 12 September 2012 available at: <http://www.bundesverfassungsgericht.de/entscheidungen/rs20120912_2bvr139012en.html>.

[103] See, respectively, Case C-208/09 *Sayn-Wittgenstein* [2010] ECR I-13693 paras 88 and 92, Case C-391/09 *Runevič-Wardyn* [2011] ECR I-3787 para 85, and Case C-202/11 *Anton Las* [2013] nyr. para 26. For more details on these cases, see the contributions by Timmermans and Millet in this book.

particular national identity of private legal orders or at least requests clarification of the relationship between the *ius commune* as the binding element and the national private legal orders as possible elements of a national identity being put on an equal footing with the concept of the republic and the concept of human dignity (or others). The second set of questions strives for a deeper analysis of the differences between private *law*, private legal *systems* (J. Dickson), and private legal *orders* (K.C. Culver/M. Giudice).[104] Dickson understands European private law as a system, whereas Culver/Giudice restrict the concept of system to national laws and advocate instead an understanding of European law as a legal order.

My intention is more modest as I focus on 'Federal Order of Competences'. If there is a link between 'essential state function', 'national identities', and national private laws then it is neither possible to hollow out the national private law systems via European regulatory private law thereby leaving no relevant space for the national private legal systems, nor to actively replace national private legal orders via a fully-fledged European Civil Code. CESL certainly does not go this far. The draft Regulation might indeed comply with Article 6 TEU. The devil, however, is in the detail. The 'essential state function' and 'national identity' argument helps to strike down *full harmonization* of private law as a constitutional means of completing the internal market, at least as long as it is advocated for as a general and universally applicable tool. Minimum harmonization neither endangers essential state functions nor national identities. A common platform is exactly what shared competence in combination in respect of the subsidiarity principle is calling for.

2. The choice of the appropriate legal tool

Whenever the European Commission discusses the completion of the internal market or, more generally, how to promote European integration, harmonization via legal means is on the agenda. The substance of EU law is, first and foremost, characterized by binding directives and more and more by directly applicable regulations.

The order of competences presented here in the field of private law in the form of minimum harmonization rules which establish a common platform, should be implemented via the means of minimum regulations. Norbert Reich[105] was the first to bring the issue up in the area of consumer protection, when he invoked Article 169(3) lit. (a) TFEU as the appropriate legal basis, which would automatically limit harmonization to the minimum level. The draft proposal on CESL equally follows the model of a regulation, though aiming at full harmonization.

[104] On the legal systems, see J. Dickson, 'Towards a Theory of European Legal Systems', and on legal orders see K.C. Culver and M. Guidice, 'Not a System but an Order: An Interinstitutional View of European Union Law', both in J. Dickson and P. Eleftheriadis (eds.), *Philosophical Foundations of European Union Law* (Oxford: Oxford University Press, 2013), 25 and 54.

[105] N. Reich, 'A European Contract Law or a European Contract Law Regulation for Consumers?' (2005) 28 *Journal of Consumer Policy* 383.

The choice of a regulation as the appropriate tool would have the advantage of considerably increasing transparency and legal certainty. For all parties involved, the regulation would serve as a platform equally and directly applicable in all Member States, available in all the languages of the European Union. The Member States would be considerably discharged from the transactions costs resulting from the transformation of directives into national law. At the same time, the national law could remain as it stands and, if the Member State so decided, provide for a higher level of social protection.

The Treaty of Lisbon does not deal with 'governance', at least not with regard to private law issues. Article 21 TEU contains general provisions on the Union's external actions. Paragraph (2) ties the promotion of an international system based on stronger multilateral cooperation and *good global governance*. No similar ruling exists with regard to the internal market or, more generally speaking, for the internal affairs of the EU. Article 15 TFEU provides guidance only on the way in which the Union's institutions are supposed to work: '[i]n order to promote good governance and ensure the participation of civil society, the Union's institutions, bodies, offices and agencies shall conduct their work as openly as possible.' In the field of private law, there was and there is much discussion on European governance in contract law.[106] Neither the *acquis* group, nor the study group, took contract governance into account. In addition, soft forms of coordination have gained considerable ground not only at the nation state level, but also in Europe. With the choice of an optional instrument in CESL, the European Commission seems ready to test a new strand of regulatory technique. The nation state legal orders remain unaffected unless the parties to the contract choose the proposed optional instrument. This regulatory technique has gained much support, in particular from law and economics-inspired scholars.[107]

Concluding Remarks

The Treaty of Lisbon paves the way for a new reading of the EU competence order in private law. It is not so much the scope but the content of the conferred powers which needs to be corrected and adjusted to a legal order which is no longer so one-sidedly dominated by the internal market logic, but which takes the social dimension of private law into account. Equally important is the new reading of the subsidiarity principles which set constitutional boundaries to maximum harmonization within the scope of shared competences and which impose a common obligation upon the Member States and upon the European Union to give shape

[106] Cf. n 21.

[107] F. Gomez and J.J. Ganuza, 'An Economic Analysis of Harmonization Regimes: Full Harmonization, Minimum Harmonization and Optional Instrument' (2011) *European Review of Contract Law* 275; S. Grundmann, 'Kosten und Nutzen eines Optionalen Europäischen Kaufrechtsrechts', paper presented within the Special conference organized by the German Association of Civil Lawyers, Zivilrechtslehrervereingung, April 2012, see in English: 'Costs and Benefits of an Optional European Sales Law (CESL)' (2013) 50 *Common Market Law Review* 225.

to the changing non-market outlook of the European Union. The interplay of minimum harmonization as a common platform in Europe, combined with the constitutionally guaranteed leeway for the Member States to go beyond the EU level of social protection, preserves the national identities of the Member States and their essential state functions, whilst leaving space for the development of a constitutional order beyond the nation state.

PART III

THE EUROPEAN COURT OF JUSTICE AND THE QUESTION OF COMPETENCE

7

ECJ Doctrines on Competences

Christiaan Timmermans

Introductory Remark and Conclusions

The plural of my subject (doctrines) is quite appropriate. If it would be at all possible to speak with regard to EU competences and division of competences of a doctrine of the Court of Justice of the European Union, then we should speak about various doctrines, varying according to the sector involved and sometimes even varying within one and the same sector. However, that being the case, I prefer to speak of approaches, rather than doctrines. The only sector where one could perhaps speak of one single doctrine is that of external relations. Marise Cremona discusses this field in another chapter of this book. Moreover, the field of external relations is the one in which the issue of competences has always been and still is the most extensively discussed. For these reasons, I shall focus my contribution on the internal competences.

Let me for once reverse the normal order of an article and start with the conclusions. This might allow some readers to stop reading any further than that. The conclusions are the following:

1. The Court has not developed a real doctrine, in the sense of a self-standing, systematically-ordered construct, on the issue of competences and the division of competences between the EU and its Member States.
2. The concept of pre-emption plays no role in the case law but it might nevertheless be useful for its understanding.
3. The Lisbon Treaty has not really codified the case law with regard to shared internal competences.
4. The Court will not necessarily have to change that case law but it might nevertheless be expected to do so.
5. The conclusion of an international agreement on a 'Fiscal Compact' to solve the euro crisis, whatever its merits, raises questions of a competence divide that should be further explored.

I. Which Approaches?

The most interesting case law on this matter is that concerning the common agricultural policy.[1] This is the case for obvious reasons because this was, and probably still is, the most elaborate and interventionist of EU policies. It may be interesting to note that this case law was particularly abundant in the 1970s and 1980s, but much less so today. The following analysis shall not include the common fisheries policy, more particularly the conservation policy on fish stocks, a subject for which the Court as early as 1976 held the EEC competence to be of an exclusive nature.[2]

In its early case law with regard to the division of competences, the Court took a fairly dogmatic position. To quote from the *Bollmann* case of 1970: '[t]o the extent to which Member States have transferred legislative powers...with the object of ensuring the satisfactory operation of a common market in agriculture they no longer have the powers to adopt legislative provisions in this field.'[3] So, the mere transfer, and not the exercise of those powers in occupying the field, deprived Member States of their powers.

However, it became quickly apparent on the basis of new cases that it would be unwise to so radically cut off a possible autonomous intervention by Member States. In the decentralized Community system, they had to implement and manage agricultural market organizations, and they were the first to be confronted with daily problems, unexpected events and lacunae in the EC rules. Completely freezing the possibility of autonomous intervention by Member States could in the end be counterproductive and hamper, more than foster, the smooth functioning of the market organizations. Moreover, in various cases, the Court was confronted with autonomous national measures that interfered with the functioning of an agricultural market organization, but that (also) pursued perfectly legitimate objectives, such as national income policy[4] or national competition policy.[5] It would have been difficult to declare such measures incompatible with market organization rules. This is how I explain the change in the case law from the originally dogmatic to a much more flexible and nuanced approach.

Looking again at this case law concerning the common agricultural policy over the last 40 years, the least one can say is that it is complex, fairly casuistic, and, some might say, not always coherent. Nevertheless, essentially, three basic approaches can be distinguished:

[1] See M. Waelbroeck, 'The Emergent Doctrine of Community Pre-emption-Consent and Re-delegation', in T. Sandalow and E. Stein (eds.), *Courts and Free Markets, Perspectives From The United States And Europe*, Vol. II (Oxford: Clarendon Press, and New York: Oxford University Press, 1982), 548; K. Boskovits, *Le juge communautaire et l'articulation des compétences normatives entre la Communauté européenne et ses Etats membres* (Athens: N. Sakkoulas, and Brussels: Bruylant, 1999).

[2] Joined Cases 3, 4, and 6/76 *Kramer* [1976] ECR 741.

[3] Case 40/69 *Bollmann* [1970] ECR 69 para 4. See also Case 74/69 *Krohn* [1970] ECR 451 para 4.

[4] Joined Cases 36 and 71/80 *Irish Creamery* [1981] ECR 735.

[5] See for more recent judgments: Case C-137/00 *Milk Marque* [2003] ECR I-7975 and Case C-462/01 *Ulf Hammarsten* [2003] ECR I-781 para 29 with further references.

1. A strict approach which still echoes somewhat the early dogmatic approach of *Bollmann*:[6] where there exists an agricultural market organisation providing for the necessary Community competences, Member States must refrain from taking any unilateral measure, even if that measure is likely to support the common Community policy. It is for the Community, and not for a Member State to seek a solution to the problems at stake and exercise Community competences to that effect.[7] This comes quite close to accepting an exclusive Community competence albeit that the Court normally does not use that qualification, perhaps considering it too provocative.[8] Examples of this approach can also be found in more recent case law.[9]

A variation of this strict approach—which seems to me less intrusive for Member States' competences but also closely resembles a situation of exclusive Union competence—is the test of completeness or exhaustiveness: if on a specific subject matter an agricultural market organisation can be considered to have established a complete regime or to contain an exhaustive body of rules, Member States have no competence to take unilateral measures.[10]

This strict approach in both its emanations comes down to a rule of competence. The criteria used serve to draw the line between Union and national competences. Any unilateral national measure concerning an issue covered by Union competence is ultra vires, irrespective of its contents.

2. The second approach consists of applying not a rule of competence, but a rule of conflict. Member States are admitted some margin to take unilateral measures, also when they enter the field covered by a market organisation, but the Court exercises a close scrutiny. The scope of this rule of conflict is very widely drawn. A national measure is already considered to be in conflict with the regime of a market organisation whenever it jeopardizes the aims or functioning of the market organisation,[11] interferes with,[12] or hinders[13] that functioning. Another oft-used criterion is to establish whether the national measure is such as to undermine or to derogate from, or to create an exception to, the market organisation.[14] There exist

[6] *Bollmann* (n 3).

[7] E.g. Case 77/76 *Cucchi* [1977] ECR 987 paras 34 and 35; Case 216/84 *Commission v France* [1988] ECR 793 para 18; Case 407/85 *3 Glocken* [1988] ECR 4233 para 26; Case 76/86 *Commission v Germany* [1989] ECR 1021 para 19; Case 90/86 *Zoni* [1988] ECR 4285 para 26; Case 274/87 *Commission v Germany* [1989] ECR 229 para 21; Case C-86/89 *Italy v Commission* [1990] ECR I-3891 para 19.

[8] For an exception see *Cucchi* (n 7) para 34.

[9] Case C-113/00 *Spain v Commission* [2002] ECR I-7601 para 74; Case C-283/03 *Kuipers* [2005] ECR I-4255 para 49.

[10] E.g. Case 222/82 *Apple and Pear Development Council* [1983] ECR 4083 paras 23 and 24; Case 16/83 *Prantl* [1984] ECR 1299 paras 13 to 16; Case 218/85 *Le Campion* [1986] ECR 3513 paras 12, 13, 15, and 16; Case C-478/07 *Budvar* [2009] ECR I-7721 paras 114 and 129.

[11] E.g. Case 31/74 *Galli* [1975] ECR 47 paras 33 and 34; Case 65/75 *Tasca* [1976] ECR 291 para 6; Joined Cases 88 to 90/75 *Sadam* [1976] ECR 323 para 6; Case 223/78 *Grosoli* [1979] ECR 2621 para 7.

[12] *Irish Creamery* (n 4) para 15.

[13] E.g. *Apple and Pear Development Council* (n 10) para 12; Case C-507/99 *Denkavit* [2002] ECR I-169 para 32.

[14] E.g. *Ulf Hammarsten* (n 5) para 28, with further references; Case C-355/00 *Freskot* [2003] ECR I-5263 para 19.

quite a variety of formulations of this test, but they all express the intention of the Court to exercise a control that goes largely beyond the actual text and contents of the rules of a market organisation.

3. The third and final approach consists of applying the classic test of controlling the compatibility of the national measure with the text of the market organisation rules.[15] This also comes down to applying a rule of conflict, but in the more traditional sense.

It should be added that these three different approaches are sometimes applied in one and the same case.[16] That is not at all problematic if this concerns different elements of the national measure under consideration. However, it also happens that the first two approaches are combined such as to blur the important distinction between the two.[17]

Another sector of Union law in which the issue of the competence divide plays an important role in the case law is that of harmonization of law, more particularly also in the field of environmental law. Here, however, the situation is much more straightforward. Apart from the classic compatibility test, it is only—as far as I am aware—the test of completeness or exhaustiveness which is being applied by the Court.[18] For the Court to conclude a loss of power of Member States to act unilaterally, it is certainly not necessary to establish the exhaustive nature of the harmonization instrument as a whole or in its entirety. It often happens that this conclusion remains limited to only one or a combination of rules of the instrument.[19] It should be noted that there seems to be no equivalent in the case law on harmonization measures to the second approach followed in the field of agriculture.

What to conclude from this too brief and condensed overview of the case law on the issue of competences, which remained limited—I repeat—to the internal competences?

The obvious conclusion must be that there is no real general doctrine. The test most generally applied to delimit Union competences from national competences is that of completeness or exhaustiveness. However, in the field of agricultural policy, we have seen that this test is applied together, sometimes alternately, with others. Particularly in that field the Court has developed a number of different approaches and criteria within those approaches, from which it is able to choose, in

15 For an example see *Le Campion* (n 10) para 13 where the third approach is mentioned together with the two other approaches.

16 *Le Campion* (n 10); for examples of applying approaches 1 and 2 see *Apple and Pear Development Council* (n 10) paras 23 (approach 1), 12, and 31 (approach 2); Case 255/86 *Commission v Belgium* [1988] ECR 693; Case C-27/96 *Danisco Sugar* [1997] ECR 6653; *Spain v Commission* and *Kuipers* (both n 9).

17 See *Galli* (n 11) paras 31 (approach 1) and 29–30 (approach 2); *Spain v Commission* (n 9) paras 73 and 74; *Kuipers* (n 9): the reasoning starts with approach 2 in para 37, but later on the Court uses competence language in paras 41 and 49.

18 E.g. Case 148/78 *Ratti* [1979] ECR 1629, paras 26 and 27; Case 60/86 *Commission v UK* [1988] ECR 3921; Case C-169/89 *Gourmetterie Van den Burg* [1990] ECR I-2143; Case C-52/92 *Commission v Portugal* [1993] ECR I-2961; Case C-491/01 *British American Tobacco* [2002] ECR I-11453 paras 76 and 77.

19 See Case C-428/08 *Monsanto* [2010] ECR I-6765; Case C-47/09 *Commission v Italy* [2010] ECR I-12083; Case C-159/09 *Lidl* [2010] ECR I-11761; Case C-495/10 *Centre Hospitalier*, judgment of 21 December 2011, nyr.

order to judge a case according to its merits, and also—at least that is my impression—according to the margin of intervention it considers appropriate to be left to Member States. So, what we are seeing here is not a real doctrine, but much more a tool box making available various tools from which the Court chooses to solve a case as it deems fit.

II. What about Pre-emption?

Until now I have made no reference to the concept of pre-emption. Deliberately so. The Court has, as far as I know, never explicitly referred to it. However, pre-emption is discussed in legal doctrine, notably to compare Union law in this respect with the constitutional law of those Member States that are federations (German *Grundgesetz*), and more particularly to compare the case law of the ECJ with that of the US Supreme Court.[20]

Allow me to make just one, more conceptual, remark. I shall not enter here into the debate on how to define pre-emption (field-, obstacle-, rule- pre-emption).[21]

As far as EU law is concerned, it seems to me that the concept of pre-emption may be useful to distinguish with regard to shared competences between two, entirely different approaches:

1. The exercise of Union competence is considered to block the exercise of national competence. Member States may not at all act unilaterally anymore in the field in which, and to the extent to which, the Union has exercised its competence. Whether or not the national measure can be considered in conflict with Union rules, is completely irrelevant. Each national measure, whatever its contents, will be invalid.[22] This approach establishes a rule of competence; it solves a conflict of competences, not of norms. Here the notion of pre-emption seems useful.

2. In the second approach national competences as such remain unaffected. Member States may continue to exercise their competence in spite of the exercise of Union competences, provided that they respect Union rules. We have to do here with a rule, not of competence, per se, but of conflict. I do not think that applying to this approach the concept of pre-emption has any added value. Where a conflict of norms arises, applying the principle of primacy of Union law will be sufficient to solve it.

The difficulty in the first approach will be how to appreciate, and according to which criteria, the extent to which Union competences must be exercised so as to entail a blockage of national competences and, if so, how far that blockage

[20] See e.g. Waelbroeck (n 1); E.D. Cross, 'Pre-emption of Member State law in the European Economic Community: A framework for analysis' (1992) 29 *Common Market Law Review* 447; R. Schütze, 'Supremacy without pre-emption? The very slowly emergent doctrine of Community pre-emption' (2006) 43 *Common Market Law Review* 1023.

[21] See on that the articles of Cross and Schütze (n 20).

[22] See Case 216/86 *Antonini* [1987] ECR 2919 paras 9 and 10.

should go. The difficulty in the second approach is entirely different: it is to establish the existence and the scope of a conflict.

So far pre-emption.

III. And what about the Lisbon Treaty?

Will the Lisbon Treaty have any consequences for the approaches followed by the ECJ as just discussed? To answer that question we must first have a quick look at the new Treaties.

Let me start with a preliminary remark. When we discuss the scope of Union competences and their relationship to national competences, we should not forget that Union law may of course also affect—and sometimes considerably so—the exercise of national competences in areas in which the Union itself has not been conferred any legislative or regulatory competence. I refer to the consequences of negative integration, the fundamental freedoms, including that of free movement of the Union citizen. In this respect, the Lisbon Treaty brings forth an important innovation by introducing in Article 4(2) EU a fairly detailed definition of what the original, quite general provision of the Maastricht Treaty that the Union shall respect the national identities of its Member States has to imply. That identity has now been defined by a reference to Member States' 'fundamental structures, [both] political and constitutional'. Moreover, according to this Article the Union shall respect the essential functions of the state, including ensuring its territorial integrity, maintaining law and order, and safeguarding national security. This enumeration of state functions—which, incidentally, is not exhaustive—, together with the reference to the fundamental constitutional and political structures, indirectly defines the hard core of national sovereignty which the Union may not affect. This new provision—which contrary to its predecessor falls within the jurisdiction of the Court—reads as a sovereignty clause, a 'réserve de souveraineté nationale'. It applies horizontally, not only to the exercise by the Union of its own competences, but also to the possible impact of the prohibitions of negative integration on the exercise of national competences. The Court has already in its recent case law paid some attention to this new provision, but there is certainly more to come.[23] Union law is entering a new era here. I cannot go into this any further apart from one obvious question.[24]

Would the application of this Article be justiciable? I think it should. The definition is not exhaustive, I must admit. Moreover, it would be hard to imagine that the ECJ would determine what belongs to the fundamental constitutional

[23] Case C-208/09 *Sayn-Wittgenstein* [2010] ECR I-13693 para 92; Case C-391/09 *Runevic-Vardyn* [2011] ECR I-3787 para 86; Case C-202/11 *Anton Las*, judgment of 16 April 2013, nyr.

[24] Another question to be raised in this context is how to interpret the reference in art 53 of the EU Charter of Fundamental Rights to the Member States' constitutions. The *Melloni* judgment of 26 February 2013 in Case C-399/11, nyr., now tells us that this Article does not allow Member States to override obligations resulting from secondary EU law instruments by invoking national constitutional specificities of fundamental rights protection.

structures of a Member State. Nevertheless, the Article clearly conveys the message that Member States discretion to define their fundamental structures and state functions, which should be considered untouchable for Union action, is not unlimited. Still more importantly, the Article imposes an obligation upon the Union and its institutions, an obligation of Union law, which the Court by its very mission to ensure the respect of that law must abide by and enforce. The Court would at least have to define the outer limits of the scope of this 'réserve de souveraineté nationale', similarly to what it has always done when interpreting the public policy exception to the fundamental Treaty freedoms.[25] And here also, the proportionality principle might be helpful. In these respects in my view the Court should have the final say, a responsibility to be handled with the greatest care and wisdom, as well as in close cooperation with national supreme and constitutional courts.[26]

Clarifying the Union's competences, and delimiting more clearly their scope and relationship to Member States competences was of course one of the main subjects put forward in the Laeken Declaration and thoroughly debated during the Convention.[27] What became of all that is, apart from Articles 4 and 5 TEU, to be found in Title I of Part I of the TFEU 'Categories and Areas of Union Competence'. This Title defines three general categories of competences (exclusive, shared, and supporting, coordinating or supplementing) and allots areas of Union activity to these categories. For exclusive competences and supportive etc. competences these areas are exhaustively listed. For the category of shared competences the main areas are indicated, but this list is not exhaustive; logically so because this category is a rest category: Union competences in areas other than those indicated in the list of exclusive and that of supporting coordinating or supplementing competences are to be considered shared competences (Article 4(1) TFEU).

[25] See Case 41/74 *Van Duyn* [1974] ECR 1337 para 18; Case C-36/02 *Omega* [2004] ECR 9609 paras 30 *et seq*; Joined Cases C-316/07, C-358/07, C-359/07, C-360/07, C-409/07 and C-410/07 *Markus Stoss* [2010] ECR 8069 paras 76, 77, and 80, with further references.

[26] The *Runevic-Vardyn* judgment (n 23) paras 86 and 91–93, might be a promising precedent. The Court gives an autonomous interpretation as to the relevance in this case of art 4(2) EU and thus 'controls' the application of this Article, but it leaves the appreciation with regard to a fair balancing between the protection of the national values involved and the protection of private and family life to the national court. The more recent judgment in the case of *Anton Las* (n 23) goes an important step further: a national measure, which the Court accepts to be able to benefit from the protection of art 4(2) EU, is submitted to a full proportionality test, which that measure fails to satisfy. For a contrary view about who should have the final say, see A. von Bogdandy and S. Schill, 'Overcoming Absolute Primacy: Respect For National Identity under The Lisbon Treaty' (2011) 48 *Common Market Law Review* 1417. On the necessary cooperation between the highest national courts and the ECJ in order to accommodate the application of the primacy principle see my contribution 'Multilevel Judicial Co-operation' in P. Cardonnel, A. Rosas, and N. Wahl (eds.), *Constitutionalising the EU Judicial System: Essays in Honour of Pernilla Lindh* (Oxford and Portland, Or.: Hart, 2012).

[27] See, also for further references, P. Craig, 'Competence: clarity, conferral, containment and consideration' (2004) *European Law Review* 323; H. Bribosia, 'Subsidiarité et repartition des competences entre l'Union et ses Etats Membres', in G. Amato, H. Bribosia, and B. De Witte (eds.), *Genèse et Destinée de la Constitution Européenne Commentaire du Traité établissant une Consitution pour l'Europe à la lumière des travaux préparatoires et perspectives d'avenir* (Brussels: Bruylant, 2007), 389; J-C. Piris, *The Lisbon Treaty: A Legal and Political Analysis* (Cambridge and New York: Cambridge University Press, 2010), 74; L.S. Rossi, 'Does the Lisbon Treaty Provide a Clearer Separation of Competences between EU and Member States', in A. Biondi, P. Eeckhout, and S. Ripley (eds.), *EU Law After Lisbon* (Oxford: Oxford University Press, 2012), 85.

The most interesting category for our subject is that of shared competences. In cases of shared competence, Article 2(2) TFEU states: '[t]he Member States shall exercise their competence to the extent that the Union has not exercised its competence.' This is diplomatic drafting. The *a contrario* is much more interesting: Member States shall not exercise their competence to the extent that the Union has exercised its competence. That this is the real meaning follows also from the next sentence: '[t]he Member States shall again exercise their competence to the extent that the Union has decided to cease exercising its competence.' So they shall not do so before the Union has taken that decision.[28] Normally, such decision will be an implicit one, for instance by withdrawing existing legislation without replacing it with any new rules.

This characteristic of shared competences, that is the blocking of the exercise of national competence to the extent the Union exercises its competence, comes down to what I have earlier called a rule of competence. You could also say this is pre-emption. National competence is neutralized; it is frozen as long as the relevant Union rules remain in force. German lawyers would call this *Sperrwirkung*. Protocol No. 25, annexed to the Treaties, on the exercise of shared competences, clarifies that this blocking effect does not extend to the whole area to which the Union action relates, but only to the part of that area which has been (in my words) effectively occupied by that action. What this exactly means, leaves some margin of appreciation and will finally have to be determined by the Court in each particular case.

This rule of blocking effect, of pre-emption, is to be distinguished from the situation of an exclusive Union competence, where there exists no national competence at all. But it is also to be distinguished from a rule of conflict regulating a conflict between rules. It is much more intrusive. It is something of a paradox that this rule of pre-emption, which could be considered as a fairly radical application of the primacy principle, has survived the operation of stripping the Treaty texts of their constitutional elements after the failure of the Constitution, whereas the primacy principle itself was removed from the Treaty.

The drafters of the Treaty have left part of their work on this Title unfinished. A number of important Union policy areas have not been clearly allotted to one or the other of the three competence categories.[29] This concerns the areas of coordination of national economic and employment policies, partly also social policy, and those of common foreign and security policy and the progressive framing of a common defence policy. These areas are mentioned in Article 2(3) and (4), the first two areas of Union action to be referred to again in Article 5, together with the coordination of Member States' social policies (but see also Article 4(2)(b) TFEU). Apparently, Member States could not agree to include these areas explicitly in the list of shared competences. Nevertheless, these areas could seem to have to be brought into that category because of the rule of Article 4(1) TFEU according to

28 See also art 4(3) and (4) TFEU where a negative formulation is used: 'Member States being prevented from.'

29 See also on this question Rossi (n 27) 101 and 102.

which any area not included in the list of exclusive or that of supporting etc. competences must be considered a shared competence. Or should one interpret the separate mentioning of these areas in the said articles as meaning that they should not be considered as belonging to any of the three categories of competence?[30]

The real question in this regard is of whether the competence rule applying to shared competences (blocking of national competence) must be considered as applying also to these areas. I would not exclude that. It would be difficult to disregard the clear provision of Article 4(1) TFEU qualifying the category of shared competences as a rest category. Neither does this provision make an exception for these areas nor has the application of the blocking rule been excluded for these areas as has been done for the areas mentioned in Article 4(3) and (4) TFEU (research and development, development cooperation, humanitarian aid). In any event it would not be possible to allot these areas to the third category of supporting etc. competences because they do not figure in the exhaustive list set out in Article 6 TFEU. Consequently, the characteristics of this category (national competences cannot be superseded, no possibility to take harmonization measures) could not be said to apply to these areas. However, it should be added immediately that the practical consequence of these questions is not very important for the areas of employment policy and the coordination of social policies by virtue of Article 153(2)(a) TFEU. Indeed, the latter provision excludes any harmonization of national laws. So does Article 149 TFEU with regard to the harmonization of employment policies.

In passing, I might draw attention to the relationship between Articles 2(2) (blocking effect in case of exercise of shared competences) and 3(2) TFEU. According to the latter provision, external competences become exclusive in three particular situations, well-known from the case law, related to the exercise of internal competences amongst which the *ERTA* situation. So, no blocking effect but exclusivity. This raises the question of whether Article 2(2) TFEU is at all applicable to the exercise of non-exclusive external competences. There should be no doubt about that. But then it is interesting to note that only the exercise of internal competences may make an external competence exclusive, not the exercise of the external competence itself. The latter may only entail the blocking effect of Article 2(2) TFEU, which, as already mentioned, is not the same as exclusivity.

And now the final question: will the Court have to change its approaches with regard to issues of competences and the competence divide?

Let us first look at the question of whether the existing approaches followed in the case law with regard to shared competences could as such be considered compatible with the new rules. I think that they can. Both criteria used within the framework of what I have called the strict approach (Union competences and procedures have been provided, so they must be used excluding unilateral national

[30] Social policy partly figures explicitly on the list of shared competences. This would seem to concern more particularly the areas covered by arts 153(2)(b) and 157(3) TFEU. This differentiation in itself would seem to make it difficult to bring the other part referred to in art 5(3) within the category of shared competences as well.

measures; the criterion of completeness or exhaustiveness) could be regarded as referring to ways of exercising the Union's shared competence so as to block or to pre-empt the exercise of national competence within the meaning of Article 2(2) TFEU. The other two approaches remain in any event unaffected by the Lisbon rules. They concern rules of conflict that do not fall within the ambit of that provision.

So, the conclusion must be that nothing will change? I do not think so. As far as shared competences are concerned, the new rules bring an important change. In future cases raising issues of competence divide, the starting point will now be the blocking rule of Article 2(2) TFEU. One might expect the parties to focus their debate on that provision, and the Court will have to answer that by interpreting the provision. This might have two consequences. First, the Court might feel inclined when interpreting the blocking rule to develop a single criterion (for instance by giving precedence to the criterion of exhaustiveness) or by merging the two existing criteria into one (for instance by regarding the situation covered by the first criterion as an example of exhaustiveness). Another consequence might be that issues of competence divide will get more attention in the case law, and even that the case law might become stricter in this respect. All that is speculation. But I am not so sure that, as has been often said, the Lisbon rules on these issues are merely codifying existing case law and will not bring changes.

Final Remark

Questions of division of competences are, and will remain, on the agenda, also the political agenda.

I may finish with a comment in that regard on the euro crisis, or if you prefer, the sovereign debt, banking and fiscal crisis, more particularly with regard to the efforts of Member States to solve that crisis by concluding intergovernmental agreements, notably the one on a 'Fiscal Compact'. When I wrote this paper for the conference, the results of which are presented in this book, the negotiations on this 'Fiscal Compact' had not yet been concluded. The final agreement was signed on 2 March 2012 and has entered into force on 1 January 2013.[31] But the comment I made in my contribution for the conference is still valid, I think. Indeed, I was struck at the time by the fact that most, if not all of the points listed in the Statement of the Euro-zone summit of 9 December 2011 were either already covered by the so-called Six-pack legislation,[32] which entered into force a few days

[31] Strangely enough, the Agreement on the 'Fiscal Compact', officially titled 'Treaty on Stability, Coordination and Governance in the Economic and Monetary Union', has not been published in the Official Journal of the European Union but on the website of the Council.

[32] Council Directive 2011/85/EU on requirements for budgetary frameworks of the Member States; Council Reg (EU) 1177/amending Reg (EC) 1467/97 on speeding up and clarifying the implementation of the excessive deficit procedure, [2011] OJ L 306/41; Reg (EU) 1176/2011 on the prevention and correction of macroeconomic imbalances, [2011] OJ L 306/25; Reg (EU) 1175/2011 amending Council Reg (EC) 1466/97 on the strengthening of the surveillance of budgetary positions and the

later, or could have been dealt with by Union legislation using existing legal bases in the Treaty, or if opposed by one Member State or another, quite probably by enhanced cooperation. I really doubt whether a Treaty amendment as originally insisted upon by Germany and supported by France was legally necessary. In any event, in the hypothesis that Union action to enact the envisaged measures would be legally possible, is it acceptable that 25 Member States take that action outside the Treaty framework and do it the intergovernmental way? I have always thought that, if there exists a Union competence, that competence should be used, even when that competence is not of an exclusive nature.[33] It seems to be an anomaly to opt for an intergovernmental approach and still more so when trying to involve the EU institutions, the Commission, and even the Court, as has been the case with the Treaty on the 'Fiscal Compact'.

However, an anomaly is not necessarily an illegality, albeit that the line between the two will easily be crossed where Member States, when opting for an intergovernmental approach, at the same time try to involve and benefit from the institutions as they deem fit. It is true that the Court has gone some way in accepting this as far as the Commission is concerned in its *Bangladesh* case law[34] but there the agreement in question involved all Member States. In any event the EU legal and institutional system is a self-standing, composite whole, not a menu from which the Member States can pick and choose according to their *gusto*. To put it in more legal terms: the conferral principle together with the impossibility of modifying the Treaties otherwise than by following the amending procedures explicitly provided for in the EU Treaty precludes that. This is not to say that, in the particular case of the 'Fiscal Compact', the role attributed to the Commission and the Court of Justice must necessarily be regarded as incompatible with Union law. Indeed, the drafters of the Agreement have been careful to underline in its recitals that the role of the Commission comes within the framework of its already existing powers, whereas that of the Court has been based on the compromissory clause of Article 273 TFEU.

The Court, as far as I know, has never—apart from the case of an exclusive EU competence—condemned an intergovernmental action by Member States because there existed a Union competence to take that action. The closest to that might be the case law on agricultural market organizations requiring Union competences and procedures to be used.[35] But, as we have seen, the Court does not systematically follow that approach.

surveillance and coordination of economic policies, [2011] OJ L 306/12; Reg (EU) 1174/2011 on enforcement measures to correct excessive macroeconomic imbalances in the euro-area, [2011] OJ L 306/8; Reg (EU) 1173/2011 on the effective enforcement of budgetary surveillance in the euro-area, [2011] OJ L 306/1.

[33] C.W.A. Timmermans, 'Division Of External Powers between Community And Member States In The Field Of Harmonization Of National Law—A Case Study', in C.W.A. Timmermans and E.L.M. Völker (eds.), *Division of powers between the European Communities and their Member States in the field of external relations* (Deventer: Kluwer, 1981), 15.

[34] Joined Cases C-181/91 and C-248/91 *European Parliament v Council and Commission* (*Bangladesh*) [1993] ECR I-3685.

[35] See the case law referred to in nn 7 and 9.

One might also think of the now—because of Article 40 TEU—defunct case law on the relationship between the former pillars requiring the use of a Community competence where it existed instead of enacting the measure within the framework of the second or third pillar.[36]

Another reference in this context might be the negotiation clauses in secondary Union legislation providing for the conclusion of an international agreement with third countries, which render the external competence exclusive (see now Article 3(2) TFEU). However, the field of external relations poses special problems because the conclusion of international agreements by Member States will normally create obligations with regard to third countries that cannot easily be undone.

In the meantime the Court has rendered its judgment in the *Pringle* case, which sheds some more light on these issues.[37] The case concerns the Treaty on the European Stability Mechanism, not the Fiscal Compact, but some of the questions the Court had to answer are similar—or at least related—to the ones I have just raised.

First of all, the Court, confirming its *Bangladesh* case law,[38] has accepted the tasks and powers entrusted by the ESM Treaty to the European Commission, the European Central Bank, and the Court of Justice respectively, as compatible with EU law. As far as the Court is concerned, the compromissory clause of Article 273 TFEU was considered a sufficiently solid legal base. This augurs well for the lawfulness of the role conferred on the EU institutions by the 'Fiscal Compact'.

Mr Pringle had argued that the ESM would encroach upon EU competences on monetary and economic policy referred to in Part I of the TFEU. Therefore, the simplified procedure of Article 48(6) TEU, which procedure is only available to amend the provisions of Part III TFEU, could not be used to amend Article 136 TFEU so as to allow the Euro-zone Member States to establish the ESM. The Court rejected the argument, the ESM not being an instrument of monetary policy—an exclusive Union competence—but of economic policy. Even so, the ESM could not be regarded as affecting economic policy powers of the EU because the Treaties did not confer 'any specific power' on the Union to establish an ESM.[39] Competences not conferred upon the Union remaining according to Articles 4(1) and 5(2) TEU with the Member States, the ESM could not be considered affecting existing EU competences on economic policy.[40] The Court reiterated this reasoning when rejecting the argument that the Member States had lost the power to conclude the ESM Treaty, the EU having acquired an exclusive treaty-making power on the subject under Article 3(2) TFEU, the provision codifying the *ERTA* effect. It is first important to note that the Court interprets this Article as also prohibiting, when the conditions for its application are being fulfilled, the Member States from concluding an agreement amongst themselves.[41] However, no Union

[36] Case C-176/03 *Commission v Council* [2005] ECR I-7879, with further references; Case C-91/05 *Commission v Council (small arms)* [2008] ECR I-3651.

[37] Case C-370/12 *Thomas Pringle v Government of Ireland*, judgment of 27 November 2012, nyr.

[38] See n 34.

[39] *Pringle* (n 37) para 64.

[40] *Pringle* (n 37) para 68.

[41] *Pringle* (n 37) para 101.

rules could be considered to be affected or having their scope altered by the ESM. Moreover, so the Court added, the EU Treaties not conferring 'a specific power' on the Union to establish a permanent stability mechanism such as the ESM, the Member States were entitled, in the light of Articles 4(1) TEU and 5(2) TEU, to act in this area.[42]

This reasoning, more particularly as invoked by the Court to reject the argument with regard to the *ERTA* effect, is most interesting because it raises at least the question of whether the conclusion would have had to be different if the Treaties had conferred such a 'specific power' on the Union. One could indeed be inclined to read the judgment as implying that if the Union Treaties provide for a specific legal base, a specific power to regulate an issue, that power must be exercised barring the Member States from opting for an intergovernmental approach. If that reading were correct, *Pringle* would bring an important clarification to the debate on the competence divide. Of course, the precise meaning of the qualification *specific* power is not so clear and may be subject to further discussion in future cases. We know already that a possible exercise of the subsidiary competence of Article 352 TFEU does not qualify as a specific power.[43]

I cannot further explore these questions to which I wanted at least to draw some attention. Let me finish, however, with a proposition for discussion. That proposition is to consider as legally barred a collective action of all Member States outside the framework of the Treaties in a situation in which Union law provides for the necessary legal basis for such action and on a subject matter on which Union legislation already has been or is in the course of being developed.

If that proposition were to be accepted, would then the conclusion have to be different in case not all Member States would be prepared to act but enhanced cooperation could be a valid alternative because the entry conditions to such cooperation were or could be reasonably expected to be met?

[42] *Pringle* (n 37) para 105.

[43] *Pringle* (n 37) para 67.

8

EU Law and Retained Powers of Member States

Lena Boucon

Introduction

The present contribution intends to shed light on a neglected and somehow overlooked phenomenon that occurs in a substantial range of negative integration cases decided by the European Court of Justice, that is jurisdictional conflicts between European powers and the retained powers of Member States. This phenomenon, which is the outcome of the Court's interpretation of the fundamental freedoms[1] and EU citizenship,[2] consists of constitutional limitations imposed on the exercise of retained powers of Member States.

The European Court of Justice has developed several doctrines the effect of which is to circumscribe the scope of Member States' powers. These doctrines include, for instance, the implied power doctrine,[3] the extensive interpretation of the so-called 'flexibility clause',[4] and the broad interpretation of Article 114 TFEU.[5] The various legal contexts in which they have emerged deserve consideration. Indeed, the Court was called upon, in each case scenario, to assess the legality of EU secondary law or, in other words, to decide whether EU institutions breached the conferral principle by impinging upon Member States' powers when adopting secondary acts of legislation. Therefore, each of these doctrines raises what can be described as 'positive integration issues'.

[1] I.e. free movement of goods (art 34 TFEU), free movement of persons (workers: art 39 TFEU, establishment: art 49 TFEU), freedom to provide services (art 56 TFEU), and free movement of capital (art 63 TFEU).

[2] Art 21 TFEU.

[3] See e.g. Cases 281, 283–285, 287/85 *Germany v Commission* [1987] ECR 3203, in which the Court held that 'it must be emphasized that where an Article of the EEC Treaty...confers a specific task on the Commission it must be accepted, if that provision is not to be rendered wholly ineffective, that it confers on the Commission necessarily and per se the powers which are indispensable in order to carry out that task'.

[4] Art 352 TFEU.

[5] See e.g. C. Barnard, *The Substantive Law of the EU. The Four Freedoms*, 2nd edn (Oxford and New York: Oxford University Press, 2007), 567 *et seq.*

However, this chapter primarily focuses on the European Court of Justice *free movement cases*, i.e. cases in which it interprets EU primary law, whether the four fundamental freedoms or EU citizenship provisions. More precisely, it looks at a specific range of cases, which differ from several of the doctrines traditionally developed in negative integration cases. Most of these cases comprise analogous formulae, whereby the Court asserts that even though the field at issue falls within Member States' powers, the latter must nonetheless exercise such powers consistently with European law. It turns out that these cases involve several rather disparate fields: direct taxation,[6] personal status (such as nationality,[7] rules governing surnames,[8] the enforcement for the recovery of debts[9]), education,[10] social protection (social security,[11] compensation of civil war victims[12]), and the right to strike.[13] The main contention here is that the

[6] See e.g. Case C-446/03 *Marks and Spencer* [2005] ECR I-10837 para 29: 'although direct taxation falls within their competence, Member States must none the less exercise that competence consistently with Community law.'

[7] See e.g. Case C-135/08 *Rottmann* [2010] ECR I-1449 paras 39 and 41: '[i]t is to be borne in mind here that, according to established case-law, it is for each Member State, having due regard to Community law, to lay down the conditions for the acquisition and loss of nationality. ... Nevertheless, the fact that a matter falls within the competence of the Member States does not alter the fact that, in situations covered by European Union law, the national rules concerned must have due regard to the latter.'

[8] See e.g. Case C-148/02 *Garcia Avello* [2003] ECR I-11613 para 25: '[a]lthough, as Community law stands at present, the rules governing a person's surname are matters coming within the competence of the Member States, the latter must none the less, when exercising that competence, comply with Community law, in particular the Treaty provisions on the freedom of every citizen of the Union to move and reside in the territory of the Member States.'

[9] See e.g. Case C-224/02 *Pusa* [2004] ECR I-5763 para 22: '[E]nforcement for the recovery of debts falls as a rule within the competence of the Member States, it is none the less the case that that competence must be exercised in compliance with Community law and, in particular, the Treaty provisions on freedom to move and reside within the territory of the Member States, as conferred by Article 18 EC.'

[10] See e.g. Case C-76/05 *Schwarz* [2007] ECR I-6849 para 70: '[w]hilst Community law does not detract from the power of the Member States as regards, first, the content of education and the organization of education systems and their cultural and linguistic diversity (Article 149(1) EC) and, secondly, the content and organization of vocational training (Article 150(1) EC), the fact remains that, when exercising that power, Member States must comply with Community law, in particular the provisions on the freedom to provide services.'

[11] See e.g. Case C-157/99 *Geraets-Smits and Peerbooms* [2001] ECR I-5473 paras 44–46: 'Community law does not detract from the power of the Member States to organize their social security systems. In the absence of harmonization at Community level, it is therefore for the legislation of each Member State to determine, first, the conditions concerning the right or duty to be insured with a social security scheme and, second, the conditions for entitlement to benefits. Nevertheless, the Member States must comply with Community law when exercising that power.'

[12] See e.g. Case C-192/05 *Tas-Hagen* [2006] ECR I-10451 paras 21–22: '[i]n that regard, it is important to bear in mind that, as Community law now stands, a benefit such as that in issue in the main proceedings, which is intended to compensate war victims for physical or mental damage which they have suffered, falls within the competence of the Member States. However, Member States must exercise that competence in accordance with Community law, in particular with the Treaty provisions giving every citizen of the Union the right to move and reside freely within the territory of the Member States.'

[13] See e.g. Case C-438/05 *Viking Line* [2007] ECR I-10779 para 40: '[e]ven if, in the areas which fall outside the scope of the Community's competence, the Member States are still free, in principle, to lay down the conditions governing the existence and exercise of the rights in question, the fact remains that, when exercising that competence, the Member States must nevertheless comply with Community law.'

Court uses such line of reasoning to subject cases involving very heterogeneous fields to a specific legal framework.

Despite their disparity, the fields affected by the Court's distinctive approach share two defining common features. On the one hand, they fall within what can be termed the 'retained powers of Member States'. This specific category of national powers may be defined as follows.[14] They correspond to fields where, first of all, EU regulatory powers are non-existent, or in any case, very limited. Thus, the Treaty explicitly excludes nationality and the right to strike from EU powers.[15] It is, moreover, silent regarding the rules governing surnames, enforcement measures for the recovery of debts, and the compensation of civil war victims. According to the conferral principle,[16] this entails that these fields remain within the hands of the Member States. Things are slightly different as far as education and cross-border health care are concerned. Articles 165, 166, and 168 TFEU confer complementary and supplementary powers to the European Union. But these provisions also comprise clauses safeguarding Member States' powers, since they exclude harmonization at the EU level and stress that the content and organization of educational and health policies remain within the ambit of the Member States.[17] Mention must finally be made of the field of direct taxation. Here, although the Treaty does not formally exclude EU action, EU secondary acts of legislation are nonetheless quasi-inexistent. This is notably due to the fact that, in this field, the unanimity rule applies.[18] The latter therefore plays a role of 'constitutional constraint' by paralyzing most EU action. Secondly, retained powers of Member States may also be described as 'originally discretionary' in the sense that they were, at the outset, excluded from the scope of EU law. This means that, with respect to the European legal order, Member States were free to exercise such powers as they

[14] A threefold distinction relating to the notion of power needs to be kept in mind in order to identify the defining features of the notion of retained powers of Member States. It is indeed necessary to distinguish the concepts of allocation of powers, exercise of powers, and scope of a given power. While the allocation of powers refers to *who* exercises a power, the exercise of powers relates to *how* powers are to be exercised. The former allows drawing a distinction between *exclusive* powers (a given power remains with a unique holder) and *shared* powers (several actors may exercise the same power). The latter pertains to the rules that regulate the conditions of exercise. A power is deemed discretionary when it is exercised freely. Conversely, a power is considered restricted when its conditions of exercise are subjected to a specific set of rules. As for the scope, it refers to the area, or field, that the power-holder may regulate.

[15] Art 20(1) TFEU: 'Citizenship of the Union is hereby established. Every person holding the nationality of a Member State shall be a citizen of the Union. Citizenship of the Union shall be additional to and not replace national citizenship.' Art 153(5) TFEU: 'The provisions of this Article shall not apply to pay, the right of association, the right to strike or the right to impose lock-outs.'

[16] Art 5(2) TEU: 'Under the principle of conferral, the Union shall act only within the limits of the competences conferred upon it by the Member States in the Treaties to attain the objectives set out therein. Competences not conferred upon the Union in the Treaties remain with the Member States.'

[17] Art 165(1) TFEU provides that the EU must exercise its complementary power in the field of education 'while fully respecting the responsibility of the Member States for the content of teaching and the organization of education systems'. Art 168(7) TFEU provides that 'Union action shall respect the responsibilities of the Member States for the definition of their health policy and for the organization and delivery of health services and medical care'.

[18] Harmonization in the field of direct taxation is explicitly excluded from the scope of Art 114 TFEU. It must therefore be made pursuant to art 115 TFEU, which provides for the unanimity rule.

pleased. However, the various developments of the Court's case law are progressively altering this discretionary character, since they tend to restrict the regulatory freedom enjoyed by Member States.

On the other hand, the fields affected by the Court's original approach raise sensitive issues. In fact, they either relate to *national sovereignty* or to *welfare state functions*. Direct taxation is, for instance, a strong expression, if not the strongest, of national sovereignty. The same goes for personal status. As for the fields relating to social security, higher education, the compensation of war victims, and the right to strike, these are at the core of national welfare states and involve national key policy choices.

The purpose of the following sections is therefore twofold. First of all, they aim to demonstrate that the Court of Justice subjects the various fields under analysis to a specific legal framework, which differs from what usually prevails in negative integration cases. Secondly, they shed light on the different implications induced by the Court's original approach.

I. A Specific Legal Framework

At first glance, it might be argued that the Court's approach in cases involving the various fields under analysis does not differ fundamentally from the one prevailing in traditional cases. As a matter of fact, the Court bases its decisions upon the same legal provisions, namely the four fundamental freedoms and EU citizenship. In the same vein, it divides its rulings into the same steps of reasoning: applicability; assessment of the restrictive character of the national measure; and appraisal of justifications, which includes their admission as well as the assessment of necessity and proportionality. Accordingly, one might think that the Court simply applies its traditional doctrine to cases involving retained powers of Member States. However, a closer look reveals that they differ from the Court's traditional line of cases in several respects. The Court's departures pertain to two fundamental elements: the scope of EU law and the justification stage.

1. The broadening of the scope of EU law

The Court of Justice interprets the scope of EU law broadly in cases involving the various fields under analysis, and has also done so in many of its negative integration cases.[19] However, when faced with the fields analysed herein, it uses innovative strategies, which are generally absent from traditional negative integration cases. These strategies notably include the use of formulae and the dissociation between the scope of EU law and the scope of EU powers.

[19] It suffices to think, for instance, of the notion of 'worker' as regards the free movement of workers or of the concept of 'remuneration' as regards the freedom to provide services.

Regarding the former, the Court iteratively states the aforementioned formulae at the applicability stage. This shows that they serve a precise function: the Court uses them to support the application of European Union law. In this regard, it is noteworthy that the Court started to use these formulae as a means to counter Member States' or national courts' doubts as regards the applicability of European law. For instance, in *Schumacker*, the first case where the formula emerged in a consolidated form, the Advocate General pointed out that:

> [n]oting that direct taxation falls within the exclusive powers of the Member States, the national court expresses doubts as to the possibility of applying Article 48 to national legislation in this sphere. In particular it states that '... nowhere does the EEC Treaty confer express authority to harmonize the direct taxes of the Member States'.[20]

It is to these 'doubts' that the Court of Justice answered by stating the formula.[21] Consequently, it appears that the Court of Justice confers a function of *justification* to these formulae. Such a way of enshrining the applicability of European Union law is systematic. Even when Member States do not challenge the applicability of European law, the Court's rulings nonetheless contain the said formulae, hence their rhetorical dimension.

Another strategy developed by the Court to broaden the applicability of EU law lies in the process of dissociation between the scope of EU law and the scope of EU powers. The Court subjects Member States to EU law requirements even in areas where the European Union either lacks regulatory powers or has not exercised such powers. In this context, Member States, and sometimes even national courts, have often contested the applicability of EU law when measures taken in the exercise of the powers retained by Member States are involved. Their arguments are very similar in each case. They boil down to claiming that, since the EU has no regulatory power in a given field, EU law should not apply to measures taken in the exercise of the national powers existing in this field. In *Morgan & Bucher*, for instance, the Court was asked whether national measures regulating the awarding of study grants fell within the scope of the Treaty. Some Member States contended that:

> the European Union has no jurisdiction over study grants granted by the Member States. Since Community matters are not involved, the rights conferred by Article 18 EC are unconnected with the facts of the questions referred for a preliminary ruling and no reply should be given to the national court, because the cases of Mrs. Morgan and Ms Bucher may be resolved in accordance with German law.[22]

[20] Opinion under Case C-279/93 *Schumacker* [1995] ECR I-225 para 16.

[21] *Schumacker* (n 20) para 21. It is to be noted here that *Schumacker* is not the first direct taxation case. The Court had already decided six cases at that time (Case 270/83 *Commission v France* [1986] ECR 273; Case C-175/88 *Biehl* [1990] ECR I-1779; Case C-204/90 *Bachmann* [1992] ECR I-249; Case C-112/91 *Werner* [1993] ECR I-429; Case C-330/91 *Commerzbank* [1993] ECR I-4017; Case C-1/93 *Halliburton* [1994] ECR I-1137). However, in none of these cases was the argument based on the nature of Member States' retained powers raised. The same goes for the other areas at hand. As regards social rights, see e.g. *Viking Line* (n 13) para 39. See also, in the field of social security, Case C-120/95 *Decker and Kohll* [1997] ECR I-1831 para 20. See, in the field of education, Cases C-11 and 12/06 *Morgan & Bucher* [2007] ECR I-9161 para 79 of the Advocate General's Opinion.

[22] Opinion under *Morgan & Bucher* (n 21) para 79. See also, in the field of direct taxation, *Schumacker* (n 20) para 16, in the field of social security; *Decker and Kohll* (n 21) para 20, in the field

Therefore, according to the Member States, there should be a strict correlation between the applicability of EU law and the scope of EU powers. This argument is tantamount to claiming that each entity—i.e. the European Union and the Member States—should be supreme only within its own spheres of powers. On the one hand, EU law should trump national laws only within the spheres of EU powers. On the other hand, Member States should be supreme within the spheres of their exclusive powers, which means that the EU primacy principle should not apply to spheres where the Member States have exclusive jurisdiction. Interestingly, this standpoint coincides with the perspective embraced by the Court in its early education cases. In *Gravier*, for instance, the Court held that:

> although educational organization and policy are not as such included in the spheres which the Treaty has entrusted to the Community institutions, access to and participation in courses of instruction and apprenticeship, in particular vocational training, are not unconnected with Community law.[23]

To reach such a conclusion it based its ruling on Article 128 EEC,[24] which empowered the Community to act in the field of vocational training, and on the secondary acts of legislation taken in the exercise of this power.[25] It recognized the existence of two distinct spheres of powers. First of all, national retained powers—educational organization and policy—for which Member States enjoy complete freedom and which fall outside the reach of EU law. Secondly, a sphere that comprises European powers and that corresponds to the scope of application of EU law. In other words, the Court held that the applicability of EU law stemmed from the vocational training regulatory powers held by the Community. The same line of reasoning led the Court to exclude the applicability of EU law from measures regulating assistance to students:

> at the present stage of development of Community, law assistance given to students for maintenance and for training falls in principle outside the scope of the EEC Treaty for the purposes of Article 7. It is, on the one hand, a matter of educational policy, which is not as

of social rights; *Viking Line* (n 13) para 39; and in personal status cases the Opinion under *Tas-Hagen* (n 12) 28.

[23] Case 293/83 *Gravier* [1985] ECR 593 para 19.

[24] *Gravier* (n 23) para 21. In this respect, S. Prechal, S. de Vries, and H. van Eijken, 'The principle of attributed powers and the "scope of EU law"', in L.F.M. Besselink, F. Pennings, and S. Prechal (eds.), *The eclipse of the legality principle in the European Union* (Aalphen an den Rijn: Kluwer Law International, 2011), 213, note at 221: 'it does not matter whether the competence to regulate an area is used in the specific situation, or what kind of competence it is (even empowering Treaty provisions and provisions on the encouragement of certain policies are sufficient in this respect).'

[25] *Gravier* (n 23) paras 20 *et seq*: arts 7 and 12 of Council Reg 1612/68 on freedom of movement for workers within the Community, [1968] OJ L 257/2, Council Decision 63/266/EEC laying down principle for implementing a common vocational training policy capable of contributing to the harmonious development both of the national economies and of the common market, [1963–1964] OJ Spec Ed 25, the 'general guidelines' laid down by the Council in 1971 for drawing up a Community program on vocational training, the resolution of the Council and of the Ministers for Education, meeting within the Council of 13 December 1976 concerning measures to be taken to improve the preparation of young people for work and to facilitate their transition from education to working life, and the Council Resolution of 11 July 1983 concerning vocational training policies in the European Community in the 1980s.

such included in the spheres entrusted to the Community institutions and, on the other, a matter of social policy, which falls within the competence of the Member States in so far as it is not covered by specific provisions of the EEC Treaty.[26]

Here, again, the mere fact that assistance given to students fell within national retained powers constituted a sufficient ground for excluding the applicability of EU law. The Court subsequently reversed this ruling by using the same grounds of justification. In *Bidar*,[27] in fact, it referred to the introduction of two Treaty provisions, namely EU citizenship and Article 149 EC,[28] in order to establish a link between EU powers and the scope of EU law.

However, nowadays, the Court seems to have abandoned this approach. In this regard, *Morgan and Bucher* marked a significant turning point. For the first time, the Court did not refer to any Treaty provision to establish the applicability of EU law in the education field. It followed the Advocate General, according to whom 'the fact that the matter concerned is governed by Community law or serves the aims of the Community constitutes at most an additional factor in the appraisal of a particular case, not an imperative requirement for the application of Article 18 EC'.[29] Further, the Court replied to the Member States' contention that EU law was not applicable by stating the formula.

The Court follows the same approach in each of the fields discussed here, as noted by the Advocate General Kokott in the *Tas-Hagen* case, which concerned rules regulating the compensation of civil war victims:

Union citizens can assert their right to free movement even if the matter concerned or the benefit claimed is not governed by Community law.... [T]he classic fundamental freedoms apply also to matters in respect of which the Treaty grants the Community no powers or otherwise contains rules. *A fortiori* the scope of the fundamental freedoms cannot be restricted merely to matters in respect of which the Community has already exercised its powers, in particular by adopting harmonization measures.[30]

Therefore, the Court's case law shows that the scope of EU law is not conditional upon the existence of Treaty provisions empowering the European Union. There is thus a disconnection between the scope of EU law and the scope of EU powers, the former being broader than the latter.[31] AG Kokott made some very important points to justify this dissociation:

[t]he fact that [EU law] can produce its effects primarily in fields which are not (yet) harmonized is consistent with the spirit and purpose of the fundamental freedoms and precisely an expression of their direct applicability. To make the application of a fundamental freedom subject to the existence of a harmonizing measure would ultimately be to deprive it of direct effect.... [I]t would be equally inconsistent with the notion of Union citizenship as the fundamental status of all Union citizens, which they enjoy irrespective of any economic activity, if the Member States did not have to observe Union citizens' right to free

[26] Cases 39/86 *Lair* [1988] ECR 3161 para 15 and 197/86 *Brown* [1988] ECR 3205 para 18.
[27] Case C-209/03 *Bidar* [2005] ECR I-2119 para 42.
[28] *Bidar* (n 27) paras 39, 40, and 41.
[29] *Morgan & Bucher* (n 21) para 85.
[30] Opinion under *Tas-Hagen* (n 12) paras 33 and 35–36.
[31] See Prechal, de Vries, and van Eijken (n 24) 215.

movement in all areas but merely in individual matters in respect of which the Treaty grants the Community specific powers or other rules of Community law exist.[32]

According to AG Kokott, disconnecting the applicability of EU law from the scope of EU powers is necessary in order to preserve the direct effect of the fundamental freedom provisions. This is because it would negate the effectiveness of the latter if Member States were allowed to act unilaterally when exercising their retained powers.

In short, the Court faces a very sensitive dilemma. On the one hand, allowing Member States to act unilaterally within the spheres of their retained powers would jeopardize the effectiveness of EU law and therefore the exercise of European powers, as well as individual rights deriving from the fundamental freedoms and EU citizenship provisions. On the other hand, however, continuously extending the scope of EU law raises legitimacy issues. The Court's line of reasoning indeed results in a substantial extension of European legality.[33] Now, all matters can potentially fall within the scope of application of EU law. As summed up by Loïc Azoulai, '[t]his extension produces a legitimacy problem, and also, in practice, a *problem of boundaries*'.[34] Indeed, the broadening of the scope of EU law may have the effect of weakening Member States' autonomy by generating important intrusions into national spheres of jurisdiction.

2. A mutual adjustment resolution

Not only does the applicability stage differ from the Court's traditional approach when the fields analysed herein are involved, but the justification stage is also original in several respects. The Court resolves these jurisdictional disputes through the implementation of what can be described as a 'mutual adjustment resolution'. This specific judicial answer is twofold. On the one hand, the Court tends to adapt its own approach to the peculiarities of the cases involving the retained powers of

[32] Opinion under *Tas-Hagen* (n 12) paras 36 and 38.

[33] This phenomenon of constant extension of the scope of EU law has been considerably amplified since the introduction of EU citizenship, as shown by E. Spaventa, 'Seeing the wood despite the trees? On the scope of Union citizenship and its constitutional effects' (2008) 45 *Common Market Law Review* 13. See also L. Azoulai, 'The Court of Justice and the social market economy: The emergence of an ideal and the conditions for its realization' (2008) 45 *Common Market Law Review* 1335, at 1340: '[b]ecause the scope of application of Community law has constantly widened, there is virtually no area of economic and social life which escapes, in principle, the effect of the Treaty rules.'

[34] Azoulai (n 33) 1340. This author justifies the Court's case law as follows at 1341–2: 'it must be assumed that in conferring on the Community the competence to implement the objectives of integration, by the privileged means of the market freedoms, the Member States also agreed that the exercise of this Community competence should result in constraints on the pursuit of all national policies. It must be assumed moreover that the Court has legitimacy to identify such constraints.' For a more critical view see Prechal, de Vries, and van Eijken (n 24) 246: '[t]he principle of attributed powers is apparently unable to stop this expansion of EU law. Viewed from the perspective of the principle of legality, legality is leaking here. That is to say, the guarantees the principle aims at—division and separation of powers, regulation of and legitimating the exercise of public authority—are safeguarded in a rather loose and flexible legal context which is perceived by the Member States and, ultimately, by the individuals in the Member States, as facilitating an unpredictable and uncontrollable competence creep.'

Member States. When the exercise of the latter is at issue, it is indeed inclined to move towards a more flexible approach than in traditional negative integration cases. On the other hand, the Court imposes peculiar obligations upon Member States, which consist of placing limitations upon the discretionary exercise of retained powers.

a) The Court

The Court's rather flexible approach regarding the eight fields under analysis is shown through two factors. First of all, the Court accepts specific justifications with regard to their substance. These justifications differ in at least two respects from the justifications usually admitted in traditional cases. According to a well-enshrined principle, '[i]t is settled case law that *economic grounds* can never serve as justification for obstacles prohibited by the Treaty'.[35] The Court's stand on this issue is based on the underlying idea that

> [i]f Member States were able to rely on economic grounds...they could stop the free movement the moment its impact is felt. Allowing Member States to limit free trade for economic reason would defeat the objective of the EC Treaty to replace purely national markets with a more efficient European one.[36]

However, when the fields of direct taxation, social security, and education are at issue, the Court allows Member States to rely on economic aims to justify their measures. It indeed recognized the following justifications: the 'balanced allocation of the power to impose taxes between Member States',[37] the 'preservation of the cohesion of the tax system',[38] and the 'prevention of tax avoidance'[39] in direct taxation cases; the 'risk of seriously undermining the financial balance of the social security system'[40] in social security cases and 'ensuring that the grant of assistance to cover the maintenance costs of students from other Member States does not become an unreasonable burden which could have consequences for the overall level of assistance'[41] in education cases. The Court has even acknowledged that such justifications aim to protect economic interests:

> [i]t must be recalled that aims of a purely economic nature cannot justify a barrier to the fundamental principle of freedom to provide services....However, it cannot be excluded that the risk of seriously undermining the financial balance of the social security system may constitute an overriding reason in the general interest capable of justifying a barrier of that kind.[42]

[35] Case C-367/98 *Commission v Portugal* [2002] ECR I-4731 para 52, emphasis added.

[36] J. Snell, 'Economic aims as justification of restrictions on free movement', in A. Schrauwen (ed.), *The Rule of Reason: rethinking another classic of European legal doctrine* (Groningen: Europa Law, 2005), 37, at 48.

[37] *Marks and Spencer* (n 6).

[38] *Bachmann* (n 21).

[39] Case C-264/96 *Imperial Chemical Industries* [1998] ECR I-4695.

[40] *Geraets-Smits and Peerbooms* (n 11).

[41] *Bidar* (n 27).

[42] Case C-158/96 *Kohll* [1997] ECR I-1831 para 41. See also *Marks and Spencer* (n 6); Case C-414/06, *Lidl Belgium* [2008] ECR I-3601 paras 32 and 46; Case C-231/05 *OyAA* [2007] ECR I-6373 para 56.

Contrary to what prevails in traditional cases, the Court also recognizes justifications that primarily seek to preserve *purely national interests*. This is verified in all of the fields that are discussed in this article. So far, it has accepted, *inter alia*: the 'preservation of the cohesion of the tax system',[43] the 'maintenance of treatment capacity or medical competence on national territory essential for public health and even the survival of the population',[44] the granting of assistance 'only to students who have demonstrated a certain degree of integration into the society of that State',[45] the preservation of the 'constitutional identity' of a Member State,[46] and the 'right to take collective action for the protection of workers of the host state against possible social dumping'.[47] Thus, the Court acknowledges that Member States may protect interests that may not be 'Europeanized'. It accordingly gives them more leeway than it usually does, by allowing them to develop a wider range of arguments. In short, the justifications based on economic grounds and purely national interests embody the need to preserve, within the European Union legal order, the autonomy of Member States.

Secondly, the Court imposes adjustment requirements upon Member States at the proportionality stage, as expressly stated in the field of social security:

> the achievement of the fundamental freedoms guaranteed by the EC Treaty inevitably requires Member States to make some *adjustments* to their systems of social security.[48]

Here, the Court does not challenge the exclusive character of the national powers. It implicitly recognizes that Member States are the sole holders of the powers relating to the fields of direct taxation, social security, education, personal status, and social rights. It focuses only on the *exercise* of these powers. There is a sharp contrast with traditional cases where the Court's judicial review is such as to exclude certain matters from the ambit of Member States' powers. As Loïc Azoulai puts it,

> [i]n the areas of competences which are reserved to the Member States, the application of the market freedoms is not equivalent to a centralized action by the Community. It does not lead to a Community competence taking the place of national competences. Instead, the market freedoms offer the Member States criteria which allow them to evaluate all policies pursued in a wider context, the trans-national context.[49]

[43] *Bachmann* (n 21). [44] *Geraets-Smits and Peerbooms* (n 11). [45] *Bidar* (n 27).

[46] Case C-208/09 *Sayn Wittgenstein* [2010] ECR I-13693. In the field of personal status, the following justifications have also been accepted, e.g.: 'ensuring that all persons of a particular nationality are treated in the same way' (Case C-353/06 *Grunkin and Paul* [2008] ECR I-7639), the protection of 'the official language by imposing the rules which govern the spelling of that language' (Case C-391/09 *Vardyn and Wardyn* [2011] ECR I-3787), the 'wish to limit the obligation of solidarity with victims of war or repression solely to those who have a connection with the Polish people' (Case C-499/06 *Nerkowska* [2008] ECR I-3993), the 'wish to protect the special relationship of solidarity and good faith between it and its nationals and also the reciprocity of rights and duties' (*Rottmann* (n 7)).

[47] Case C-341/05 *Laval* [2007] ECR I-11767.

[48] Case C-490/09 *Commission v Luxembourg* [2011] ECR I-247 para 45, emphasis added. See also Case C-385/99 *Müller-Fauré and Van Riet* [2003] ECR I-4509 para 102 and Case C-372/04 *Watts* [2006] ECR I-4325 para 121. See more developments on the adjustment requirement issue in the following section.

[49] Azoulai (n 33) 1342.

All in all, it seems that the Court's approach moves towards greater flexibility. This is a logical consequence of the Court's strict assessment of the applicability and restriction stages. It is also the demonstration of its willingness to strike a balance between European and national interests. And since retained powers of Member States comprise highly sensitive interests, the Court gives more weight to national concerns than it usually does. As noted by Jukka Snell:

> in certain circumstances, the constitutional structure of the Union as a divided powers system may mandate a more permissive approach towards economic aims. Member States remain solely or primarily responsible for many important policy areas. Sometimes the only reasonable practical way of discharging these responsibilities involves the adoption of measures the immediate aim of which is economic but that ultimately serve as a means for pursuing a legitimate public interest aim.[50]

This statement can also be applied to justifications protecting purely national interests. In both cases, the justifications reflect the fundamental need to preserve the organization and/or functioning of a given policy area. Such preservation can often only be achieved through the maintaining of obstacles that aim to safeguard the level of national budgetary resources or purely national interests. By way of consequence, not only does the Court incorporate national retained powers into the European legal order; it also includes a new range of interests that are, at first glance, inconsistent with the free movement principle. It attempts to reconcile national arrangements, which are irreducibly linked to the territoriality principle, with the core non-discrimination doctrine, which, by essence, seeks to transcend national boundaries.

b) The Member States

As mentioned earlier, the Court imposes adjustment requirements upon Member States through the assessment of the necessary and proportionate characters of the national measures suspected of impinging upon the free movement principle or EU citizenship provisions. Four concrete examples illustrate the extent to which Member States must adapt the conditions of exercise of their retained powers.

It is, perhaps, in the field of cross-border health care that the ECJ is the most explicit.[51] Before the Court began to limit Member States' powers in social security matters,[52] patients seeking cross-border health care were required, in most countries, to obtain an authorization prior to receiving medical services abroad. The Court held that such authorizations, outside hospital settings, constituted unlawful restrictions to the freedom to provide services. As for care provided in a hospital environment, it decided that:

> in order for a prior administrative authorization scheme to be justified…, it must, in any event, be based on objective, non-discriminatory criteria which are known in advance, in such a way as to circumscribe the exercise of the national authorities' discretion, so that it is not used arbitrarily.…Such a prior administrative authorization scheme must likewise

[50] Snell (n 36) 49. [51] See n 55. [52] *Decker and Kohll* (n 21).

be based on a procedural system which is easily accessible and capable of ensuring that a request for authorization will be dealt with objectively and impartially within a reasonable time and refusals to grant authorization must also be capable of being challenged in judicial or quasi-judicial proceedings.[53]

This statement shows that the adjustment requirement imposed upon Member States is twofold. Member States must make substantial adaptations in order to comply with the non-discrimination principle. Furthermore, they must conform to procedural requirements, according to which patients must be enabled to challenge any administrative refusal to grant them an authorization.

The issue relating to the conditions under which Member States grant benefits is also an interesting illustration. Member States must confer the same benefits upon nationals and non-EU nationals or on residents and non-EU residents so long as non-nationals and/or non-residents fulfil the non-discriminatory conditions established by the national legal systems. In this regard, cases decided in the field of direct taxation show that Member States are gradually compelled to adjust their tax systems with respect to non-resident workers:

as far as the exercise of the powers of taxation so allocated is concerned, the Member States must comply with the Community rules, and, more particularly, respect the principle of national treatment of nationals of other Member States and of their own nationals who exercise the freedoms guaranteed by the Treaty.[54]

The Court has decided since *Biehl*[55] that the state of employment of non-residents must grant them the same tax benefits as residents, provided that they receive most of their income in this state.[56] In other words, states of employment must adapt their tax systems in such a way as to take into account the 'personal and family circumstances' of non-resident workers. They are nonetheless free to choose the means to implement such adjustments:

Community law does not lay down specific requirements with regard to the manner in which the state of residence must take account of the personal and family circumstances of a taxpayer who, during the year in question, has received income in that state and in another Member State. However, the conditions as to that taking into account must not constitute discrimination, either direct or indirect, on grounds of nationality, or an obstacle to the exercise of a fundamental freedom guaranteed by the Treaty.[57]

[53] *Geraets-Smits and Peerbooms* (n 11) 90.

[54] Case C-385/00, *De Groot* [2002] ECR I-11819 para 94.

[55] *Biehl* (n 21). In this case, unlike residents, non-residents employed in Luxembourg were not entitled to the repayment of overdeductions of income tax. The Court held at 16 that: '[a] national provision such as the one at issue is liable to infringe the principle of equal treatment in various situations. That is so in particular where no income arises during the year of assessment to the temporarily resident taxpayer in the country he has left or in which he has taken up residence. In such a situation, that taxpayer is treated less favorably than a resident taxpayer because he will lose the right to repayment of the overdeduction of tax which a resident taxpayer always enjoys.'

[56] See also, among others: *Schumacker* (n 20); Case C-87/99 *Zurstrassen* [2000] ECR I-3337; *De Groot* (n 54); Case C-169/03 *Wallentin* [2004] ECR I-6443; Case C-520/04 *Turpeinen* [2006] ECR I-10685; Case C-182/06 *Lakebrink* [2007] ECR I-6705; Case C-527/06 *Renneberg* [2008] ECR I-7735.

[57] Opinion under *De Groot* (n 54) para 72.

Similarly, in the field of education, the Court compels Member States to grant assistance to non-national students provided that the latter demonstrate 'a certain degree of integration into the society' of the host state.[58] It imposes requirements analogous to the field of social security:

[Member States] must accept that EU citizens, who have been lawfully resident within their territory for a relevant period of time, may equally be eligible for such assistance where they fulfill the objective conditions set for their own nationals. In this respect, they must ensure that the criteria and conditions for granting such assistance do not discriminate directly or indirectly between their own nationals and other EU citizens, that they are clear, suited to attaining the purpose of the assistance, are made known in advance and that the application is subject to judicial review.[59]

Cases decided on the granting of surnames provide another example of what adjustment requirements consist of. For instance, in *Garcia Avello*, a case in which Belgium refused to register children of dual nationality with the surname of both parents following the Spanish tradition, the Advocate General emphasized that

Belgium has a procedure whereby surnames can be changed if sufficiently serious grounds are present. The only point of which Belgian practice appears to conflict with Community law lies in the systematic refusal to consider a situation such as that of Mr. Garcia Avello and his children as constituting such grounds.[60]

The Court took a similar approach in *Grunkin and Paul*.[61] This decision concerned Germany's refusal to recognize a child's double-barrelled surname as determined and registered in Denmark, where he lived, because the child was a German national. The Court stressed that:

German law does not wholly preclude the possibility of conferring double-barreled surnames on children of German nationality. As the German government confirmed at the hearing, where one of the parents has the nationality of another State, the parents may choose to form the child's surname in accordance with the law of that State.[62]

Therefore, EU law does not oblige Member States to establish arrangements that do not already exist in their legal systems. It does, however, require them to extend the possibility to rely on existing mechanisms to non-nationals or non-residents.

This brief look at the Court's approach invites us to make several observations. First, it is notable that the Court of Justice implements the same judicial strategy in the various cases involving retained powers of Member States, which consist of compelling the latter to adapt the conditions of exercise of such powers. Member States are not precluded from exercising their powers, but rather they must exercise

[58] *Bidar* (n 27) para 57. [59] Opinion under *Bidar* (n 27) para 32.
[60] *Bidar* (n 27) 75. [61] *Grunkin and Paul* (n 46).
[62] *Grunkin and Paul* (n 46) para 37. See also the Opinion of the Advocate General in *Grunkin and Paul* (n 46) para 91: 'my approach would not require any major change to Germany's substantive or choice of law rules in the field of names, but would simply require them to allow greater scope for recognizing a prior choice of name validly made in accordance with the laws of another Member State. To that extent, it involves no more than an application of the principle of mutual recognition which underpins so much of Community law.'

them *differently*. Secondly, it is noteworthy that cases involving the retained powers of Member States all have the effect of restricting Member States' discretion and arbitrariness in fields where they have exclusive jurisdiction. Thirdly, the various cases relating to the fields analysed here reveal that the Court of Justice imposes three main types of adjustment requirements on Member States, often combined with one another. It has indeed compelled Member States to implement the principle of mutual recognition in, for instance, the fields relating to the recognition of nationality, and the rules governing surnames.[63] It has, moreover, imposed substantive requirements. In this respect, it is striking that one obligation in particular has been imposed in most of the aforementioned fields. The Court has indeed, on multiple occasions, compelled Member States to take into account the personal circumstances of individuals who exercise their rights derived both from the four freedoms, and from EU citizenship. The Court has finally imposed a range of requirements, this time of a procedural nature, in several of the fields under analysis, namely direct taxation, higher education, cross-border health care and the rules governing surnames. Such requirements consist of compelling Member States to enforce the principles of legal certainty and transparency. Their decisions must be based on clear criteria, known in advance and subject to judicial review. All in all, it appears that the three types of requirements share a defining feature. In cases involving retained powers of Member States, the Court of Justice goes beyond imposing negative obligations upon Member States; it also imposes *positive obligations*. Fourthly, it is worth mentioning that the intensity of the Court's assessment of the proportionality principle varies from context to context, which means that the obligations incumbent upon Member States may be more or less burdensome. For instance, the Court is reluctant to control national measures that involve substantive areas of nationality law.[64] However, at the other end of the spectrum, the Court takes a hard-line approach in nationality cases pertaining to the conditions of recognition of nationality, as well as cases concerning cross-border treatments outside hospital settings and not involving the use of major medical equipment. The same holds true for taxation cases relating to the free movement of workers. Between these two extremes, there are cases in which the Court allowed Member States to maintain restrictions, provided that certain conditions, laid down by the Court itself, are met. Thus, in the field of cross-border health care, Member States may require prior authorizations if their legislation complies with substantive requirements such

[63] See Case C-369/90 *Micheletti* [1992] ECR I-4239 (nationality); *Garcia Avello* (n 8), *Grunkin and Paul* (n 46) (rules governing surnames).

[64] See Case C-192/99 *Kaur* [2001] ECR I-1237. This decision involved issues pertaining to the attribution of nationality and the content of the rights related to it. Mrs Kaur was born in Kenya in 1949 and became thereby citizen of the UK and colonies. British law subsequently changed and she became a British Overseas citizen, a status that conferred on her no right to enter or remain in the UK. Accordingly, she could not exercise any right derived from EU law. She claimed that EU citizenship required the UK to fix the criteria for attribution and the content of nationality in such a way as to allow her to move and reside freely within the European Union. The Court relied entirely on a 1972 Declaration annexed to the Treaty of Accession of the United Kingdom in which the latter unilaterally defined the category of UK nationals falling within the scope of the EU Treaties (paras 23–27). In other words, the Court refused to put any limitation on the discretion enjoyed by the United Kingdom as regards the rules on acquisition of nationality.

as the taking into account of patients' personal circumstances and procedural requirements. Similarly, Member States may limit the granting of students' financial support to those who can demonstrate a certain degree of integration with their society. The same goes for the compensation of war victims, which might be reserved to those who share specific bonds with the Member State providing such benefits.[65]

3. Proposed explanatory framework

One might wonder, at this stage, why the Court endorses a distinctive approach when faced with national retained powers. Two reasons might explain this trend. First, the fields covered by the retained powers share common defining features despite their apparent heterogeneity. Secondly, the integration of these powers into the European legal order raises similar issues.

a) The common features of the fields under review

The fields under analysis are, from a substantial point of view, expressions of Member States' essential functions. Some of them indeed represent core expressions of national sovereignty. This is the case of direct taxation, for the survival of a state depends on its ability to levy taxes. The same goes for certain matters covered by the field of personal status. It suffices to think of the rules governing nationality, which relate to the states' ability to determine who is to become their citizens or, in other words, who is to be subject to a specific set of rights and duties. Similarly, the fields of social security, higher education, mechanisms relating to the compensation of war victims, and social rights are all key components of national welfare states, a notion which is itself intrinsically linked to the idea of national sovereignty, as underlined by Maurizio Ferrera,

> [t]he European nation state has typically become a *welfare state*; the social components of citizenship are no less important than its civil and political components; the right to decide about the forms and substance of social citizenship in its turn has come to be considered a crucial aspect of national sovereignty.[66]

As a consequence, the five fields at issue are reflections of national key policy choices. This explains why Member States regulate them in very different ways. As shown by the European Commission,[67] national tax systems vary greatly from one another: Member States implement disparate tax arrangements, rates, and tax bases. The rules governing surnames also show that Member States have made different policy choices, as Advocate General Jacobs underlined in his opinion in

[65] *Tas-Hagen* (n 12), *Nerkowska* (n 46), and Case C-221/07 *Zablocka* [2008] ECR I-9029.

[66] M. Ferrera, *The boundaries of welfare: European integration and the new spatial politics of social protection* (Oxford: Oxford University Press, 2005), 11. See also G. Esping-Andersen, 'After the golden age? Welfare state dilemmas in a global economy', in G. Esping-Andersen (ed.), *Welfare states in transition: National adaptations in global economies* (London and Thousand Oaks: SAGE Publications Ltd., 1996), 1.

[67] Report on *Taxation trends in the European Union*, Eurostat, Statistical book, 2012 edn, available at: <http://ec.europa.eu/taxation_customs/resources/documents/taxation/gen_info/economic_analysis/tax_structures/2012/report.pdf>.

Garcia Avello.[68] By way of illustration, in Belgium, a child bears only his father's surname, while in Spain a child bears a double surname (the first element of his father's surname and the first element of his mother's surname). The same goes for the fields of social security and education. On the one hand, national health care systems are all based on the principle of solidarity,[69] and '[f]rom this fundamental principle stems the role played by the state in the definition, organization, development and the control of the health care system'.[70] Broadly speaking, there exist two main types of health care systems in Europe: social insurance systems and national health care services. The former comprises reimbursement systems (e.g. Belgium, France, Luxembourg) and benefit-in-kind systems (e.g. Austria, Germany, and the Netherlands). It is based on the compulsory insurance of categories of persons. The latter group, a model which exists in the UK and Spain, is financed through public taxation and provides universal health coverage.[71] On the other hand, it is noteworthy that European educational systems share important common features: they are all based on the territoriality principle and are largely public in nature. They, moreover, pursue efficiency and social justice objectives.[72] But various educational systems nonetheless coexist within the European Union.[73] They differ in three main respects: structure and content of courses, organization, and funding. Thus, for instance, some Member States have opted for restricted access; others have opted for open access; while another range combines both procedures.[74] Public contributions to expenditure also vary. Consequently, the level of tuition fees differs substantially from one state to another.[75] Similarly, the conditions under which Member States provide financial support depend on national discretion.[76]

All in all, a fundamental feature is emerging: the existence of boundaries, which plays a crucial role for the coherence of all the aforementioned national policies. In this regard, Ferrera identified two types of boundaries: territorial and membership

[68] Opinion under *Garcia Avello* (n 8) paras 10 *et seq.*

[69] H. Lewalle, 'Systèmes de santé et intégration européenne', in P. Nihoul and A-C. Simon (eds.), *L'Europe et les soins de santé. Marché intérieur, sécurité sociale, concurrence* (Brussels: Larcier, 2005), 36.

[70] Lewalle (n 69) para 37: '[d]e ce principe fondamental découle le rôle de l'État dans la définition, l'organisation, le développement et le contrôle du système de santé.'

[71] See T. Hervey, 'The current legal framework on the right to seek health care abroad in the European Union' (2006–07) 9 *The Cambridge Yearbook of European Legal Studies* 261, at 267, Lewalle (n 69) 38–9, Ferrera (n 66) 124 *et seq.* Ferrera noted at 205: '[c]ompulsory insurance operates as a boundary because it "locks" entire segments of the population (or in certain cases the whole population) into redistributive schemes resting on the authority of the state, which impose obligations and confer entitlements on those who are "in" while rigorously keeping out all those who do not qualify, those who do not meet the requirements for admission.'

[72] A.P. Van der Mei, *Free movement of persons within the Community: cross-border access to public benefits* (Oxford and Portland, Or.: Hart, 2003), 337.

[73] For a historical perspective, see E. Hackl, 'Towards a European area of higher education. Change and convergence in European higher education', *EUI Working Papers RCS* 2001/09, 3–6.

[74] Education and Culture DG, *Key Data on Higher Education in Europe*, 2007 edn, available at: <http://eacea.ec.europa.eu/education/eurydice/documents/key_data_series/088EN.pdf>, 21 *et seq.*

[75] Education and Culture DG (n 74) 85 *et seq.*

[76] Education and Culture DG (n 74) 99 *et seq.* Financial support can take several forms (grants, reduced payments, etc.), it can be directly granted to students or to the students' parents, and its level greatly varies from one Member State to another.

ones. The first relate to the geographical territory, while the second pertain to the substantial conditions that must be fulfilled to be included into a national arrangement such as residence, nationality, age, and so forth. The same author used these two criteria to define the notion of welfare state:

> the welfare state is definitely a geographical space, with a recognizable territorial scope demarcated by administrative borders. But at the same time it is a membership space, or, more precisely, a bundle of membership space.... Seen in this light, the welfare state has always had a 'spatial politics', that is, conflicts on inclusion and exclusion rules and on the relative positioning of different social groups within the bundle of sharing arrangements.[77]

Even if the fields under review are not all direct expressions of welfare state functions, their internal coherence is nonetheless also primarily based on boundaries.[78] It suffices to think here of the area relating to direct taxation: the whole logic of national tax systems relies on the territoriality principle and on the definition of inclusion and exclusion rules.

b) The specific issues raised by retained powers of Member States

It is precisely in relation to boundaries that the European legal order becomes involved, insofar as it allows individuals to challenge the boundaries defined and imposed by the Member States. In this context, the Court is systematically faced with the same kind of claims when retained powers are involved. On the one hand, Member States argue against entry to or exit from their national arrangements, while individuals develop 'for entry' and 'for exit' arguments. These conflicts raise fundamental issues. Granting rights to enter into or rights to exit from the national arrangements taken in the exercise of retained powers is likely to have substantial implications for essential state functions. Therefore, more than in any other areas, the Court is asked to draw a balance between the preservation of European powers and the necessary protection of Member States' autonomy.[79] It must carry out the difficult task of ensuring that the same rights be applied within very different national contexts, which reflect national key policy choices.

Another element shows that the cases under review raise specific issues. They indeed share common conceptual foundations. This is verified by the fact that the formulae iteratively used by the Court have a common conceptual origin. It is true that their wording varies, depending on the field at stake. It is also true that they appeared at different periods of time: in 2007 in the areas of education and social rights,[80] in 2003 in cases relating to personal status,[81] and in 1998 in the field of social security.[82] The first 'consolidated' formula seems to have been used within the field of direct taxation, in the 1995 *Schumacker*[83] case. In this respect, a defining factor shows that these

[77] Ferrera (n 66) 6.

[78] See in this regard Ferrera (n 66) 20 who more generally notes that: '[i]t was through boundary-setting that European states and nations were built.'

[79] See art 4(2) EU according to which the European Union must respect essential state functions.

[80] *Morgan & Bucher* (n 21) and *Viking Line* (n 13).

[81] *Garcia Avello* (n 8).

[82] *Decker and Kohll* (n 21).

[83] *Schumacker* (n 20).

formulae have a common origin. Indeed, as they emerged, the Court reasoned by analogy by making cross-references to formulae from other areas. Thus, the Court of Justice referred, whether directly or indirectly, to the social security formula in *Garcia Avello*,[84] *Morgan & Bucher*,[85] and *Viking Line*.[86] In *Decker and Kohll*, there is a direct reference to *Schumacker*.[87] Accordingly, this shows that the Court has transferred, and adapted, the direct taxation formula to the four other fields under analysis.

The various cases show that the formulae are based upon strong conceptual foundations. In this respect, it is noteworthy that the formula used in *Schumacker*[88] contains a reference to another decision that forms part of the *Factortame* litigation.[89] Remembered more these days for its implications for the primacy principle, the powers of national courts, and the British parliamentary supremacy principle, the *Factortame* series, however, also has important implications for retained powers of Member States. Indeed, the Court held in *Commission v United Kingdom* that:

> as Community law stands at present, it is for the Member States to determine, in accordance with the general rules of international law, the conditions which must be fulfilled in order for a vessel to be registered in their registers and granted the right to fly their flag, but, in exercising that power, the Member States must comply with the rules of Community law.[90]

Thus, similarly to the fields of direct taxation, social security, personal status, education, and social rights, the Court distinguished, in this case, the existence of the power from the conditions of its exercise to justify the applicability of European Union law to an area—the registration of vessels—where the European Union (at the time the European Economic Community) had no jurisdiction. In this regard, it is worth examining the opinion of Advocate General Mischo, which strongly influenced the Court's rulings. The first steps of his reasoning consist of the drawing of a distinction between the existence and the exercise of Member States' powers.[91] What is very interesting here is *how* he established this distinction. Indeed, his argument is based on reasoning by analogy. He inferred that what applied in

[84] The *Garcia Avello* formula (n 8) para 25, refers to Cases C-336/94 *Dafeki* [1997] ECR I-6761 and C-135/99 *Elsen* [2000] ECR I-409. *Dafeki* concerned German provisions under which certificates of civil status are accorded different probative value, depending on whether they are German or foreign. At 16–20, the Court acknowledged that there were differences and variations between the national legal orders but nonetheless set limits on Member States, stating that the 'exercise of the rights arising from the freedom of movement of workers must be effective'. The *Elsen* case, at 33, comprised the social security formula and a direct reference to *Decker and Kohll* (n 21).

[85] *Morgan & Bucher* (n 21). The formula refers to the *Schwarz* formula (n 10), used at the justification stage, which itself refers to *Watts* (n 48), a social security case.

[86] *Viking Line* (n 13). The formula refers to the *Decker and Kohll* formula (n 21) and to direct taxation cases, which also comprise the formula.

[87] *Decker and Kohll* (n 21). [88] *Schumacker* (n 20).

[89] The facts in issue are well-known. They concerned several fishing companies, incorporated under the laws of the United Kingdom, most of whose directors and shareholders were Spanish nationals. The passage of the Merchant Shipping Act 1988 prevented them from reregistering their fishing vessels in the UK. This law was passed to combat 'quota hopping', i.e. the practice whereby fishing companies flew British flags to benefit from its fishing quotas but that lacked any genuine link with this country.

[90] Case C-246/89 *Commission v United Kingdom* [1991] ECR I-4585 para 15.

[91] *Commission v United Kingdom* (n 90) paras 5 and 6 respectively.

the field of monetary policy also held true for the registration of vessels. In the former field, the Court had long since ruled that 'the fact that Member States retain certain monetary powers does not entitle them to take unilateral measures prohibited by the Treaty'.[92] AG Mischo deduced that:

> [c]onsequently, without having to decide whether the right of registration is a retained power or whether the Community could legislate at any time in that field, it must be held that in exercising that competence the Member States must comply with the general rules of the Treaty.[93]

Accordingly, the principle according to which Member States cannot rely on the retained character of their powers to take unilateral measures, as expressed by the formulae, ultimately goes back to cases decided in the monetary policy field. In the Joined Cases 6 and 11/69 *Commission v France*, for instance, the Court was faced for the first time with the issue as to whether the nature of retained powers of Member States automatically legitimates possible encroachments upon European powers when the former are being exercised. The Court answered negatively by putting forward two main arguments. First, it held that admitting unilateral actions would negate European powers.[94] Secondly, it stated that this would be contrary to the principle of loyal cooperation.[95] In other words, the Court refused to recognize the existence of a 'nucleus of sovereignty that Member States c[ould] invoke, as such, against the Community'.[96]

Therefore, the formulae used in contemporary cases originate from the Court's conception of European integration and its continuous willingness to preserve European powers. They express the idea underlying the 1969 cases that the exercise of retained powers of Member States must comply with the Treaty requirements. In short, Member States cannot circumvent the obligations provided for in the Treaty and decide to act unilaterally, so long as the exercise of their retained powers is likely to jeopardize the integrity of European powers.

[92] Case 127/87 *Commission v Greece* [1988] ECR 3333 para 7, quoted in AG Mischo's Opinion para 7. See also Case 57/86 *Greece v Commission* [1988] ECR 2855 para 9: [a]s regards the argument that the repayment of interest is merely monetary in character, it is sufficient to point out that the Court has held... that the exercise by the Member States of the powers retained by them in the monetary field do not permit them unilaterally to adopt measures prohibited by the Treaty.'

[93] Case 6 and 11/69 *Commission v France* [1969] ECR 523 para 8.

[94] *Commission v France* (n 93) para 15: 'Articles 108(3) and 109(3) confer powers of authorization or intervention on the Community institutions which would be otiose if the Member States were free, on the pretext that their action related only to monetary policy, unilaterally to derogate from their obligations under the provisions of the Treaty and without being subject to control by the institutions.'

[95] *Commission v France* (n 93) para 16: 'the solidarity which is at the basis of these obligations as of the whole of the Community system in accordance with the undertaking provided for in Article 5 of the Treaty, is continued for the benefit of the states in the procedure for mutual assistance provided for in Article 108 where a Member State is seriously threatened with difficulties as regards its balance of payment.'

[96] Terms borrowed from K. Lenaerts, 'Constitutionalism and the Many Faces of Federalism' (1990) 38 *American Journal of Comparative Law* 205, at 220. See also, by the same author, *Le juge et la Constitution aux États-Unis d'Amérique et dans l'ordre juridique européen* (Brussels: Bruylant, 1988), 482 *et seq.*

II. Implications

The fact remains, however, that the Court's approach entails substantial implications. Such implications primarily concern the substance and extent of Member States' retained powers. They also pertain to the fundamental freedom provisions.

1. The substance of retained powers of Member States

Regarding, first, the implications for the substance of national retained powers—defined as encompassing the personal, territorial, and material scopes of such powers—, the purpose of this section is to demonstrate that the Court's original approach has the effect of reshaping national boundaries and redrawing the internal coherence of national policies.

a) The reshaping of boundaries

One of the main results of the Court's approach is the reshaping of national boundaries.[97] Subjecting the exercise of their retained powers to EU law requirements leads Member States to modify the original design of national boundaries in at least three different ways. They must, first, reshape the conditions of access to their national arrangements. This happens for instance in the areas of education and personal status. In the area of education, Austria and Belgium had to change the specific conditions of access they had set up for non-nationals.[98] In the area of personal status, specifically the rules governing surnames, Member States are required to give access to procedures to new categories of EU citizens. Secondly, host Member States are often compelled to amend the conditions in which they grant benefits so that a broader category of individuals can be included. Thus, in the case of the taxation of workers, they are compelled to grant the same tax advantages to non-resident workers as to residents. The same goes for financial assistance in the field of higher education. The last way in which the European legal order reshapes national boundaries is when Member States of origin must continue to grant benefits to their nationals when the latter have exercised their rights to free movement. Examples of this are when war victims have moved their residence to another Member State, or when students require from their state of origin financial assistance to study abroad. The case of social security is the most emblematic example of this trend: 'it is as if European patients are allowed to "sneak out" of their schemes of affiliation, without giving notice, and then re-enter them and "voice" for compensation.'[99]

[97] As defined above: see *supra* 77.

[98] Case C-147/03 *Commission v Austria* [2005] ECR I-5969, and Case C-73/08 *Bressol* [2010] ECR I-2735.

[99] M. Ferrera (n 66) 129. The same author adds at 130 that the ECJ rulings in the field of social security have 'not only severely restricted the discretion of national authorities in shaping their authorization policy, but also widened, [...], the range of (vocal) exit options beyond those envisaged by the 1971 coordination regime'.

These various examples show that Member States are gradually compelled to adapt the inclusion and exclusion rules which were set up to form the basis of the internal coherence of their various policies. Therefore, this ultimately leads to a *reconfiguration of both territorial and internal membership boundaries*. This reconfiguration consists of an extension of the scope of inclusion rules and, simultaneously, of a narrowing of the scope of exclusion rules. As regards national welfare state functions, Ferrera pointed out that: '[b]y challenging national boundaries and by redrawing these boundaries along different geographical, socio-economic, and institutional lines... European integration can undermine—and thus *destructure*—deep-seated social and political equilibriums.'[100] This statement can also be applied to the fields that do not directly pertain to welfare state functions, given the fact that their internal coherence is dependent upon the edification of boundaries.

b) The redrawing of the internal coherence of national policies

The interpretation of the fundamental freedoms also affects the internal coherence of national policies. Two examples illustrate this idea. First, the submission of the exercise of retained powers to EU law requirements results in the redrawing of the internal coherence of national social security systems. As regards social insurance systems, Member States have been forced to open national contracting arrangements to new health care providers.[101] This stems from the *Geraets-Smits and Peerbooms* and *Müller-Fauré and Van Riet* rulings.[102] The *Watts* ruling had an even greater impact upon national health care services. In this case, the Court decided that the freedom to provide services applied to the UK National Health Service (hereafter 'NHS'). It furthermore ruled that British patients could challenge the waiting list system. In the UK, however, the NHS enjoys a wide degree of discretion since the whole system is based on prior approvals[103] and on the setting of waiting lists.[104] In this regard, Jonathan Montgomery underlined that 'it could be said that there is almost no prospect for individuals to enforce rights to receive care under domestic law',[105] before adding that '[c]onsiderable state control is exercised over the scope of services that can be funded under the NHS'.[106] Therefore, the dynamic created by the Court in the field of health care fundamentally goes against the internal logic of both the NHS and the UK procedural system.[107] It allows

[100] Ferrera (n 66) 51. [101] Ferrera (n 66) 130.

[102] *Geraets-Smits and Peerbooms* (n 11) and *Müller-Fauré and Van Riet* (n 48).

[103] J. Montgomery, 'Impact of European Union law on English healthcare law', in E. Spaventa and M. Dougan (eds.), *Social Welfare and EU Law* (Oxford: Hart, 2005), 145, at 150.

[104] Opinion under *Watts* (n 48) para 7: '[u]nder the NHS system the type, location and timing of hospital treatment are determined on the basis of clinical priority and the availability of resources by the relevant NHS body, and not at the choice of the patient.... the NHS applies its finite resources by according priorities to different treatments and by having regard to individual cases. This results in waiting lists for less urgent treatment.... NHS bodies are free to determine the allocation and weighting of clinical priorities within national guidelines.'

[105] Montgomery (n 103) 147. [106] Montgomery (n 103) 149.

[107] Montgomery (n 103) 147: '[i]n the cases under English domestic law, the courts had consistently accepted that it was not their role to make judgments about how scarce budgets should be allocated, nor about clinical judgments on the appropriateness or urgency of particular treatments.'

patients to circumvent two core principles of the NHS: when they seek health care abroad, they can both choose their providers and challenge the waiting list system. In other words, EU law requires the UK to 'introduce fundamental changes into English healthcare law'.[108]

Another illustration drawn from cases dealing with access to education systems also shows that EU law may alter the internal coherence of national policies. As seen earlier, Member States may either decide to set up free or restricted access to higher education. Austria and Belgium have both opted for the first option. This means that any individual holding a secondary education diploma can have access to higher education. However, such liberal arrangements originally only concerned students holding Austrian or Belgian diplomas. Other students had to fulfil additional conditions. In this context, non-holders of Austrian or Belgian diplomas respectively claimed that these measures were contrary to Article 12 EC and Article 18 EC. In both cases, the Court found that the additional conditions imposed on non-residents amounted to indirect discrimination.[109] Austria and Belgium developed interesting arguments to justify their domestic arrangements. The former relied on the safeguarding of the homogeneity of the Austrian higher or university education system[110] and on the prevention of abuse of Community law.[111] The latter claimed that if non-residents could freely access its education system, this would create excessive burdens on the financing of higher education,[112] and would jeopardize the protection of the homogeneity of the higher education system[113] and of public health, with a risk of a significant reduction in the quality of teaching in the medical and paramedical courses and of a shortage of qualified medical personnel throughout the territory.[114] Austria and Belgium were faced with the same issues, as summed up by their respective governments:

> [u]nrestricted access would create the risk of the more liberal Austrian system being flooded by applications from students not admitted to higher education in more restrictive Member States. That influx would entail serious financial, structural and staffing problems and pose a risk to the financial equilibrium of the Austrian education system and, consequently, to its very existence.[115]
>
> Concern has been expressed that, having regard to the budgetary, human and material resources available to the teaching institutions concerned, this is jeopardizing the quality of teaching—and, because of the nature of the programs at issue [courses in the medical and paramedical fields], public health.[116]

See also C. Newdick, 'The ECJ, transnational health care, and social citizenship. Accidental death of a concept?' (2009) 26 *Wisconsin International Law Journal* 845, and 'Citizenship, free movement and health care: Cementing individual rights by corroding social solidarity' (2006) 43 *Common Market Law Review* 1645.

108 Montgomery (n 103) 155.
109 *Commission v Austria* (n 98) para 47 and *Bressol* (n 98) para 47.
110 *Commission v Austria* (n 98) paras 60 *et seq*.
111 *Commission v Austria* (n 98) paras 69 *et seq*.
112 *Bressol* (n 98) paras 50 *et seq*.
113 *Bressol* (n 98) paras 53 *et seq*.
114 *Bressol* (n 98) paras 56 *et seq*.
115 Opinion under *Commission v Austria* (n 98) para 26.
116 Opinion under *Bressol* (n 98) para 19.

The Court followed a strict approach in the case of Austria. It stressed that access to higher education 'constitutes the very essence of the principle of freedom of movement for students guaranteed by the Treaty'[117] and ultimately rejected all of Austria's contentions.[118] It was, however, more cautious in *Bressol*, since it did not expressly reject the justifications. Rather, it referred for the most part to the national court.[119] Nonetheless, these two cases undoubtedly show that EU law can have important implications for the internal logic governing the rules of access to higher education. In the case of Austria, for instance, the Advocate General mentioned two less restrictive measures: the establishment of an entry examination or the controlling of the correspondence of foreign qualifications with those required from holders of Austrian diplomas,[120] and expressly admitted that: '[c]learly the adoption of these less discriminatory measures would require change to the current system of unrestricted public access'.[121] If Member States theoretically remain free to opt for unrestricted or restricted access, they must in any event comply with EU law. And, as noted by the Advocate General in *Bressol*, if they favour unlimited access, 'they must however be prepared to offer unlimited free access for all students regardless of nationality.'[122] This shows that Member States may be compelled to significantly alter the philosophy of access to their education system. Indeed, offering unlimited access to all students is very likely to lead to further additional costs in order to safeguard the quality of the education systems. And, if they decide to implement restricted access in order to safeguard the financial balance of their education system, they will thus have to relinquish one crucial principle, namely the principle of ensuring broad and democratic access to the education system.[123]

These developments have therefore shown that the adjustment requirements imposed on Member States have significant implications, both for the exercise of national retained powers, and for their substance. In addition, the gradual inclusion of this specific category of powers into the European legal order also has notable effects on the interpretation of the fundamental freedom provisions.

[117] *Commission v Austria* (n 98) para 70.

[118] One of the decisive factors that might have influenced the Court resides in the fact that 'no estimates relating to other courses have been submitted to the Court... the Republic of Austria has conceded that it does not have any figures in that connection. Moreover, the Austrian authorities have accepted that the national legislation in question is essentially preventive in nature' (para 65).

[119] *Bressol* (n 98) paras 66, 70, 76, 78, 80. But several authors have noted that the Court strictly guided the national court and developed a strict proportionality control. See S. Garben, 'Case C-73/08, *Nicolas Bressol and Others, Céline Chaverot and Others v Gouvernement de la Communauté française*, Judgment of the Court of Justice (Grand Chamber) of 13 April 2010' (2010) 47 *Common Market Law Review* 1493, S. Grosbon, 'Libre circulation et systèmes de sélection universitaire: une équation complexe' (2009-10) *Revue des Affaires Européennes* 635–41.

[120] Opinion under *Commission v Austria* (n 98) para 52.

[121] *Commission v Austria* (n 98) para 53. Similarly, at 108, the Advocate General in *Bressol* argued that '[i]t seems to me very possible that implementing less discriminatory measures may mean abandoning the current system of unrestricted public access to higher education for all Belgians.'

[122] Opinion under *Bressol* (n 98) para 106. [123] Grosbon (n 119) 640.

2. The fundamental freedom provisions

The fundamental freedom provisions are of crucial importance for European integration. They constitute concrete expressions of the free movement principle and therefore form the pillar of the internal market, the establishment and functioning of which was historically the primary goal of the European Union.[124] On that account, they are usually seen as economic freedoms, from which corresponding economic rights derive: '[t]he Court of Justice... by interpreting the Treaty's free movement provisions as particular applications of the principle of nondiscrimination on grounds of nationality..., has purposefully linked fundamental freedoms of movement with fundamental and justiciable economic rights arising under Community law.'[125] Pierre Pescatore also noted in this regard that '[b]asic to these diverse forms of freedom is a philosophy that is inspired by a regard for private initiative and the free development of the human person as far as economic and professional activities are concerned'.[126]

However, cases involving retained powers of Member States confirm a substantial shift in the interpretation of the four freedoms. The Court, indeed, does not exclusively rely on their economic dimension to assess the restrictive character of national measures taken in the exercise of retained powers. This is verified by the nature of the individual rights arising from the Court's case law. Thus, for instance, one of the main outcomes of cases relating to social security is the creation of trans-border patients' rights. Such rights are first and foremost social in nature. They apply to any patient seeking cross-border health care, irrespective of whether they are economically active. The same holds true, to a certain extent, for direct taxation. Recognizing new tax rights certainly amounts to providing non-resident taxpayers with tax burden reductions, i.e. economic benefits. But such rights also contain a social dimension, in the sense that they allow non-resident individuals to benefit from the solidarity of their state of employment, and a certain degree of integration in the host society. The *Schwarz*[127] ruling constitutes an even more appealing illustration of this tendency. This case concerned a German tax rule according to which payments of school fees to certain schools located in the German territory, but not payments to schools located in other Member States, could be treated as special expenditure leading to a reduction of income tax. The Court successively examined whether the national measure was compatible with the freedom to provide services and EU citizenship. In this regard, it is striking that it came up with very similar interpretations of the two provisions. In particular, it looked at the German rule in light of the same ranges of justifications[128] and reached identical conclusions.

[124] See art 26(1) and (2) TFEU.

[125] C.A. Ball, 'The making of a transnational capitalist society: The Court of Justice, social policy and individual rights under the European Community's legal order' (1996) 37 *Harvard International Law Review* 307, at 339. For a critique of the traditional Court's approach see e.g. J. Coppel and A. O'Neill, 'The European Court of Justice: Taking rights seriously?' (1992) 29 *Common Market Law Review* 669.

[126] P. Pescatore, 'Fundamental rights and freedoms in the system of European Communities' (1970) 18 *American Journal of Comparative Law* 343, at 349.

[127] *Schwarz* (n 10).

[128] *Schwarz* (n 10) paras 95 and 96.

Accordingly, this case corroborates the idea that a freedom that was originally purely economic and EU citizenship may now both protect rights of an analogous nature, in this case the right to seek education abroad. Therefore, in cases involving national retained powers, the Court does not intrinsically link the fundamental freedoms to the economic objectives of the Treaty. Rather, it construes the fundamental freedom provisions in such a way as to recognize rights of a social nature.[129] In other words, cases involving retained powers of Member States are the sign of the gradual *objectification* of the fundamental freedoms provisions. They must be understood as aiming to enshrine the free movement principle viewed as a neutral, i.e. not necessarily economic—right conferred on European nationals.

Conclusion

The present contribution has shown that the Court takes a distinctive approach when retained powers of Member States are involved in negative integration cases. And such an approach has defining implications. First, it tends to give more leeway to Member States at the justification stage, by allowing them to rely on a wider range of grounds of justification. Secondly, however, the fact remains that it gives rise to intrusions into national spheres of powers. The Court compels the Member States to adapt, and even redefine, national policies that are core expressions of national sovereignty and/or welfare state functions. It therefore limits Member States' autonomy even in fields where the European Union has no regulatory powers. Thirdly, this original approach also has important implications for EU constitutional law. It confirms that the scope of EU law must be distinguished from the scope of EU powers, the former being broader than the latter. It moreover validates the idea that the free movement principle can no longer be seen as a purely economic principle. The Court, on the contrary, seems to interpret the four traditional freedoms, and particularly the free movement of persons and the freedom to provide services, in a way that is increasingly similar to the interpretation of EU citizenship provisions.

These various elements ultimately invite us to reconsider the usual perspective used to analyse negative integration cases. Such a perspective traditionally distinguishes negative integration cases depending on the freedom at issue. Another angle can, however, be used as a starting point of the analysis. Instead of focusing exclusively on the freedoms, the *nature of the national powers* involved seems to be a relevant criterion for drawing distinctions between different categories of negative integration cases. The shared or retained character of national powers seems indeed to be the primary source of variations in the Court's approach.

[129] It is to be noted that this trend is not exclusively developed in cases involving retained powers of Member States. It notably emerged in the context of free movement of persons. See Ball (n 125) 352 *et seq.* See also N.N. Shuibhne, 'The Outer Limits of EU Citizenship: Displacing Economic Free Movement Rights?', in C. Barnard and O. Odudu (eds.), *The Outer Limits of European Union Law* (Oxford and Portland, Or.: Hart Publishing, 2009), 167.

9

The Protection of Fundamental Rights and the Allocation of Competences in the EU: A Clash of Constitutional Logics

Edouard Dubout

Introduction

Is it possible that the European Union has gone from an 'insufficient' protection of fundamental rights to a position where it does 'too much'? It is useful to analyse how and why—in a relatively short period of time—the objective of fundamental rights protection attributed to the European Union has become a threat to the basic principle of conferral of competences. This is not a new phenomenon, but it creates an expansion of EU law, which in turns engenders feelings of uncertainty.

The protection of fundamental rights is among the objectives pursued by the European Union and the values upon which it is based (Article 2 TEU). This assertion is no longer contested. Yet, it is also known that the European Union is not competent, or in any event has only little competence, in the matter of fundamental rights protection.[1] If the competence cannot be conceived of without the objective, the objective itself provides the competence in this instance. The phenomenon is both banal and singular.

One can detect a genetic form of inconsistency, a manifestation of the ambivalent attitude of the Member States towards the organization that they have created and that they will continue to shape via Treaty revisions. This contradiction consists of projecting upon the Union their most ambitious aims and ideals without giving the Union sufficient capacity to achieve them. This schizophrenic attitude includes assigning to the Union the objective of protecting fundamental rights without allocating the corresponding competence to ensure such protection. An attempt to explain this discrepancy would argue that EU primary law, through the unbridled use of objectives, cedes to a more profound phenomenon, namely the *finalization of the* law. In contemporary Western legal systems legal standards are

[1] Opinion 2/94 *Accession by the Communities to the European Convention on Human Rights* [1996] ECR I-1759.

assigned ever wider—and often vague—aims, without the realization of such aims being properly guaranteed. The objectives thus embody the 'imaginary' of the legal system. This entails the risk of some loss of normativity, a risk of dilution of the dividing-line between law and policy.[2]

Behind its seeming banality, yet this phenomenon signals essential changes in the legal system of the European Union. The objective of protecting fundamental rights gives the Union the opportunity to be thought of, and to think of itself, as 'something else' (better, something more) than a sum of originally national powers exercised in common: namely, a societal project to be constructed, which needs to go beyond the strict limits of its own competences and organizational capacities. Through the protection and reconciliation of the various values that it prescribes and upholds, the Union is able to participate in the definition of a consensus around the values that are at the core of our putative European society. Ultimately, the development of the objective of fundamental rights protection represents a means of transition towards a more 'complete' integration of the peoples of Europe.

Though gradually integrated into the objectives of the European Union, the objective of protection of fundamental rights has transcended its own remit. It allows the EU to apply its fundamental rights in an increasing number of situations, even if such situations are outside the scope of its competences. It is possible to identify three main phases in this process. The first phase deals with the decisions in *Stauder* and *Internationale Handelsgesellschaft*, which first established that the acts of the institutions and bodies of the Union must respect fundamental rights.[3] The second phase includes the *Wachauf* and *ERT* judgments, which extended the fundamental rights jurisdiction of the ECJ also to national measures that implement Union law or derogate from this latter.[4] The third phase, which is still ongoing, is represented by the *Kücükdeveci* and *Ruiz Zambrano* judgments, which expanded the reach of EU fundamental rights to situations far beyond the previous sphere.[5] For the moment, it is difficult to detect any consistency in this latest phase. One of the reasons for this is that in the *Ruiz Zambrano* judgment the protection of fundamental rights is only indirect, as the Court decided the case by relying on European citizenship.

This brief overview suggests that the control on respect for fundamental rights by the Court of Justice has played (and still plays) a crucial role in defining the respective powers of the Union and its Member States. In particular, the control of the protection of fundamental rights by the ECJ has been accomplished by relying on the nebulous 'scope of Community law' formula (which has subsequently

[2] J. Caillosse, 'Les rapports de la politique et du droit dans la formulation d'"objectifs"', in B. Faure (ed.), *Les objectifs dans le droit* (Paris: Dalloz, 2010), 13.

[3] Case 29-69 *Stauder* [1969] ECR 419, and Case 11-70 *Internationale Handelsgesellschaft* [1970] ECR 1125.

[4] Case 5/88 *Wachauf* [1989] ECR 2609, and Case C-260/89 *ERT* ECR I-2925.

[5] Case C-555/07 *Kücükdeveci* [2010] ECR I-365, and Case C-34/09 *Ruiz Zambrano* [2011] ECR I-1177.

shifted to 'scope of European Union law'), established in the *ERT* judgment. According to this formula

> where national rules do fall within the scope of Community law, and reference is made to the Court for a preliminary ruling, it must provide all the criteria of interpretation needed by the national court to determine whether those rules are compatible with the fundamental rights the observance of which the Court ensures.[6]

Such statement has allowed for the review of the compatibility with EU fundamental rights and also of national measures adopted by the Member States in the exercise of exclusive competences or retained powers—that is powers that the Union has not yet exercised—, or in any event falling within areas in which the Union has only limited powers. It is therefore not a case of dereliction of the allocation of competences in the classical sense, but rather a certain (deliberate) ignorance of the distribution of powers in matters interfering with issues related to the protection of EU fundamental rights. The European Union intends to impose a standard of protection of fundamental rights that goes beyond the capacity for action conferred on the Union by the founding treaties.

How to justify this? Let us note at this point that the nature of the rules in question—'fundamental' rights—is probably not unrelated to it. While it is possible to define the fundamental nature of the norms in different ways and via different criteria, it remains the case that the special standards of protection applied to fundamental rights are explained primarily by the function that they perform within a legal system. These are standards that make it possible to achieve concord between validity and legitimacy in a legal system, thereby contributing to that system's effectiveness and sustainability. These standards respond directly to the aspirations of their recipients, namely the population. In national law, this particular characteristic of human rights causes a horizontal displacement of the normative power of the legislative and executive authorities, ultimately towards the judicial authorities, entrusted with the task of interpreting and determining the scope of such rights. In EU law, the unique nature of human rights also produces disruptions, not only horizontally in the relationship between the legislature and the Courts of the Union, but also vertically, in the relationship between the Union and its Member States.[7] The general idea is that EU law creates new situations that lie beyond the scope of the European competences and are subject to a *European* standard of protection.

As a result, the national authorities are required to comply with EU fundamental rights, even in cases when the European Union has, in principle, no competence to intervene in the area or situation in question. This expansion is a source of 'constitutional uncertainty' because it goes beyond the will of the Member States.[8]

[6] *ERT* (n 4), esp para 42.

[7] K. Lenaerts and J-A. Gutiérrez-Fons, 'The Constitutional Allocation of Powers and General Principles of EU Law' (2010) 47 *Common Market Law Review* 1629; A. Knook, 'The Court, the Charter, and the Vertical Division of Powers in the European Union' (2005) 42 *Common Market Law Review* 367.

[8] N. Shuibhne, 'The Constitutional Uncertainty of EU Law' (2010) 29 *Yearbook of European Law* 496.

The balance struck between the requirements of fundamental rights protection and respect for the competences of the various authorities represents another manifestation of the current state of the European integration process. This process not only remains deeply precarious: it has also created shadowy areas. These areas mainly arise from the activist judicial doctrines progressively realized by the Court of Justice, which has been the main instigator of the rise of fundamental rights in the EU legal order. However, the Court took care to justify the extension of its control over fundamental rights by establishing connections to the scope of EU law. In the absence of such connection, the Court remains reluctant to exercise control, ruling that fundamental rights 'cannot in themselves have the effect of broadening the scope of the treaty beyond the jurisdiction of the Community'.[9] The problem is to identify these connections. In the future, fundamental rights are also likely to become increasingly important in the EU as a consequence of growing mainly secondary legislation that is closely linked to them (either because it consolidates fundamental rights or, conversely, sets limits to their protected scope). The incorporation of the Charter of Fundamental Rights into EU primary law is also likely to contribute to this phenomenon. Inevitably, this perpetual and non-linear movement creates a form of legal insecurity, and acts as a permanent source of disturbance. To remedy this, the Court should strive to build a solid doctrine of judicial review of fundamental rights, which is currently lacking. What is needed is an overall perspective of the rationales and logic lying behind such extensions.

In addition, another element urges such an overall perspective. Some national courts increasingly perceive the approach of the Court of Justice as an unbridled intrusion in their traditionally 'reserved' domain, namely the protection of fundamental rights. One shall admit that there is a certain irony in this: the EU discourse on fundamental rights, which was originally developed by the ECJ in order to reassure the Member States, now scares them. However, nascent tensions on the issue are a matter of fact.

The collision of the objective of protecting fundamental rights and the need to respect the allocation of competences stands at the constitutional heart of European integration. The European objective of the protection of fundamental rights seems to be indifferent to the *existence* of limited European competences. The question then is *to what extent* this objective influences the *exercise* of national competences.

I. The Protection of Fundamental Rights and the Definition of the Union's Competence

Perhaps more than any of the other overall objectives of the European Union, the protection of fundamental rights is characterized by a form of supreme indifference to the limits of the EU's capacity for action. In the EU system, the protection of fundamental rights is one of the few goals that have been pursued while not

[9] Case C-249/96 *Grant* [1998] ECR I-261, esp para 45.

being accompanied by a corresponding transfer of competence. The first question is how the objective came to exist without a corresponding Union's competence (1). The second question is how the objective has grown outside the remit of Union's competence (2).

1. The protection without a competence

Can we (still) say that the European Union is not competent in the matter of the protection of fundamental rights? Ever since Opinion 2/94, EU law has experienced changes of 'constitutional significance', which challenged the idea that the EU is deprived of any competence in the field of the protection of fundamental rights.[10] There are, first of all, specific legal bases which permit normative action regarding human rights. The first of these is Article 19 TFEU, which empowers the Union to adopt measures to fight against discrimination on certain grounds. This provision contradicts the assumption of total lack of competence of the Union. Even the legal bases for the internal market can serve as grounds for the adoption of European standards of fundamental rights protection.[11] And yet, the above is not enough to consider that the EU has 'general' jurisdiction regarding the protection of fundamental rights.

More problematic, then, is the adoption of the Charter of Fundamental Rights of the European Union. Its incorporation into EU primary law since the Lisbon Treaty almost forgets the fact that the Charter first took the form of an inter-institutional agreement. No specific legal basis permitted the adoption of such a Charter: its adoption was decided within the European Council, which issued a specific mandate. So, how can an organization that is incompetent in the matter of the protection of fundamental rights develop a catalogue that appears as the most up-to-date and most complete text in this area? On the basis of the Charter, there is now a real institutional system for the monitoring and evaluation of human rights, which frontally challenges the idea that the Union has no power to act in this area. Finally, is it not the case that permitting (better, mandating) the Union to seek accession to the European Convention on Human Rights entails—by a sort of reversal of the principle of parallelism of competences *in foro interno/in foro externo*—that the Union is implicitly competent for the protection of fundamental rights? It is difficult to understand why an entity would otherwise participate in a protection system that does not concern it.

The above represent surprising contradictions, the resolution of which may possibly be found in the correlation of the concepts of 'competence' and 'fundamental rights'. What does it mean, to be 'competent' for the protection of 'fundamental rights'? In order to answer this question attention must be paid to two different—though connected—types of legal discourse. One might refer to the distinction

[10] C. Blumann, 'Les compétences de l'Union européenne en matière de droits fondamentaux' (2006) 1 *Revue des Affaires Européennes* 11.

[11] J-P. Jacqué, 'Communautés des internautes et protection des libertés individuelles dans l'Union européenne' (2010) 46 *Revue Trimestrielle de Droit Européen* 271.

between power-conferring norms and norms of prescription. These two types of norms are not at the same level of legal language: while the first is concerned with identifying the *scope* (*ratione personae* and *ratione materiae*) of the action, the second intends to regulate the *content* of the action. The power-conferring norms—or if one prefers, the rules of competence—necessarily require the identification of a specific sector of the legal reality. The notion of competence involves a material definition of the normative capacity, the identification of a sphere of legitimate normative action. However, fundamental rights are essentially prescriptive norms: they indicate the possibility of doing something, or not doing it.[12] They create standards in light of which other norms are assessed. The logic of human rights does not coincide with a sectorial division of segments of activity.[13] There may be elective areas of application of certain fundamental rights (e.g. criminal or civil cases for the right to a fair trial). However, generally speaking, it would constitute a contradiction to say that fundamental rights do not apply to a particular subject.

The function performed by fundamental rights may aid in explaining this. The so-called 'fundamental rights' correspond to norms that a legal system *S* considers at a moment *t* to be values which are the object of an enhanced protection. In some respects, fundamental rights are specifically concerned with the essential attributes of the human person. However, this specificity is difficult to grasp, inasmuch as any attempt to define precisely the boundaries of these particular standards seems destined to fail. It is difficult to delineate the area of legal reality belonging to fundamental rights by virtue of a substantive criterion. All spheres of legislative action are thus susceptible to be concerned with fundamental rights issues. Fundamental rights in their entirety do not constitute, therefore, a specific policy area. They cannot be relied upon as a 'policy' per se, but rather serve as justifications for political action, notably to legitimize it more than to substantialize it.

This is probably one of the reasons for which the 'purpose' of fundamental rights protection has arisen, even in the absence of general European competence conferred to that effect. However, this is not enough to explain why this purpose has been gradually developing outside of the scope of the Union's competences.

2. The protection beyond the competence

Gradually, control of the respect of fundamental rights has been extended to situations that the Union does not have the legislative power to regulate directly. The debate focuses mainly on measures adopted by the national authorities acting within their reserved area of competence. What pressing need is there for the Union to engage in an extension of its competence despite the constitutional allocation of competences?

[12] Sometimes, however, the standards of protection of fundamental rights set out themselves certain regulatory powers, such as references to the legislature to define the limits of fundamental rights.

[13] See P. Alston and J.H.H. Weiler, 'Vers une politique des droits de l'homme authentique et cohérente pour l'Union européenne', in P. Alston and others (eds.), *L'Union européenne et les droits de l'homme* (Brussels: Bruylant, 2001), 3.

What are the situations in which it is possible to say that the objective of fundamental rights protection is effective, though they fall outside the scope of formal EU competence? EU fundamental rights apply to Member States action in two classical types of situations.[14] We must now add two new ones. Of these four cases, at least the last three can be considered to be outside the scope of EU competences.

The first situation can probably be considered as respecting the allocation of competences. Initiated by the *Wachauf* judgment, it concerns cases of national implementation of EU law.[15] Since the Member States essentially act as 'agents' of the Union, their action is deemed to fall within the EU standards of protection. This decision contrasts sharply with the case law of the US Supreme Court prior to the adoption of the Fourteenth Amendment, which limited the review in light of the fundamental rights enshrined in the Federal Constitution only to the actions of the Federal Government, and not also of state authorities.[16] One could argue that the Court of Justice went beyond the strict separation of competences by subjecting national authorities to constraints that were not explicitly provided by the founding treaties. In practice, however, the application of EU fundamental rights to state measures implementing Union law only really becomes relevant if the EU measure that is implemented at national level was adopted within the competences of the Union.[17] From this perspective, it cannot be considered that the protection of the purpose of fundamental rights goes beyond the allocation of competences. Note, however, that this situation raises a crucial question: the identification of situations that relate to the 'implementation' of EU law.[18] The situations concerned are those in which the Member States have competences related to the *proper implementation* of EU legislation.[19] Recently, the Court has considered that a criminal sanction, not directly related to EU law, but adopted to enforce an obligation that derives from EU law, falls within the scope of Union

[14] We shall put to one side the question of control of fundamental rights by the measures adopted by the institutions and bodies of the Union, which does not call for comment within the scope of that which concerns us here. In this case, control of the protection of fundamental rights is generally conditioned by compliance with powers, and it is only after having verified the compliance with the latter that compliance with fundamental rights will be checked.

[15] *Wachauf* (n 4), esp para 19. Constantly upheld since Case C-2/92 *Bostock* [1994] ECR I-955, esp para 16; Case C-351/92 *Graff* [1994] ECR I-3361, esp para 17; Case C-292/97 *Karlsson e.a.* [2000] ECR I-2737, esp para 37; Case C-349/07 *Sopopré* [2008] ECR I-10369, esp para 34.

[16] *Barron v Baltimore* 32 US 243 (1833).

[17] However, it has been the case that the Court of Justice has come to review fundamental rights with regard to national measures, even though it was questionable whether the legislation at the origin of its attachment to the field of law of the European Union actually gives it competence to do so: in this sense, Knook (n 7), esp at 386–90, referring to Case C-138/01 *Österreichisser Rundfunk et a.* [2003] ECR I-4989, and Case C-101/01 *Lindqvist* ECR I-12971.

[18] That is the meaning of the phrase 'to the extent possible' found in point 19 of *Wachauf* (n 4), according to F. Jacobs: see '*Wachauf* and the Protection of Human Rights in EC Law', in M. Poiares Maduro and L. Azoulai (eds.), *The Past and Future of EU Law* (Oxford and Portland: Hart Publishing, 2010), 133.

[19] Joined Cases C-20/00 and C-64/00 *Booker Aquaculture et Hydro Seafood* [2003] ECR I-7411, esp paras 88 *et seq.*

law; therefore, it must comply with EU fundamental rights.[20] Moreover, the Court of Justice imposes an obligation for Member States to use the flexibility offered by the EU legislation in a manner consistent with respect for fundamental rights.[21]

First introduced by the important judgment *ERT*, the second type of situation consists of submitting the national authorities to respect for fundamental rights when they *derogate from the freedoms of movement*, whether on the basis of the public policy provisions of the Treaty,[22] or on the grounds of objective of general interests,[23] or by secondary legislation.[24] All freedoms of movement are concerned, including that of the EU citizens to move freely within the territory of the Union.[25] The point is that the national measure in question is to be reviewed not only in terms of respect for freedom of movement but also in terms of respect for fundamental rights as general principles of Union law, as an *additional* condition of its compatibility with Union law.[26] The margin for national discretion is further reduced by the Court of Justice, which does not hesitate to apply EU law (or EU fundamental rights) within areas of competence reserved to the states (social protection, taxation, personal status, etc.).[27] Through the combination of the broad scope of application of the freedoms of movement and the *ERT*-case law, the protection of EU fundamental rights enters what remains the heart of state *imperium*.[28] Though quantitative in appearance, this jump forward is also, in reality, qualitative. As noted by Damien Chalmers, through the extension of the sphere of protection of fundamental rights, the Union offers additional resource for protection.[29]

The third scenario that triggers the application of EU fundamental rights concerns national measures in an area already partially covered by the EU secondary law. This scenario is still in the process of developing. At first sight, this is not a problematic situation in terms of the allocation of competences. If an EU norm has already been adopted, this means that a European competence exists, even if it eventually comes into conflict with a reserved competence of the Member States.[30] But even if EU competence exists, it is not necessarily 'complete' and

[20] Case C-617/10 judgment of 26 February 2013 *Åkerberg Fransson* nyr., esp paras 24 *et seq*. In this case, the Court focuses notably on the link between the national measure and the EU's own resources which are part of European competences (esp para 26).

[21] Case C-540/03 *Parlement v Conseil* [2006] ECR I-5769, esp para 105.

[22] *ERT* (n 4).

[23] Case C-368/95 *Familiapress* [1997] ECR I-3689, esp para 24.

[24] Joined Cases C-482/01 and C-493/01 *Orfanopoulos* [2004] ECR I-5257, esp para 97.

[25] Case C-145/09 *Tsakouridis* [2010] ECR I-11979, esp para 52.

[26] P. Eeckhout, 'The EU Charter of Fundamental Rights and the Federal Question' (2002) 39 *Common Market Law Review* 945, esp at 962–7.

[27] L. Azoulai, 'The "Retained Powers" Formula in the Case Law of the European Court of Justice: EU Law as Total Law?' (2011) 4 *European Journal of Legal Studies* 192.

[28] For a particularly symptomatic example, see Case C-60/00 *Carpenter* [2002] ECR I-6279. It has even happened that applicants artificially operate a movement within the Union to benefit from the protection of fundamental rights by the Court of Justice: Case C-109/01 *Akrich* [2003] ECR I-6907.

[29] D. Chalmers, 'Looking Back at *ERT* and its Contribution to an EU Fundamental Rights Agenda', in Azoulai and Poiares Maduro (n 18) 140, esp at 145.

[30] E.g. the application of the directive on gender equality to the question of the organization of the armed forces is part of a reserved competence of the states: Case C-273/97 *Sirdar* [1999] ECR I-7403, and Case C-285/98 *Kreil* [2000] ECR I-69. G. Anagnostaras, 'Sex Equality and Compulsory

can accommodate a sphere of incompetence, either substantive (the whole of the area is not affected by the transfer of competence) or instrumental (the Union does not have the monopoly of the legal instruments in the area transferred). It is therefore conceivable that the application of fundamental rights extends beyond the limits of the allocated competences in certain cases. Until now, these cases were concerned with procedural issues related to the right to effective judicial protection.[31] But now new cases have emerged that concern the 'horizontal' application of directives. Horizontal application is generally excluded, according to the Court, due to the distinction between the nature of directives and regulations and the division of powers between the Union and the Member States.[32] The limitation of the legislative competence of the Union acting via directives justifies the inability of directives to directly apply to national law in horizontal situations. However, the Court of Justice ruled that such cases were still subject to fundamental rights requirements via the application of the general principles of Union law. This position is that of the *Mangold* judgment, in which the Court concluded that the applicability of the European principle of non-discrimination on grounds of age should be extended to horizontal situations falling within the field covered by the directive on fixed-term employment.[33] The following *Kücükdeveci* decision confirms this position, using the combined application of the same principle (this time as enshrined in the Charter of Fundamental Rights) and the same directive against discrimination in order to exclude contrary national law in a horizontal situation.[34] This complex reasoning was justified by Advocate General Bot by reference to the specific secondary legislation aiming at ensuring the protection of fundamental rights.[35] It would seem, then, that the scope of the protection of fundamental rights extends to situations that the legislator of the Union does not have the formal authority to deal with directly.[36] However, this phenomenon remains unclear in scope.[37]

The emergence of a fourth case of protection of fundamental rights against national measures has emerged via the Union's citizenship status, which, according to the Court's formula, 'is destined to be the fundamental status of nationals of Member States'. The situation has emerged in the *Ruiz Zambrano* case. This involved a Colombian father of Belgian children (therefore, EU citizens), who challenged an expulsion order of which he was the addressee. The Court worked out an original

Military Service: the Limits of National Sovereignty over Matters of Army Organisation' (2003) 28 *European Law Review* 713.

[31] Case C-276/01 *Steffensen* [2003] ECR I-3735, esp paras 70 *et seq.*

[32] Case C-91/92 *Faccini Dori* [1994] ECR I-3325, esp para 24. Sharing this reasoning, D. Simon, *La directive européenne* (Paris: Dalloz, 1997), esp 73–4. See equally the Opinion of AG Mazak in Case C-411/05 *Palacios de La Villa* [2007] ECR I-4531, esp para 138.

[33] Case C-144/04 *Mangold* [2005] ECR I-9981.

[34] *Kücükdeveci* (n 5).

[35] In particular para 90 of the Opinion.

[36] Editorial Comments, 'The Scope of Application of General Principles of Union law: An Ever Expanding Union?' (2010) 47 *Common Market Law Review* 1589.

[37] See the remarks of AG Trstenjak in her Opinion in Case C-282/10 *Dominguez*, nyr., esp paras 154 *et seq.*

solution: despite the fact that none of the parties involved had exercised their freedom of movement within the Union, the Court, in an unusually terse decision, held that 'Article 20 TFEU precludes national measures which have the effect of depriving citizens of the Union of the genuine enjoyment of the substance of the rights conferred by their status citizen of the Union'.[38] Situations of deportation from the territory of the Union may be regarded as incompatible with the rights attached to European citizenship. It is true that, in the *Ruiz Zambrano* judgment, the issue of fundamental rights is not specifically mentioned. Yet, a violation of the fundamental right to family life is at stake here, which in turn affects the rights attached to citizenship. Citizenship is a 'Trojan horse' for the protection of fundamental rights. Advocate General Sharpston justified this extension of the scope of EU law by relying on the existence of a shared competence with regard to European citizenship, which in her view would not be limited to transnational situations, despite the fact that only transnational situations are contemplated by the current secondary law.[39] One is left not entirely convinced by this analysis,[40] the main drawback being the confusion of citizenship as a status (Articles 20 TFEU and 21(1) TFEU) and as an object of secondary legislation (Article 21(2) and (3) TFEU). Here, the status alone justifies the application of EU law, and not the existence of a 'competence' in the field. This question is of fundamental importance for the evolution of the European integration. A new trigger is then created for a given situation to be subject to the application of EU fundamental rights: no longer mobility, but rather a form of 'vulnerability', that is a situation that exposes a vulnerable EU citizen to the prospect of being forced to leave the Union.[41]

How to explain the incursions of the objective of protecting fundamental rights outside the scope of the existing EU competences? One reason is the *effectiveness* of Union law, which requires uniformity in the application of EU standards and primacy of EU law. In the *ERT* case, the main argument used to justify the

[38] *Ruiz Zambrano* (n 5), esp point 42.

[39] In particular para 163 of the Opinion. The AG proposes to trace the scope of the control on the jurisdiction, whether it has been exercised or not, as 'transparency and clarity require that we can determine with certainty that the "scope of European Union law" extends to the protection of the fundamental rights of the European Union. It seems to me that in the long term, the clearest rule would be one that would subordinate the availability of protection of fundamental rights of the European Union not to the direct applicability of a provision of the Treaty and the adoption of secondary law, but rather *to the existence and extent of a material competence of the European Union.* In other words, the rule provides that, provided that the European Union shall have jurisdiction (whether sole or joint) in a particular field of law, fundamental rights of EU citizens are protected by the European Union, *even if the jurisdiction has not yet been exercised*'.

[40] Surprisingly, the Advocate General does not propose to the Court to engage immediately in the line of reasoning reproduced in the preceding note, since the facts of the case took place before the entry into force of the Lisbon Treaty and the Charter of Fundamental Rights. However, it is clear that the legislative competence for citizenship justifying control (despite the fact that it had not been much exercised) has existed since the Maastricht Treaty. Ergo, we do not know whether the proposed reasoning, consisting of aligning the field of control with the existence of jurisdiction, is chosen for its theoretical rigour or because of the 'constitutional' dimension taken on by EU primary law since the Lisbon Treaty (which also seems rather more restrictive than extensive concerning the question of the scope of control).

[41] Case C-256/11 *Dereci et a.* judgment of 15 November 2011 nyr., and Joined Cases C-356/11 and C-357/11 *O.* and *S.* judgment of 6 December 2012 nyr.

application of EU fundamental rights was to ask what would be 'the state of the common market if each member state could determine, by reference to its own laws and values—without any reference to Community law—what is or is not covered by the prohibition and the exceptions to this rule'.[42] In short, it is the requirement of uniformity which justifies the solution. One can remain sceptical about this reasoning: Where is the need, *from the point of view of the effectiveness of the freedom of movement*, to engage in additional protection of fundamental rights? One might consider that a breach of a fundamental right is, in itself, an infringement of the freedom of movement.[43] In the *Kücükdeveci* case, the argument put forward was to preserve the 'full effect'[44] and thus the uniformity of EU law, together with the primacy of the principle of non-discrimination on grounds of age. In the *Ruiz Zambrano* case, the requirements of effectiveness and uniformity are at the heart of the Opinion of Advocate General Sharpston.

The argument of *effectiveness/uniformity/primacy* used to justify the extension of the protection of fundamental rights is not entirely convincing. There is no dispute that effectiveness plays a role within the scope of Union law. It is much more debatable that it justifies an expansion of this scope. This sort of reasoning amounts to reversing the relationship between causes and consequences: the requirement of effectiveness can only be invoked *within* the scope of protection, not to justify the expansion; otherwise we are left in an endless spiral of expansion.

Another argument may be put forward. Let us call it the *compensation* argument. It consists of explaining the extension of the application of fundamental rights by the need to take into account the disadvantages suffered by those who find themselves, *in extremis*, excluded from benefits conferred by the law of the Union. Using the terminology of Advocate General Poiares Maduro it is possible to call them 'residual' situations of EU law,[45] since they have no meaning and existence, except in connection with EU law. This represents a sort of border or boundary area between national law and EU law that simply does not exist in the absence of the latter. As a matter of fact, the three types of situations previously identified may be characterized in this way. The fact that EU law tolerates a national measure that derogates from free movement singles out the person who is subject to this measure, relative to a counterpart who could take full advantage of his freedom of movement. Similarly, excluding situations involving horizontal application of a

[42] J.H.H. Weiler and S.C. Fries, 'Une politique des droits de l'homme pour la Communauté et l'Union européenne: la question des compétences', in Alston and others (n 13), esp at 164. Similarly, K. Lenaerts, 'Fundamental Rights in the European Union' (2000) 25 *European Law Review*, esp at 590.

[43] In this sense, see the Opinion of AG Jacobs in Case C-168/91 *Konstantinidis* [1993] ECR I-851, esp para 46. In any event, it is necessary to consider that the control for the respect of fundamental rights is included in that relating to free movement, and not that it is attached as a post hoc appendage thereto.

[44] In particular para 53 of *Kücükdeveci* (n 5). See also in this vein, K. Lenaerts and T. Corthaut, 'Of Birds and Hedges: the Role of Primacy in Invoking Norms of EU Law' (2006) 31 *European Law Review*, esp at 290–1.

[45] Opinion of AG Poiares Maduro in Case C-72/03 *Carbonati Apuani* [2004] ECR I-8027, esp para 58.

directive singles out those faced with a purely private dispute, as distinct from those involved in a similar administrative dispute, in which they would have succeeded in invoking their rights. Finally, the situation of the 'static' citizen may be contrasted with that of the 'mobile' citizen, who had the luck or foresight to cross a Member State frontier. It is possible to argue that people in such situations should receive at least a minimum level of protection from the system that generates their legal deprivation. This minimum level of protection should come in the form of a defence of the core values that underpin the system itself and ensure its legitimacy, namely the fundamental rights of the European Union. From this perspective, it is precisely because the EU has only limited competences that the protection of its fundamental values should be applied to situations that are not a priori covered by EU law. These situations only exist because of the presence of Union law, of which they illustrate the incompleteness. In this way, the EU includes within European society people who are in principle excluded from its competence and who suffer a disadvantage because of this exclusion. The question now is how far the overflow of competence extends in relation to the protection of this objective.

II. The Protection of Fundamental Rights and the Exercise of National Competences

The extension of the fundamental rights protection beyond the strict framework of the legislative powers of the Union requires us to define the contours of its application. Since the protection of fundamental rights has already crossed the 'yellow line' of competence in order to encompass borderline situations, why not bring this process to its most far-reaching consequences by universalizing the protection? Such a hypothesis seems premature, and the current state of EU law is more complex.

1. The delimitation of the protection of fundamental rights vis-à-vis national competences

What is meant by the formula whereby a national measure '*falls within the scope of application of Union law*'? One could draw a 'negative' boundary by identifying cases in which the Court of Justice ruled that the situation fell outside of the scope of EU law. Two main situations shall be distinguished: that of national measures not intended to apply EU secondary law, or lying outside the (material or personal) scope thereof,[46] and that of national measures against which the freedoms of movement cannot be opposed owing to a lack of a cross-border element[47] or an absence of restriction.[48] The problem is that the 'new' situations related to

[46] See Case C-144/95 *Maurin* [1996] ECR I-2909, and Case C-309/96 *Annibaldi* [1997] ECR I-7493.

[47] Case C-299/95 *Kremzow* [1999] ECR I-2629.

[48] Case C-159/90 *Grogan* [1991] ECR I-4685. Further, in an apparently isolated domain, the Court proceeded to review the respect of fundamental rights despite the fact that the measure was not considered as a restriction to free movement; see Case C-71/02 *Karner* [2004] ECR I-3025.

anti-discrimination directives and the citizenship status undermine this conventional analysis. Can we therefore consider a more 'positive' form of delimitation? It seems that the Court of Justice builds its own connecting factors in the form of *specific interests*. Much like a state is defined by reference to a population and territory (themselves subject to organized power), the Court of Justice attempts to *define the EU's own dimensions of integration* by tracing the limits of the protection of fundamental rights it is able to offer. To do this, it puts forward a set of specific interests, unrelated to those of the Member States, which must be protected by national authorities, even when they are, in principle, free to act on the basis of the constitutional allocation of competences. The difficulty is that these interests are not clearly defined. The scope of protection may be defined both *ratione personae* and *ratione loci*.

Ratione personae. Member State nationals are privileged EU law subjects, and by extension their family members, all of whom somehow constitute the Union's 'people'. This goes so far that the Court of Justice allows itself to scrutinize—though in a limited and shy manner—the conditions for granting and withdrawal of nationality by the Member States, a matter that nevertheless falls entirely within the scope of national competence.[49] Not only economic operators but the European citizen becomes, as such, the custodian of a specifically European interest, which links his particular situation to the protection offered by EU law. This includes people who are not engaged in economic activity (such as children, students, but also unemployed or no longer economically active persons) into the sphere of European interests. This may seem insignificant, or even marginal. However, this actually represents a historic extension, entailing that the European project is changing its nature, from a market project to that of a real society.

The situation of nationals of third countries who are not part of the family of European citizens still remains somewhat more nebulous. The protection of fundamental rights is not completely ruled out, but it depends on different criteria. A detailed analysis of this point goes beyond the purpose of this work. However, it can be noted that those criteria essentially relate to the regularity and duration of the stay of third country nationals in the Union, the existence of an agreement between the home country and the European Union, and their status as an asylum seeker or refugee. Some sources of secondary law relating to the protection of fundamental rights (for instance, in terms of social rights and the fight against discrimination) are addressed to 'any person' within the jurisdiction of a state. A shift to a more general protection of third country nationals (non-family members of a citizen) 'embedded' in European society should not be ruled out. The 'people' of the European Union is defined as a form of social integration, including all those persons who are considered sufficiently 'integrated' into the society of a Member State, and hence into the Union.

Ratione loci. The 'territory' of the European Union is essentially transnational. Although such 'purely internal' situations have become less common, owing to the

[49] Case C-135/08 *Rottmann* [2010] ECR I-1449.

broad interpretation of the cross-border element promoted by the Court, these situations remained in principle excluded from the scope of protection of fundamental rights provided by the law of the Union. In particular, they create what has been labelled as 'reverse discrimination'. The initially transnational field tends to invade progressively more and more domestic situations, although the uncertainties here are still numerous. First, we must ask the question as to which situations are actually covered by EU secondary law. The idea is gaining ground that purely national situations covered by the scope of EU secondary law are subject to control for the respect of fundamental rights, including cases which do not involve any supranational element. This is the case, as we have seen, in situations involving the prohibition of discrimination based on age, where the fundamental right claimed is itself specified by the text of a directive.[50] If we follow the Opinion of Advocate General Sharpston in the *Bartsch* case, such control even extends to all areas covered by secondary law, whether or not such law is specifically intended to contribute to the protection of fundamental rights.[51] Then there is the question of the role of the Union's citizenship status as a means of bringing situations within the Court's scope of review. This extension appears to have occurred in two cases. First, the situation of persons having dual nationality appeared to present sufficient specificity to be directly related to the scope of Union law, including in cases not involving any transnational element. This was the case in *Garcia Avello*, which involved the exercise of a competence reserved to the domestic legislator notably the rules concerning civil status and family name.[52] However, the *McCarthy* case nuanced the previous conclusion, holding that the dual nationality of the applicant was deemed insufficient in the eyes of the Court to make the appropriate connection to EU law.[53] Secondly, the *Ruiz Zambrano* case clearly extended the control of the Court to situations which were formerly 'purely internal' in nature, lacking any cross-border element.[54] As a result, the European citizen is now *better protected* than the original addressees of Community law provisions, that is economic operators, who still have to move to another Member State in order to be held to be in a situation triggering the protection of fundamental rights. One must

[50] This is the position of the decisions in *Mangold* (n 33) and *Kücükdeveci* (n 5) respectively.

[51] See the Opinion of AG Sharpston in Case C-427/06 *Bartsch* [2008] ECR I-7245, esp para 69: '[i]n particular, the compatibility of national measures with general principles can be invoked only when they fall within the scope of Community law. For that to happen, the national rule in question should generally be part of one of the following three categories. Either it must implement Community law (regardless of the discretion retained by the Member State and whether the national measure goes beyond what is strictly necessary for the implementation of Community law), or it must rely on a derogation permitted by Community law, *or again it must relate in one way or another to the scope of Community law because of a positive rule of law that applies to the situation in question*' (emphasis added). Read *a contrario*, this last hypothesis extends the control of European fundamental rights to national measures in any situation already covered by EU secondary law.

[52] Indeed, in this case, although the disadvantage of a possible deportation was found to hinge upon the lack of citizenship on the part of the parents, the scope of review by the Court seems to have been expanded owing to the bi-national children, whose parents demanded the inclusion of the double name: Case C-148/02 *Garcia Avello* [2003] ECR I-11613.

[53] Case C-434/09 *McCarthy* [2011] ECR I-3375, esp paras 49 and 54.

[54] *Ruiz Zambrano* (n 5).

wonder whether this development represents a first step towards a universalization of EU fundamental rights. Fearing to appear as a real Supreme Court for the protection of fundamental rights, the Court has decided to limit its control in respect of the deprivation of 'the substance of the rights' of citizens.

Although more neglected in literature, the question of the degree of review is also crucial to measuring the real impact of this protection on matters that essentially relate to national competences. It is not easy to precisely evaluate the reach of the review carried out by the Court of Justice. The question of the degree of control may vary depending on the degree of connection to EU law, as suggested by Advocate General Poiares Maduro in his Opinion in the *Centro Europa* 7 case.[55] As it stands, it appears that the different situations I have identified are not subject to the same standard of protection. In particular, it seems that the standard of protection is not the same as the control carried out with respect to 'classic' cases involving the implementation of EU law. Thus, the fundamental rights of a 'mobile' citizen are probably better protected than those of a 'static' citizen, for whom only the 'substance' of the rights attached to citizenship status is protected under EU law. This makes sense in terms of respect for national competences, but much less so in terms of the protection of fundamental rights. Another example is the protection of the right to family life of a 'static' citizen facing the deportation of a family member. In the *Ruiz Zambrano* case, the separation of minor children from their parents triggered the EU law protection, while in the *McCarthy* case the deportation of a spouse did not. What consistency can be found in these radically different solutions, when the cases themselves displayed some similarities? It should be noted that the legal basis chosen is not exactly the same: Article 20 TFEU in one case and Article 21 TFEU in the other. This, however, adds to the inconsistency rather than diluting it. However, with a certainly subtlety, it is still possible to find some logic in this apparent contradiction, notably in terms of the relationship of the European Union vis-à-vis the definition of its territory, depending on whether a person is forced to leave the territory or is looking to enter it.[56]

2. The vindication of national competences against the protection of fundamental rights

The review of national measures in light of EU fundamental rights leads to a form of competition between systems of protection. It is being challenged, both by states acting as Masters of the Treaties, which may see the expansion of EU law as

[55] In his Opinion in Case C-380/05 *Centro Europa* 7 [2008] ECR I-349, AG Poiares Maduro upheld the idea of a generalized protection of fundamental rights beyond all links of attachment to Union law by the Court, but with a degree of control restrained (only) to 'structural' violations—that is serious and persistent—of fundamental rights.

[56] *Dereci* (n 41), esp para 66: '[i]t follows that the criterion relating to the denial of the genuine enjoyment of the substance of the rights conferred by virtue of European Union citizen status refers to situations in which the Union citizen has, in fact, to leave not only the territory of the Member State of which he is a national but also the territory of the Union as a whole.'

a non-consented limitation upon their constitutional competence, and by national courts that are deprived of part of their jurisdiction.

Article 51 of the Charter reveals the resistance of the Member States. Its first paragraph stipulates that the provisions of the Charter 'are addressed to the institutions and bodies of the Union with due regard for the principle of subsidiarity and to the Member States only when they are implementing Union law'. The second paragraph of the same provision then adds that the Charter 'does not establish any new power or task for the Community or the Union, or modify powers and tasks as defined in the Treaties'.[57] At first sight, three main limitations are thereby provided. First, this wording excludes the protection of fundamental rights in horizontal situations.[58] However, it was precisely in a case between private parties that the Court extended the benefit of the protection of the principle of non-discrimination on grounds of age, as enshrined in Article 21 of the Charter.[59] Secondly, the protection is supposed to apply only in relation to the 'implementation' of EU law, thereby excluding *ERT*-types of situation. However, the Court subsequently referred to Article 7 of the Charter relating to respect for private and family life in order to rule on the compatibility of a national measure derogating from freedom of movement in the case of *Runevič-Vardyn and Wardyn*.[60] In the *Asparuhov Estov* ruling,[61] the Court found that its jurisdiction to interpret the Charter was not established, since no evidence existed that the national decision in question 'was a measure of implementation of EU law or that it presents other elements which are attached thereto'. In *Äkerberg Fransson*, the Court confirmed that the requirement to respect fundamental rights is binding on the Member States when they act 'in the scope of Union law'. It follows that 'the applicability of European Union law entails applicability of the fundamental rights guaranteed by the Charter'.[62] Finally, according to Article 51(2) of the Charter of Fundamental Rights, the scope of the protection afforded by the Charter is supposed not to exceed that of the powers conferred to the Union. However, this did not prevent the Court from referring to the Charter again in situations falling within the reserved powers of Member States.[63] In contrast, in other cases, the Court took due consideration of this limit. In the judgment, handed down under the urgent preliminary ruling procedure, the Court, in accordance with the position of the Advocate General, focused on the lack of EU competence in the regulation of custody rights, in order to use the Charter only for interpretative purposes vis-à-vis EU law, and not to directly review the contested

[57] H. Kaila, 'The Scope of Application of the Charter of Fundamental Rights of the European Union in the Member States', in P. Cardonnel, A. Rosas, and N. Wahl (eds.), *Constitutionalising the EU Judicial System—Essays in Honour of Pernilla Lindh* (Oxford: Hart Publishing, 2012), 291.

[58] In this vein, see also the Opinion of AG Trstenjak in *Dominguez* (n 37), esp para 80 *et seq* and the case law cited therein.

[59] *Kücükdeveci* (n 5).

[60] Case C-391/09 *Runevic-Vardyn and Wardyn* [2011] ECR I-3787, para 89.

[61] C-339/10 *Asparuhov Estov e.a.* [2010] ECR I-11465, esp para 14; as well as Joined Cases C-267/10 and 268/10 *Rossius* and *Colliard* [2001] ECR I-81, esp para 19.

[62] *Äkerberg Fransson* (n 20) paras 20 and 21.

[63] In the matter of family names, see *Runevic-Vardyn and Wardyn* (n 60) and, more ambiguously, Case C-208/09 *Sayn-Wittgenstein* [2010] ECR I-13693.

national measure.[64] Similarly, in the *Vino* cases, the Court expressly referred to Article 51(2) and ruled that the situation was not within the scope of Union law and the protection of fundamental rights.[65]

As it stands, it seems that the Court has partially overcome state resistance. How can we explain this? Firstly, it is true that some ambiguity remains with regard to the *Explanatory Notes* attached to the Charter, which replicate the broad wording of the 'scope' of EU law.[66] It is difficult to say what was the precise intention of the majority of the authors of the Charter, but there is no doubt that some of them had a significantly restrictive vision.[67] Secondly, the argument commonly advanced is that of the unity of fundamental rights protection, whatever the normative instrument used. It is argued that even if the limitations imposed by Article 51 of the Charter would be met, it would remain open to the Court to maintain a more extensive protection of fundamental rights on the basis of EU general principles of law.[68] Advocate General Bot even argues that the distinction between two different regimes of protection of fundamental rights within the Union (that of the Charter and that of the general principles) could weaken the overall level of protection and contradict Article 53 of the Charter, which is a principle of non-regression of the standard of protection.[69] It is not uncommon for a court to use its power of interpretation to change the meaning of a 'constitutional' text. However, it is less common that it ignores subsequent changes to the constitutional text. Therefore, determining the exact scope of Article 51 should be seen as a particularly sensitive issue, which could potentially significantly and irreparably degrade the relative confidence that Member States attach to the Court of Justice.[70] The issue is not only the protection of rights per se, but rather the ability of the organization to emancipate itself from the will of its constituent states, in order to win the trust of the ultimate recipients of the integration project, namely individuals.

If the Court of Justice seems to ignore some of the limits imposed by primary law to extend the scope of fundamental rights, can it go as far as to turn a deaf ear to protests on the part of national courts? Brandishing the argument of ultra vires or that of constitutional identity, some national constitutional courts purport to define by themselves the influence of EU law on national measures. Emblematic of the call for respect for democratic principles is the *Lisbon* decision of the German

[64] Case C-400/10 PPU *McB.* [2010] ECR I-8965, esp para 51.

[65] Case C-20/10 *Vino* [2010] ECR I-148, in esp para 52, and Case C-161/11 *Vino* [2011] ECR I-91, esp paras 23 *et seq.*

[66] According to which 'it results without ambiguity from the case law of the court that the obligation to respect fundamental rights defined within the Union framework is only imposed upon Member States when they act within the sphere of application of Union law'.

[67] F. Jacobs, 'Human Rights in the EU: the Role of the Court of Justice' (2001) 26 *European Law Review* 331, esp at 338.

[68] On this question, see Lenaerts and Gutiérrez-Fons (n 7), esp 1657–60; T. Tridimas, *The General Principles of EU Law*, 2nd edn (Oxford and New York: Oxford University Press, 2006), 363; A. Egger, 'EU-Fundamental Rights in the National Legal Order: The Obligations of Member States Revisited' (2006) 25 *Yearbook of European Law*, esp at 547–50.

[69] Opinion of AG Bot in Case C-108/10 *Scattolon* [2011] ECR I-7491, esp para 120.

[70] As is demonstrated by the British and Polish refusal to see themselves as bound by the Charter, despite its art 51.

Constitutional Court.[71] This Court emphasized that the expansion of EU competences should not ignore the sovereign consent of the German state, and thus deny the free self-determination of its people speaking either directly or through the voice of their representatives. However, from the point of view of the protection of fundamental rights, this admonition does not seem justified. Indeed, if the European standard of protection is more protective than the national one, the 'democratic' argument becomes untenable, insofar as it can ultimately only favour democracy in the material sense (namely human rights) over democracy in the procedural sense (the position of the majority). However, if the European standard appears less protective or different, nothing prevents the national standard of protection from continuing to apply, where possible, by reference to the national constitutional identity. As some have noted, there is some bad faith in the challenge brought by certain constitutional courts to the Court of Justice's dynamic interpretation of the scope of fundamental rights, since those courts adopt similar standards of interpretation.[72] What bothers national constitutional courts is not that the Court of Justice supervises national authorities, but that they see their own interpretation of fundamental rights challenged by another power. However, in the end, it is barely credible that a true conflict should arise.[73] In its *Honeywell* decision, the German Constitutional Court finally acknowledged that the *Mangold* case, establishing the principle of non-discrimination on the grounds of age and applying it to relationships between individuals, did not constitute a breach of the principle of conferral.[74]

Ultimately, the question is not one of respective scope of the rights, rather one concerning the diverging interpretation of these rights. Is it possible to avoid any power of the last word on the matter, in a pure form of multilevel constitutional pluralism?[75] The desire of the Union to create its own ties with the recipients of rights requires the imposition of its own interpretation of rights, and its own system of values. However, it is also obvious that the integration process cannot do without the cooperation of national courts that have the real ability to force national authorities to act and think 'European'. Therefore, the resolution of the conflict in gestation should be achieved through a form of mutual recognition of national and European courts, and collaborative research alignment of standards

[71] Bundesverfassungsgericht, Judgment of June 2009, 2 BvE 2/08. See F. Mayer, 'Rashomon à Karlsruhe' (2010) 46 *Revue Trimestrielle de Droit Européen* 77.

[72] In this vein, P. Craig, 'The ECJ and *Ultra vires* Action: A Conceptual Analysis' (2011) 48 *Common Market Law Review*, esp at 403 *et seq.*

[73] J. Ziller, 'Le dialogue judiciaire et la Cour de Karlsruhe—Quelques réflexions à propos du jugement de la Cour constitutionnelle fédérale allemande concernant le Traité de Lisbonne' (2010) 46 *Revue Trimestrielle de Droit Européen*, esp at 97–8.

[74] Bundesverfassungsgericht, Judgment of July 2010, 2 BvR 2661/06.

[75] M. Kumm, 'Who is the Final Arbiter of Constitutionality in Europe? Three Conceptions of the Relationship between the German Federal Constitutional Court and the European Court of Justice' (1999) 36 *Common Market Law Review* 351; M. Poiares Maduro, 'Contrapunctal Law: European Pluralism in Action', in N. Walker (ed.), *Sovereignity in Transition* (Oxford: Hart Publishing, 2003), 501; D. Ritleng, 'De l'utilité du principe de primauté du droit de l'Union' (2009) 45 *Revue Trimestrielle de Droit Européen Revue Trimestrielle de Droit Européen* 677; N. Walker, 'The Idea of Constitutional Pluralism' (2002) 65 *Modern Law Review* 317.

of protection.[76] Fundamental rights provide a suitable normative support to the judicial dialogue, and allow exchanges between legal systems that coexist in the same space.[77] The European Court of Human Rights is expected to play the role of arbiter in this quest for consistency, a sort of high guarantor of European judicial pluralism. The avoidance of open conflict in case of minor encroachments is the price of any form of constitutional tolerance.

Conclusion

In the confrontation between the objective of protecting fundamental rights and the need to respect the allocation of competences, there is more than just a legal issue. The reproach of 'not enough protection' has given way to 'too much protection' of fundamental rights, reflecting a major change in the evolution of European integration. At a time when the European Union no longer finds sufficient legitimacy in the construction of an economic space that is the guarantor of stability and prosperity, it seeks justification elsewhere for its existence. Providing an additional and original degree of protection of fundamental rights allows it to appear as the emanation of a real society. The protection granted to EU fundamental rights increasingly tends to exceed the limits of the powers of the Union in an ever more frequent fashion, in order to embrace a larger number of situations. These situations are mainly situations that can be identified as 'borderline'. In these situations, the Court of Justice applies the protection of fundamental rights in order to compensate for specific disadvantages resulting from the limitation of the sphere of EU competence. In so doing, the EU has built an identity in relation to a community of people whose boundaries still need to be rigorously systematized. The aim is not to deprive Member States of their competences. What the Union claims is not the power to impose a standard of protection of fundamental rights that is completely new, but rather to establish a framework for the development of a common standard, which would reflect the aspirations of the European society it intends to create.

[76] Case C-127/07 *Arcelor* [2008] ECR I-9895 represents a good example here.

[77] E. Dubout and S. Touzé (eds.), *Les droits fondamentaux: charnières des rapports entre ordres et systèmes juridiques* (Paris: Pedone, 2010), 336.

PART IV

POLITICAL AND LEGAL LIMITS TO EU COMPETENCES

10

Limits to the Union's 'Internal Market' Competence(s): Constitutional Comparisons

*Robert Schütze**

Introduction

The enumeration principle forms the constitutional core of every federation, and structures the division of powers in the United States and the European Union.[1] Federal constitutions thereby present a picture of thematically limited competences. Yet this picture is—partly—misleading. Many federal unions enjoy a functional competence that cuts horizontally across (almost) all other policy areas. This competence typically relates to the establishment and functioning of a Union-wide market. The advantages of an economic 'unity in diversity' were identified early on by the American founding fathers:

> [a]n unrestrained intercourse between the States themselves will advance the trade of each by an interchange of their respective productions, not only for the supply of reciprocal wants at home, but for exportation to foreign markets. The veins of commerce in every part will be replenished, and will acquire additional motion and vigor from a free circulation of the commodities of every part. Commercial enterprise will have much greater scope, from the diversity in the productions of different States.[2]

* This chapter draws extensively on my *From Dual to Cooperative Federalism: The Changing Structure of European Law* (Oxford and New York: Oxford University Press, 2009).

[1] For the US Constitution, see art I, s 1 (emphasis added): '[a]ll legislative Powers *herein granted* shall be vested in a Congress of the United States, which shall consist of a Senate and House of Representatives'; as well as the Tenth Amendment: '[t]he powers not delegated to the United States by the Constitution, nor prohibited by it to the States, are reserved to the States respectively, or to the people.' For the EU this follows from the 'principle of conferral' as expressed in art 5(2) TEU: '[u]nder the principle of conferral, the Union shall act only within the limits of the competences conferred upon it by the Member States in the Treaties to attain the objectives set out therein. Competences not conferred upon the Union in the Treaties remain with the Member States.'

[2] A. Hamilton, 'Federalist No. 11', in A. Hamilton, J. Madison, and J. Jay, *The Federalist* (Cambridge and New York: Cambridge University Press, 2003), 46, at 51.

Trade and commerce were consequently of central concern to the Federation. The free circulation of commodities would increase the wealth of the 'nation(s)'.[3] The same point would be made, almost 200 years later, on the other side of the Atlantic:

> [t]he object of a European common market should be to create a vast zone of common economic policy, constituting a powerful unit of production and permitting a continuous expansion, an increased stability, an accelerated raising of the standard of living, and the development of harmonious relations between its Member States. To attain these objectives, a fusion of the separate markets is an absolute necessity.[4]

Both Union-wide markets would have to be created by federal law aiming to establish a degree of legal 'unity' amidst the diverse state markets.[5] But to what extent should such legal unity be created through federal legislation? Would *any* diversity among state laws—like 'labour law' or 'public health laws'—undermine free commerce and trade?

These constitutional questions have been raised in the United States and the European Union, and this Chapter wishes to analyse their respective answers. Section I starts with the—older—American 'internal market' competence: the 'Commerce Clause'. The latter allows Congress 'to regulate Commerce…among the several States'.[6] It has been the chief competence to deregulate and re-regulate the American federal market.[7] The European Union's internal market competence(s) will be analysed in section II. We shall see here that Article 114 TFEU has—like the US 'Commerce Clause'—been given an (almost) unlimited scope. Nonetheless: both the American and the European internal market powers have encountered *some* political and legal limits, and section III will compare these constitutional limitations by means of a 'Conclusion'.

I. The 'Internal Market' Competence in the United States

One of the central tasks of the 1787 US Constitution had been the creation of an internal market. The ability of the states to create obstacles to trade had been obstructive for federal commerce,[8] and the (second) American Constitution

[3] On the impact of Adam Smith on the American Founders, see S. Fleishacker, 'Adam Smith's reception among the American founders, 1776–1790' (2002) 59 *William & Mary Quarterly* 897.

[4] Comité Intergouvernemental Crée par la Conference de Messine, Rapport des Chefs De Delegation ('Spaak Report'), as translated by J.J.A. Ellis, 'Source Material for Article 85(1) of the EEC Treaty' (1963) 32 *Fordham Law Review* 247, at 249.

[5] Cf. A. Hamilton, 'Federalist No. 22', in Hamilton and others (n 2) 98: '[t]he want of a power to regulate commerce is by all parties allowed to be of the number. The utility of such a power has been anticipated under the first head of our inquiries; and for this reason, as well as from the universal conviction entertained upon the subject, little need be added in this place. It is indeed evident, on the most superficial view, that there is no object, either as it respects the interests of trade or finance, that more strongly demands a federal superintendence.'

[6] US Constitution, art I, s 8 (Clause 3).

[7] On the (deregulatory) 'dormant' part of the 'Commerce Clause', see J.N. Eule, 'Laying the Dormant Commerce Clause to Rest' (1982) 91 *Yale Law Journal* 425; as well as M. Tushnet, 'Rethinking the Dormant Commerce Clause' (1979) *Wisconsin Law Review* 125.

[8] Under Articles of Confederation, there had been no 'Commerce Clause'.

therefore provided Congress with the power 'to regulate Commerce... among the several States'.[9] This provision would soon prove to be the broadest power of the American Federation.[10] However, the scope of this power had to be limited. Even the most 'nationalist' reading of the Constitution could not deny this: federal powers were enumerated powers; and 'enumeration presupposes something not enumerated'.[11] But where would interstate commerce begin and intrastate commerce end? What were the constitutional or political limits to the American 'internal market' competence? These questions have received different answers in the constitutional history of the United States.

1. The 'Commerce Clause' before the 'New Deal': internal and external constitutional limits

In the early history of the 'Commerce Clause', the Supreme Court had devised two strategies to restrict this Union competence. The first strategy was to develop *internal* limitations to the competence. This was complemented by a second strategy that would impose *external* boundaries to the 'Commerce Clause'.

We find a good illustration of the first strategy in *Hammer v Dagenhart*.[12] Would the 'Commerce Clause' generally allow the Federal Government to prohibit or ban interstate commerce with regard to a product? The 'Federal Child Labor Act' had aimed at standardizing the ages at which children could be employed in mining and manufacture. And, in the absence of a specific power to regulate working hours, Congress had used its general competence under the 'Commerce Clause' by simply prohibiting interstate commerce in those goods that shared in the 'original sin' of child labour. Would 'the power to *regulate* given to Congress incidentally include[] the authority to *prohibit* the movement of ordinary commodities'?[13] The Supreme Court did not think so. It invalidated the federal law, since it could not

[9] US Constitution, art I, s 8 (cl 3).

[10] The provision is often supported by the 'Necessary and Proper Clause'. This is the last clause in art I, s 8, and provides Congress with the power '[t]o make all Laws which shall be necessary and proper for carrying into Execution the foregoing Powers, and all other Powers vested by this Constitution in the Government of the United States'. In American constitutional practice, the clause can only be used in combination with one of the 'foregoing powers'. The 'sweeping clause' is thus 'not a self-contained power' as it 'must always be tied to the exercise of some other identifiable constitutional power of the national government' (G. Lawson and P.B. Granger, 'The "Proper" Scope of Federal Power: A Jurisdictional Interpretation of the Sweeping Clause' (1993-94) 43 *Duke Law Journal* 267, at 274–5). The 'Necessary and Proper Clause' thus requires the presence of an expressly enumerated power in the Constitution. In this sense: R. Beck, 'The New Jurisprudence of the Necessary and Proper Clause' (2002) *University of Illinois Law Review* 581, at 592: '[t]he clause merely confirmed the existence of lesser powers, not expressly detailed in the Constitution, which would serve as the means of carrying the enumerated powers into effect.' The 'Necessary and Proper Clause' may then best be identified with a rule of interpretation for the scope of an express power. It allows the—very—wide exercise of a 'pre-existing' power, see *McCulloch v Maryland* 17 US 316 [1819], 421: '[l]et the end be legitimate, let it be within the scope of the constitution, and all means which are appropriate, which are plainly adapted to that end, which are not prohibited, but consistent with the letter and spirit of the constitution, are constitutional.'

[11] *Gibbons v Ogden* 22 US 1 [1824].

[12] *Hammer v Dagenhart* 247 US 251 [1918].

[13] *Hammer v Dagenhart* (n 12) 270, emphasis added.

be shown to have any positive effect on interstate commerce. The power to regulate commerce was 'directly the contrary of the assumed right to forbid commerce from moving and thus destroying it as to particular commodities'.[14] The power to regulate commerce was a power to 'regulate', not to 'prohibit'.[15] Could the 'Commerce Clause' nonetheless be used to remove distortions of competition flowing from disparities in state labour laws? The Court categorically rejected this view.[16]

More important was a second limitation strategy applied to the 'Commerce Clause'. It was informed by the idea that the 1787 Constitution had split the atom of sovereignty,[17] and had established a governmental system of *dual* federalism. 'The United States are sovereign as to all the powers of Government actually surrendered: Each State in the Union is sovereign as to all the powers reserved.'[18] '[T]he powers of the General Government, and of the State, although both exist and are exercised within the same territorial limits, are yet separate and distinct sovereignties, acting separately and independently of each other within their respective spheres.'[19] The philosophy of dual federalism, while advocating the idea of autonomous federal powers, thus insisted on the idea of 'implied limitations'.[20] What were these implied—external—boundaries that were limiting the 'Commerce Clause'? Prior to the 'New Deal', the Supreme Court here drew on the idea of *exclusive* state police powers.

We find a good illustration of this type of reasoning in *United States v Knight*.[21] The case involved a challenge to the 1890 'Sherman (Antitrust) Act', which had tackled unlawful restraints and monopolies. To what extent could the Union regulate competition law? The Supreme Court thought that 'the power of a state to protect the lives, health, and property of its citizens, and to preserve good order and the public morals' was 'a power originally and always belonging to the states, not surrendered by them to the general government, nor directly restrained by the Constitution of the United States, and essentially exclusive'. 'The relief of the citizens of each state from the burden of monopoly and the evils resulting from the restraint of trade among such citizens was left with the states.' However, the Court equally recognized that it was

> vital that the independence of the commercial power and of the police power, and the delimitation between them, however sometimes perplexing, should always be recognized and observed, for, while the one furnishes the strongest bond of union, the other is essential to the preservation of the autonomy of the states as required by our dual form of government.[22]

[14] *Hammer v Dagenhart* (n 12).

[15] See *Champion v Ames* (*Lottery Cases*) 188 US 321 [1903]: '[t]he authority given to Congress was not to prohibit, but only to regulate.'

[16] *Hammer v Dagenhart* (n 12) 273.

[17] *US Term Limits Inc v Thornton* 514 US 779 [1995], 838 (Justice Kennedy, concurring).

[18] *Chisholm v State of Georgia* 2 US 419 [1793], 435.

[19] *Ableman v Booth* 62 US 506 [1859], 516.

[20] W.F. Dodd, 'Implied Powers and Implied Limitations in Constitutional Law' (1919) 29 *Yale Law Journal* 137.

[21] *United States v Knight* 156 US 1 [1895].

[22] *United States v Knight* (n 21) 11 and 13.

From this, the Court concluded that since 'commerce succeeds to manufacture, and is not a part of it',[23] the federal power could not extend to the regulation of the latter. The exclusive powers of the states would thus limit the (exclusive) federal power to regulate commerce.

2. The 'Commerce Clause' after the 'New Deal': From 'constitutional' to 'political' safeguards?

Reforms follow crises. The 'reformation' of American federalism followed the Great Depression of 1929. The spirit of the time was this:

> [a]rchitecturally we have an antiquated frame of government when we lack nation-wide power to deal with nation-wide conditions that can not be dealt with effectively by the several states. It is abundantly clear that the states could not do much to revive agriculture and industry. If it were clear that the nation by national regulation could do a lot to revive and maintain agriculture and industry, it would then be clear that the nation ought to have the power to do it.[24]

The economic crisis had affected the entire Union market, and thus demanded Union-wide solutions. To reinvigorate the American economy, a series of statutes had been enacted to regulate the federal market.[25] (Yet this 'new nationalism' was first blocked by a dual federalist Supreme Court.[26] The reforms were judicially vetoed, and it was only after the Roosevelt administration threatened to 'pack' the Court, that the 'switch in time that saved the nine' endorsed the birth of a new era.) The subsequent 'nationalist' re-interpretation of the 'Commerce Clause' gradually discarded any internal and external limitations around that federal competence.

We can see this new constitutional spirit at work in *Jones & Laughlin*.[27] This case concerned the constitutionality of the 'National Labor Relations Act' (1935), which had been challenged 'as an attempt to regulate all industry, thus invalidating

[23] *United States v Knight* (n 21) 12. The well-known passage from *Kidd v Pearso*n 128 US 1 [1888], 20–22 reads: '[n]o distinction is more popular to the common mind, or more clearly expressed in economic and political literature, than that between manufactures and commerce. Manufacture is transformation—the fashioning of raw materials into a change of form for use. The functions of commerce are different. The buying and selling and the transportation incidental thereto constitute commerce; and the regulation of commerce in the constitutional sense embraces the regulation at least of such transportation.... If it be held that the term [commerce] includes the regulation of all such manufactures as are intended to be the subject of commercial transactions in the future, it is impossible to deny that it would also include all productive industries that contemplate the same thing. The result would be that Congress would be invested, to the exclusion of the states, with the power to regulate, not only manufacture, but also agriculture, horticulture, stock-raising, domestic fisheries, mining,—in short, every branch of human industry. For is there one of them that does not contemplate, more or less clearly, an interstate or foreign market?'

[24] T.R. Powell, 'Some Aspects of Constitutionalism and Federalism' (1935-36) 14 *North Carolina Law Review* 1, at 26.

[25] For a brief summary, see R.L. Stern, 'The Commerce Clause and the National Economy, 1933–1946' (1945-46) 59 *Harvard Law Review* 645, at 653.

[26] The Supreme Court dealt with the 'Agricultural Adjustment Act' in *United States v Butler et al* 297 US 1 [1936]; and the 'National Industrial Recovery Act' *in Schechter Poultry Corp v United States* 295 US 495 [1935].

[27] *National Labor Relations Board v Jones & Laughlin Steel Corp* 301 US 1 [1937].

the reserved powers of the States over their local concerns'.[28] In its judgment, the Court abruptly abandoned the interpretative approach that had tried to distinguish between 'commerce' and 'production':

> [t]he congressional authority to protect interstate commerce from burdens and obstructions is not limited to transactions which can be deemed to be an essential part of a 'flow' of interstate or foreign commerce. Burdens and obstructions may be due to injurious action springing from other sources. The fundamental principle is that the power to regulate commerce is the power to enact 'all appropriate legislation' for its 'protection or advancement'; to adopt measures 'to promote its growth and insure its safety'; 'to foster, protect, control, and restrain.' *That power is plenary and may be exerted to protect interstate commerce 'no matter what the source of the dangers which threaten it.'* Although activities may be intrastate in character when separately considered, if they have such a close and substantial relation to interstate commerce that their control is essential or appropriate to protect that commerce from burdens and obstructions, Congress cannot be denied the power to exercise that control.[29]

Instead of concentrating on the thematic distinction between (interstate) *commerce* and (intrastate) *production*, the Court here concentrated exclusively on the effects of the federal legislation. The Court's new effect-centred test thereby cut across all the categories of dual federalism that had previously tried to protect exclusive state powers. Focusing on the consequences and not the 'nature' of activities, this new test could capture all activities—even 'trivial' or 'local' ones—whose accumulative effect might be 'far from trivial'.[30] Were there thus no external limits to the 'Commerce Clause'? For a time, not even the Tenth Amendment appeared to provide any external boundaries for the 'Commerce Clause'.[31] The Supreme Court indeed seemed to totally abdicate its judicial review function by relying on the

[28] *National Labor Relations Board v Jones & Laughlin Steel Corp* (n 27) 29, emphasis added.

[29] *National Labor Relations Board v Jones & Laughlin Steel Corp* (n 27) 36–37, emphasis added.

[30] *Wickard v Filburn* 317 US 111 [1942], 127–128: '[t]he maintenance by government regulation of a price for wheat undoubtedly can be accomplished as effectively by sustaining or increasing the demand as by limiting the supply. The effect of the statute before us is to restrict the amount which may be produced for the market and the extent as well to which one may forestall resort to the market by producing to meet his own needs. That appellee's own contribution to the demand for wheat may be trivial by itself is not enough to remove him from the scope of federal regulation where, as here, his contribution, taken together with that of many others similarly situated, is far from trivial.'

[31] Cf. *United States v Darby* 312 US 100 [1941], 124: '[t]he amendment state[d] but a truism that all is retained which has not been surrendered'. Instead of constituting an independent limit on the 'Commerce Clause', the Tenth Amendment must be 'construed as not depriving the national government of authority to resort to all means for the exercise of a granted power which are appropriate and plainly adapted to the permitted end'. In *National League of Cities v Usery* 426 US 833 [1976], the Supreme Court had still found the 'truism' to be of some significance. This 'exception' to the inoperability of the Tenth Amendment as an external limit on the 'Commerce Clause' was explicitly overruled in *Garcia v San Antonio Metropolitan Transit Authority* 469 US 528 [1985], where the Supreme Court held: '[w]e therefore now reject, as unsound in principle and unworkable in practice, a rule of state immunity from federal regulation that turns on a judicial appraisal of whether a particular governmental function is "integral" or "traditional".... We doubt that courts ultimately can identify principled constitutional limitations on the scope of Congress' Commerce Clause powers over the States merely by relying on a priori definitions of state sovereignty' (*Garcia v San Antonio Metropolitan Transit Authority* 446–548).

theory of the 'political safeguards of federalism'.[32] This new reasoning is exemplified in *Garcia v San Antonio Metropolitan Transit Authority*:

[i]t is no novelty to observe that the composition of the Federal Government was designed in large part to protect the States from overreaching by Congress.... The States were vested with indirect influence over the House of Representatives and... were given more direct influence in the Senate, where each State received equal representation and each Senator was to be selected by the legislature of his State. The significance attached to the States' equal representation in the Senate is underscored by the prohibition of any constitutional amendment divesting a State of equal representation without the State's consent... *Of course, we continue to recognize that the States occupy a special and specific position in our constitutional system and that the scope of Congress' authority under the Commerce Clause must reflect that position. But the principal and basic limit on the federal commerce power is that inherent in all congressional action—the built-in restraints that our system provides through State participation in federal governmental action. The political process ensures that laws that unduly burden the States will not be promulgated.*[33]

The denial of any—internal or external—constitutional safeguards of federalism was the strongest expression of the 'new nationalism' following the New Deal. The Court here left the scope of the 'Commerce Clause' completely in the hands of the federal legislator.

However, this theory of the political safeguards of federalism is difficult to defend;[34] and the Supreme Court's celebration of judicial passivism was indeed not to last. The Court thus revived the idea of *some* constitutional boundaries around the 'Commerce Clause' in *United States v Lopez*.[35] The respondent had violated the 1990 'Gun-Free School Act' by knowingly carrying a firearm on school premises, and challenged the federal law as an unconstitutional exercise of the 'Commerce Clause' power. Reasserting the importance of judicial review, the Court emphatically confirmed that the 'Commerce Clause' 'is subject to outer limits'.[36]

But wherein lay these 'outer limits'? Systematizing its past precedents, the Court distinguished three classes of legitimate federal legislation:

[f]irst, Congress may regulate the use of the channels of interstate commerce. Second, Congress is empowered to regulate and protect the instrumentalities of interstate commerce, or persons or things in interstate commerce, even though the threat may come only from intrastate activities. Finally, Congress' commerce authority includes the power to regulate activities having a substantial relation to interstate commerce.[37]

[32] On the theory of the political safeguards of federalism, see H. Wechsler, 'The Political Safeguards of Federalism: The Role of the States in the Composition and Selection of the National Government' (1954) 54 *Columbia Law Review* 543.

[33] *Garcia v San Antonio Metropolitan Transit Authority* (n 31) 550–551 and 556, emphasis added.

[34] L. Tribe, *American Constitutional Law*, Vol. 1 (New York: Foundation Press, 2000), 865–6: '[t]he political safeguards of federalism cannot always be counted on to prevent state-subordinating excesses of federal legislative power. The fact that Congress is made up of (and represents) individuals obviously does not guarantee that that body... will always act in accordance with individual rights; so too the fact that Congress is made up of (and reflects) the elected representatives of states does not assure that the nation's legislature will always adequate respect to the rights of states.'

[35] *United States v Lopez* 514 US 549 [1995].

[36] *United States v Lopez* (n 35) 557.

[37] *United States v Lopez* (n 35) 558–559, references omitted.

Undoubtedly, it was this third class of federal laws that would pose the greatest threat to the legislative autonomy of the states. And the Court therefore 'clarified' that the 'Commerce Clause' could only be of federal avail to regulate an economic activity that would '*substantially* affect' interstate commerce.[38]

This first—internal—limitation would be joined by a second limitation in *National Federation of Independent Business v Sebelius*.[39] The case involved a challenge to the 2010 'Patient Protection and Affordable Care Act'. The latter required all individuals—unless exempted—to purchase a minimum health insurance policy. The plaintiffs alleged that the individual mandate exceeded the boundaries of the 'Commerce Clause'. The Government objected that this was not the case, since a failure to purchase the insurance would have 'a substantial and deleterious effect on interstate commerce'.[40] This argument chartered new constitutional territory: the federal law compelled individuals to become active in the market on the grounds that their *inactivity* would (substantially) affect interstate commerce.[41] However, should the power to regulate commerce not 'presuppose . . . the existence of commercial *activity* to be regulated'? The Supreme Court indeed thought so:

> [c]onstruing the Commerce Clause to permit Congress to regulate individuals precisely because they are doing nothing would open a new and potentially vast domain to congressional authority. Every day individuals do not do an infinite number of things. In some cases they decide not to do something; in others they simply fail to do it. Allowing Congress to justify federal regulation by pointing to the effect of inaction on commerce would bring countless decisions an individual could potentially make within the scope of federal regulation, and—under the Government's theory—empower Congress to make those decisions for him . . . *The proposition that Congress may dictate the conduct of an individual today because of prophesied future activity finds no support in our precedent. We have said that Congress can anticipate the effects on commerce of an economic activity. But we have never permitted Congress to anticipate that activity itself in order to regulate individuals not currently engaged in commerce.*[42]

The power to 'regulate' commerce thus did *not* entail the power to 'create' commerce. The individual mandate could thus not be based on the 'Commerce Clause'.

Would the *post*-New Deal jurisprudence also see the revival of *external* constitutional limits to the 'Commerce Clause'? Judicial intervention indeed revived in relation to the Tenth Amendment. To maintain the 'etiquette of federalism',[43] the Federal Government would not be able to rely on the 'Commerce Clause' to

[38] *United States v Lopez* (n 35) 560.

[39] *National Federation of Independent Business v Sebelius* 567 US [2012]. An electronic copy of the judgment is available at: <http://supreme.justia.com/cases/federal/us/567/11-393>.

[40] *National Federation of Independent Business v Sebelius* (n 39) 17.

[41] *National Federation of Independent Business v Sebelius* (n 39) 18: '[b]ut Congress has never attempted to rely on that power to compel individuals not engaged in commerce to purchase an unwanted product. Legislative novelty is not necessarily fatal; there is a first time for everything. But sometimes "the most telling indication of [a] severe constitutional problem . . . is the lack of historical precedent" for Congress's action.'

[42] *National Federation of Independent Business v Sebelius* (n 39) 20 and 26, emphasis added.

[43] M.D. Adler and S.F. Kreimer, 'The New Etiquette of Federalism: New York, Printz, and Yeskey' (1998) *Supreme Court Review* 71.

'commandeer' the 'States as States' to implement federal laws.[44] Thus 'even where Congress has the authority under the Constitution to pass laws requiring or prohibiting certain acts, it lacks the power directly to compel the States to require or prohibit those acts'.[45] What was the philosophy behind this constitutional prohibition? 'States are not mere political subdivisions of the United States. State governments are neither regional offices nor administrative agencies of the Federal Government.' And having retained a 'residuary and inviolable sovereignty', the Union could not 'compel the States to enact or administer a federal regulatory program'.[46] The non-commandeering principle would thus externally limit the 'Commerce Clause'. The latter could not be used as a constitutional basis to force the states to adopt 'harmonized' state laws.

II. The 'Internal Market' Competence(s) of the European Union

The principal idea behind the European (Economic) Community was the creation of a 'common market'. The gradual unification of national markets was to be achieved by two complementary mechanisms. In the first place, the Treaties themselves would 'negate' certain national barriers to intra-European trade.[47] A second constitutional instrument was 'positive integration'. Europe would be competent to adopt legislation for the 'approximation of the laws of Member States to the extent required for the proper functioning of the common market'.[48] The original harmonisation competence for the 'common market' was contained in Articles 115 TFEU.[49] It was the European equivalent of the

[44] In *New York v United States* 505 US 144 (1992), petitioners had not contended that the Tenth Amendment limited the power of Congress to act in relation to the subject matter at issue (and the Court would affirm that Congress had power over the issue). They had only contended that the manner in which Congress had exercised its power was unconstitutional. The question was, whether 'Congress may use the states as implements of regulation; that is, whether Congress may direct or otherwise motivate the states to regulate in a particular field or a particular way'.

[45] *New York v United States* (n 44) 166.

[46] *New York v United States* (n 44) 188 (with reference to the Federalist No. 39). According to E.H. Caminker, 'State Sovereignty and Subordinancy: May Congress Commandeer State Officers to implement Federal Law?' (1995) 95 *Columbia Law Review* 1001, this formal understanding of the states as institutionally autonomous entities is 'quite new': '[u]ntil quite recently, the Supreme Court attempted to secure its view of the proper allocation of power between the two governmental systems through efforts to circumscribe the substantive content of enumerated federal power.'

[47] Art 3(a)–(c) of the original EEC Treaty. In its subsequent titles, the Treaty would lay down specific provisions on the free movement of goods, persons, services, and capital. The most well-known of these 'dormant Commerce Clauses' is art 34 TFEU. The provision reads: '[q]uantitative restrictions on imports and all measures having equivalent effect shall be prohibited between Member States.'

[48] Art 3(h) of the EEC Treaty.

[49] The Union's harmonization competences were scattered across the Treaty. Examples at the time of the adoption of the EEC Treaty were: ex-art 27 for the harmonization of customs legislation; ex-Art 54(3)(g) in the field of company law; ex-art 56(2) in the area of justified restrictions on the freedom of establishment and free provision of services; ex-art 57(2) and (3) concerning access and exercise of professional activities; ex-art 70 gave a specific harmonization competence as regards free movement of capital; ex-art 99 was confined to indirect taxation; and ex-art 117 was to permit the harmonization of social systems.

'Commerce Clause' and allowed the European Union to 'issue *directives* for the *approximation* of such provisions laid down by law, regulation or administrative action in Member States as *directly affect* the establishment or functioning of the common market'.

From the very beginning, the scope of Article 115 TFEU appeared 'quite simply unlimited'.[50] The Court had given wide interpretations to the concepts of 'directive' and 'approximation',[51] and had conveniently swept the need to show that national legislation 'directly affect[ed]' the common market under the constitutional carpet.[52] The (almost) unlimited scope of the Union's original internal market competence nonetheless encountered a *political* limit. For any Union law adopted under Article 115 TFEU requires the unanimous consent of the Member States in the Council. This political safeguard of federalism would substantially limit the exercise of the competence in the Union's early life.[53] The 1986 Single European Act however gave the Union's harmonization competence a 'brilliant assistant': Article 114 TFEU.[54] The constitutional neighbour textually widened the Union's internal market competence;[55] and—importantly—it no longer required a unanimous decision of all Member States.[56] Would the rise of decisional supranationalism—and the consequent decline in the political safeguards of federalism—induce the Court to strengthen the judicial safeguards of federalism? Would the Court consequently develop internal or external constitutional limits to the Union's (supranational) internal market competence?

[50] P. Leleux, 'Le rapprochement des législations dans la communauté economique européenne' (1968) 4 *Cahiers De Droit Européen* 129, at 138.

[51] On the 'transformation' of the directive into a directly effective and (potentially) field-pre-emptive instrument, see R. Schütze, *European Constitutional Law* (Cambridge and New York: Cambridge University Press, 2012), 323 *et seq*, as well as 371 *et seq*. On the wide notion of 'approximation', see section II.1.a.

[52] On the function and scope of art 115 TFEU in the Union legal order, see F. Marx, *Funktion und Grenzen der Rechtsangleichung nach Art.100 EWG-Vertrag* (Cologne, Berlin, Bonn, and Munich: Heymanns, 1976); and C. Eiden, *Die Rechtsangleichung gemäß Art.100 des EWG-Vertrages* (Berlin: Duncker & Humblot, 1984).

[53] On this point, see A. Dashwood, 'Hastening Slowly: The Community's Path Towards Harmonization', in H. Wallace, W. Wallace, and C. Webb (eds.), *Policy-Making in the European Community* (London and New York: Wiley & Sons Ltd, 1983), 177.

[54] D. Vignes, 'The Harmonisation of National Legislation and the EEC' (1990) 15 *European Law Review* 358, at 367.

[55] Constitutionally, art 114 TFEU no longer contained the—by now obsolete—references to 'directives' as instruments of harmonization; nor did it mention the 'direct [e]ffect' of national laws on the internal market.

[56] This reinforcement of the Union's harmonization power would, however, be thematically limited, since the new competence could 'not apply to fiscal provisions, to those relating to the free movement of persons nor to those relating to the rights and interests of employed persons' (art 114(2) TFEU). Obstacles to trade or distortions of competition arising from regulatory barriers within these areas would thus still have to be eliminated by recourse to art 115, or one of the special legal bases provided for in the Treaty (e.g. art 113 for the harmonization of indirect taxation).

1. Internal limits: harmonization for the internal market

a) *The concept of 'approximation' or 'harmonization'*

Would the idea of 'approximation' or 'harmonization' conceptually require the *prior* and *subsequent* existence of national laws regulating trade within the European market?[57]

For a long time, European constitutional thought strongly linked the concept of harmonization to the *subsequent* approximation of national laws. Originally, this was the result of the harmonization instrument of the 'directive'.[58] Directives require Member States to adopt national legislation that will implement the European command. The result of a directive would thus be 'harmonized' *national* rules; and it seemed that the *subsequent* existence of national rules was a conceptual characteristic of the notion of harmonization. This however changed with the Single European Act, which decoupled the idea of harmonization from the 'directive'. The Union could henceforth adopt any measure under its internal market competence, and this included 'regulations' as instruments of *direct* Union legislation.[59]

But would harmonization measures not have to be at least generally applicable? For how could an individual decision—an executive act—ever harmonize national laws? In *Germany v Council*,[60] this constitutional delicacy was placed on the judicial table. Germany argued that the power to 'harmonize' precluded the executive power from adopting decisions;[61] and since Article 9 of the Product Safety Directive granted such a power in certain situations, the provision had to be void.[62] The Court held otherwise:

> [t]he measures which the Council is empowered to take under that provision are aimed at 'the establishment and functioning of the internal market'. In certain fields, and particularly

[57] In this sense: J. Usher, 'Harmonisation of Legislation', in D. Lasok and others (eds.), *Les Communautés Européennes en Fonctionnement* (Brussels: Bruylant, 1981), 171, at 174, arguing that the concept of 'approximation' 'would appear necessarily to imply that the matter in question is governed by national rules in the first place, and remains governed by national rules after they have been harmonized'.

[58] According to art 288(3) TFEU, '[a] directive shall be binding, as to the result to be achieved, upon each Member State to which it is addressed, but shall leave to the national authorities the choice of form and methods'.

[59] On the Union instrument of 'regulation', see Schütze (n 51) 317 *et seq*.

[60] Case C-359/92 *Germany v Council* [1994] ECR I-3681.

[61] Germany's principal claim in this respect is quoted in para 17: '[t]he German Government objects to that argument essentially on the ground that the sole aim of Article [114] et seq. of the [FEU] Treaty, and of Article [114 (1)] in particular, is the approximation of laws and that those articles do not therefore confer power to apply the law to individual cases in the place of the national authorities, as permitted by Article 9 of the directive.'

[62] Directive 92/59/EEC on general product safety, [1992] OJ L 228/24, which is now replaced by Directive 2001/95/EC on general product safety, [2002] OJ L 11/4. Art 9 provided as follows: '[i]f the Commission becomes aware, through notification given by the Member States or through information provided by them, in particular under Article 7 or Article 8, of the existence of a serious and immediate risk from a product to the health and safety of consumers in various Member States and if: (a) one or more Member States have adopted measures entailing restrictions on the marketing of the product or requiring its withdrawal from the market, such as those provided for in Article 6(1) (d) to (h); (b) Member States differ on the adoption of measures to deal with the risk in question;

in that of product safety, the approximation of general laws alone may not be sufficient to ensure the unity of the market. *Consequently, the concept of 'measures for the approximation' of legislation must be interpreted as encompassing the Council's power to lay down measures relating to a specific product or class of products and, if necessary, individual measures concerning those products.*[63]

Article 114 TFEU would thus entitle the Union to adopt executive decisions. (Yet, since the ruling dealt with a *state*-addressed decision, its constitutional impact might have been confined to that category.) Yet, could the provision also be employed for the establishment of a centralized authorization procedure operated by the Commission or even the creation of the Union's own executive infrastructure?[64]

Subsequent jurisprudence clarified that Article 114 could indeed be used for both purposes. For the adoption of decisions addressed to individuals, the cause célèbre is *United Kingdom v Parliament and Council*.[65] The case concerned the validity of Regulation 2065/2003, which tried to ensure the effective functioning of the internal market through a Union authorization procedure. The legislative measure delegated the power to grant or reject authorizations to the Commission; and its decisions were addressed to the individual applicant.[66] The British Government protested: 'The legislative power conferred by Article [114 TFEU] is a power to *harmonise* national laws, *not a power to establish [Union] bodies or to confer tasks on such bodies, or to establish procedures for the approval of lists of authorised products*.'[67] Yet in its judgment, the Court confirmed this very power.[68] The Union legislator would enjoy 'a discretion, depending on the general context and the specific circumstances of the matter to be harmonised, as regards the harmonisation technique'.[69] This granted the Union an (almost) total freedom with regard to the

(c) the risk cannot be dealt with, in view of the nature of the safety issue posed by the product and in a manner compatible with the urgency of the case, under the other procedures laid down by the specific [Union] legislation applicable to the product or category of products concerned; and (d) the risk can be eliminated effectively only by adopting appropriate measures applicable at [Union] level, in order to ensure the protection of the health and safety of consumers and the proper functioning of the common market, the Commission, after consulting the Member States and at the request of at least one of them, may adopt a decision, in accordance with the procedure laid down in Article 11, requiring Member States to take temporary measures from among those listed in Article 6(1)(d) to (h).'

63 *Germany v Council* (n 60) paras 37–38, emphasis added.

64 For a recent and critical analysis of this question in the context of the European Banking Authority, see E. Fahey, 'Does the Emperor have Financial Cloth? Reflections on the Legal Basis of the European Banking Authority' (2011) 74 *Modern Law Review* 581.

65 Case 66/04 *United Kingdom v Parliament and Council* [2005] ECR I-10553. In relation to the use of art 114 TFEU to create a Union body, see Case C-217/04 *United Kingdom v Parliament and Council* (*ENISA*) [2006] ECR I-3771, esp para 44: '[t]he legislature may deem it necessary to provide for the establishment of a [Union] body responsible for contributing to the implementation of a process of harmonisation in situations where, in order to facilitate the uniform implementation and application of acts based on that provision, the adoption of non-binding supporting and framework measures seems appropriate.'

66 Art 9(1)(b) of the Regulation; and see also: art 11(1) of the Regulation.

67 *United Kingdom v Parliament and Council* (n 65) para 18, emphasis added.

68 *United Kingdom v Parliament and Council* (n 65) para 64.

69 *United Kingdom v Parliament and Council* (n 65) para 45. This was confirmed in: Case C-217/04 *United Kingdom v Parliament and Council* (2006) ECR I-3771 para 43.

formal type of harmonization action. This freedom of form complemented the substantive freedom of the Union legislator. For the Court has never identified the concept of harmonization with a 'medium' regulatory standard, and indeed grants the Union legislator a wide substantive discretion.[70]

What about the *prior* existence of national laws as a precondition for Article 114 TFEU? This question was the subject of *Spain v Council*.[71] The European legislator believed the national protection period for medicinal products to be insufficient, and saw this insufficiency as penalizing European pharmaceutical research. It had therefore created a supplementary protection certificate, which could be granted under the same conditions as national patents by each of the Member States.[72] Two major constitutional hurdles seemed to oppose the legality of this European law. First, Article 114 TFEU could theoretically not be used to create *new* rights as it could only harmonize *existing* rights.[73] Secondly, at the time of its adoption only *two* Member States had legislation concerning a supplementary certificate.

The Court took the first hurdle by force. It simply rejected the claim that the European law created a new right.[74] Concentrating on the second hurdle, the Court then addressed the question whether Article 114 required the *pre*-existence of diverse national laws. In the eyes of the Court, this was not the case. The Union could use its internal market competence 'to prevent the heterogeneous development of national laws leading to further disparities which would be likely to create obstacles to the free movement of medicinal products within the [Union] and thus directly affect the establishment and the functioning of the internal market'.[75] The Union was thus entitled to use its harmonization power to prevent the *potential* fragmentation of the internal market.[76]

[70] For an early version of this argument, see T. Vogelaar, 'The Approximation of the Laws of the Member States under the Treaty of Rome' (1975) 12 *Common Market Law Review* 211, at 213. The Union standard will nonetheless be subject to the principle of proportionality (cf. art 5(4) TEU). One substantive orientation for the Union harmonization standard can be found in art 114 (3) TFEU, which reads: '[t]he Commission, in its proposals envisaged in paragraph 1 concerning health, safety, environmental protection and consumer protection, will take as a base a high level of protection, taking account in particular of any new development based on scientific facts. Within their respective powers, the European Parliament and the Council will also seek to achieve this objective.'

[71] Case C-350/92 *Spain v Council* [1995] ECR I-1985. But see now also Case C-58/08 *Vodafone and others v Secretary of State for Business, Enterprise and Regulatory Reform* (2010) ECR I-4999.

[72] Reg 1768/92 concerning the creation of a supplementary protection certificate for medicinal products [1992] OJ L182/1.

[73] Legislation for the creation of new rights will have to be based on Art 352 TFEU, cf. *Spain v Council* (n 71) para 23 (with reference to Opinion 1/94 on the competence of the Community to conclude international agreements concerning services and the protection of intellectual property, [1994] ECR I-5267 para 59).

[74] *Spain v Council* (n 71) para 27.

[75] *Spain v Council* (n 71) para 35 (with reference to the sixth recital of Regulation 1768/92).

[76] On the idea of 'preventive' harmonization in the internal market, see M. Seidel, 'Präventive Rechtsangleichung im Bereich des Gemeinsamen Marktes' (2006) 41 *Europarecht* 26. For some limits, see however: Case C-436/03 *Parliament and Council* [2006] ECR I-3733 para 44, emphasis added. The Court here confirmed and extended the point made in relation to intellectual property law (cf. *Spain v Council* (n 71); as well as Case C-377/98 *Netherlands v Council and Parliament* [2001] ECR I-7079) to 'new legal forms in addition to the national forms of cooperative societies' (para 40).

b) The 'establishment' or 'functioning' of the Internal Market

The Union's competence to harmonize national laws is a functional competence. It is not thematically limited, and applies to *any* measure that affects the establishment or functioning of the internal market.[77] The former alternative concerns obstacles to intra-Union trade; whereas the latter alternative captures distortions of competition resulting from disparities between national laws. However, *to what extent* would Union legislation have to serve the 'establishment' or 'functioning' of the internal market? What effects would the Union law have to have on the internal market?

Until the end of the twentieth century, the jurisprudence of the Court had unequivocally confirmed the widest possible reading of the European 'Commerce Clause'. Yet, the Court finally confirmed the existence of constitutional limits in *Germany v Parliament and Council* (*Tobacco Advertising*).[78] The bone of contention was a European law that banned the advertising and sponsorship of tobacco products.[79] Could a prohibition or ban be based on the Union's *Commerce* Clause? Germany objected to the idea. It argued that the Union's internal market power could only be used to promote the internal market; and this was not so in the event, where the federal legislation constituted, in practice, a total prohibition of tobacco advertising.[80] Further, even if total bans could legitimately be based on Article 114 on the grounds of removing distortions of competition, this second alternative would have to be limited to cases where the distortion was 'considerable'.[81]

The Court accepted—to the surprise of many—these invitations and annulled, for the first time in its history, a European law on the grounds that it went beyond the Union's 'Commerce Clause'. Emphatically, the Court pointed out that the latter could not grant the Union a general power to regulate the internal market:

> *[t]o construe that article as meaning that it vests in the [Union] legislature a general power to regulate the internal market would not only be contrary to the express wording of the provisions cited above but would also be incompatible with the principle embodied in Article [5 TEU] that the powers of the [Union] are limited to those specifically conferred on it.* Moreover, a measure adopted on the basis of Article [114] of the Treaty must genuinely have as its object the improvement of the conditions for the establishment and functioning of the internal

[77] Cf. S. Weatherill, 'The Limits of Legislative Harmonization Ten Years after Tobacco Advertising: How the Court's Case Law has become a "Drafting Guide"' (2011) 12 *German Law Journal* 827, at 831: '[a]rticle [114] is functionally driven: any national measure may be harmonized provided that leads to an improvement in the functioning of the internal market envisaged by Article 26 TFEU[.]'

[78] Case C-376/98 *Germany v Parliament and Council* (*Tobacco Advertising*) [2000] ECR I-8419.

[79] Directive 98/43/EC on the approximation of the laws, regulations and administrative provisions of the Member States relating to the advertising and sponsorship of tobacco products [1998] OJ L 213/9.

[80] Germany had pointed out that the sole form of advertising allowed under the Directive was advertising at the point of sale, which only accounted for 2 per cent of the tobacco industry's advertising expenditure (*Tobacco Advertising* (n 78) para 24).

[81] *Tobacco Advertising* (n 78) para 29. There was case law to support this claim, e.g. Case 91/79 *Commission v Italy* [1980] ECR 1099 para 8; as well as Case C-300/89 *Commission v Council* (*Titanium Dioxide*) [1991] ECR I-2867 para 23.

market. If a mere finding of disparities between national rules and of the abstract risk of obstacles to the exercise of fundamental freedoms or of distortions of competition liable to result therefrom were sufficient to justify the choice of Article [114] as a legal basis, judicial review of compliance with the proper legal basis might be rendered nugatory.[82]

What consequences did the Court draw from this statement of principle? The Court split its analysis into an 'establishment' and 'functioning' part and analysed, in turn, the two alternative applications of the Union's harmonization power.

Regarding the elimination of obstacles to free movement, the Court qualified its generous ruling in *Spain v Council.* While accepting that 'recourse to Article [114] as a legal basis is possible if the aim is to prevent the emergence of future obstacles to trade resulting from multifarious development of national laws', the Court nonetheless insisted that '*the emergence of such obstacles must be likely* and the measure in question must be designed to prevent them'.[83] Were future obstacles to intra-Union trade in tobacco advertising likely? The Court accepted this for press products. 'However, for numerous types of advertising of tobacco products, the prohibition under Article 3(1) of the Directive cannot be justified by the need to eliminate obstacles to the free movement of advertising media or the freedom to provide services in the field of advertising'.[84] In the light of this, the European legislature had not been entitled to rely on its internal market power on the grounds that the measure would eliminate obstacles to free movement.

However, recourse to the competence could still have been justified by means of the second alternative in Article 114: the elimination of distortions of competition. Here, though, the Court accepted Germany's invitation and introduced a second internal limitation: the distortion of competition would have to be *appreciable.* In the absence of such a requirement, the powers of the [Union] legislature would be practically unlimited. Constitutionally, the federal legislator could thus not pass laws under Article 114 'with a view to eliminating the smallest distortions of competition'.[85] And since the national laws at issue had only a 'remote and indirect' effect on competition, disparities between them could not lead to distortions that were appreciable.[86] The Directive could thus neither have been legitimately based on the second prong of the internal market power and the Court consequently annulled the European law.

With *Tobacco Advertising*, the Court consequently accepted *some* effects-related internal limits on the Union's internal market power. First, a simple disparity in national laws will not be enough to trigger the Union's Commerce Clause. The disparity must give rise to obstacles in trade or appreciable distortions in competition. While Article 114 TFEU can be used to 'harmonize' *future* disparities in national laws, it must be 'likely' that the divergent development of national laws leads to obstacles in trade. (The Court has—strangely—come to verbalize this requirement by extending the constitutional criterion of a 'direct effect'—textually mandated

82 *Tobacco Advertising* (n 78) paras 83–84.
83 *Tobacco Advertising* (n 78) para 86, emphasis added.
84 *Tobacco Advertising* (n 78) paras 97 and 99.
85 *Tobacco Advertising* (n 78) paras 106–107.
86 *Tobacco Advertising* (n 78) para 109.

only in Article 115 TFEU—to Article 114 TFEU.)[87] And secondly, the Union measure must actually contribute to the elimination of obstacles to free movement or distortions of competition.[88] These two constitutional limits to the Union's 'Commerce Clause' were confirmed *in abstracto* by subsequent jurisprudence; yet, their concrete application has led to renewed accusations that Article 114 grants the Union a general competence for the internal market.[89]

2. External limits: constitutional 'saving clauses' for state 'police powers'?

From the beginning, certain provisions within the Treaties could be read as constitutional guarantees for national exclusive powers. Apart from the mysterious Article 345 TFEU,[90] one of the prominent candidates was Article 36 TFEU. The provision allows states to justify a violation of the free movement of goods on grounds of, *inter alia*, public morality, public policy, and public security. Had these policy fields remained within the exclusive powers of the states? The European Court gave short shrift to that argument in *Simmenthal*.[91] Pointing out that Article 36 TFEU was 'not designed to reserve certain matters to the exclusive jurisdiction of Member States',[92] the Member States could not insist on their stricter national laws where Union legislation provided for the necessary protection of the interests in Article 36 TFEU. Reacting to this early defeat, the Member States have increasingly used subsequent Treaty amendments to insert provisions designed to protect national powers within the Treaty. The most important species of these clauses

[87] Cf. Case C-210/03 *Swedish Match* [2004] ECR I-11893 para 29; as well as Case 380/03 *Germany v Parliament and Council* (*Tobacco Advertising II*) [2006] ECR I-11573 para 37. See also: Case C-58/08 *R, on the application of Vodafone Ltd and Others v Secretary of State for Business, Enterprise and Regulatory Reform* (2010) ECR I-4999 para 32 (emphasis added): '[w]hile a mere finding of disparities between national rules and the abstract risk of infringements of fundamental freedoms or distortion of competition is not sufficient to justify the choice of Article [114 TFEU] as a legal basis, the [Union] legislature may have recourse to it in particular where there are differences between national rules which are such as to obstruct the fundamental freedoms and thus have a direct effect on the functioning of the internal market.'

[88] Case C-491/01 *British American Tobacco* [2002] ECR I-11453 para 60.

[89] This has led D. Wyatt, 'Community Competence to Regulate the Internal Market', *Oxford Faculty of Law Research Paper* 9/2007, 23 to query whether *Tobacco Advertising* was a 'false dawn'. For an analysis of legislative and judicial practice after *Tobacco Advertising*, see also the excellent analysis by Weatherill (n 77).

[90] The provision reads: '[t]his Treaties shall in no way prejudice the rules in Member States governing the system of property ownership.'

[91] Case 35/76 *Simmenthal v Italian Minister of Finance* [1976] ECR 1871.

[92] *Simmenthal v Italian Minister of Finance* (n 91) para 14. However, for a judicial 'slip of the tongue', see Case 265/95 *Commission v France* [1997] ECR I-6959 paras 32–33: '[a]rticle [34 TFEU] therefore requires the Member States not merely themselves to abstain from adopting measures or engaging in conduct liable to constitute an obstacle to trade but also, when read with Article [4(3) TEU] of the Treaty, to take all necessary and appropriate measures to ensure that that fundamental freedom is respected on their territory. In the latter context, the Member States, which retain exclusive competence as regards the maintenance of public order and the safeguarding of internal security, unquestionably enjoy a margin of discretion in determining what measures are most appropriate to eliminate barriers to the importation of products in a given situation.'

excludes the Union from harmonizing national laws within a specific policy area.[93] For example: within its 'public health' competence under Article 168 TFEU, the Union is entitled to adopt health measures '*excluding any harmonisation* of the laws and regulations of the Member States'.[94]

Would these 'saving clauses' externally limit the Union's internal market competence? The European Court has expressed a negative inclination in *Germany v Parliament and Council (Tobacco Advertising)*.[95] While admitting that '[t]he national measures *affected* [were] to a large extent inspired by public health policy objectives',[96] the Union harmonization measure was nonetheless legitimate. For Article 168 (5) TFEU did 'not mean that harmonizing measures adopted on the basis of other provisions of the Treaty cannot have any impact on the protection of human health'.[97] '[T]he [Union] legislature cannot be prevented from relying on that legal basis on the ground that public health protection is a decisive factor in the choices to be made.'[98] The express saving clause would thus *not* operate as an external limitation on Article 114 TFEU. Where Union legislation served an internal market objective, the Union legislator could enter into health-related fields. However, the Court conceded that these saving clauses did have some constitutional significance: the Union must not use its internal market power 'to circumvent the express exclusion of harmonisation laid down in Article [168 (5)] of the Treaty'.[99]

While these local 'savings clauses' do consequently not directly limit Article 114 TFEU, the latter will nonetheless find an absolute external limit in the 'constitutional identity' of the European Union.[100] And since the Lisbon Treaty introduced Article 4(2) TEU, the new provision might potentially even extend this external limit to the protection of the constitutional identity of the Member States.[101]

[93] For an overview of the various types of constitutional 'saving clauses' in the Union legal order, see R Schütze, 'The European Community's Federal Order of Competences: A Retrospective Analysis', in M. Dougan and S. Currie (eds.), *Fifty Years of the European Treaties—Looking back and Thinking Forward* (Oxford and Portland, Or.: Hart, 2009), 63, at 87–90.

[94] Art 168(5) TFEU, emphasis added.

[95] *Germany v Council (Tobacco Advertising)* (n 78).

[96] *Germany v Council (Tobacco Advertising)* (n 78) para 76, emphasis added.

[97] *Germany v Council (Tobacco Advertising)* (n 78) para 78.

[98] *Germany v Council (Tobacco Advertising)* (n 78) para 88.

[99] *Germany v Council (Tobacco Advertising)* (n 78) para 79.

[100] For this argument, albeit in the context of art 352 TFEU, see Opinion 2/94, *Accession by the European Community to the ECHR* [1996] ECR I-1759.

[101] Art 4(2) TEU states: '[t]he Union shall respect the equality of Member States before the Treaties as well as their national identities, inherent in their fundamental structures, political and constitutional, inclusive of regional and local self-government. It shall respect their essential State functions, including ensuring the territorial integrity of the State, maintaining law and order and safeguarding national security. In particular, national security remains the sole responsibility of each Member State.' The meaning of art 4(2) TEU remains highly controversial. For an excellent overview of the provision—and its potential as a future constitutional tool—see B. Guastaferro, 'Beyond the *Exceptionalism* of Constitutional Conflicts: The *Ordinary* Functions of the Identity Clause' (2012) 31 *Yearbook of European Law* 263.

III. Comparisons and Conclusions

The creation of an 'internal market' is a classic task of many federations. The United States and the European Union both enjoy a legislative competence to achieve this aim. Owing to its functional scope, this internal market competence has been subject to intense constitutional debates on both sides of the Atlantic. For, while there must—in theory—be constitutional limitations to its scope, the extent to which the two federations have exercised their competence has almost continuously expanded in constitutional practice.

This expanding federal universe can best be traced in the history of the United States' 'Commerce Clause'. The extent to which economic 'unity within diversity' could be created has here, however, changed over time. Prior to the 'New Deal', the Union's 'Commerce Clause' was internally and externally limited by solid constitutional safeguards. Internally, the Clause's reference to the 'regulat[ion]' of commerce was taken to exclude general 'prohibitions' of commerce. Further, according to the—then dominant—philosophy of dual federalism, particular policy areas were completely outside the scope of the 'Commerce Clause'. Both constitutional limitations were to wither away in the aftermath of the New Deal, in the course of which the Supreme Court left the federal balance to the political safeguards of federalism. However, should the federal legislator be entitled to autonomously determine the scope of the 'Commerce Clause' without any constitutional limitations? This view was ultimately rejected in *Garcia*, where the Court revived the idea of *judicial* safeguards of federalism. What constitutional boundaries would limit the 'Commerce Clause'? We saw earlier that the Court insists upon three principal limitations. First, federal legislation must regulate (or prohibit[102]) an economic activity that would '*substantially* affect' interstate commerce.[103] Secondly, while federal legislation can 'regulate', it cannot 'create' federal commerce.[104] Thirdly, there is an external limit to the 'Commerce Clause' in the form of the non-commandeering rule.[105] Federal commerce legislation cannot require state legislatures to adopt 'harmonized' state laws.

What about the European Union's internal market competence? Textually, the latter seemed—at least in one respect—more limited than its American counterpart. For the Union's power to establish its common market appeared to hinge on the 'harmonization' of existing national laws. Yet the European Court of Justice managed to gradually transform this 'harmonization' power into a 'regulatory' power that was—almost—completely independent of the existence of national legislation. This liberation was achieved by means of the doctrine of 'preventive' harmonization, as well as the judicial acceptance of an (almost) unlimited Union discretion with regard to its 'harmonization' techniques. The sole constitutional

[102] Cf. *United States v Lopez* (n 35); as well as: *Gonzales v Raich* 545 US 1 [2005].
[103] Cf. *United States v Lopez* (n 35) 560.
[104] Cf. *National Federation of Independent Business v Sebelius* (n 39).
[105] Cf. *New York v United States* (n 44).

limit that the Court still appears—at least rhetorically—to confirm is the inability of 'harmonization measures' to create 'new rights'.[106] What about the reference to the 'establishment' or 'functioning' of the internal market? That a federal law adopted under Article 114 TFEU could not just 'regulate' but also generally 'prohibit' was confirmed in *Tobacco Advertising*.[107] However, the Court here clarified that those commercial prohibitions, if not likely to remove obstacles to trade, must 'appreciably' serve the functioning of the internal market. The federal legislator could thus not pass laws 'with a view to eliminating the smallest distortions of competition'. The opposite view would be incompatible with the principle of conferred powers on which the Union's federal structure was based.[108]

In conclusion: the internal market competences of both federal unions are horizontal competences that mainly concentrate on the effects of federal legislation. The effects-based test has meant that there are no a priori thematic exclusions from the scope of the Union competences. (The sole external limitation accepted in US jurisprudence is of a formal nature: the states cannot be 'commandeered' into harmonizing national law.) In the absence of any tangible internal or external *thematic* limitations on both competences, the only 'real' limits have been the political safeguards of federalism. These safeguards appear much stronger in the European Union. For unlike the simple state majority in the US Senate, a qualified majority of states continues to be required to back Union legislation. This higher political hurdle will (partly) diminish, however, once the (new) Lisbon voting system comes into operation.[109] The European Union will thus—even in this respect—follow in the footsteps of the American 'Commerce Clause'.

[106] Cf. Case C-350/92 *Spain v Council* [1995] ECR I-1985.

[107] *Germany v Parliament and Council* (*Tobacco Advertising*) (n 78).

[108] *Germany v Parliament and Council* (*Tobacco Advertising*) (n 78) paras 106–107.

[109] From 1 November 2014 a completely new system of voting is to apply in the Council. This revolutionary change is set out in art 16(4) TEU: '[a]s from 1 November 2014, a qualified majority shall be defined as at least 55 per cent of the members of the Council, comprising at least 15 of them and representing Member States comprising at least 65 per cent of the population of the Union. A blocking minority must include at least four Council members, failing which the qualified majority shall be deemed attained. The other arrangements governing the qualified majority are laid down in Article 238(2) of the Treaty on the Functioning of the European Union.'

11

Subsidiarity as a Procedural Safeguard of Federalism

Xavier Groussot and Sanja Bogojević *

Introduction

The subsidiarity principle is of obvious importance in a federal legal order built on conferred competences. Here, the federal order refers to a dual-levelled form of governance, that is the central and the national that operate in constitutional plurality, or, in other words, the legal order of the European Union (the Union). In such mode of organization, the key issue is establishing and enforcing mechanisms whereby the efficiency of the federal structure is ensured while avoiding excessive centralization of regulatory power.[1] The core ethos of the subsidiarity principle is thus to deal with the division of fields of competences between the Union and its Member States, or to ensure that the Union has not become a super-state, but indeed stays within its conferred competences.[2] To put it bluntly, the principle of subsidiarity is 'important in allaying fears about the "F" word (federalism)'.[3]

The ancient roots of the subsidiarity principle are well documented.[4] In the EU legal context, subsidiarity was first tied to the regulation of the environment but soon developed to respond to the loss of the right to veto decision-making procedures at the EU level following the Treaty of Maastricht. The role bestowed on subsidiarity was a judicially enforceable mechanism that prevents the excessive use of non-exclusive Union powers, pre-empting Member State legislative action. In this sense, the principle of subsidiarity serves as a substitute for the political safeguards protecting the Member States' residual powers.[5] In deploying such mechanisms, however, the EU

* This research was generously sponsored by Ragnar Söderberg Stiftelse, to which we are grateful.

1 That is, maintaining the distinction between 'federal' and 'state' power, see P. Craig, 'Subsidiarity: A Political and Legal Analysis' (2012) 50 *Journal of Common Market Studies* 72, at 73.

2 R. Schütze, *From Dual to Cooperative Federalism: The Changing Structure of European Law* (Oxford: Oxford University Press, 2009), 247.

3 Craig (n 1).

4 The subsidiarity principle is often described to be as old as the Roman Empire: see A. Estella, *The EU Principle of Subsidiarity and its Critique* (Oxford: Oxford University Press, 2002) and Schütze (n 2).

5 K. Lenaerts, 'The Principle of Subsidiarity and the Environment in the European Union: Keeping the Balance of Federalism' (1993) 17 *Fordham International Law Journal* 846, at 851–2.

has frequently been criticized for failing to protect the autonomy of national powers.[6] Indeed, a recurring argument is that, if European federalism is to be safeguarded, new mechanisms should be sought.[7]

The argument to be advanced in this chapter is that two distinct approaches to monitoring subsidiarity, focused on procedural tests of competence, have the capability of providing a new approach to the judicial control of subsidiarity.[8] More precisely, the Lisbon Treaty brings an increase in *ex ante* political control by empowering national parliaments to issue 'early warning' signals for breaches of the subsidiarity principle. The *ex post* legal control remains as a crucial complement, which, moreover, is strengthened by the new legal framework.[9] In our view, this constitutional provision of the Lisbon Treaty, together with the parallel rise of the impact assessments used as an EU institutional policy, reflect a general move towards proceduralization. This shift in mood, or *zeitgeist*, is starting to show in judicial review exercised by the Court of Justice of the European Union (ECJ) in subsidiarity cases that will be explored in this chapter.

More precisely, this chapter starts by examining the procedural competence tests that are available in the *post*-Lisbon era. Our starting point is the competence test layered on top of Article 5 TEU; that is, the political safeguard vested with the national parliaments enabling them to warn the Commission of potential infringements of the subsidiarity principle. Describing first the functionality of such assessment, we then discuss the possible implications that these changes may lead to with regard to process-based review. The following part of this chapter discusses the second competence-based tool in monitoring the subsidiarity principle: the obligations imposed on the Commission to carry out impact assessment in the pre-legislative phase. Subsequently, the earlier case law involving the principle of subsidiarity is examined, followed by an analysis of the way in which the Court interprets subsidiarity cases in light of the two new process-based approaches. In the concluding part, the findings in the chapter are summarized and the high aspirations for the new safeguards of federalism are confirmed.

[6] See e.g. G. Davies, 'Subsidiarity: The Wrong Idea, in the Wrong Place, at the Wrong Time' (2006) 43 *Common Market Law Review* 63; D. Edwards, 'Fearing Federalism's Failure: Subsidiarity in the European Union' (1996) 44 *American Journal of Comparative Law* 537; G. Martinico, 'Dating Cinderella: On subsidiarity as a political safeguard of federalism in the European Union' (2011) 17 *European Public Law* 649. Cf. P. Syrpis, 'In Defence of Subsidiarity' (2004) 24 *Oxford Journal of Legal Studies* 323.

[7] L. Azoulai, 'Introduction', *EUI Working Paper* 2012/06, available at: <http://cadmus.eui.eu/bitstream/handle/1814/21298/LAW_2012_06_Rev2.pdf>.

[8] The argument about procedure-based review is inspired by K. Lenaerts, 'The European Court of Justice and Process-oriented Review' (2013) 32 *Yearbook of European Law* 3.

[9] An argument similarly furthered by D. Wyatt, 'Could a "Yellow Card" for National Parliaments Strengthen the Judicial as well as the Political Policing of Subsidiarity?' (2006) 2 *Croatian Yearbook of European Law & Policy* 1.

I. Political Competence Test in the Post-Lisbon Era

Following the implementation of the Lisbon Treaty, a number of procedural tests are available to check the use of competences in the EU federal legal order. The most important and obvious provision is listed in Article 5 TEU, which is transposed word-by-word from the previous treaty. This provision establishes a test of competences directed towards the institutions and monitored by the ECJ in case of litigation. The test is based on the *existence* (this is, the 'can' question is asked) and the *use* (this is, the 'who' and 'how' questions are raised) of Union competences. As stated in Articles 5(3) and (4) TEU, once it is found that the aims of the Union action can best be achieved at the central level (paragraph 3), the legislator must not go beyond what is necessary to achieve these aims (paragraph 4). Here, it is worth listing the two paragraphs:[10]

> 3. Under the principle of subsidiarity, in areas which do not fall within its exclusive competence, the Union shall act only if and *in so far as* the objectives of the proposed action cannot be sufficiently achieved by the Member States, either at central level or at regional and local level, but can rather, by reason of the scale or effects of the proposed action, be better achieved at Union level. The institutions of the Union shall apply the principle of subsidiarity as laid down in the Protocol on the application of the principles of subsidiarity and proportionality. National Parliaments ensure compliance with the principle of subsidiarity in accordance with the procedure set out in that Protocol.
>
> 4. Under the principle of proportionality, the content and form of Union action shall not exceed what is necessary to achieve the objectives of the Treaties. The institutions of the Union shall apply the principle of proportionality as laid down in the Protocol on the application of the principles of subsidiarity and proportionality.

It is in the assessment of the *use* of Union competences that the principle of subsidiarity comes into play with the principle of proportionality. Indeed, a quick reading of Article 5 TEU shows that the test of proportionality in Article 5(4) TEU should be addressed having first assessed 'who' is responsible to take the specific action according to Article 5(3) TEU. The subsidiarity question is thus not about the objective pursued but *whether* the pursuit of that objective requires Union action.[11] Yet, on a closer reading of Article 5(3) TEU, proportionality—as expressed in the text by the words 'in so far as'—constitutes an integral part of the subsidiarity calculus.[12] As stated by de Búrca,

> [t]he more precisely the aims of an action are defined for the purpose of Article 5(3) TEU, the more this overlaps with Article 5(4) TEU and becomes also a question of 'How' or what kind of Union power should be exercised.[13]

[10] Emphasis added.

[11] See AG Maduro, Case C-58/08 *Vodafone* [2010] ECR I-4999 para 30. This approach reflects the distinction between the so-called 'subsidiarity in the strict sense' *contra* 'subsidiarity in the wide sense': see Lenaerts (n 5) 875.

[12] Schütze (n 2) 250, discusses the textual ambivalence of art 5(2) EC. Since art 5(3) TEU is a copy-paste of art 5(2) EC, it can thus similarly be described as 'a textual failure'.

[13] G. de Búrca, 'The Principle of Subsidiarity and the Court of Justice as an Institutional Actor' (1998) 36 *Journal of Common Market Studies* 217, at 220.

To phrase it differently, proportionality has 'cannibalized' the principle of subsidiarity. This 'cannibalization' is also visible within the reasoning of the ECJ in a number of subsidiarity cases.[14] This means that the 'who' and the 'how' are inherently tied together. This situation clearly adds fuel to the argument that subsidiarity should be understood in terms of 'federal proportionality',[15] an argument to which we will return.

The relevant point in this overview of Article 5(3) TEU is that the EU's conferral of competences involves a series of procedural steps, including establishing 'who' should legislate.[16] In this regard, Protocol No. 2 on the application of the principles of subsidiarity and proportionality annexed to the Lisbon Treaty is of key importance, since it offers specific guidelines for rendering subsidiarity an operational principle. It is worth remarking here that the Amsterdam Protocol (Protocol No. 13) is almost entirely rewritten by Protocol No. 2. Indeed, in contrast to the Amsterdam Protocol, the new Protocol focuses almost exclusively on procedural aspects.[17] It is to this new competence test that we now turn.

1. National parliaments as political safeguards

In the *post*-Lisbon era, national parliaments play an important role in the decision-making process at EU level. This role stems from the duty imposed on the Commission to consult widely before proposing legislative acts,[18] and to forward its draft legislative acts to national parliaments at the same time as to the Union legislator.[19] Here the Commission must provide a 'detailed statement' concerning proposed legislation so that compliance with subsidiarity can be assessed.[20] This statement must contain some assessment of the financial impact of the proposals, as well as qualitative and, wherever possible, quantitative indicators to substantiate the conclusion that the objective can be better attained at EU level.[21]

Within eight weeks following the initiation of the consultation period, the national parliaments can issue a so-called 'yellow' or 'orange' card, thereby signalling a risk of breach of the subsidiarity principle. The 'yellow card' follows where non-compliance with subsidiarity is claimed by national parliaments that represent one-third of all the votes assigned to such parliaments. In accordance with Protocol No. 2, the Commission must then review its proposal and thereafter decide to maintain, amend, or withdraw the proposal, giving reasons for the decision.[22] The 'orange card' emerges in the case of legislative acts being decided upon following the ordinary legislative procedure, and where reasoned opinions on non-compliance

[14] E.g. Case C-84/94 *United Kingdom v Council* [1996] ECR I-5755 (*Working Time Directive* case) and also, more recently, the *Vodafone* case of the Grand Chamber (n 11).

[15] See e.g. Schütze (n 2) 263 *et seq* and Davies (n 6) 63 *et seq*.

[16] A. Biondi, 'Subsidiarity in the Courtroom', in A. Biondi, P. Eeckhout, and S. Ripley (eds.), *EU Law After Lisbon* (Oxford: Oxford University Press, 2012), 211, at 213.

[17] J-V. Louis, 'The Lisbon Treaty: The Irish "No": National Parliaments and the Principle of Subsidiarity—Legal Options and Practical Limits' (2008) 4 *European Constitutional Law Review* 429.

[18] Art 2 of Protocol No. 2.

[19] Art 4 of Protocol No. 2.

[20] Art 5 of Protocol No. 2.

[21] Art 5 of Protocol No. 2.

[22] Art 7(2) of Protocol No. 2.

with subsidiarity represent at least a simple majority of votes cast by national parliaments. In the case of such a scenario, the Commission *must* review the proposal and, if it decides to maintain it, it must issue a reasoned opinion explaining why the proposal complies with the subsidiarity principle.[23]

Entrusting national parliaments with the role of the 'watchdogs of subsidiarity'[24] in the manner described has given rise to a series of concerns regarding its effectiveness and function. To start with, the national parliaments are limited by the provision that only legislative acts are reviewable in the light of subsidiarity checks. Also, these national institutions are empowered to review EU legislation for conformity with subsidiarity but not with proportionality (its so-called 'sister principle').[25] In light of the earlier discussion on the interwoven nature of the principles of subsidiarity and proportionality, this is a clear drawback. Concerns are also raised with regard to the complexity and inconsistency of Commission's arguments in favour of Union action and the very short period (eight weeks) for the national parliaments to respond.[26] More importantly, since the Commission's opinions are not binding, the risk is thought to be that the responses of the national parliaments will be found to be ineffective.[27]

Examining the first periods following the implementation of the Lisbon Treaty, it seems that a certain level of scepticism that existed prior to the adoption of Protocol No. 2 was unfounded. First, the time limit has proven not to be a real factor. During 2010, three-quarters of the opinions received under the subsidiarity control mechanism were received within the eight weeks' time frame, indicating that national parliaments managed to react to the Commission's proposals.[28] The following year, in 2011, the Commission received 60 per cent increase in the number of reasoned opinions from national parliaments compared to 2010.[29] From this perspective, the implementation of the subsidiarity control mechanism has 'run very smoothly',[30] although the number of opinions from national parliaments on a

[23] Art 7(3) of Protocol No. 2.

[24] I. Cooper, 'The Watchdogs of Subsidiarity: National Parliaments and the Logic of Arguing in the EU' (2006) 44 *Journal of Common Market Studies* 281. Note that this comment is set out against the backdrop of the early warning systems as codified in the Constitutional Treaty.

[25] Cooper (n 24) 283.

[26] G.A. Bermann, 'The Lisbon Treaty: The Irish "No". National Parliaments and Subsidiarity: An Outsider's View' (2008) 4 *European Constitutional Law Review* 453, at 458.

[27] Bermann (n 26) 459. Ultimately, there are about 10,000 national parliamentarians, operating now in 28 different political landscapes and according to 28 political agendas that need, to a certain extent, to cooperate under the new procedures; see P. Kaczynski, *Paper Tigers or Sleeping Beauties? National Parliaments in the post-Lisbon European Political System* (Special Report: 'Thinking ahead for Europe', Centre for European Policy Studies, 2011), 2.

[28] More precisely, during 2010 the Commission sent 82 draft legislative acts to national parliaments for subsidiarity scrutiny and received 211 opinions, of which 15 per cent raised subsidiarity concerns: see COM (2011) 345 final, 'Annual Report 2010 on Relations between the European Commission and National Parliaments', 3.

[29] COM (2012) 373 final, 'Report from the Commission on Subsidiarity and Proportionality' (19th Report on Better Lawmaking covering the year 2011), 4, and COM (2012) 375, Report from the Commission, 'Annual Report 2011 on Relations between the European Commission and National Parliaments', 4.

[30] Annual Report 2010 (n 28), 2.

particular draft legislative act failed to trigger the 'yellow' and 'orange' card mechanisms in the first two years of application.[31] Recent evidence of the post-Lisbon rules, however, indicates that the Commission will listen to concerns from national parliaments, even where the number expressing such concerns has not reached the formal trigger required by the Protocol.[32] The Commission has also made clear that while subsidiarity controls only apply to draft legislative acts, it will, nonetheless, consider opinions of national parliaments on other acts within the framework of the political dialogue,[33] as well as all—and not only subsidiarity-centred—motivations as to the non-compliance with the principle of subsidiarity.[34]

On 30 May 2012, the Commission received its first 'yellow card'.[35] The subsidiarity-related concerns were raised with regard to the Commission's proposal for a Council Regulation on the exercise of the right to take collective action within the context of the freedom of establishment and the freedom to provide services.[36] This so-called 'Monti II' Regulation aimed to lay down general EU-based principles and rules for collective action within an internal market context.[37] The Danish Parliament (Folketing) was one of numerous national parliaments that raised subsidiarity-concerns in this context. It argued, *inter alia*, that the proposal failed to clarify the relationship between the respective interests of ensuring freedom of movement, on the one hand, and the right of workers to take collective action, on the other.[38] As such, the Commission was seen as simply interfering with, and disturbing, national labour systems. The United Kingdom House of Commons argued that the Commission's objective to 'express more committed political approach' indeed could not replace the 'evidence of necessity for the EU to act'.[39] The bulk of the reasoned opinions from the national parliaments questioned the added value of this legislative action, and pointed to the fact that the Treaty explicitly excluded the right to strike from competences conferred on the

[31] As such, national parliaments could be seen as mere 'paper tigers'; see Kaczynski, (n 27).

[32] Annual Report 2010 (n 28) 3.

[33] Annual Report 2010 (n 28) 4. Obviously, and as noted by Craig (n 1) 85, the Commission's willingness to consider subsidiarity concerns raised by individual Member States is to be welcomed, although one must be mindful of the dangers of diluting such concerns if they merely become part of the general political dialogue between the Commission and the Member States.

[34] Annual Report 2011 (n 29) 5.

[35] The subsidiarity concerns were raised by national Parliaments in Belgium, Denmark, France, Finland, Latvia, Luxembourg, Malta, Poland, Portugal, Sweden, the United Kingdom, and the Netherlands.

[36] See COM (2012) 130 final, Proposal for a Council Regulation on the exercise of the right to take collective action within the context of the freedom of establishment and the freedom to provide services.

[37] For an overview of the Commission's proposal see F. Fabbrini and K. Granat, 'Yellow card, but no foul: The role of the national parliaments under the Subsidiarity Protocol and the Commission proposal for an EU Regulation on the right to strike' (2013) 50 *Common Market Law Review* 115, at 130–5.

[38] Reasoned opinion by the Danish Parliament (Folketing) on the Proposal for a Council Regulation on the exercise of the right to take collective action within the context of the freedom of establishment and the freedom to provide services, available at: <http://www.ipex.eu>.

[39] Reasoned opinion by the House of Commons on the Proposal for a Council Regulation on the exercise of the right to take collective action within the context of the freedom of establishment and the freedom to provide services, available at: <http://www.ipex.eu>.

Union, meaning that the proposed Regulation falls outside of the scope of EU law.[40] Following Protocol No. 2, the Commission re-examined its proposal against the said reasoned opinions, and concluded, only three months following the signalling of the yellow card, to withdraw it. However, it did so not on the basis of the principle of subsidiarity—indeed, it found the proposal justifiable in this regard—but because it thought it was 'unlikely to gather the necessary political support within the European Parliament and Council'.[41] The withdrawal has been hailed for showing the 'national parliaments' growing role in EU legislation'[42] but it has also fuelled further scepticism about this control system, as it seemingly allows legislative actions to be struck down based on mere political motivation.[43]

What we want to focus on in this chapter, however, is not the specific outcome concerning the 'Monti II' Regulation, but rather the obligation imposed on the Commission to publish reasons for its decision, as set out in Protocol No. 2. Indeed, the group of reasoned opinions that the Commission received in the first year following the implementation of the Lisbon Treaty relate in great part to the lack of or insufficient subsidiarity justification in the explanatory memoranda of the relevant proposals.[44] In this context, the national parliaments also questioned the objectivity of the criteria used by the Commission in transferring powers to the Union institutions as opposed to keeping these vested with Member States.[45] What this shows is that the failure to give reasons for regulating at the EU level is seen as a breach of the subsidiarity principle.[46] The Protocol, however, has the potential to serve as a framework for developing the legislating rationale at EU level. In order for this to be effective, the national parliaments need actively to engage with the procedures set out in the Protocol, so as to ensure that it does not become a 'dead letter'.[47] If Protocol No. 2 is regarded through the lens of federal proceduralism, it is clear that it has an additional, important, competence-control function.

Here, it should be borne in mind that judicial scrutiny of the appropriateness of the reasons stated for Union action is about the only practical route for the ECJ to supervise the respect by the political institutions of the principles of subsidiarity and proportionality flowing from Article 5 TEU. The idea behind this kind of supervision is that the political institutions ought to be forced to express their reasoning with regard to the operation of subsidiarity and proportionality as limits

[40] See e.g. the reasoned opinion by the Swedish Riksdag on the Proposal for a Council Regulation on the exercise of the right to take collective action within the context of the freedom of establishment and the freedom to provide services, available at: <http://www.ipex.eu>.

[41] M Šefčovič, Vice-President of the European Commission, Letter to the Speaker of the House of Common, available at: <http://ec.europa.eu/dgs/secretariat_general/relations/relations_other/pdf/pdfletters/uk_house_of_commons_-_letter_vp_sefcovic_on_monti_ii_-_withdrawal_procedure_com20120130.pdf>.

[42] *EurActiv*, 'EPP Group welcomes the withdrawal of Monti II', available at: <http://pr.euractiv.com/pr/monti-ii-epp-group-welcomes-withdrawal-monti-ii-decision-shows-national-parliaments-growing-role>.

[43] Fabbrini and Granat (n 37), 116.

[44] Commission Annual Report 2010 (n 28) 4.

[45] Commission Annual Report 2010 (n 28).

[46] Commission Annual Report 2010 (n 28).

[47] As cited in S. Weatherill, 'The Limits of Legislative Harmonization Ten Years after Tobacco Advertising: How the Court's Case Law has become a "Drafting Guide"' (2011) 12 *German Law Journal* 827, at 853.

intra vires to Union action. In this manner, Union institutions will also be more directly subject to the political control of the Member States, their sub-national authorities, and interested citizens.[48] Indeed, and as argued by Derrick Wyatt, giving teeth to subsidiarity by entrusting national parliaments with responsibility for monitoring its application, and reinforcing that responsibility with an appropriate judicial response from the ECJ, could enhance a sense of 'ownership' of the European project at national level.[49]

For some, the strengthening of *ex ante* political scrutiny will confirm the Court in its position, consisting of exercising a mostly formal control, bearing mainly upon the reasoning. For others, greater pressure to provide reasons and the reasoned opinion allow the national parliament to influence the consideration of a judgment. According to George A. Bermann, 'the subsidiarity review called for by the Protocols will leave an analytic and documentary trail'[50] that could be of great use and value to the ECJ if it were inclined to take a 'harder look' at the implementation of the subsidiarity principle.[51] In other words, a 'vigorous national parliamentary examination will lighten the pressure on the Court to "*do something*"'.[52] This will not only improve the quality and clarity of the political dialogue but also provides a solid ground for the ECJ to engage in procedural review in relation to the assessment of subsidiarity, should the matter be adjudicated.

It is possible that the use of the new *ex ante* monitoring system will provide the basis for a more intensive *ex post* control by the Court.[53] The idea here is that in case the objections of numerous national parliaments are swept aside by the Commission, or the other Union institutions with thin reasoning, the Court might be inclined to find the legislative action invalid. In this way, the Court could add to the 'shift in the presumption',[54] meaning that the Commission would need to show something similar to a manifest error of appraisal in the objections in order to be able to proceed with the proposal. As argued by Stephen Weatherill, the threat of such *ex post* control might helpfully induce political actors at EU level to take seriously *ex ante* critical input by national parliaments.[55] This control would then focus on the steps in the law-making process, in which compliance with the principle of subsidiarity ought to be most transparent. That is, the legislative proposal, the justification of that proposal in subsidiarity terms by the Commission, the objections by national parliaments to that proposal on subsidiarity grounds, and the response by the Commission to those objections. Whether the Commission maintains or amends a draft legislative act in response to a 'yellow card', the procedure would provide a workable mechanism for judicial scrutiny of compliance with the principle of subsidiarity, which would strike a new and appropriate balance between political assessment and judicial control.[56] As predicted by the House of Lords' EU Committee Report: 'if national parliaments operate the

[48] Lenaerts (n 5) 894. [49] Wyatt (n 9) 1. [50] Bermann (n 26) 458.
[51] Bermann (n 26) 457–8. [52] Bermann (n 26).
[53] An argument set forward by Weatherill (n 47) 853. [54] Weatherill (n 47).
[55] Weatherill (n 47). [56] Wyatt (n 9) 16.

mechanism effectively it would be hard for the Commission and the Council to resist such sustained political pressure.'[57]

II. Impact Assessments as a Competence Test

The second procedural competence test that we wish to examine is embedded in impact assessment requirements. These form an important part of a Union-based initiative to improve, or 'smarten' the regulatory environment.[58] In a nutshell, impact assessment corresponds to:

> a set of steps to be followed when policy proposals are prepared, altering political decision makers to the advantages and disadvantages of policy options by assessing their potential impacts. The results of this process are presented in an Impact Assessment Report.[59]

The relevance of such reports to this chapter is that, following the introduction of impact assessments in 2004/05, the Commission is under the obligation to include subsidiarity and proportionality assessments as part of the impact assessment method.[60] In effect, the Commission's impact assessments are 'the main vehicle for addressing subsidiarity and proportionality issues' during the pre-legislative phase.[61] In the Impact Assessment Guidelines issued in 2005,[62] the Commission defines the pre-conditions of the subsidiarity principle by reference to Protocol No. 2; that is, satisfying the 'Necessity Test',[63] the 'Added Value' test,[64] and the 'Boundary Test'.[65] However, in the Impact Assessment Guidelines published in 2009,[66] the Commission understands compliance with subsidiarity to be based on a 'Necessity Test' and an 'EU Value Added Test'.[67] Interestingly, the 'Boundary

[57] Wyatt (n 9) 15, and House of Lords European Union Committee, 'Strengthening national parliamentary scrutiny of the EU—the Constitution's subsidiarity early warning mechanism', 14th Report of Session, London, 5 April 2005, available at: <http://www.publications.parliament.uk/pa/ld200405/ldselect/ldeucom/101/101.pdf>, para 126.

[58] COM (2002) 278 final, Action Plan 'Simplifying and improving the regulatory environment'. See A. Meuwese and P. Popelier. 'Legal Implications of Better Regulation: A Special Issue' (2011) 17 *European Public Law* 455, at 456. The authors describe the relationship between impact assessment and better regulation (renamed 'smart regulation'). The impact assessment is viewed as the flagship tool of this new policy. See also COM (2002) 276 final, Communication from the Commission on Impact Assessment.

[59] Craig (n 1) 11.

[60] Commission on Impact Assessment (n 58) 4.

[61] Report 2011 (n 29) 10.

[62] SEC(2005) 791 final, Impact Assessment Guidelines.

[63] Impact Assessment Guidelines (n 62) 18.

[64] Impact Assessment Guidelines (n 62) 31.

[65] '[T]he scope of EU action shall be limited to what Member States cannot achieve satisfactorily and to what the Union can do better (boundary test).' The 'Boundary Test' corresponds to the political aspect and condition of subsidiarity in Art 5 EC which states that the 'Community shall take action, in accordance with the principle of subsidiarity, only if and so far as the objectives of the proposed action cannot be sufficiently achieved by the Member States', see Impact Assessment Guidelines (n 62).

[66] SEC(2009) 92 final, Impact Assessment Guidelines.

[67] Impact Assessment Guidelines (n 66) section 5.2, at 21. The test reworks the language of art 5 TEU into a justification for Union action rather than a limiting condition precedent, that is, the following two questions are asked: (1) Why can the objectives of the proposed action not be achieved sufficiently by Member States (Necessity Test)? (2) As a result of this, can objectives be better achieved by action by the Community (EU Value Added test)?

Test' from the 2005 Guidelines is considered a question relating to proportionality rather than subsidiarity.[68] This policy shift corroborates the view taken previously regarding the close relationship between proportionality and subsidiarity (the so-called 'inherently-tied approach').[69]

The questions regarding the exact role that impact assessments play in the EU adjudication and the extent to which, if at all, they may significantly impact judicial review in subsidiarity cases, remain to be answered.[70] It is argued that, since impact assessments include a quantification of both costs and benefits, it will be easier for the plaintiff to collect and rely on this information in the proceedings before the ECJ.[71] After all, if the Court were to use qualitative and quantitative data gathered for impact assessments in establishing whether an action is better regulated at European rather than at the domestic level, this would have the potential of decreasing the present difficulty in adjudicating the principle of subsidiarity.[72] On this note, Paul Craig contends that the impact assessment report does provide a helpful framework within which to address 'competence creep' or 'competence anxiety' concerns.[73] Ultimately, this approach is a constructive move towards facilitating the scrutiny of justificatory arguments issued by Union institutions. In turn, this should ease judicial review.

Obviously, it should not be accepted too easily that impact assessments are the ultimate instruments to rely on in judicial review. Although the European Court of Auditors finds them useful in this context, in its 2010 Report it indicated that impact assessment reports are not always updated nor sent to the Parliament and the Council early enough in the decision-making process to have a real impact.[74] In addition, it is not always possible to invoke the impact assessment report in judicial proceedings, since the European Parliament and Council can make amendments to the Commission's proposal and are thus not bound by the impact assessment report.[75] Still, it is worth noting that in such circumstances, the Parliament and Council are obliged to carry out their own impact assessment on the proposed amendments to the Commission's proposal.[76] In the end, the impact assessments' subsidiarity check has the potential of strengthening the enforceability of the subsidiarity principles, and in doing so, also raise the low rate of cases founded on

[68] Impact Assessment Guidelines (n 66) section 7.2.

[69] Impact Assessment Guidelines (n 66) section 2.

[70] See A. Alemanno, 'The Better Regulation Initiative at the Judicial Gate: A Trojan Horse within the Commission's Walls or the Way Forward?' (2009) 15 *European Law Journal* 391. A parallel can be drawn with regulatory review using cost-benefit analysis in the US; see S. Shapiro, 'The Evolution of Cost-Benefit Analysis in US Regulatory Decision-making', *Jerusalem Papers in Regulation and Governance*, Working Paper No 5, May 2010; C. Sunstein, 'Cost-Benefit Default Principles' (2000-01) 99 *Michigan Law Review* 1651. Sunstein supports the judicial review of cost-benefit analyses since they are reasonable and likely to enhance the consistency of regulations.

[71] A. Alemanno, 'A Meeting of Minds on Impact Assessment' (2011) 17 *European Public Law* 485.

[72] Alemanno (n 71).

[73] See P. Craig, 'The ECJ and *Ultra Vires* Action: A Conceptual Analysis' (2011) 48 *Common Market Law Review* 395, at 412 as quoted in Lenaerts (n 8) 8.

[74] Special Report No. 3 2010, 'Impact Assessments in the EU Institutions: Do they support decision-making?', § 38, 49.

[75] Lenaerts (n 8) 9.

[76] See Alemanno (n 71) 503.

subsidiarity review, as well as the intensity of such review. As we shall see next, the increase in intensity of review, however, is not a *sine qua non* condition for an increase in legislative annulment based on the ground of subsidiarity.

III. Subsidiarity and Adjudicative Federalism

Since the insertion of the subsidiarity principle with the Treaty of Maastricht, only about 20 cases have been brought before the ECJ, making it approximately one judgment per year.[77] Out of these 20 cases, only 10 are thought of as raising 'real' subsidiarity challenges in the sense that they were not misplaced and substantially evidenced by the plaintiff.[78] In fact, it is often the case that the claimant does not bring enough proof as to the breach of the principle of subsidiarity.[79] Moreover, in many cases the subsidiarity-centred challenge is often contested, or disagreed upon by different Member States, and as concluded by Paul Craig, '[a]ny idea that Member States take a uniform view concerning the application of subsidiarity in a particular case is therefore untenable'.[80] Yet, analyzing subsidiarity as a mere tool of judicial review ('overt subsidiarity') reflects in our opinion a narrow vision of its adjudicative role in a federal order of competences. Subsidiarity should also be conceptualized as a tool of legal interpretation ('covert subsidiarity').[81] The latter conception mirrors a broad understanding of judicial subsidiarity, which is encountered, in particular, when the ECJ relies on derogations in economic freedom cases,[82] Article 4(2) TEU, or when it engages in methodological issues relating to EU fundamental rights and their scope of application.[83] Owing to the limited scope of this essay, however, only the 'overt' aspect of subsidiary will next be discussed in relation to subsidiarity-based judicial review in EU federalism.

1. Analytical framework in judicial review

To start with the obvious, the principle of subsidiarity is justiciable. Indeed, Article 8 of Protocol No. 2 offers a clear sign that subsidiarity should be taken seriously in terms of judicial application by extending the standing under Article 263 TFEU to include the Committee of Regions in bringing actions for annulment on subsidiarity grounds. In the past, however, the case law showed that the ECJ does not easily overturn an EU action on the grounds that the legislative act fails to comply with the principle of subsidiarity. In fact, the CJEU has never

[77] Craig (n 1) 17. [78] Craig (n 1).

[79] See Case C 176/09 *Luxembourg v Parliament and Council* [2011] ECR I-03727.

[80] Craig (n 1) 17. [81] See recital 1, Protocol No. 2.

[82] See Case C-36/02 *Omega* [2004] ECR I-9609; Case C-42/07 *Liga Portuguesa* [2009] ECR I-7633, and Case C-208/09 *Sayn-Wittgenstein* [2010] ECR I-13693.

[83] Here it can be referred to the use of comparative methodology by the ECJ in elaborating fundamental rights or the discussion surrounding the application of fundamental rights in situation of implementation or derogation. See, in relation to the latter point, Case C-256/11 *Dereci* [2011] nyr., para 72.

done so.[84] Here, it is important to understand the logic of the Court in the few real subsidiarity cases, as in that sense, a pattern or, analytical framework can be identified.

First of all, the ECJ insists on the importance of the intent of the legislator to harmonize.[85] This element is often lucidly viewed as a circular argument, reflecting the use of a tautological reasoning by the Court.[86] The second element emphasized by the ECJ is that the legislature must be allowed a wide discretion, leaving the Court to review whether a manifest error or misuse of powers can be proven, or whether it can be shown that the EU institutions concerned have manifestly exceeded their limits of discretion.[87] The result of this is a light-touch standard of judicial review.

This low level of scrutiny is often accompanied by a 'procedural check'. For instance, in *Deposit Guarantee Scheme*[88] the importance of the statement of reasons upon which the institutions adopt legislation is clearly underlined.[89] Moreover, AG Jacobs confirms that the procedure of examining compliance with the principle of subsidiarity is mainly concerned with the question whether the institutions have fulfilled their duty to comment—even implicitly—on compliance with the principle of subsidiarity.[90] Indeed, it is only in cases concerning manifest violation that the Court looks to matters of substance in reviewing legislative acts on the grounds of subsidiarity.

The sign of the Court taking a more 'structured review' first showed in the *Imperial Tobacco* case.[91] Here, the ECJ, for the first time, firmly distinguishes between the subsidiarity argument (that is, the 'who' question, which is subsidiary in the 'strict sense')[92] from the proportionality argument (referring to the 'how' question, or subsidiarity in the 'wide sense').[93] The intensity of this review, however, is considered weak because the Court continued granting wide discretion to Union institutions in the case of policy choices. Next we will examine, in light of the most recent jurisprudence, whether there has been a shift in the Court's framework of reasoning.

2. *Vodafone* and 'procedural proportionality'

Vodafone,[94] a ruling that concerns the validity of a Regulation on roaming in the electronic communications sector, is a significant case in demonstrating that the ECJ applies 'procedural proportionality' in cases dealing with vertical allocation of

[84] Report from the Commission on Subsidiarity and Proportionality (n 29) 1.

[85] See e.g. *UK v Council* (n 14), and the case law on the EU Emissions Trading Scheme as analysed in S. Bogojević, *Emissions Trading Schemes: Markets, States and Law* (Oxford: Hart Publishing, 2013), ch. 5.

[86] *UK v Council* (n 14) para 47.

[87] *UK v Council* (n 14) para 48.

[88] Case C-233/94 *Germany v EP and Council* [1997] ECR I-2405.

[89] *Germany v EP and Council* (n 88) paras 25–26.

[90] See AG Jacobs, 'On monitoring by the Court of Justice of the principle of subsidiarity', Working Group I on Subsidiarity, intervention delivered on 25 June 2002 (Brussels, 28 June 2002) (CONV 156/02 WGI 5).

[91] Case C-491/01 *Imperial Tobacco* [2002] ECR I-11453.

[92] *Imperial Tobacco* (n 91) paras 180–183.

[93] *Imperial Tobacco* (n 91) para 184.

[94] *Vodafone* (n 11).

regulatory powers.[95] In this regard, the analytical framework developed in *Vodafone* is different from other subsidiarity cases. As usual, the ECJ starts by highlighting the broad discretion of the Union legislature in regulatory areas that involve political, economic, and social choices, and in which it is called upon to carry out complex assessments and evaluations.[96] The important point in this case, however, is that the Court finds that limits must be had to this discretion, and that the Union legislature must base its policy choices on objective criteria. Furthermore, in assessing the burdens associated with various possible measures, the Court states that the Union legislator must examine whether the objectives pursued by the measure chosen are such so as to justify even substantial negative economic consequences for certain operators. In doing so, the Court relies on a study drafted by the Commission summarized in the relevant impact assessment report.[97] This report shows that the Commission examined various regulatory scenarios, including the option of regulating retail charges only, wholesale charges only, or both, and that it assessed the economic impact of those various types of regulation, as well as their effects.[98]

Considering that *Vodafone* is the first preliminary ruling procedure in which the Court relies on an impact assessment report when examining the alleged infringement of the principle of proportionality, it seems fair to say that, in this context, the judgment in *Vodafone* is revolutionary.[99] The focus on the procedural aspects of proportionality suggests that the Union institutions must show that they took 'all the relevant factors and circumstances of the situation the act was intended to regulate'[100] into account before exercising their discretion to adopt the relevant legislative act. The direct advantage of this approach is that it does not require the Court to second-guess the policy choices adopted by the EU legislature, as these will be clearly listed.[101]

The ECJ followed the same approach in *Luxembourg v Parliament and Council*.[102] Indeed, just like in *Vodafone*, the Court recites its mantra on the broad discretion accorded to the legislature, and in examining the impact assessment report it concludes that the Commission's review of several regulatory options satisfies the burden imposed by the regulatory action.[103] While Luxembourg lost its subsidiarity plea on the basis that it failed to articulate how subsidiarity was infringed,[104] the Court approached the objection in precisely the same way it had in *Vodafone*: it first considered the proportionality plea, and then the subsidiarity plea. These two

[95] See Lenaerts (n 8). [96] *Vodafone* (n 11). [97] *Vodafone* (n 11) paras 52–54.

[98] *Vodafone* (n 11) para 55.

[99] The ECJ referred to the findings set out in the impact assessment report on six occasions and to the explanatory memorandum on five occasions.

[100] Case C-310/04 *Spain v Council* [2006] ECR I-7285 para 122. [101] Lenaerts (n 8) 7.

[102] *Luxembourg v Parliament and Council* (n 79).

[103] *Luxembourg v Parliament and Council* (n 79) paras 60–65.

[104] *Luxembourg v Parliament and Council* (n 79) para 80. Here the ECJ states that '[i]n the present case, the Grand Duchy of Luxembourg has not stated its third plea in law in detail sufficient as to permit review by the Court of the extent to which national rules could be sufficient to achieve the objective pursued by Directive 2009/12 in a Member State in which the main airport does not reach the minimum size laid down in Article 1(2) of that directive'.

cases thus appear to herald a change in the way that efforts to examine a potential breach of the principle of proportionality (subsidiarity 'in the wide sense') are carried out using impact assessments. However, as long as these assessments make a favourable finding, it seems that the Court will accept those reasons on their face value.

This proceduralization of proportionality has its roots in monopoly and internal market case law, that is, in areas where the Member States have typically been granted a wide margin of discretion.[105] It has now spilled over in the jurisprudence relating to the judicial review of Union legislative acts (another area of wide discretion), two such examples being *Tetra Laval*[106] and *Spain v Council*.[107] In *Tetra Laval*, a merger case, the Court recognized that, whilst the Commission has a margin of discretion with regard to economic matters, this does not entail that the Court must refrain from reviewing the Commission's interpretation of information of an economic nature. Not only should the Court establish whether the evidence relied upon is factually accurate, reliable, and consistent, but also whether it contains all the relevant information in order to be able to assess a complex situation, and to draw conclusions from it.[108] What this shows is that the control of the factual situation allows the Court to scrutinize the discretion granted to the EU institution. This, however, is not to say that the Court will substitute the legislature's assessment underpinning a particular regulatory action. Rather, it simply means that the Court is able to demand that regulatory objectives are clearly set out and substantiated for the legislative act to be held valid before the Court.

Similarly, in *Spain v Council*, a case concerning an annulment action of a regulatory act establishing a Union-based support system for specific crops—the Court confirms the importance of judicial review of facts:

> It is also true that the Community legislature's broad discretion, which implies limited judicial review of its exercise, applies not only to the nature and scope of the measures to be taken but also, to some extent, to the finding of the *basic facts*... *However*, even though such judicial review is of limited scope, it requires that the Community institutions which have adopted the act in question *must be able to show before the Court* that in adopting the act they actually exercised their discretion, which presupposes the taking into consideration of all the *relevant factors and circumstances of the situation* the act was intended to regulate.... It follows that the institutions must at the very least *be able to produce and set out clearly and unequivocally the basic facts* which had to be taken into account as the basis of the contested measures of the act and on which the exercise of their discretion depended.[109]

[105] See Case C-189/95 *Franzén* [1997] ECR I-5909 paras 44 and 51; Case C-438/02 *Hanner* [2005] ECR I-4551 paras 38–39; Case C-320/03 *Commission v Austria* [2005] ECR I-9871, para 87 and Case C-244/06 *Dynamic Medien* [2008] ECR I-505, paras 49–50.

[106] Case C-12/03 P *Commission v Tetra Laval* [2005] ECR I-987.

[107] *Spain v Council* (n 100).

[108] See *Tetra Laval* (n 106) paras 38–39. The ECJ refers to Cases C-68/94 and C-30/95 *France v Commission* (*Kali and Salz*) [1998] ECR I-1375 paras 223–224.

[109] *Spain v Council* (n 100) paras 122–123, emphasis added. This case clearly counts to recent examples of jurisprudence that allows greater intensity of factual judicial review. Indeed, *Spain v Council* para 123, clearly echoes para 39 in *Tetra Laval* (n 106), although this link is not acknowledged.

What this shows is that the Union institutions must at the very least be able to clearly set out the rationale and facts upon which their legislative actions depend. Here, the Court annulled the contested regulation on the basis that the Council failed to take into consideration all the relevant factors, such as the labour costs linked to cotton growing. Notably, the lack of an impact study by the legislature arguably led the Court to establish a breach of the principle of proportionality.[110] On this basis, it seems fair to say that a shift is noticeable in the intensity of judicial review of facts, and in the application of proportionality in a procedural fashion. Moreover, *Spain v Council* relates to a wider issue of transparency of the legislative process.[111] In the end, it may be said that the development of a culture of transparency goes hand in hand with the development of a culture of subsidiarity since both have similar end goals; that is, to enhance the public confidence in relation to decision-making at the EU-level. Thus, the application of 'procedural proportionality' constitutes not only the common judicial denominator of both cultures, but also appears as an appropriate tool of adjudication in areas of broad discretion.

Another important point to make here relates to the burden of proof in judicial review cases. As stated earlier, the Court, on the basis of the lack of proof, often disregards subsidiarity-based pleas. The burden of proof is by tradition placed on the application, a view confirmed in the recent case *Luxembourg v Parliament and Council*.[112] Here, the Court refused the review on the basis that 'the Grand Duchy of Luxembourg has not stated its third plea in law in detail sufficient as to permit review by the Court'.[113] Similarly in *Germany v Council*, the Court rejected the applicant's claim on the basis that it 'has not shown that the Council adopted measures which were manifestly inappropriate or that it carried out a manifestly erroneous assessment of the information available to it at the time when the Regulation was adopted'.[114] In *Spain v Council*, it appears that the Advocate General and the Court followed a similar approach.[115] In this regard, it seems that

[110] AG Sharpston, *Spain v Council* (n 100) paras 94–96, treats the lack of an impact study as a decisive factor in concluding that proportionality has been breached. However, the ECJ did not attach similar importance to the absence of an official impact study.

[111] See AG Geelhoed, Cases C-154 and C-155/04 *Alliance for Natural Health v Secretary of State for Health* [2005] ECR I-6451 para 85. The principle of proportionality might also constitute an effective tool for achieving more clarity in the adoption of the Union legislation, which may boast in certain circumstances 'the transparency of a black box'.

[112] *Luxembourg v Parliament and Council* (n 79).

[113] *Luxembourg v Parliament and Council* (n 79) para 80.

[114] Case C-280/93 *Germany v Council* [1994] ECR I-4973 para 95. See also Case C-122/95 *Germany v Council* [1998] ECR-973 para 79.

[115] *Spain v Council* (n 100) para 127, and AG Sharpston in *Spain v Council* para 93. However, note that in para 122, the ECJ states that in the context of judicial review of facts, 'the Community institutions which have adopted the act in question must be able to show before the Court that in adopting the act they actually exercised their discretion, which presupposes the taking into consideration of all the relevant factors and circumstances of the situation the act was intended to regulate'. The Court concludes, in para 133, that the Council has not shown before the Court that in adopting the new system it actually exercised its discretion, involving the taking into account of basic facts, such as labour costs. One might interpret such statements as meaning that it is for the Union institution to demonstrate that there is no manifest error of factual appreciation. If this reading is accurate, it means that there is a reversal of the burden of proof.

the use of impact assessments, and the Commission's statements on the basis of Protocol No. 2, may be of great benefit to future litigants. Considering that these assessments contain quantification both of the costs and the benefits of legislative action, it will inevitably be easier for plaintiffs to gather information, and in this way, will add to an increased review of subsidiarity.

IV. Federal Proportionality and Process Federalism

The debate so far is, at its core, concerned with whether the principle of subsidiarity should be understood in terms of federal proportionality. That is, abandoning the 'manifest test' and instead explicitly recognizing proportionality *stricto sensu*, or in other words, balancing the added value to the Union against any possible harm to national interests.[116] By analyzing the 'in-so-far' aspect of Article 5(3) TEU, the test will clearly become more substantive. The correct question in defining subsidiarity would then be 'has the European legislator unnecessarily restricted national autonomy?',[117] or 'is the importance of the Union measure sufficient to justify its net effect on Member States?'.[118] According to Robert Schütze, 'a subsidiarity analysis that will not question the federal proportionality of a European law is bound to remain an empty formalism. Subsidiarity properly understood is federal proportionality'.[119] From this viewpoint, a substantive test is more suitable than a procedural approach in judicial review.

Unfortunately, subsidiarity viewed in a strict sense—meaning, asking the question 'who' should implement the regulatory objective—does not set out a methodology for weighing, on the one hand, the interests of the Member States, and the interests of the Union, on the other. A fully-fledged application of the principle of proportionality (proportionality *stricto sensu*), however, could provide a method through which it could be assessed whether the EU norm disproportionately infringes upon Member States' values. Still, this would mean that the ECJ would have to conduct a competence-based proportionality test, which is not enlisted in Article 5(3) TEU.[120] One may also contend that the Treaty scheme already balances Member States and EU interests, and that the EU 'objective' is fashioned via an interplay of political forces.[121] From this perspective, embracing federal proportionality would risk undermining the qualified majority voting system, particularly where a majority of Member States adopt a harmonized measure and thereby agree that the set legislation does not impinge upon national values.[122]

[116] See Schütze (n 2) 263 and Davies (n 6) 63.

[117] R. Schütze, *European Constitutional Law* (Cambridge: Cambridge University Press, 2012), 184.

[118] See J. Hettne and F. Langdal, 'Does Subsidiarity Ask the Right Question?' (2011) *Think Global—Act European* (*TGAE*) 350, at 354, available at: <http://www.sieps.se/sv/publikationer/tgae-2011-the-contribution-of-16-european-think-tanks-to-the-polish-danish-and-cypriot-trio-presidenc>.

[119] R. Schütze, 'Subsidiarity after Lisbon: Reinforcing the Safeguards of Federalism' (2009) 68 *Cambridge Law Journal* 525, at 533.

[120] Craig (n 1) 21. [121] Craig (n 1). [122] Craig (n 1) 22–23.

The application of federal proportionality would certainly lead the Court to second-guess the policy choices of the Union institutions. However, this is not the path that tends to be followed by the ECJ. As this chapter has shown, the Court refuses to make use of the full-scale review and instead relies on a wide margin of discretion granted to the legislature, *Vodafone* being a clear example thereof.[123] In contrast, AG Maduro provides a far more searching test. He does not follow the Court's usual practice of pointing to the importance of the legislator's intention to harmonize, subsequently accepting every harmonising regulatory action. Instead, AG Maduro argues that the framework of analysis must consider the impact on the Member States' autonomy, meaning that the outcome of the case ought to depend on whether the pursuit of the objectives for legislative action *requires* Union action, as opposed to examining the objectives per se.[124] From this perspective, the Court should assess

> whether the legislature's decision on how to address the problem of high roaming charges was proportionate in terms of both the goals of Article 95 EC [114 TFEU] relating to the establishment of the internal market and the policy objective of consumer protection when balanced against the loss of autonomy on the part of Member States and the interference with the rights of the claimants.[125]

What AG Maduro thus suggests is that a balancing exercise takes place in assessing the 'who' question relating to the principle of subsidiarity. This balancing exercise renders the subsidiarity test more substance-oriented.

Similarly to the Court's ruling, AG Maduro relied upon the impact assessment report in examining whether the regulatory action ought to be dealt by the central, or the national authorities.[126] By going through the arguments underpinning the main regulatory justifications—namely that the objectives of the set Roaming Regulation is to secure, which includes adequate consumer protection that cannot be achieved by the Member States in a harmonized and timely manner—AG Maduro came to the conclusion that the legislation does not violate the principle of proportionality, and as such ought to be adopted at the Union level.[127] A key element in his argumentation is that the impact assessment report is particularly useful in determining that the Union legislator intervened as a last resort for regulating the area.[128] This evidences the utility of the impact assessment report; they contain a systematic examination of the possible impact on the national public authorities, as well as constitute an integral part of the process of designing policy proposals that allows the ECJ a higher scrutiny. This show that the impact assessment report and all other preparatory studies, including the Commission's statement for regulatory action issued under Protocol No. 2, are helpful in verifying whether the balance between Union harmonization and Member State autonomy

[123] See *Vodafone* (n 11). In para 69, the ECJ appears to introduce a three-pronged proportionality test. See *contra* M. Brenncke, 'Annotation in Case C-58/08 Vodafone' (2010) 47 *Common Market Law Review* 1793, at 1811.

[124] AG Maduro, *Vodafone* (n 11) para 30.

[125] AG Maduro, *Vodafone* (n 11) para 37.

[126] AG Maduro, *Vodafone* (n 11) para 39.

[127] AG Maduro, *Vodafone* (n 11) para 44.

[128] AG Maduro, *Vodafone* (n 11) para 39.

has been realized by the EU lawmaker. It could be argued that this type of procedural review contains an element of federal proportionality. Although federal proportionally may appear less substantive than a review of proportionality based on a competence test, Andrea Biondi rightly concludes that 'in any form of judicial review, procedure is always substantial and it all depends on the intensity of the scrutiny'.[129]

In sum, when the ECJ reviews whether the EU legislator has respected the subsidiarity principle, it not only enters the analysis of various regulatory options and the assessment of their economic, social, and environmental impact, but it also ensures that the (political) balancing of interests have been taken into consideration. The ECJ is thus able to monitor principles that have a manifest political nature by verifying whether the political safeguards are truly 'safeguarded'. The crux of all of this is that procedural safeguards do not compel the Court to substitute its judgment for that of the Union legislator. Rather, they oblige the Court to take subsidiarity seriously.[130] This means that instead of dictating substantive results, the ECJ intervenes only when the 'market'—in our case, the political market—is malfunctioning.[131] This 'proceduralization of proportionality', or 'process federalism' comes close to the technique used by the US Supreme Court in certain areas knows as 'rational basis review' or 'structuralism'.[132] In the EU context—despite the 'textual failure of Article 5(3) TEU',[133] and the lack of its explicit recognition in Protocol No. 2—'process federalism', as developed by the ECJ, underlines the presence and paramount significance of the principle of proportionality within the 'subsidiarity calculus'. It is in this sense that subsidiarity after Lisbon stands as a procedural safeguard of federalism.

Conclusion: One Vision of Federal Safeguards?

In summary, it is useful to briefly look to the US where the understandings of the concept of 'federalism' and 'federal safeguards' are many. Herbert Wechsler who, in essence, argues that the political and judicial safeguards are highly interrelated, offers one powerful vision.[134] Simply put, the existence of effective political safeguards leads, in Wechsler's view, to a low level of scrutiny of the law of state-federal relations.[135] In 1985, the US Supreme Court delivered the *Garcia* case, which is often described as a judicial recognition of the theory of political safeguards.[136]

[129] Biondi (n 16) 12. [130] See Lenaerts (n 8) 8.

[131] This analogy is set out in J.H. Ely, *Democracy and Distrust: A Theory of Judicial Review*, 14th edn (Cambridge: Harvard University Press, 2002), 103. Ely calls it an antitrust approach to constitutional adjudication.

[132] Ely (n 131) 78–9. [133] Schütze (n 117) 178.

[134] See H. Wechsler, 'The Political Safeguards of Federalism' (1954) 54 *Columbia Law Review* 543.

[135] G.A. Bermann, 'Subsidiarity as a Principle of U.S. Constitutional Law' (1994) 42 *American Journal of Comparative Law* 555. See also, by the same author, 'Taking Subsidiarity Seriously: Federalism in the European Community and the United States' 94 (1994) *Columbia Law Review* 341.

[136] *Garcia v San Antonio Transit Auth.* 469 U.S. 528 (1985).

Looking at this judgment more closely, it appears that the adjudicator emphasizes the *process* rights, and not the substantive rights. The interests of the states are said to be safeguarded best by the states' participation in the national political procedures, and not by judicial constraints on national policy.[137]

In the EU, the Lisbon Treaty brings an increase in *ex ante* political control by empowering national Parliaments to issue 'early warning' signals for breach of the subsidiarity principle. The *ex post* legal control, however, remains as a complement, and what is more, it is strengthened by the new legal framework. An analysis of the few 'real subsidiarity' cases reveals that the ECJ trusts the political safeguards of federalism and adopts, in turn, a self-restraint approach when it comes to judicial review of the law of state-federal relations. The recent jurisprudential developments are, notably, marked by an increased proceduralization of judicial review, and by a reliance on preparatory documents, such as the impact assessment reports. These changes should be hailed and used to highlight the capacity for providing a new approach to the judicial control of subsidiarity in terms of intensity, but not in terms of substance. In contrast to the US Supreme Court, the ECJ has, thus far, only provided us with one vision of federalism: that of a procedural one.

[137] *Garcia* (n 136). See *contra* Powell, at 566, dissenting. Powell suggests that limiting state control over state governmental functions weakens democracy because it 'disregards[s] entirely the far more effective role of democratic self-government at the state and local levels'.

12

The Respect for National Constitutional Identity in the European Legal Space: An Approach to Federalism as Constitutionalism

*François-Xavier Millet**

'Federalism should not be seen only as a static pattern or design, characterized by a particular and precisely fixed division of powers between governmental levels. Federalism is also and perhaps primarily the process of federalizing a political community, that is to say, the process by which a number of separate political communities enter into arrangements for working out solutions, adopting joint policies, and making joint decisions on joint problems, and, conversely, also the process by which a unitary political community becomes differentiated into a federally organized whole' (Carl J. Friedrich, *Trends of Federalism in Theory and Practice*, London: Pall Mall Press, 1968, 7).

Introduction

Traditional accounts on federalism claim that federal institutional arrangements are characterized by at least two major elements or even 'laws', as the French lawyer and sociologist Georges Scelle used to put it: the *loi de participation* and the *loi d'autonomie*.[1] According to the first 'law', as an inherent element of the federative phenomenon, local entities should be able to contribute significantly to the decision-making process at the federal level. More broadly, they should have a say on any matter concerning the upper level, including for instance, the composition of the federal bodies, as Herbert Wechsler, the renowned legal expert

* I am indebted to Camille Aynès, Loïc Azoulai, Olivier Beaud, Michal Bobek, Bruno de Witte, Giuseppe Martinico, and Hanna Schebesta for their insightful comments. The usual disclaimer however applies. This is a more elaborate version of an earlier paper published in Loïc Azoulai, Lena Boucon, and François-Xavier Millet (eds.), 'Deconstructing Federalism Through Competences', *EUI Law Working Paper* 2012/06, 53 and see more extensively F.-X. Millet, *L'Union européenne et l'identité constitutionnelle des Etats membres* (Paris: LGDJ-Lextenso, 2013).

[1] G. Scelle, *Précis du droit des gens. Principes et systématiques* (Paris: Libr. De Recueil Sirey (original publication), 1932-34, subsequently republished by CNRS, 1984), 198–200.

on federalism in the US, once mentioned in a seminal article.[2] According to the 'law of autonomy', both the federal and the federated bodies should have a certain set of competences that they are to exercise in an autonomous manner, irrespective of what the other level may decide. It follows from this requirement that federal structures should contain a clear and a priori allocation of powers[3] so that each level knows in advance what it can or cannot do.[4] This classical view implies that a supposedly 'true' federal system will put emphasis on four elements: power (both in the technical and in the political sense), the identity of the competence-holder, the autonomy of the different levels of government, and legal certainty (through anticipation). Accordingly, any institutional structure that would actually merit the label of 'federal' should admittedly stress the dimension of power through a clear-cut, *ex ante* vertical distribution of competences, which would then be exercised in an independent manner by each actor. This will, for instance, explain why countries such as Germany or Switzerland are usually described as federal states. We can indeed find within their constitutions several provisions that not only set out lists of competences, but also empower their highest courts to enforce them.[5]

When it comes to the European Union as the object of our enquiry, we may wonder whether it fits into this traditional scheme. We know that the EU has gradually developed along objectives and rights while the issue of the distribution of competences has long been eschewed.[6] On the theoretical plane, *does that actually mean that the absence of a clear and effective vertical order of competences necessarily implies the absence of federalism in the EU?* We seem bound to reach such a conclusion if we assume that the a priori allocation of powers is still a major feature of federalism. However, we may also consider that, despite the ineffectiveness of the distribution of competences, the practices in the European Union in relation to the issue of powers will signal the existence of a new kind of federalism, calling for new theoretical approaches.

As a matter of fact, in the light of the past and current functioning of the EU, in this contribution I wish to challenge the idea that an *ex ante* vertical distribution of competences is a necessary condition for having a *federal* form of governance. In the first part of this chapter, I will argue that, despite the changes introduced by the Lisbon Treaty, the EU will probably remain not primarily concerned

[2] H. Wechsler, 'The Political Safeguards of Federalism: the Role of the States in the Composition and Selection of the National Government' 1954 *Columbia Law Review* 543.

[3] I do not make any difference here between powers and competences. I will therefore use them interchangeably.

[4] D. Elazar, *American Federalism: A View from the States*, 3rd edn (New York: Harper and Row Publishers, 1984), 2; K. Lenaerts, 'Constitutionalism and the Many Faces of Federalism' (1990) 38 *American Journal of Comparative Law* 205.

[5] For Germany, see arts 73, 74, and 93 I 4 of the Basic Law; as to Switzerland, a whole chapter with 71 Articles distributes the respective competences of the Confederation and the Cantons (see Title 3, Chapter 2 on powers: arts 54 to 125). Enforcement by the Federal Supreme Court is guaranteed under art 189 of the Swiss Constitution.

[6] See notably L. Azoulai's introduction in this volume. Also, A. von Bogdandy and J. Bast, 'The European Union's Vertical Order of Competences: The Current Law and Proposals for its Reform' (2002) 39 *Common Market Law Review* 227.

with the question '*Who* holds or exercises the competence X or Y?' in the near future, but will keep giving more weight to the question '*How* to exercise the competence X or Y?'. In support of this claim, I will first show, in the light of the US experience and in view of the integrationist *telos* of the European Union, why the vertical distribution of powers may prove to be only formal in nature, and may fail to be actually enforced in the EU. Turning then to the exercise of the competences of the European Union, I will examine the actual and potential use of national constitutional identity, and will contrast it with another important control mechanism, namely subsidiarity. In the second part, I will move on to the theoretical implications for EU federalism that derive from the salience of the question of '*How*' in the European legal space[7] in light of national constitutional identity, grasped both as an ideologically-loaded narrative and as a technical check on powers. As the latter concept includes the idea of limitation of power through law, together with maximization of diversity, I will contend that respect for national constitutional identity departs from the modern language of sovereignty and power politics. Therefore, when it comes to determining what kind of federalism, if any, it promotes, I will conclude that constitutional identity does not fit well in Carl Schmitt's political and institutional vision of federalism (lately rediscovered by Oliver Beaud) but can be better captured through a cosmopolitan, differentiated approach to constitutionalism that could actually find its roots in Althusius' societal federalism.

I. From '*Who* Should Hold a Competence?' to '*How* to Exercise a Competence?'

In relation to the exercise of competences, while the question *Who?* does not sound that important in the EU in spite of the recent changes brought in by the Lisbon Treaty, the question *How?* seems paramount.

1. The inconclusiveness of the vertical division of powers in the EU

Considering that the vertical separation of powers is one of the classical features of federal polities, the EU Treaties now contain a clearer catalogue of competences. In light of the US experience and with regard to the structure of the EU, such a list would, however, be hard to enforce.

[7] I refer intentionally here to the idea of a 'European legal space' with a view to distinguishing it from the traditional concept of legal order and making it inclusive: the European legal space will indeed comprise not only the EU legal order but also the domestic ones, together with the ECHR legal system. See later for the related developments on integrity in the European legal space.

a) Allocation of powers after Lisbon

Built as a functional polity, the EC did not initially bother with a division of powers. It was meant to reach broadly defined objectives. To that end, the European institutions did not hesitate to use and overuse the various available and well-known instruments. In fact, the issue of the division of powers has become salient only since the Maastricht Treaty but the dramatic shift took place in the past decade in the follow-up to the Laeken Declaration attached to the Treaty of Nice. Heads of states and governments then required, amongst other things, a clear division of powers between the supranational and the national levels.

Following the recommendations of the Group on Complementary Competences within the European Convention, the Constitutional Treaty and later the Lisbon Treaty firmly established the principle of conferred competences[8] and distinguished three types of competences,[9] namely exclusive competences of the EU, shared competences, and complementary competences.[10] Like most federal systems based on conferral of powers, the Treaties do not expressly provide for competences reserved to the Member States, however. Even if Article 4(2) TEU states that 'the Union shall respect their essential State functions, including ensuring the territorial integrity of the State, maintaining law and order and safeguarding national security', it does not explicitly grant powers to the Member States; in addition, it would be inaccurate to speak about reserved competences when it comes to areas where 'the Union shall have competence to carry out actions to support, coordinate or supplement the actions of the Member States'.[11] At best, these are 'retained' powers, on which EU law will have an impact. In any case, by clarifying the issue of competences, the Lisbon Treaty has made a valuable effort in order to safeguard unity and autonomy for all political actors. However, it is doubtful that the Court of Justice will start enforcing the relevant provisions any time soon.

b) Enforcement difficulties in the light of the American experience and the EU integrationist ideal

The provisions regulating the division of powers in the EU may prove hard to enforce for reasons pertaining to the practices of federalism, as illustrated by the paradigmatic US example, as well as for reasons pertaining to EU integration.

Comparative analysis shows that division of competences is not always stringently enforced in federal polities. In the United States, under the Tenth Amendment to the Federal Constitution, 'the powers not delegated to the United States by the Constitution nor prohibited by it to the States, are reserved to the States respectively or to the people'. Despite this provision dating back to 1791,

[8] See arts 4(1), 5(1) and (2), and 6 TEU. [9] See art 2 TFEU.

[10] For an overview of the changes introduced by the Treaty of Lisbon, see L. Serena Rossi, 'Does the Lisbon Treaty Provide a Clearer Separation of Competences between EU and Member States?', in A. Biondi, P. Eeckhout, and S. Ripley (ed.), *EU Law after Lisbon* (Oxford: Oxford University Press, 2012), 85.

[11] Articles 2(5) and 6 TFEU.

the Supreme Court has proved reluctant to strike down pieces of federal legislation adopted under the 'Commerce Clause',[12] which would be impinging upon the states' sphere of autonomy. It did so for the first time in 40 years in 1976 in the famous *National League of Cities* case.[13] Since the New Deal policy and up to this date, the Supreme Court had taken a very open stance on the 'Commerce Clause', thereby allowing the Congress to legislate in matters—especially social matters—that may have been primarily regulated by the states.[14] In this decision, taken shortly after the advent of the federalist-minded Burger Court—as opposed to the human rights-minded Warren Court—the Supreme Court held that national legislation making the 1938 'Fair Labour Standards Act' provisions for overtime pay applicable to virtually all state and local employees was unconstitutional. This was on the basis that it violated the limitations imposed on the scope of the federal commerce power by the Tenth Amendment. Some five years later, the Court refined its case law and came up with four requirements that had to be fulfilled in order for a state not to be subject to federal legislation based on the 'Commerce Clause':[15] among them, federal acts could not regulate areas pertaining to attributes of state sovereignty or could not directly impinge upon states' power to freely organize activities corresponding to traditional governmental functions. It seems as though the Supreme Court was at that time quite eager to enforce the Tenth Amendment even at the expense of social breakthroughs.

However, this attempt was rather short-lived, as the Court reversed its case law in 1985 in the landmark *Garcia* ruling.[16] In this case, the abovementioned 'Fair Labour Standards Act' was again at stake. The question—this time concerning a minimum wage—was whether employees of a local public transportation company would benefit from the federal legislation. Relying on the *Hodel* test, the employer argued that transportation came under the category of 'traditional state function' and that the company would therefore not fall within the scope of application of the federal act. Yet, the Supreme Court strongly criticized the state sovereignty approach and decided to jettison the *Hodel* test. Interestingly enough, the Supreme Court not only based its judgment on the lack of objective criteria to determine what would qualify as a 'traditional state function', but also emphasized the futility of a priori definitions of state sovereignty, especially in a

[12] Under art I, s 8, cl 3 of the US Constitution, the US Congress shall have 'power to regulate commerce with foreign Nations, and among the several States, and with the Indian Tribes'. The 'Commerce Clause' has been extensively used since the New Deal in order to empower the Congress, at the expense of states' rights, over not only interstate commerce but also over several aspects of intrastate commerce as well as non-commerce.

[13] *National League of Cities v Usery* 426 US 833 [1976] (states-rights-minded Justice Rehnquist delivering the opinion of the Court).

[14] See Robert Schütze's chapter in this volume, esp for a comparison with arts 114 and 115 TFEU (former arts 94 and 95 EC).

[15] *Hodel v Virginia Surface Mining* 452 US 264 [1981].

[16] *Garcia v San Antonio Metropolitan Transit Authority* 469 US 528 [1985]. See A. Rapaczynski, 'From Sovereignty to Process: The Jurisprudence of Federalism after *Garcia*' (1985) *Supreme Court Review* 341, noting that *Garcia* reveals the absence of a theory of federalism on the part of judges and calling for one.

context where federal law and institutions have become so prominent. The Court concluded that

> any substantive restraint on the exercise of 'Commerce Clause' powers must find its justification in the procedural nature of the basic limitation [that the Constitution imposes to protect the States] and it must be tailored to compensate for possible failings in the national political process rather than to dictate a sacred province of State autonomy.[17]

Nevertheless, such an approach is quite striking as it entirely disregards the a priori division of powers as being an inadequate safeguard of federalism. It is all the more noteworthy that, before the Civil War, 'dual federalism' and 'states rights' used to be paramount in the US, as a consequence of the American conception of separation of powers. Such centralizing trends in a country where, as opposed to Europe, a rigid distribution of powers prevails (both horizontally and vertically) make us doubt that the European Union would rate better that the United States in this respect, especially in view of its integrationist *telos*.

Despite the adoption of the Lisbon Treaty, the European Union seems to be structurally at odds with an effective enforcement of distribution of competences, both because it is placed in a situation of path dependency and because it pursues an integrationist aim. First, in the past, the ECJ has struck down on just one occasion a piece of EU legislation on the ground of competences, in the *Tobacco* cases.[18] In a way, this is no surprise in a functional polity that used to be—and is still—organized around objectives. Unlike other federal polities such as Germany or Switzerland, we still cannot find any ad hoc provision in the Lisbon Treaty empowering the ECJ to enforce the division of powers between the Member States and the European Union.[19] In this context, the incentives for the ECJ to change its case law are few, and we can therefore expect it to keep going in the same direction, especially if the domestic constitutional courts fail to take a strong decentralizing stance on this matter.[20] Secondly, unlike the US, there has never been such a thing as dual federalism in Europe because of the integrationist *telos* of the EU. The EU faces structural constraints that impede it from effectively sanctioning the vertical division of powers. These constraints have to do with the parent ideas of integration, 'ever closer union', integrative federalism and *acquis communautaire*. Indeed the mere concept of integration supports a centripetal force leading to the granting of new powers to the European Union, such an attribution of competences being meant to be definitive, as emphasized by the *Costa v Enel* ruling.

It would not be particularly useful here to present in detail the numerous devices that have been used by the ECJ to create new powers for the EU and to broaden

[17] In emphasizing political guarantees of federalism, the judges were probably inspired by Wechsler (n 2).

[18] See K. Lenaerts, 'L'encadrement par le droit de l'Union européenne des compétences des Etats membres', in G. Cohen-Jonathan and J-P. Jacqué, *Chemins d'Europe. Mélanges en l'honneur de Jean-Paul Jacqué* (Paris: Dalloz, 2010), 421.

[19] Art 263 TFEU (lodging a normal action for invalidity) could obviously fulfil this task. However, it has never proved very successful in this respect. Furthermore, the mere existence of a specific provision would be quite telling and meaningful on the symbolic plane.

[20] See the *Honeywell* ruling of the German Federal Constitutional Court.

the scope of application of EU law beyond EU competences *stricto sensu*. The very extension of EU powers—a phenomenon which is better known as 'creeping competences'—seems so limitless that a high-profile scholar and practitioner of EU law even stated that there was 'simply no nucleus of sovereignty that the Member State can invoke as such against the Community'.[21] It is therefore clear that the EU has never been so keen on regulating the way in which powers are distributed between the Member States and the EU. When it comes to competences, the European Union seems more concerned with the *modalities* of their exercise.

2. The salience of the *How* question: the requirement to respect national constitutional identity

In the EU, I would argue that the main issue relating to competences is *how* to exercise them, irrespective of *who* exercises them. We can indeed find several checks within EU law on the way in which the Member States and the EU exercise their own competences. What immediately come to the mind are the proportionality and the subsidiarity reviews (I will look at the latter in due course). However, other types of checks exist. In this volume, Lena Boucon has discussed the fact that Member States' 'retained' powers have to respect certain substantive rules of EU law.[22] Conversely, it appears that the European Union should use its competences in a way which is sympathetic towards certain norms of domestic law, namely those reflecting the 'constitutional identity' of the Member States. Qualifying as a gateway between the EU and the domestic legal orders, the recently devised narrative of national constitutional identity practically works as a check on EU competences. We will see that the scope of this check is quite broad, though not unlimited.

a) *The emergence of a common narrative to settle the constitutional conflict*

A new and rather enigmatic discourse known as 'constitutional identity' is gradually emerging, both in the EU, and in some domestic legal orders, such as France, Germany, and Poland. Those words first came to prominence in the early 2000s in the framework of the debate on the Constitutional Treaty. In the absence of a common ethnic identity in Europe, the aim was to create a new European identity founded on universal principles and values devised by reason.[23] This civic identity, stressing the need for enhanced deliberation through communication in Europe, was meant to be the source of a new type of patriotism, namely what Habermas dubbed 'constitutional patriotism'.[24]

[21] Lenaerts (n 4) 220. [22] See ch. 8 of this volume.

[23] See A. von Bogdandy, 'The European Constitution and European Identity: Text and Subtext of the Treaty establishing a Constitution for Europe' (2005) 3 *International Journal of Constitutional Law* 473; M. Rosenfeld, 'The European Treaty-Constitution and Constitutional Identity: A View from America' (2005) 3 *International Journal of Constitutional Law* 316; W. Sadurski, 'European Constitutional Identity?', *EUI Working Paper Law* 2006/33.

[24] See F. Michelman, 'Morality, Identity and 'Constitutional Patriotism' (2001) 14 *Ratio Juris*, 253; J.-W. Müller, 'A European Constitutional Patriotism? The Case Restated' (2008) 14 *European Law*

Recently, the notion of constitutional identity has migrated from the European level to the national one. Indeed it has started to be applied to the Member States by national courts but also, to a lesser extent though, by the ECJ. It first appeared in the case law of the French, the German, and the Polish constitutional courts.[25] The three upper courts used this new terminology in order to set a new limit to the action of the European institutions, in other words, a constitutional reservation that may partially overlap with the previously defined reservations such as sovereignty, ultra vires, or fundamental rights.

At this stage, one may legitimately wonder why three major constitutional courts in Europe such as these came up with such a dubious concept. In fact, by resorting to constitutional identity, these courts have proved quite cunning, because the concept at stake here is implicit in the EU Treaty itself. Following the Lisbon Treaty in fact, Article 4(2) TEU now reads: 'The Union shall respect the equality of Member States before the Treaties as well as their *national identities, inherent in their fundamental structures, political and constitutional*, inclusive of regional and local self-government.' Prior to this, the constitutional dimension of national identity was absent from the wording of the Treaty. Originally, Article F(1) TEU in its Maastricht version (which became Article 6(3) TEU in Amsterdam) was quite straightforward, mentioning that the EU should respect the national identities of the Member States. By connecting those identities and the fundamental constitutional structures, the Lisbon Treaty has given the national courts the opportunity to coin the concept of constitutional identity. Through this concept, it has allowed them to justify their basic constitutional claim that EU law itself preserves at least the core provisions of the constitutions of the Member States. In doing this, coalescing constitutional courts have found an entry point to EU primary law. However, this attempt on the part of national courts to justify their claim of—relative—primacy of their constitutions on the basis of EU law could have remained dead letter, had the ECJ chosen not to respond favourably to that claim. At first sight, there was indeed little hope of seeing the ECJ vindicating this kind of claim, above all against the background of its seminal ruling in *Internationale Handelsgesellschaft* where the Luxembourg judges made it clear that national constitutional provisions should by no means impede the uniform application of EU law.[26]

Nevertheless, contrary to the widespread view, the ECJ has certainly always been careful not to expressly open a Pandora's box, but it has simultaneously often proved willing to accommodate national constitutional claims to the greatest possible extent.[27] First, a handful of Advocates General have not shied away from

Journal 542; also from the same author, 'A General Theory of Constitutional Patriotism' (2008) 6 *International Journal of Constitutional Law* 72.

[25] Conseil constitutionnel, case no 2006-540 DC, 27 July 2006, *Law on copyright and related rights in the information society, Rec.* 88; Bundesverfassungsgericht, 2 BvE 2/08, *Lissabon-Urteil* of 30 June 2009; Polish Constitutional Tribunal, K 32/09, *Lisbon-judgment* of 24 November 2010.

[26] Case 11-70 *Internationale Handelsgesellschaft* [1970] ECR 1125.

[27] See N.N. Shuibhne, 'Margins of Appreciation: National Values, Fundamental Rights and EC Free Movement Law' (2009) 34 *European Law Review* 230; D. Ritleng, 'Le droit au respect de l'identité constitutionnelle nationale', in J-C. Barbato and J-D. Mouton (eds.), *Vers la reconnaissance de droits*

using the very narrative of 'constitutional identity' in their opinions, the most elaborate version being AG Poiares Maduro's in the *Michaniki* case.[28] In this Greek case on public procurement and the media,[29] the Advocate General explained that respect for constitutional identity dated back to the origin of the European construction and called for a qualified respect of the most important principles of domestic constitutions, subject to a proportionality test.

Secondly, even where the notion of constitutional identity is absent, the ECJ does in any case take national constitutional provisions into account. It even seems to be increasingly sympathetic to considerations deriving from national identity, although it usually bypasses the hurdle by delivering a decision primarily based upon other grounds. While in 1996 the ECJ only saw in the preservation of national identity a '*legitimate aim*',[30] it has recently begun referring to Article 4(2) TEU. In *Runevic-Vardyn*,[31] the Court considered that the protection of Lithuania's national official language flowed from Article 4(2) EU. It therefore decided that the domestic rules governing the spelling of that language constituted a legitimate interest capable of justifying restrictions on the rights of freedom of movement and residence provided for in Article 21 TFEU.[32] Even more interesting for us is the decision in *Sayn-Wittgenstein*.[33] In this case, the plaintiff was a 65-year-old Austrian citizen. In the wake of her adoption by a German prince some 20 years earlier, she took both his name and nobility title, namely 'Fürstin von Sayn-Wittgenstein'. However, the Austrian authorities decided to challenge—belatedly—the use of such a title on the basis of a decision issued by Austria's Constitutional Court in a similar case. The constitutional judges had held that the law on the abolition of nobility, which is of constitutional status, precluded an Austrian citizen from acquiring a surname that included a title of nobility. Mrs Sayn-Wittgenstein, who was involved in the sale of castles, objected, arguing that such a decision infringed her right to freedom of movement across the EU, together with her right to name and personal identity. Upon a preliminary reference sent by the Administrative Court of Austria, the ECJ ruled that the Austrian constitutional prohibition on nobility titles was compatible with EU law on two grounds: first, this ban was justified on the basis of public policy and, secondly, 'in accordance with Article 4(2) TEU, the European Union is to respect the national identities of its Member States, which include the status of the State as a Republic'. This judgment, which reminds

fondamentaux aux Etats membres de l'Union européenne? (Brussels: Bruylant, 2010), 22; J. Gerards, 'Pluralism, Deference and the Margin of Appreciation Doctrine' (2011) 17 *European Law Journal* 80.

[28] Case C-213/07 *Michaniki* [2008] ECR I-9999.

[29] See the case note by V. Kosta in (2009) *European Constitutional Law Review* 501.

[30] Case C-473/93 *Commission v Luxembourg* [1996] ECR I-3207.

[31] Case C-391/09 *Runevic-Vardyn* [2011] I-3787.

[32] See also Case C-202/11 *Anton Las*, judgment of 16 April 2013. In this ruling, the Court examined the obligation for companies established in the Dutch-speaking region of Belgium to draft employment contracts in Dutch. They decided that the objective of promoting and encouraging the use of Dutch in Belgium was a legitimate interest that is protected under art 4(2) TEU and justifies a restriction on the free movement for workers. However, the domestic norm under review failed the proportionality test and was therefore declared incompatible with EU law.

[33] Case C-208/09 *Sayn-Wittgenstein* [2010] ECR I-3696.

us of *Omega*,[34] is quite illustrative of the attention paid by the ECJ to issues related to core national constitutional provisions although national identity still looks like an unsophisticated second order reason to restrict the basic market freedoms.

In these cases, the ECJ unfortunately did not seem to grasp the importance of explicitly referring to 'constitutional' national identity.[35] While constitutional identity will in all probability not always have the same meaning in EU law as in domestic law, what is crucial here is that the same expression should be used in both spheres. It could therefore qualify as a gateway between both legal orders and, thus, be apt to resolve the constitutional conflict under the obvious proviso that the ECJ should not take too restrictive a view of constitutional identity while domestic constitutional courts should refrain from overstretching it. In any case, it is already striking to note how broad the scope of constitutional identity can be as a check on the exercise of the competences of the European Union.

b) A broad check on the exercise of EU competences

When it comes to the EU, the subsidiarity principle is usually considered to be the best concept in terms of guaranteeing the autonomous action of the Member States.[36] However, now focusing solely on the EU standpoint and leaving aside the purely national dimension, it appears that respect for constitutional identity may transpire to be a more effective check on the exercise of EU competences than subsidiarity. While admittedly the same bottom-up political philosophy underlies both principles, subsidiarity is primarily an operative tool aimed at deciding along rather technical lines which level of governance is the most suitable to take action, while national constitutional identity serves as a substantive check, enhancing diversity through the taking into account of national specificities.

Subsidiarity is fundamentally about the vertical distribution of competences. To be more precise, it does not aim at vesting powers in the Member States, but is merely a flexible tool regulating *ex post* the *exercise* of certain EU competences in order to ensure the efficiency of political action. Even though the subsidiarity check was substantially improved in Lisbon, we may still have doubts as to its effectiveness.[37] First, its scope is limited to shared competences. Therefore, it should theoretically not impact upon EU exclusive competences nor, *a fortiori*, on the scope of application of EU law. Secondly, numerous hurdles should be overcome before the decision is taken to brush aside a draft EU legislative act for breach of subsidiarity: one-third of national parliaments have to raise such a

[34] Case C-36/02 *Omega Spielhallen* [2004] ECR I-9609.

[35] Admittedly, the European Court of Justice is wary in the use of the constitutional identity rhetoric for fear of seriously jeopardizing the principle of primacy of EU law over domestic constitutions.

[36] E.g. G.A. Bermann, 'Taking Subsidiarity Seriously: Federalism in the European Community and the United States' (1994) 94 *Columbia Law Review* 331; G. Martinico, 'Dating Cinderella: On Subsidiarity as a Political Safeguard of Federalism in the European Union' (2011) 17 *European Public Law* 649.

[37] On the functioning of subsidiarity under the Lisbon treaty, see Xavier Groussot's contribution to this volume.

breach in a reasoned opinion sent to the EU institutions. It is ultimately up to the Commission to withdraw, amend, or maintain the text.[38] Thirdly, subsidiarity (as it is designed) seems to be more concerned with economic efficiency, rational choice, and—to a certain extent—democratic legitimacy, than with respect for specific national characteristics. While such a respect does not necessarily entail the exercise of a competence by the Member States, one must keep in mind that subsidiarity is essentially about that. Furthermore, a *specific* feature cannot be effectively taken into account by a control mechanism that requires a qualified minority of national parliaments.

Against this background, together with proportionality, respect for national constitutional identity looks more apt to be a political and judicial safeguard of a kind of federalism that would put more emphasis on diversity and respect for specificities rather than on the autonomy of the different political actors involved. I assume from the outset that constitutional identity will not be about allocating competences between the EU and the Member States although, from the standpoint of some national judges, this concept may admittedly be instrumental in retaining competences. From the EU perspective, not only did we see earlier that the issue has never been salient within the European Union—at least until Lisbon—but we would hardly understand why respect for constitutional identity would have the same function as subsidiarity. I contend that, in practice, the former is very different from the latter in the way in which it actually works. To start with, the scope of the respect for national constitutional identity is quite broad. Indeed, it flows from the very wording of Article 4 TEU that it encompasses virtually all areas of competences of the European Union, including exclusive competences. It will therefore regulate the exercise of EU powers. Moreover, it can be seen as an interpretive principle within the broad scope of application of EU law, requiring constructions of EU norms in conformity—or at least compatibility—with constitutional identity.[39] It will therefore be advanced not only against secondary EU acts, but equally against primary law and domestic implementation measures.

That being said, a great deal of issues remain unsettled. To name just a few, we may first wonder what national constitutional identity actually *is*, whether it is all-encompassing under EU law, and how it shall be enforced by courts. Is it only a shorthand, merely referring to the features of national identity that are reflected in the domestic constitution? What are those specificities to be taken into account by the EU? Who should decide on the constitutional identity 'exception'? In view of the lack of space afforded to us and keeping in mind our primary aim in this contribution, I will only address the second problem: drawing on the Hungarian example, I argue that the respect for constitutional identity will *not* include all national rules, values, and principles of constitutional significance that

[38] See Protocol No. 2, attached to the Lisbon Treaty, on the application of the principles of subsidiarity and proportionality.

[39] Advocating already such an interpretation back in the early 90s, B. de Witte, 'Droit communautaire et valeurs constitutionnelles nationales' (1991) 14 *Droits* 87, 95–6.

are deemed worthy of respect against contradicting EU norms as that would be too far-fetched.[40]

c) A necessarily 'constitutional' constitutional identity

From the EU perspective, the respect for certain provisions of the constitutions of the Member States can only be limited in its scope. It could otherwise prove too divisive and potentially dangerous. Therefore, not all national specificities endowed with constitutional status shall reasonably be accepted in EU law. The latter will set a framework within which the former can be deemed acceptable. This framework will be designed along the lines of constitutionalism, that is to say, around the core values of the EU, namely the respect for human rights, democracy, and the rule of law[41] but also the principle of non-discrimination on grounds of nationality,[42] in connection with EU citizenship.[43]

This means that in practice, a Member State cannot simply put forward its own national identity, albeit enshrined in its constitution, if it does not comply with the broadly defined standards of constitutionalism. As Germans might put it, the '*Verfassungsidentität*' should be '*konstitutionnell*', i.e. in line with the values and principles aimed at ensuring limitation of power through law. In other words, the respect for 'national' constitutional identity will find its boundaries in the respect for 'European' constitutional identity. In this regard, the new Hungarian Constitution may offer a compelling case study.

Hungary adopted a very controversial constitution in the spring of 2011 with a strong conservative and Catholic imprint. This new constitution, which entered into force on 1 January 2012,[44] has attracted the attention of journalists, politicians, and lawyers given the fact that it might actually breach human rights. The criticisms are twofold. First, from a formal perspective, the constitution-making process has not fully complied with traditional democratic procedures, as it hardly involved the civil society or the opposition parties. Moreover, the Constitution was not put to the people through a referendum, but was adopted by a two-thirds majority of Parliament, i.e. by the ruling party. Its very content seems to be equally problematic and may violate several human rights together with the rule of law. Not only does the new Fundamental Law rest on an ethnic and potentially

[40] Setting out some interesting prospects as to the judicial enforcement of national constitutional identity both by the ECJ and the domestic courts, see A. Von Bogdandy and S. Schill, 'Overcoming Absolute Primacy: the Respect for National Identity under the Lisbon Treaty' (2011) 48 *Common Market Law Review* 1417, esp at 1447 *et seq.* I contend that the ECJ is likely to enforce constitutional identity after engaging with the other main actors, namely national courts. Such a dialogue is made necessary by the dual use of the concept of constitutional identity and its function as a gateway between conflicting legal orders. Unilateral claims would make little sense as they would undoubtedly fuel disagreement instead of alleviating it.

[41] Art 2 TEU. [42] Art 18 TFEU.

[43] See A. Von Bogdandy and others, 'Reverse *Solange*–Protecting the essence of fundamental rights against EU Member States' (2012) 49 *Common Market Law Review* 489.

[44] For an overview of the constitution-making process and the substantial changes brought in by the new Constitution, see K. Kovacs and G.A. Toth, 'Hungary's Constitutional Transformation' (2011) 7 *European Constitutional Law Review* 183.

exclusive conception of the nation,[45] but it is also rooted in Catholic values: it stresses the sanctity of marriage by limiting it to the union between a man and a woman[46] and states that the life of the foetus shall be protected from the moment of conception.[47] Such provisions may legitimately be seen as hindering gay marriage and also the right to abortion. Furthermore, in relation to the rule of law, the new constitution was criticized for the reductions it made to the jurisdiction of the Constitutional Court, especially in budgetary matters.[48] Together with the Hungarian media legislation (which may endanger pluralism) and the doubts as to the independence of the Central Bank, these issues created some suspicion about the conformity of the new Hungarian Constitution with human rights[49], especially with Article 2 TEU.[50] Do they potentially create 'a clear risk of a serious breach of the values referred in Article 2' that could ultimately lead to the suspension of Hungary's rights under the Treaties?[51] At this stage, we do not have enough elements to answer this question. However, it is quite interesting to see the proposals that it triggered to confront this kind of situation, which are objectively 'purely internal situations' where EU fundamental rights should normally not be applicable.[52]

In this context, it becomes clearer why speaking of 'constitutional' identity and not only of 'national' identity does really matter. On the functional plane, the explicit mention of 'constitutional' identity in EU law itself would send a positive and amicable signal to the domestic courts in using their own terminology. On the substantial plane, this means that, under EU law, national constitutional identity should be truly constitutional within the meaning of the liberal political thought.

Against this background, it appears that the emergence of constitutional identity together with the actual features of the vertical distribution of competences in the EU underlines new practices of federalism, requiring new theoretical approaches. Nowadays, it is extremely difficult to determine *ex ante* who should exercise a competence X or Y. In a pluralist legal space characterized by intertwined and overlapping legal orders, we can hardly revive a dualist approach[53] and we should instead rely on new remedies.

[45] See the preamble and art D dealing with Hungarian minorities abroad and non-Hungarian nationalities living on the Hungarian territory.

[46] Art L. [47] Art II. [48] See Art 24.

[49] For an assessment of the new constitution with regard to human rights and the rule of law, see the Opinion no 621/2011 of the Venice Commission (Council of Europe, 17–18 June 2011), available at: <http://www.venice.coe.int>; see also the Amicus Brief for the Venice Commission on the Transitional Provisions of the Fundamental Law and the Key Cardinal Laws (February 2012, edited by Gabor Halmai and Kim Lane Scheppele).

[50] Pursuant to art 2 TEU, 'the Union is founded on the values of respect for human dignity, freedom, democracy, equality, the rule of law and respect for human rights, including the rights of persons belonging to minorities. These values are common to the Member States in a society in which pluralism, non-discrimination, tolerance, justice, solidarity and equality between women and men prevail'.

[51] See art 7 TEU.

[52] See esp the 'Heidelberg proposal' (or '*Reverse-Solange*') by Von Bogdandy and others (n 43).

[53] Dualist federalism is in our view an expression of dualism between legal orders. It no longer fits the new relationships between orders.

For those who yearn for order, it would certainly be more satisfactory to adopt a dualist approach. However, this is no longer possible, nor even appropriate. Even the national judges for whom division of powers was paramount have started minimizing it, the best illustration of this being Germany. In fact, in its *Maastricht* ruling, the Federal Constitutional Court had insisted that it would not refrain from declaring inapplicable on the German territory EU acts that it would deem ultra vires. If it repeated its stance in its *Lisbon* judgment, the Court qualified it to a large extent in the *Honeywell* ruling under which a breach of Member States' competences on the part of the European bodies will be punished only if it is sufficiently qualified and leads to a structurally significant shift to the detriment of the Member States.[54]

What then, are the theoretical implications for EU federalism of the shift illustrated by constitutional identity together with the fact that the question '*how* competences are exercised' seems to matter more than the issue '*who* exercises them' in the European legal space?

II. A New Kind of Federalism in the European Union

Federalism is one of those blurred concepts of public law that are highly difficult to grasp. Most people would have only a fairly vague idea as to its precise meaning. They would be unable to explain exactly what it is about. Such a gap could probably remain unproblematic if the concept at stake was a minor one. However it is not. We do seem to be witnessing a large-scale phenomenon that could be referred to—in a slightly exaggerated fashion—as a 'federalization of the world'. There is, in fact, an increasing trend towards advocating and inventing federal solutions for a broad range of situations. For now, we may just think of the calls for fiscal federalism in Italy or the establishment of a federal regime in Iraq. In many respects, federalism nowadays seems to be the ideal political form. In this context, scholars have to tackle the issue by examining what federalism actually means and implies. Several factors have contributed to the present state of uncertainty as to the messy concept of federalism. This situation derives from the overuse and often misuse of federalist language. A good understanding of federalism is indeed fraught with difficulties pertaining to its focus, its perception, and its methodology.

First of all, federalism is confronted with its multiple functions and focuses. It pursues various different aims, which range from economic efficiency, accommodation of cultural diversity, or vindication of states' rights, to limiting power and creating a community of feelings. Its focus would then evolve between the individual and the polities, as federalism can be embraced both from an individualistic or from a holistic perspective, depending on whether it is inspired by a liberal or a communitarian philosophy.

[54] Bundesverfassungsgericht, 2 BvR 2661/06, 6 July 2010.

Secondly, federalism also has to face perception-related difficulties. The mere word has different meanings attached to it from one country to another. We all know how much the 'F-Word' is taboo in the EU context. Its very use was already extremely controversial at the time of the foundation of the United States: the so-called 'Federalists' were the actual proponents of a strong central authority, whereas those who were in favour of strong states' rights were branded 'Anti-Federalists'.[55] The same strict dichotomy also strikingly applies in the EU although federalism is essentially about unity *and* diversity. That is the reason why it is hard today to use a discredited narrative that is embroiled in partisan quarrels. In any scientific debate on federalism, the scholar will therefore always have to issue a disclaimer in order to avoid accusations of ideological bias.

Thirdly, there is a general lack of epistemology of federalism,[56] whereas there is a pressing need to have one. In fact, we tend to rely on a priori or historically-rooted definitions to interpret the 'federative phenomenon',[57] without asking whether such an approach is adequate in order to grasp a concept which is so elusive and unstable in several regards. Not only does that impoverish and constrain the understanding of federalism, but it questions the very relevance of an institutionally-oriented definition of a phenomenon that might be better understood as a process.

From this set of hurdles originates a situation of path dependency that prevents us from an accurate understanding of federalism, especially in the EU context. It is therefore necessary to deconstruct federalism, in other words to get rid of the numerous preconceived ideas about federalism by relying on Descartes' *doute méthodique* or Derrida's theory (or rather practical epistemology). According to the latter, there is no direct relation between the signifier and the signified and the meaning of the signifier does not result from a priori categories, but is the outcome of experience. We should therefore make *tabula rasa* of our preconceptions and discover meanings in an inductive manner. When it comes to federalism, I suggest first examining legal arrangements to ascertain its features.[58] My reasoning will be based on a single and straightforward assumption that is supposedly the common and unchallengeable thread of federalism: *federalism is about striking a fair balance between unity and diversity*. Several leading scholars emphasized what may be seen as the backbone of federalism. According to Daniel Elazar, 'federalism has to do with the need of people and polities to unite for common purposes, yet remain

[55] Rightly, Shapiro prefers distinguishing nationalists ('those who advocate strong central authority') and federalists ('those who advocate substantial diffusion of authority between the national governments and the states'): D.L. Shapiro, *Federalism: a Dialogue* (Evanston, Ill.: Nortwestern University Press, 1995), 10–11.

[56] Among the few books devoting a substantial part to methodology, see J.-F. Gaudreault-DesBiens and F. Gélinas (ed.), *Le fédéralisme dans tous ses états. Gouvernance, identité et méthodologie/The states and moods of federalism. Governance, identity and methodology* (Brussels: Bruylant, 2005), esp J.-F. Gaudreault-DesBiens, B. Théret, and V. Jackson's contributions. Also J. Kincaid (ed.), *Federalism* (London and Thousand Oaks, Calif.: SAGE, 2011), bringing together the classical and contemporary articles that have been most influential in the understanding of federalism.

[57] Scelle (n 1) 187.

[58] Already following this approach, G. Héraud, *Les principes du fédéralisme et la fédération européenne. Contribution à la théorie juridique du fédéralisme* (Paris: Presses d'Europe, 1968), 14–19.

separate to preserve their respective integrities. It is rather like wanting to have one's cake and eat it'.[59] The same idea was conveyed by Pierre Pescatore for the EC: 'federalism is a political and legal philosophy which adapts itself to all political contexts...wherever and whenever two basic prerequisites are fulfilled: the search for unity, combined with genuine respect for the autonomy and the legitimate interests of the participant states.'[60]

Therefore, genuine technical and political safeguards of federalism will preserve *both* unity and diversity. Why, then, is constitutional identity likely to be an adequate safeguard of federalism, i.e. both of unity and diversity, while it sounds so disruptive and divisive? Not only does national constitutional identity contribute to diversity, but I claim that it also contributes to unity in different ways, both in its functioning (as a check on EU competences, it ensures functional unity) and in its content (it fosters substantial unity around the main principles of constitutionalism). That leads us to look at federalism from different perspectives, namely those of integrity (federalism in action) and cosmopolitan constitutionalism (federalism in theory).[61]

1. Federalism in action: from integration to integrity

When it comes to analyzing the European Union, 'integration' is one of the main key words to describe the centripetal, neofunctionalist process that has led to the successive transfers of Member States' competences to the EU. Integration is indeed usually seen by political scientists as 'the process whereby political actors in several, distinct national settings are persuaded to shift their loyalties, expectations and political activities toward a new centre, whose institutions possess and demand jurisdiction over the pre-existing national states'.[62] Both the word and the idea behind it emphasize the establishment of a hierarchically organized unity[63] made up of an upper and a lower level.

[59] D.J. Elazar, *Exploring Federalism* (Tuscaloosa: University of Alabama Press, 1987), 33. See also K. Nicolaidis, 'Constitutionalizing the Federal Vision?', in A. Menon and M. Schain (ed.), *Comparative Federalism: The European Union and the United States in Comparative Perspective* (Oxford: Oxford University Press, 2006), 59, notably at 64; also 'The Federal Vision, Levels of Governance and Legitimacy', in K. Nicolaidis and R. Howse, *The Federal Vision: Legitimacy and Levels of Governance in the United States and the European Union* (Oxford and New York: Oxford University Press, 2001), 1, at 27: 'unity of purpose, diversity of place and belonging.'

[60] P. Pescatore, 'Foreword' in T. Sandalow and Eric Stein (eds.), *Courts and Free Markets. Perspectives from the United States and Europe* (Oxford: Clarendon Press, and New York: Oxford University Press, 1982). Also A. Von Bogdandy, 'The European Union as a supranational federation. A conceptual attempt in the light of the Treaty of Amsterdam' (2000) *Columbia Journal of European Law* 6, at 27.

[61] Note that asserting that constitutionalism serves as an update of federalism does not necessarily mean that the traditional understanding of federalism is utterly irrelevant to grasp the nature of the EU. Per se, that does not indeed disqualify federalism and its emphasis on institutional arrangements. I merely wish to stress here that the very narrative of constitutional identity tends to shift the focus towards the constitutionalist dimension of federalism, in the wake of Johannes Althusius' and C.J. Friedrich's works.

[62] E. Haas, *The Uniting of Europe: Political, Social and Economic Forces 1950-57* (Stanford, Calif: Stanford University Press, 1958), 16.

[63] See G. Itzcovich, 'Integrazione giuridica. Un'analisi concettuale' (2005) 3 *Diritto pubblico* 749, at 771.

In my view, the latest developments in the EU hint at an evolution of the European *telos*, namely a gradual replacement of integration by integrity.[64] As a matter of fact, the integration process has stalled and distrust towards European institutions is growing. It seems that unity can no longer arise from a top-down approach mainly based on power but rather from the equal and loyal involvement of all actors seeking to enhance the EU's legitimacy and authority.[65] In the wake of Ronald Dworkin, Samantha Besson coined the term 'European integrity' to refer to this new kind of unity which is sought. It involves ensuring the coherence of the past and present decisions taken by both the domestic and European authorities, especially the judges. Requiring, above all, mutual loyalty, integrity will result in a more horizontal and heterarchical unity, taking into account the competing claims of the different actors. Although this word had not previously been used as an explanatory concept, it is remarkable that the ECJ seems to have already called for integrity in its *Cilfit* decision back in 1982.[66] It made clear that the interpretation of EU law should be conducted 'in the light of the provisions of Community law *as a whole*'. One could infer from these terms that the EU and the domestic legal orders cannot be regarded either in a dualistic or in a monistic and hierarchical way: there is a European legal space in which every judge, be he or she national or supranational, is part of a community of interpreters who are required to take into account the existence of competing principles and rules, above all those embodying the identity of the respective legal orders.[67]

In its very functioning, respect for national constitutional identity will contribute to integrity. Daniel Halberstam distinguished between two approaches to federalism in connection with competences. Comparing the US, the EU, and Germany, he contrasted the entitlements approach with the loyalty approach.[68] The former 'takes a federal constitution as granting each level or unit of government a set of regulatory tools that may be used without regard to whether the exercise of these powers serves the system of democratic governance as a whole' while the latter 'insists that each level or unit of government must always act to ensure the proper functioning of the system of governance as a whole'.[69] In the context of the European Union, the entitlements approach seems largely to coincide with the

[64] Suggesting the existence of such a shift, see especially S. Besson, 'From European Integration to European Integrity: Should European Law Speak with Just One Voice?' (2004) 10 *European Law Journal* 257; also P. Eleftheriadis, 'Pluralism and Integrity' (2010) 23 *Ratio Juris* 365.

[65] As Alain Supiot mentioned in light of the ever-growing success of independent agencies, we are witnessing a comeback of the old medieval distinction between *auctoritas* and *potestas* that the sovereign state had erased: nowadays, systems of power can no longer be self-referential but need external sources of legitimacy. See A. Supiot, *Homo Juridicus. Essai sur la fonction anthropologique du droit* (Paris: Editions du Seuil, 2005; English translation: *Homo Juridicus. On the Anthropological Function of the Law* (London, New York: Verso, 2007)).

[66] Case 283/81 *Srl Cilfit* [1982] ECR I-3415.

[67] Apart from Samantha Besson's article quoted above, see M. Poiares Maduro, 'Interpreting European Law: Judicial Adjudication in a Context of Constitutional Pluralism' (2007) 1 *European Journal of Legal Studies* 2 (available online at <http://www.ejls.eu>).

[68] D. Halberstam, 'Of Power and Responsibility: The Political Morality of Federal Systems' (2004) 90 *Virginia Law Review* 731.

[69] Halberstam (n 68) 732–4.

division of powers doctrine whereas the loyalty approach—which echoes *Cilfit*—fits particularly well with the integrity thesis: irrespective of its actual holder, a competence shall not be exercised in isolation but always with due regard for the other actors within the system.

As a matter of fact, this approach, which proves particularly well suited to the European Union, finds further support in the way in which retained competences are handled. The requirement of European integrity is buttressed by two parallel moves: not only is the Union to exercise its powers with due regard and respect for the constitutional identity of the Member States, but the Member States should exercise their own powers with due regard and respect for EU law, as illustrated by the retained powers.[70] Both trends lead to embracing the EU *as a whole*, by building a European legal space rather than a proper legal order in the classical sense. In this broad legal space where the different normative orders are so interwoven, each autonomous system of norms will have to loyally ensure the protection of their respective core provisions. In other words, integrity seeks to make sure that both the constitutional identity of the EU and the constitutional identity of the Member States are respected, thus reflecting the need for mutual accommodation within an encompassing, larger framework of a *constitutional* nature.

2. Federalism in theory: cosmopolitan constitutionalism

Moving on to substance, national constitutional identity contributes to enhancing constitutionalism at the EU level, albeit not in the traditional sense which was prevailing some 10 years ago. On the surface, one could believe that the respect for constitutional identity would buttress traditional federalism and also complement state sovereignty. However, I contend that constitutional identity is essentially different from sovereignty. As a consequence, I see the EU moving away from Carl Schmitt and Olivier Beaud's *political* model of the federation to embrace a better-suited kind of federalism, which may nowadays be labelled 'cosmopolitan constitutionalism'.

a) *Away from the political model of the federation towards the societal pattern of federalism*

The very narrative of constitutional identity, with its focus on limitation of power through law together with maximization of diversity, bears far-reaching consequences in terms of substantive discussions on federalism in the EU. It entails moving away from the holistic and power-oriented model of the federation—lately propounded by Olivier Beaud—to adopt a more societal and somehow Protestant approach to federalism as process.

In the wake of Carl Schmitt,[71] Olivier Beaud has come up with a learned theory of the federation that boldly attempts to understand the federative phenomenon

[70] See Lena Boucon's contribution in this volume.

[71] C. Schmitt, *Constitutional Theory* (Durham: Duke University Press, 2008).

beyond the traditional divide between the federal state and the confederation, potentially in order to understand the peculiar nature of the European Union.[72] In his model, the federation is a political and holistic institution pursuing two contradictory aims, which account for the dialectic between unity and diversity. On the one hand, the different Member States are supposed to come together and unite for the sake of security and prosperity; on the other hand, they should keep their own political existence and remain themselves. At first sight, the latter aim seems to include respect for the constitutional identity of the Member States. However, it does not fully do so in my view. In spite of the fact that Olivier Beaud strives to push sovereignty aside on the epistemological plane, this key concept of modern state theory is still very salient in the theory of the federation.[73] Yet, a European Union founded upon constitutional identity brushes aside the issue of sovereignty, which is not in keeping with the definition of the EU as a process meant to ensure peace through law and trade, as opposed to power politics. In EU law, words definitely matter, since the construction of a new legal order needs symbols to enhance its legitimacy and establish some roots.[74] It is striking to note that at present, the narrative of sovereignty is absent at the European level whereas it is still paramount in domestic law and international law. We can easily understand such a complete silence since—absolute—sovereignty has always been blamed by the founding fathers for encouraging warfare. The sovereignty rhetoric is therefore not particularly welcome in Europe. What if the narrative of constitutional identity smuggles sovereignty in through the back door? I see both concepts as essentially different. On the one side, sovereignty still tends to be associated with absolute power, the primacy of politics over law, of the collective over the individual. On the other side, constitutional identity carries opposite values: limitation of power, the reign of law, the primacy of the individual over the group, and of identity politics over power politics.

[72] O. Beaud, *Théorie de la Fédération*, 2nd edn (Paris: Presses Universitaires de France, 2007); see also ch. 1 of this volume.

[73] Several authors have insisted upon the fact that sovereignty and federalism collided. Most of them did so on the basis of Bodin's absolute and indivisible conception of sovereignty. They saw a mere technical or formal incompatibility where there is arguably a structural problem. Carl J. Friedrich stressed on his part the antinomy between federalism and unity-oriented, hierarchy-minded sovereignty: 'we have federalism only if a set of political communities coexist and interact as autonomous entities, united in a common order with an autonomy of its own. No sovereign can exist in a federal system: autonomy and sovereignty exclude each other in such a political order.... No one has the "last word". The idea of a compact is inherent in federalism, and the "constituent power", which makes the compact, takes the place of the sovereign' (C.J. Friedrich, cited in the epigraph to this chapter, at 7–8). The reader may object that we could equally deconstruct sovereignty in order to make it fit with federalism. I actually doubt it, since the interpretation of sovereignty has to face textual and etymological constraints. In the wake of Carl J. Friedrich, I hold the view that sovereignty will necessarily therefore be a concept referring to ultimate political power, eventually exercised in a revolutionary or semi-revolutionary way by one person or a group of people that decide or 'call the shots'.

[74] For instance, about the European 'Constitution', M. Poiares Maduro, 'The Importance of Being Called Constitution. Constitutional authority and authority of constitutionalism' (2005) 3 *I.CON* 332.

In fact, respect for national constitutional identity actually fits better within the Protestant federalist mindset, especially societal federalism as propounded by Johannes Althusius in his *Politica* (1603).[75] Althusius is one of those important political theorists whose name had fallen into oblivion before being rediscovered by authors such as Otto von Gierke,[76] Carl J. Friedrich,[77] and Daniel Elazar.[78] While von Gierke relied on Althusius with a view to building up the nascent German state at the end of the 19th century, Friedrich and Elazar were more interested in the federalist model expounded by Althusius at a time of crisis and transition between pre-modernity and modernity. Already back in the early-17th century in the context of the wars of religion between Catholics and Protestants and of the rise of the absolutist state, Althusius—brought up in the Calvinist faith—built a bottom-up federalist theory on the basis of the situated man, namely the individual who is embedded in different communities and who will therefore have multiple identities. In doing so, he wanted to justify the Dutch separation from Spain and the establishment of a commonwealth (*consociatio symbiotica*) based on a covenant and where sovereignty would belong to the people. Although Althusius was influenced by Bodin, he did not endorse his conception of an absolute sovereignty of the new modern territorial state that would later be supported by Hobbes, albeit from a different starting point. Swimming against the tide, he was furthermore in favour of the limitation of power, which could ultimately justify tyrannicide. He was therefore the precursor of constitutionalism as opposed to sovereignty.[79]

Unlike Schmitt and Beaud's institutional and political federalism, societal federalism seems to be more in line with what the EU yearns to be, namely a postmodern space of peace and prosperity shying away from power politics (above all, from the Schmittian conception of politics) and constraining it through the rule of law. First, as much as Althusius helps us to understand the transition from medieval social structures to modernity, he can equally be 'a source of ideas and models for a postmodern federalism'.[80] Secondly, while Bodin mainly defined

[75] J. Althusius, *Politica* (Indianapolis, Liberty Fund, 1995). On Althusius' federalism, see T.O. Hueglin, *Early Modern Concepts for a Late Modern World. Althusius on Community and Federalism* (Waterloo: Wilfried Laurier University Press, 1999); C. Millon-Delsol, *L'Etat subsidiaire. Ingérence et non-ingérence de l'Etat: le principe de subsidiarité aux fondements de l'histoire européenne* (Presses Universitaires de France, 1992), 47 *et seq.*

[76] O. von Gierke, *Johannes Althusius und die Entwicklung der naturrechtlichen Staatstheorien. Zugleich ein Beitrag zur Geschichte der Rechtssystematik* (Breslau: Koebner, 1880).

[77] C.J. Friedrich, *Johannes Althusius und sein Werk im Rahmen der Entwicklung der Theorie von der Politik* (Berlin: Duncker & Humblot, 1975). In English, see his introduction to *Politica Methodice Digesta of Johannes Althusius* (Cambridge: Harvard University Press, 1932).

[78] See his foreword in the 1995 English edition of Althusius' *Politica*.

[79] T. Hueglin, 'Johannes Althusius: Medieval Constitutionalist or Modern Federalist?' (1979) 9 *Publius: The Journal of Federalism* 9.

[80] As stated by Elazar, 'premodern federalism, before the seventeenth century, had a strong tribal or corporatist foundation, one in which individuals were inevitably defined as members of permanent, multigenerational groups and whose rights and obligations derived entirely or principally from group membership. Modern federalism broke away from this model to emphasize polities built strictly or principally on the basis of individuals and their rights, allowing little or no space for recognition or legitimation of intergenerational groups. A postmodern federalism must reckon with one of the basic principles of postmodern politics, namely that individuals are to be secured in their individual rights, yet groups are also to be recognized as real, legitimate, and requiring an appropriate status. Althusius

politics as a hierarchical system of organized public power with state sovereignty as the ultimate source of authority, Althusius takes a wider view of politics as a 'horizontal process of communication among a plurality of groups or communities which all possess their own rights and obligations'.[81] Thirdly, the main focus of Althusius' federalism is not the polity with its abstract individual but Aristotle's *zoon politikon*. In the current EU, it is striking that such an approach seems to underlie the multilevel protection of human rights and the conception of citizenship. In terms of the former, Article 53 of the EU Charter of Fundamental Rights recognizes the plurality of the sources of protection, and hence the belonging of each individual to a particular community stressing specific rights.[82] As to the latter, Article 20 TFEU connects the acquisition of EU citizenship with the possession of the nationality of a Member State. These two illustrations account for a conception of the EU that is above all a community of communities where the concrete individual is paramount.[83] In this context, respect for the constitutional identity of the Member States cannot be entirely understood from either a purely individualistic or a purely holistic point of view. Against the first perspective, its identity dimension will naturally underline the specific past and present features of a community. Against the second perspective, its constitutional dimension will naturally underline the place of the individual. Therefore, the constitutional identity of the Member State will mainly refer to the identity of the individual who is part of a specific national community (thus, not only to domestic institutional arrangements).[84] Such an approach stresses the fact that societal federalism might in fact be one and the same thing as what we would nowadays call '*cosmopolitan constitutionalism*'. Thereby, it transpires that constitutional identity departs from traditional approaches to collective identity by enabling the individuals to emancipate

is the first, and one of the few political philosophers who has attempted to provide for this synthesis. Needless to say, his late-medieval thought cannot be transposed whole into the postmodern epoch in the latter part of the twentieth century. However, in part because he wrote in a period of epochal transition from the late-medieval to the modern epoch, much of his system, its ideas, and even its terminology, may be adaptable to or at least form the basis for a postmodern federalism' (D. J. Elazar, 'Althusius' Grand Design for a Federal Commonwealth', in Althusius, *Politica* (n 75) xl).

[81] T. Hueglin, 'Federalism at the Crossroads: Old Meanings, New Significance' (2003) 36 *Canadian Journal of Political Science* 275, esp 279.

[82] Adopting a restrictive interpretation of art 53 of the EU Charter by the European Court of Justice, see Case C-399/11 *Melloni* [2013], judgment of 26 February 2013, nyr., para 60: 'Article 53 of the Charter confirms that, where an EU legal act calls for national implementing measures, national authorities and courts remain free to apply national standards of protection of fundamental rights, provided that the level of protection provided for by the Charter, as interpreted by the Court, and the primacy, unity and effectiveness of EU law are not thereby compromised.'

[83] It is quite amusing to note also that Althusius was born in the county of Sayn-Wittgenstein, the very name that gave rise to the seminal ruling of the ECJ mentioned earlier.

[84] Such a conception is very close to Kymlicka and his liberal approach of collective rights being actually rights of individuals belonging to a certain community: W. Kymlicka, *Multicultural Citizenship* (Oxford: Clarendon Press, and New York: Oxford University Press, 1997). We can also refer to Joseph Weiler's republican conception of rights which take into account societal interests: see, notably, his essay 'Fundamental rights and fundamental boundaries: on the conflict of standards and values in the European legal space', in J.H.H. Weiler, *The Constitution of Europe. 'Do the new clothes have an emperor?' and other essays on European integration* (Cambridge: Cambridge University Press, 1999), 102.

themselves from their purely national kinship and embrace a more cosmopolitan sense of belonging.

b) The case for cosmopolitan constitutionalism as an update of societal federalism

Prima facie, we might argue that enhancing constitutional identity would take place at the expense of constitutionalism and would rather benefit intergovernmentalism. It is striking that most accounts of European constitutionalism stress unity-oriented principles to describe it and, therefore, to set apart constitutionalism and intergovernmentalism. They will invariably address primacy and direct effect, *effet utile*, the rule of law, and the protection of fundamental rights. It seems as if the autonomy of the EU legal order would be enhanced were the EU to declare its independence from the Member States.

I would argue that such an approach reflects a one-sided conception of constitutionalism. To a large extent it embodies the voluntary and centripetal approach specific to French and American constitutionalism: building up a 'people' through the universal ideals of the rule of law.[85] Yet, such a conception is probably outdated following the demise of the Constitutional Treaty, which seems to have put an end to the revolutionary idea of the 'constitutional moment', the constitutional 'grand soir'. Nevertheless, that does not mean that constitutionalism in Europe has been buried for good, the former concept having always taken different forms.[86]

When it comes to the EU, we can identify a specific type of constitutionalism, namely cosmopolitan constitutionalism. Some leading scholars have put forward the idea of constitutional pluralism to highlight the actual kind of constitutionalism prevailing in Europe, namely the multiplicity of competing constitutional claims in a broad constitutionalist framework.[87] Constitutional pluralism is therefore admittedly meant to capture the unity and the diversity of the European legal space.[88] This has notably led one of its advocates, Mattias Kumm, to suggest setting

[85] For a comparative analysis of French and American constitutionalism as opposed to the German and British versions, see C. Möllers, 'Pouvoir constituant – Constitution – Constitutionnalisation', in A. Von Bogdandy and J. Bast (eds.), *Principles of European Constitutional Law* (Oxford: Hart, 2005), 183.

[86] See M. Avbelj, 'Questioning EU constitutionalisms', (2008) 9 *German Law Journal* 1.

[87] See N. MacCormick, 'Juridical Pluralism and the Risk of Constitutional Conflict', in *Questioning Sovereignty. Law, State and Nation in the European Commonwealth* (Oxford: Oxford University Press, 1999), 97; N. Walker, 'The Idea of Constitutional Pluralism' (2002) 65 *Modern Law Review* 317; J.H.H. Weiler, 'In Defence of the *Status Quo*: Europe's *Sonderweg*', in M. Wind and J.H.H. Weiler, *European Constitutionalism Beyond the State* (Cambridge: Cambridge University Press, 2003), 7; M. Poiares Maduro, 'Contrapunctual Law: Europe's Constitutional Pluralism in Action', in N. Walker (ed.), *Sovereignty in Transition* (Oxford and Portland, Or.: Hart, 2003), 501; M. Avbelj and J. Komarek (eds.), *Constitutional Pluralism in the European Union and Beyond* (Oxford: Hart, 2011).

[88] Note that the pluralist dimension of constitutional pluralism has often been seen as actually lacking: see N. Krisch, *Beyond Constitutionalism: The Pluralist Structure of Postnational Law* (Oxford: Oxford University Press, 2010); also F-X. Millet, 'L'ordre juridique international et les doctrines constitutionnalistes: au-delà du monisme et du dualisme', in A. Hamann, E. Lagrange, and J-M. Sorel (eds.), *Si proche, si loin: la pratique du droit international en France et en Allemagne. Perspectives de jeunes chercheurs* (Paris: Société de Législation Comparée, 2012), 27.

aside any EU norm that contravenes a clear and specific provision of a domestic constitution, in other words, the constitutional identity of a Member State.[89] Kumm has lately refined his approach under the label 'cosmopolitan constitutionalism'.[90] Even though he does not use these terms in a 'thick' way, he relies on a somehow all-inclusive conception of constitutionalism. For him, the legal practices nowadays prevailing in the EU are not dualist, nor monist but rather constitutionalist. Following a global approach, he seems to embrace both the social and communitarian dimensions of actual constitutions, but also the political, democratic, and procedural conception of constitutionalism against the statist approach, which is solely based on the democratic legitimacy of the people as constitution-maker.

Cosmopolitan constitutionalism is actually not only a label bereft of an ontological meaning, but it indicates a substantial trend with its roots in political thought, namely in Althusius' societal federalism, of which it constitutes an update. Such an assertion is controversial. As illustrated by Carl J. Friedrich's quote in the epigraph, federalism used to be primarily a theory on power politics or, to be more precise, a theory on power arrangements. Likewise, under a federal system, 'the protected freedom is [admittedly] less the freedom of the individual than the freedom of the people or of the nations'.[91] That may be historically true. However, we have seen that federalism in the European Union is *sui generis* like the EU itself, since politics and the technical distribution of powers seem to matter less than limitation of power together with the care for the actual citizen. Federalism in its Althusian version is therefore quite close to a cosmopolitan approach to constitutionalism. First, cosmopolitan constitutionalism signals the existence of a broad unity-oriented framework of constitutionalist principles that primarily aim at limiting power in a fashion that Althusius would most probably not have rejected. Secondly, the emphasis put on the cosmopolitan aspect of constitutionalism is very much in line with the *Homo europeus*. Indeed, cosmopolitanism usually refers to the *homme situé* with his or her multiple identities and loyalties. Drawing on liberal and post-national political thoughts, it fosters the emergence of constitutional patriotism without entirely depriving the citizen of his essential bonds. In doing so, cosmopolitan constitutionalism puts the state into perspective, together with the classic concept of an absolute and indivisible sovereignty. While it might be seen as weakening the sacrosanct primacy principle, it will still enhance the legitimacy of EU law in the eyes of the citizens, thus strengthening its *effet utile*, which, more than orthodox primacy, is the true condition for the perennial existence of the European Union.

[89] M. Kumm, 'The Jurisprudence of Constitutional Conflict: Constitutional Supremacy in Europe before and after the Constitutional Treaty' (2005) 11 *European Law Journal* 262, esp 296–8.

[90] M. Kumm, 'The Cosmopolitan Turn in Constitutionalism: On the Relationship between Constitutionalism in and beyond the State', in J.L. Dunoff and J.P. Trachtman (eds.), *Ruling the World: Constitutionalism, International Law and Global Governance* (Cambridge and New York: Cambridge University Press, 2009), 258.

[91] O. Beaud, 'Fédéralisme et souveraineté, notes pour une théorie constitutionnelle de la fédération' (1998) 1 *Revue du droit public et de la science politique en France et à l'étranger* 88, esp at 94–8.

Reference List

Adler, M.D. and Kreimer, S.F., 'The New Etiquette of Federalism: New York, Printz, and Yeskey' (1998) *Supreme Court Review* 71

AFDA, *La compétence* (Paris: Litec, 2008)

Alemanno, A., 'The Better Regulation Initiative at the Judicial Gate: A Trojan Horse within the Commission's Walls or the Way Forward?' (2009) 15 *European Law Journal* 391

——, 'A Meeting of Minds on Impact Assessment' (2011) 17 *European Public Law* 485

Althusius, J., *Politica* (Indianapolis: Liberty Fund, 1995)

Alston, P. and Weiler, J.H.H., 'Vers une politique des droits de l'homme authentique et cohérente pour l'Union européenne', in P. Alston and others (eds.), *L'Union européenne et les droits de l'homme* (Brussels: Bruylant, 2001), 3

Anagnostaras, G., 'Sex Equality and Compulsory Military Service: the Limits of National Sovereignty over Matters of Army Organisation' (2003) 28 *European Law Review* 713

Arendt, H., *On Revolution* (Harmondsworth: Penguin Books, 1973)

Aroney, N., 'The Ghost in the Machine: Exorcising Engineers', in J. Stone (ed.), *Upholding the Australian Constitution*, Vol. 14 (Sydney: Samuel Griffith Society, 2002, available at: <http://samuelgriffith.org.au/papers/pdf/Vol14.pdf>)

——, 'Formation, Representation, Amendment, in Federal Constitutions' (2006) 54 *American Journal of Comparative Law* 277

——, *The Constitution of a Federal Commonwealth: The Making and the Meaning of the Australian Constitution* (Cambridge and New York: Cambridge University Press, 2009)

Atienza, M. and Ruiz Manero, J., *Las piezas del derecho. Teoría de los enunciados jurídicos* (Barcelona: Ariel, coll. 'Ariel Derecho', 1996)

Assmann, H.D., Brüggemeier, G., Hart, D., and Joerges, C., *Zivilrecht als Teil des Wirtschaftsrechts* (Königstein: Athenäum, 1980)

Aubert, J.-F., *Traité de droit constitutionnel suisse* (Neuchâtel: Ides et Calendes, 1967)

——, 'Notion et fonctions de la Constitution', in D. Thürer, J.-F. Aubert, and J.-P. Müller (eds.), *Verfassungsrecht der Schweiz. Droit constitutionnel suisse* (Zürich: Schultheiss, 2001)

Avbelj, M., 'Questioning EU constitutionalism' (2008) 9 *German Law Journal* 1

—— and Komarek, J. (eds.), 'Four Visions of Constitutional Pluralism', *EUI Working Paper* 2008/21

——, *Constitutional Pluralism in the European Union and Beyond* (Oxford: Hart, 2011)

Azoulai, L., 'The Court of Justice and the social market economy: The emergence of an ideal and the conditions for its realization' (2008) 45 *Common Market Law Review* 1335

——, 'The "Retained Powers" Formula in the Case Law of the European Court of Justice: EU Law as Total Law?' (2011) 4 *European Journal of Legal Studies* 192

——, 'Introduction', *EUI Working Paper* 2012/06, available at: <http://cadmus.eui.eu/bitstream/handle/1814/21298/LAW_2012_06_Rev2.pdf>

—— and Coutts, S., 'Restricting Union citizens' residence on grounds of public security. Where Union citizenship and the AFSJ meet (Case C-348/09 P.I.)' (2013) 50 *Common Market Law Review* 553

Baere, G. de, *Constitutional Principles of EU External Relations* (Oxford and New York: Oxford University Press, 2008)

Ball, C.A., 'The making of a transnational capitalist society: The Court of Justice, social policy and individual rights under the European Community's legal order' (1996) 37 *Harvard International Law Journal* 307

Barendrecht, M., Jansen, C., Loos, M., Pinna, A., Cascao, R., and Gulijk, S. von, *Service Contracts (PEL SC)* (Munich: Sellier, 2007)

Barnard, C., *The Substantive Law of the EU. The Four Freedoms*, 2nd edn (Oxford and New York: Oxford University Press, 2007)

Basdevant, J., 'Règles générales du droit de la paix' (1936) IV 58 *Recueil des cours de l'Académie de la Haye* 471

Basedow, J., 'A common contract law for the common market' (1996) 33 *Common Market Law Review* 1169

——, 'Grundlagen des Europäischen Privatrechts' (2004) *JuS* 89

——, 'Mangold, Audiolux und die allgemeinen Grundsätze des europäischen Privatrechts', in S. Grundmann and others (eds.), *Festschrift für Klaus J. Hopt* (Berlin and New York: De Gruyter, 2010), 27

Beaud, O., 'La notion de pacte fédératif. Contribution à une théorie constitutionnelle de la Fédération', in H. Mohnhaupt and J.-F. Kervégan (eds.), *Liberté sociale et contrat dans l'histoire du droit et de la philosophie* (Frankfurt: Klostermann, coll. *Ius Commune*, 1997)

——, 'Fédéralisme et souveraineté, notes pour une théorie constitutionnelle de la fédération' (1998) 1 *Revue du droit public et de science politique en France et à l'étranger* 88

——, 'De quelques particularités de la justice constitutionnelle dans un système fédéral', in C. Grewe and others (eds.), *La notion de justice constitutionnelle* (Paris: Dalloz, 2005)

——, *Théorie de la Fédération*, 2nd edn (Paris: Presses Universitaires de France, coll. *Léviathan*, 2007)

——, 'Compétence et souveraineté', in *Association française pour la Recherche en Droit administratif, La compétence* (Paris: Litec, 2008), 5

Beck, J.R., 'The New Jurisprudence of the Necessary and Proper Clause' (2002) *University of Illinois Law Review* 581

Begg, I., 'Lisbon as economic governance: Fusion by dif-fusion?', in U. Diedrichs and others (eds.), *Europe Reloaded* (Baden-Baden: Nomos, 2011), 331

Bentham, J., *Deontology Together with A Table of the Springs of Action and the Article on Utilitarianism* (Oxford: Clarendon Press, 1983)

Bermann, G.A., 'Taking Subsidiarity Seriously: Federalism in the European Community and the United States' (1994) 94 *Columbia Law Review* 331

——, 'Subsidiarity as a Principle of U.S. Constitutional Law' (1994) 42 *American Journal of Comparative Law* 555

——, 'The Role of Law in the Functioning of Federal Systems', in K. Nicolaidis and R. Howse (eds.), *The Federal Vision: Legitimacy and Levels of Governance in the United States and the European Union* (Oxford and New York: Oxford University Press, 2001)

——, 'The Lisbon Treaty: The Irish "No". National Parliaments and Subsidiarity: An Outsider's View' (2008) 4 *European Constitutional Law Review* 453

Besson, S., 'From European Integration to European Integrity: Should European Law Speak with Just One Voice?' (2004) 10 *European Law Journal* 257

Biondi, A., 'Subsidiarity in the Courtroom', in A. Biondi, P. Eeckhout, and S. Ripley (eds.), *EU Law After Lisbon* (Oxford: Oxford University Press, 2012)

Blumann, C., 'Les compétences de l'Union européenne en matière de droits fondamentaux' (2006) 1 *Revue des Affaires Européennes* 11

Bobbitt, P., *The Shield of Achilles: War, Peace and the Course of History* (New York: Knopf, 2002)

Bogdandy, A. von, 'The European Union as a supranational federation. A conceptual attempt in the light of the Treaty of Amsterdam' (2000) 6 *Columbia Journal of European Law* 27

——, 'The European Constitution and European Identity: Text and Subtext of the Treaty establishing a Constitution for Europe' (2005) 3 *International Journal of Constitutional Law* 473

—— and Bast, J., 'The European Union's Vertical Order of Competences: The Current Law and Proposals for its Reform' (2002) 39 *Common Market Law Review* 227

—— and Bast, J., 'The Federal Order of Competences', in A. von Bogdandy and J. Bast (eds.), *Principles of European Constitutional Law*, 2nd edn (Oxford: Hart Publishing and Munich: Verlag CH Beck oHG, 2010), 276

—— and Schill, S., 'Overcoming Absolute Primacy: the Respect for National Identity under the Lisbon Treaty' (2011) 48 *Common Market Law Review* 1417

—— and others, 'Reverse Solange–Protecting the essence of fundamental rights against EU Member States' (2012) 49 *Common Market Law Review* 489

Bogojević, S., *Emissions Trading Schemes: Markets, States and Law* (Oxford: Hart Publishing, 2013)

Böhm, F., 'Privatrechtsgesellschaft und Marktwirtschaft' (1966) 17 *ORDO* 75

Boskovits, K., *Le juge communautaire et l'articulation des compétences normatives entre la Communauté européenne et ses Etats membres* (Athens: N. Sakkoulas, and Brussels: Bruylant, 1999)

Bowie, R. and Friedrich, C. (eds.), *Studies on Federalism* (Boston: Little Brown, 1954)

Brenncke, M., 'Annotation in Case C-58/08 Vodafone' (2010) 47 *Common Market Law Review* 1793

Breyer, S., *The Supreme Court: Making Democracy Work* (Oxford: Oxford University Press, 2010)

Bribosia, H., 'Subsidiarité et répartition des compétences entre l'Union et ses Etats Membres', in G. Amato, H. Bribosia, and B. De Witte (eds.), *Genèse et Destinée de la Constitution Européenne Commentaire du Traité établissant une Consitution pour l'Europe à la lumière des travaux préparatoires et perspectives d'avenir* (Brussels: Bruylant, 2007)

Bridel, M., *Précis de droit constitutionnel et public suisse* (Lausanne: Payot, 1965)

Búrca, G. de, 'The Principle of Subsidiarity and the Court of Justice as an Institutional Actor' (1998) 36 *Journal of Common Market Studies* 217

Burgess, M., *Federalism and European Union. The Building of Europe 1950-2000* (London and New York: Routledge, 2000)

Cafaggi, F. and Muir Watt, H. (eds.), *Making European Private Law: Governance Design* (Cheltenham, UK, and Northampton, MA: Edward Elgar, 2008)

——, 'The Regulatory Functions of European Private Law' (Cheltenham, UK, and Northampton, MA: Edward Elgar, 2009)

Caillosse, J., 'Les rapports de la politique et du droit dans la formulation d'"objectifs"', in B. Faure (ed.), *Les objectifs dans le droit* (Paris: Dalloz, 2010), 13

Caminker, E.H., 'State Sovereignty and Subordinancy: May Congress Commandeer State Officers to implement Federal Law?' (1995) 95 *Columbia Law Review* 1001

Cengiz, F., *Antitrust federalism in the EU and the US* (Abingdon: Routledge, 2012)

Chalmers, D., 'Looking Back at ERT and its Contribution to an EU Fundamental Rights Agenda', in M. Poiares Maduro and L. Azoulai (eds.), *The Past and Future of EU Law* (Oxford and Portland: Hart Publishing, 2010)

——, Davis, G., and Monti, G., *European Union Law: Text and Materials* (Cambridge: Cambridge University Press, 2006)

Cloots, E., De Baere, G., and Sottiaux S. (eds.), *Federalism in the European Union* (Oxford and Portland: Hart, 2012)
Collins, H., *The European Civil Code—The Way Forward* (Cambridge and New York: Cambridge University Press, 2008)
——, 'The Constitutionalisation of European Private Law as a Path to Social Justice', in H.-W. Micklitz (ed.), *The Many Concepts of Social Justice in European Private Law* (Cheltenham: Edward Elgar, 2011), 133
Combacau, J., 'Conclusions générales', in *Les compétences de l'Etat en droit international: Colloque de Rennes* (Paris: Pédone, 2005)
Comparato, G., 'Europe's steps towards a financially inclusive private law', to be published as an EUI Working Paper
Constantinesco, V., *Compétences et pouvoirs dans les Communautés européennes. Contribution à l'étude de la nature juridique des Communautés* (Paris: Pichon & Durand-Auzias, 1974)
——, 'Brève note sur la répartition des compétences comme clé de la future constitution européenne' in *Mélanges en hommage à Guy Isaac. 50 ans de droit communautaire*, Vol. I (Toulouse: Presses de l'Université des Sciences Sociales de Toulouse, 2004), 155
Cooper, I., 'The Watchdogs of Subsidiarity: National Parliaments and the Logic of Arguing in the EU' (2006) 44 *Journal of Common Market Studies* 281
Coppel, J. and O'Neill, A., 'The European Court of Justice: Taking rights seriously?' (1992) 29 *Common Market Law Review* 669
Corwin, E.S., *The Commerce Power versus States' Rights* (Princeton, NJ: Princeton University Press, 1936)
Craig, P., 'Competence: clarity, conferral, containment and consideration' (2004) 29 *European Law Review* 323
——, 'The ECJ and *Ultra Vires* Action: A Conceptual Analysis' (2011) 48 *Common Market Law Review* 395
—— 'Subsidiarity: A Political and Legal Analysis' (2012) 50 *Journal of Common Market Studies* 72
Crane, D., *The Institutional Structure of Antitrust Enforcement* (Oxford, Oxford University Press, 2011)
—— 'Competence and Member State Autonomy: Causality, Consequence and Legitimacy' in H.-W. Micklitz and B. De Witte (eds.), *The European Court of Justice and the Autonomy of the Member States* (Antwerp: Intersentia, 2012), 11
Cremona, M., 'Defending the Community Interest: the Duties of Cooperation and Compliance', in M. Cremona and B. de Witte, *EU Foreign Relations Law: Constitutional Fundamentals* (Oxford and Portland: Hart Publishing, 2008), 125
——, 'Defining Competence In EU External Relations: Lessons from the Treaty Reform Process', in A. Dashwood and M. Maresceau (eds.), *Law and Practice of EU External Relations: Salient Features of a Changing Landscape* (Cambridge and New York: Cambridge University Press, 2008), 34
——, 'Balancing Union and Member State interests: Opinion 1/2008, choice of legal base and the common commercial policy under the Treaty of Lisbon' (2010) 35 *European Law Review* 678
——, 'Case C-246/07 Commission v Sweden, judgment 20 April 2010 (Grand Chamber)' (2011) 48 *Common Market Law Review* 1639
Cross, E.D., 'Pre-emption of Member State law in the European Economic Community: A framework for analysis' (1992) 29 *Common Market Law Review* 447
Cruz Villalón, P., *La constitución inedita. Estudios ante la constitucionalización de Europa* (Madrid: Trotta, 2004)

Culver, K.C. and Giudice, M., 'Not a System but an Order: An Interinstitutional View of European Union Law', in J. Dickson and P. Eleftheriadis (eds.), *Philosophical Foundations of European Union Law* (Oxford: Oxford University Press, 2013), 54

Dahinden, P., 'The division of powers between the state and common laws of Switzerland' (D.Phil thesis, Lausanne University, 1979)

Damjanovic, D. and Witte, B. de, 'Welfare Integration through EU Law: The Overall Picture in the Light of the Lisbon Treaty', in U. Neergard, R. Nielsen, and L.M. Roseberry (eds.), *Integrating Welfare Functions into EU Law—From Rome to Lisbon* (Copenhagen: DJØF, 2009), 53

Dashwood, A., 'Hastening Slowly: The Community's Path Towards Harmonization', in H. Wallace, W. Wallace, and C. Webb (eds.), *Policy-Making in the European Community* (London and New York: Wiley & Sons Ltd, 1983), 177

——, 'The Limits of European Community Powers' (1996) 21 *European Law Review* 113.

——, 'The Draft EU Constitution—First Impressions' (2002-03) 5 *Cambridge Yearbook of European Legal Studies* 395

——, 'The Relationship Between the Member States and the European Union/European Community' (2004) 41 *Common Market Law Review* 355

Davies, G., 'Subsidiarity: The Wrong Idea, in the Wrong Place, at the Wrong Time' (2006) 43 *Common Market Law Review* 63

Delgado Casteleiro, A., 'EU Declarations of Competence to Multilateral Agreements: A Useful Reference Base?' (2012) 17 *European Foreign Affairs Review* 491

—— and Larik, J., 'The Duty to Remain Silent: Limitless Loyalty in EU External Relations' (2011) 36 *European Law Review* 524

Dicey, A., *Introduction to the Study of Constitutional Law* (Indianapolis: Liberty Fund, 1982)

Dickson, J., 'Towards a Theory of European Legal Systems', in J. Dickson and P. Eleftheriadis (eds.), *Philosophical Foundations of European Union Law* (Oxford: Oxford University Press, 2013), 25

Dodd, W.F., 'Implied Powers and Implied Limitations in Constitutional Law' (1919) 29 *Yale Law Journal* 137

Dominicé, C., 'Fédéralisme coopératif' (1969) 88 *Revue de droit suisse* 743

Dougan, M., 'The Convention's Draft Constitutional Treaty: Bringing Europe Closer to its Lawyers?' (2003) 28 *European Law Review* 763

Drexl, J., 'Competition Law as Part of the European Constitution', in A. von Bogdandy and J. Bast (eds.), *Principles of European Constitutional Law*, 2nd rev. edn (Oxford: Hart Publishing and Munich: Verlag CH Beck oHG, 2011)

——, 'La Constitution économique européenne—L'actualité du modèle ordolibéral' (2011) *Revue internationale de droit économique* 419

Dubey, B., *La répartition des compétences au sein de l'Union européenne à la lumière du fédéralisme suisse: systèmes, enjeux et conséquences* (Geneva: Helbing et Lichtenhahn, and Brussels: Bruylant, 2002)

Dubout, E. and Touzé S. (eds.), *Les droits fondamentaux: charnières des rapports entre ordres et systèmes juridiques* (Paris: Pedone, 2010)

Dutheil de la Rochère, J., 'Fédéralisation de l'Europe? Le Problème de la clarification des compétences entre l'Union et les Etats', in O. Béaud and others (eds.), *L'Europe en voie de constitution* (Brussels: Bruylant, 2004), 317

Dworkin, R.M., *Taking Rights Seriously*, 2nd edn (Cambridge, Mass.: Harvard University Press, 1978)

Edwards, D., 'Fearing Federalism's Failure: Subsidiarity in the European Union' (1996) 44 *American Journal of Comparative Law* 537

Eeckhout, P., 'The EU Charter of Fundamental Rights and the Federal Question' (2002) 39 *Common Market Law Review* 945

——, 'Bold Constitutionalism and Beyond', in M. Poiares Maduro and L. Azoulai (eds.), *The Past and Future of EU Law* (Oxford and Portland: Hart Publishing, 2010), 218

——, *EU External Relations Law*, 2nd edn (Oxford and New York: Oxford University Press, 2011)

——, 'Exclusive External Competences: Constructing the EU as an International Actor', in A. Rosas, E. Levits, and Y. Bot (eds.), *The Court of Justice and the Construction of Europe: Analyses and Perspectives on Sixty Years of Case-Law* (The Hague: Asser Press, Springer, 2013), 613

Egger, A., 'EU-Fundamental Rights in the National Legal Order: The Obligations of Member States Revisited' (2006) 25 *Yearbook of European Law* 515

Eiden, C., *Die Rechtsangleichung gemäß Art.100 des EWG-Vertrages* (Berlin: Duncker & Humblot, 1984)

Eisenmann, C., *Centralisation et décentralisation. Esquisse d'une théorie générale* (Paris: LGDJ, 1948)

——, 'Le droit administratif et le principe de légalité' (1957) *Etudes et documents du Conseil d'Etat* 25

——, 'Quelques problèmes de méthodologie des définitions et des classifications en science juridique' (1966) 11 *Archives de philosophie du droit* 25

Elazar, D.J., *American Federalism: A View from the States*, 3rd edn (New York: Harper and Row Publishers, 1984)

——, *Exploring Federalism* (Tuscaloosa: University of Alabama Press, 1987)

——, 'Althusius' Grand Design for a Federal Commonwealth', foreword to J. Althusius, *Politica* (Indianapolis, Liberty Fund, 1995)

Eleftheriadis, P., 'Pluralism and Integrity' (2010) 23 *Ratio Juris* 365

Ellis, E. (ed.), *The Principle of Proportionality in the Laws of Europe* (Oxford: Oxford University Press, 1999)

Ely, J.H., *Democracy and Distrust: A Theory of Judicial Review*, 14th edn (Cambridge: Harvard University Press, 2002)

Esping-Andersen, G., 'After the golden age? Welfare state dilemmas in a global economy', in G. Esping-Andersen (ed.), *Welfare states in transition: National adaptations in global economies* (London and Thousand Oaks: SAGE Publications Ltd., 1996), 1

Estella, A., *The EU Principle of Subsidiarity and its Critique* (Oxford: Oxford University Press, 2002)

Eule, J.N., 'Laying the Dormant Commerce Clause to Rest' (1982) 91 *Yale Law Journal* 425

Fabbrini, F. and Granat, K., 'Yellow card, but no foul: The role of the national parliaments under the Subsidiarity Protocol and the Commission proposal for an EU Regulation on the right to strike' (2013) 50 *Common Market Law Review* 115

Fabbrini, S. (ed.), *Democracy and Federalism in the European Union and the United States. Exploring Post-national Governance* (London and New York: Routledge, 2005)

Fahey, E., 'Does the Emperor have Financial Cloth? Reflections on the Legal Basis of the European Banking Authority' (2011) 74 *Modern Law Review* 581

Feeley, M. and Rubin, E., *Federalism. Political Identity and Tragic Compromise* (Ann Arbor: University of Michigan Press, 2008)

Ferrer Beltrán, J., *Las normas de competencia. Un aspecto de la dinámica jurídica* (Madrid: Centro de estudios políticos y constitucionales—Boletín oficial del Estado, col. 'El Derecho y la Justicia', 2000)

Ferrera, M., *The boundaries of welfare: European integration and the new spatial politics of social protection* (Oxford: Oxford University Press, 2005)
Fleishacker, S., 'Adam Smith's reception among the American founders, 1776-1790' (2002) 59 *William & Mary Quarterly* 897
Foucault, M., *Discipline and Punish: The Birth of The Prison* (London: Allen Lane, 1977)
Frank, J., *Law and the Modern Mind*, 6th edn (London: Stevens & Sons, 1949)
Frey, B.S. and Eichenberger, R., *The New Democratic Federalism for Europe: Functional, Overlapping, and Competing Jurisdictions* (Cheltenham and Northampton, Mass.: Edward Elgar, 1999)
Friedrich, C.J., 'Introduction' to *Politica Methodice Digesta of Johannes Althusius* (Cambridge: Harvard University Press, 1932)
——, 'Federal Constitutional Theory and Emergent Proposals', in A.W. MacMahon (ed.), *Federalism: Mature and Emergent* (Garden City, N.Y.: Doubleday, 1955), 510
——, *Trends of Federalism in Theory and Practice* (London: Pall Mall Press, 1968)
——, *Johannes Althusius und sein Werk im Rahmen der Entwicklung der Theorie von der Politik* (Berlin: Duncker & Humblot, 1975)
Garben, S., 'Case C-73/08, Nicolas Bressol and Others, Céline Chaverot and Others v Gouvernement de la Communauté française, Judgment of the Court of Justice (Grand Chamber) of 13 April 2010' (2010) 47 *Common Market Law* 1493
Gaudreault DesBiens, J.-F., 'Le fédéralisme et le législateur fédéral' (2009) 2 *Journal of Parliamentary and Political Law Revue de droit parlementaire et politique* 427
——, 'In Praise of Principles, or Beyond the Toolbox Approach to Federalism', Contribution in the 'Congrès international de droit constitutionnel' (Mexico, December 2010)
—— and Gélinas, F. (eds.), *Le fédéralisme dans tous ses états. Gouvernance, identité et méthodologie/The states and moods of federalism. Governance, identity and methodology* (Brussels: Bruylant, 2005)
Gerards, J., 'Pluralism, Deference and the Margin of Appreciation Doctrine' (2011) 17 *European Law Journal* 80
Gerstenberg, O., 'Private Law and the New Constitutional Settlement' (2004) 10 *European Law Journal* 766
Gerven, W. Van, *The European Union: A Polity of States and Peoples* (Oxford: Hart Publishing, 2005)
Gierke, O. von, *Johannes Althusius und die Entwicklung der naturrechtlichen Staatstheorien. Zugleich ein Beitrag zur Geschichte der Rechtssystematik* (Breslau: Koebner, 1880)
——, *Die Soziale Aufgabe des Privatrechts* (Berlin: Julius Springer, 1889)
Glencross, A. and Trechsel, A.H. (eds.), *EU Federalism and Constitutionalism. The Legacy of Altiero Spinelli* (Lanham, Md.: Lexington Books, 2010)
Gomez, F. and Ganuza, J.J., 'An Economic Analysis of Harmonization Regimes: Full Harmonization, Minimum Harmonization and Optional Instrument' (2011) 7 *European Review of Contract Law* 275
Goodman, N., *Ways of Worldmaking* (Hassocks: Harvester Press, 1978)
Goucha Soares, A., 'The Division of Competences in the European Constitution' (2005) 11 *European Public Law* 603
Grauwe, P. de, *Economics of monetary union*, 9th edn (Oxford: Oxford University Press, 2009)
Grosbon, S., 'Libre circulation et systèmes de sélection universitaire: une équation complexe' (2009-10) *Revue des Affaires Européennes* 635
Grundmann, S., 'Kosten und Nutzen eines Optionalen Europäischen Kaufrechtsrechts', paper presented within the Special conference organised by the German Association of Civil Lawyers, Zivilrechtslehrervereingung, April 2012

Guastaferro, B., 'Beyond the *Exceptionalism* of Constitutional Conflicts: The Ordinary Functions of the Identity Clause' (2012) 31 *Yearbook of European Law* 263

Guastini, R., 'Invalidity' (1994) 7 *Ratio Juris* 212

——, *Teoria e dogmatica delle fonti* (Milan: Giuffrè, 1998)

Gutman, K., 'The Commission Green Paper on European Contract law: Reflections on Union Competence in Light of the Proposed Options' (2012) 20 *European Review of Contract Law* 151

——, *The Constitutional Foundations of European Contract Law: A comparative Analysis* (OUP, forthcoming)

Haas, E., *The Uniting of Europe: Political, Social and Economic Forces 1950-57* (Stanford, Calif: Stanford University Press, 1958)

Habermas, J., *Questa Europa è in crisi* (Bari: Laterza, 2012)

Hackl, E., 'Towards a European area of higher education. Change and convergence in European higher education', *EUI Working Papers* RCS 2001/09

Häde, U., 'Die Wirtschafts—und Währungsunion im Vertrag von Lissabon' (2009) *Europarecht* 200

Halberstam, D., 'Of Power and Responsibility: The Political Morality of Federal Systems' (2004) 90 *Virginia Law Review* 731

——, 'Federalism: A Critical Guide' (2011) *University of Michigan Law School Public Law and Legal Theory Working Paper Series*, No. 251

Hamilton, A., 'Federalist No. 11', in A. Hamilton, J. Madison, and J. Jay, *The Federalist* (Cambridge and New York: Cambridge University Press, 2003), 46

Hart, H.L.A., *The Concept of Law* (Oxford: Clarendon Press, 1961)

Hartkamp, A., 'The General Principles of EU Law and Private Law' (2011) *RabelsZ* 241

Heller, T. and Pelkmans, J., 'The Federal Economy: Law and Economic Integration and the Positive State–The U.S.A. and Europe Compared in an Economic Perspective', in M. Cappelletti, M. Seccombe, and J.H.H. Weiler (eds.), *Integration through Law*, Vol. I Book 1 (Berlin and New York: Walter de Gruyter, 1986), 245

Hentschelmann, K., 'Der Stabilitäts–und Wachstumspakt', *Discussion Paper 1/10*, Europa-Kolleg Hamburg, Institute for European Integration, available at <http://www.wirtschaftsdienst.eu/downloads/getfile.php?id=2333>

Héraud, G., *Les principes du fédéralisme et la fédération européenne. Contribution à la théorie juridique du fédéralisme* (Paris: Presses d'Europe, 1968)

Hernández Marín, R., *Introducción a la teoría de la norma jurídica* (Madrid and Barcelona: Marcial Pons, 1998)

Hervey, T., 'The current legal framework on the right to seek health care abroad in the European Union' (2006-07) 9 *The Cambridge Yearbook of European Legal Studies* 261

Hesselink, M., Mak, C., and Rutgers, J.W., 'Constitutional Aspects of European Private Law: Freedoms, Rights and Social Justice in the Draft Common Frame of Reference', *Centre for the Study of European Contract Law Working Paper Series*, No. 05/2009, also available at: <http://ssrn.com/abstract=1413089>

Hesselink, M.W., *CFR & Social Justice: a short study for the European Parliament on the values underlying the draft Common Frame of Reference for European private law: what roles for fairness and social justice?* (Munich: Sellier, 2008)

Hettne, J. and Langdal, F., 'Does Subsidiarity Ask the Right Question?' (2011) *Think Global—Act European (TGAE)* 350

Hillion, C. and Koutrakos P. (eds.), *Mixed Agreements Revisited: The EU and its Member States in the World* (Oxford: Hart Publishing, 2010)

Lord Hoffmann, 'The Universality of Human Rights Judicial Studies Board', Annual Lecture of 19 March 2009, available at: <http://www.judiciary.gov.uk/media/speeches/2009/speech-lord-hoffman-19032009>

Hohfeld, W.N., *Fundamental Legal Conceptions as Applied in Judicial Reasoning* (Westport, Conn.: Greenwood Press, 1978)

Hueglin, T.O., 'Johannes Althusius: Medieval Constitutionalist or Modern Federalist?' (1979) 9 *Publius: The Journal of Federalism* 9

——, *Early Modern Concepts for a Late Modern World. Althusius on Community and Federalism* (Waterloo: Wilfried Laurier University Press, 1999)

——, 'Federalism at the Crossroads: Old Meanings, New Significance' (2003) 36 *Canadian Journal of Political Science* 275

Itzcovich, G., 'Integrazione giuridica. Un'analisi concettuale' (2005) 3 *Diritto pubblico* 749

Jackson, V., 'Fédéralisme. Normes et territoires', in D. Chagnollaud and M. Troper (eds.), *Traité international de droit constitutionnel*, Vol. II (Paris: Dalloz, 2012), 23

Jacobs, F., 'Human Rights in the EU: the Role of the Court of Justice' (2001) 26 *European Law Review* 331

——, 'Wachauf and the Protection of Human Rights in EC Law', in M. Poiares Maduro and L. Azoulai (eds.), *The Past and Future of EU Law* (Oxford and Portland: Hart Publishing, 2010), 133

Jacqué, J-P., *Droit institutionnel de l'Union européenne*, 6th edn (Paris: Dalloz, 2010)

——, 'Communautés des internautes et protection des libertés individuelles dans l'Union européenne' (2010) 46 *Revue Trimestrielle de Droit Européen* 271

Joerges, C., 'A Renaissance of the European Economic Constitution', in U. Neergard, R. Nielsen, and L.M. Roseberry (eds.), *Integrating Welfare Functions into EU Law—From Rome to Lisbon* (Copenhagen: DJØF, 2009), 29

——, 'Europe's Economic Constitution in Crisis', *ZenTra Working Paper in Transnational Studies No. 06/2012*

Kaczynski, P., *Paper Tigers or Sleeping Beauties? National Parliaments in the post-Lisbon European Political System* (Special Report: 'Thinking ahead for Europe', Centre for European Policy Studies, 2011)

Kaila, H., 'The Scope of Application of the Charter of Fundamental Rigths of the European Union in the Member States', in P. Cardonnel, A. Rosas, and N. Wahl (eds.), *Constitutionalising the EU Judicial System—Essays in Honour of Pernilla Lindh* (Oxford: Hart Publishing, 2012), 291

Katz, E., 'United States of America', in R. Blidenbacher and A.J. Ostien (eds.), *Dialogues on Distribution of Powers and Responsibilities in Federal Countries* (Montréal: McGill-Queen's Press, 2005), 301

Kelemen, R.D., *Eurolegalism* (Cambridge, MA: Harvard University Press, 2011)

Kelsen, H., 'La garantie juridictionnelle de la Constitution' (1928) *Revue du droit public* 258

——, *Reine Rechtslehre* (Vienna: Franz Deuticke, 1960)

——, *General Theory of Law and State* (New York: Russell and Russell, 1961)

——, 'Derogation', in R.A. Newman (ed.), *Essays in Jurisprudence in Honor of Roscoe Pound* (Indianapolis and New York: The Bobb Merrill & Co., 1962), 339

——, Ringhofer, K., and Walter, R., (eds.), *Allgemeine Theorie der Normen* (Vienna: Manz, 1979)

Kincaid, J., (ed.), *Federalism* (London and Thousand Oaks, Calif.: SAGE, 2011)

Knook, A., 'The Court, the Charter, and the Vertical Division of Powers in the European Union' (2005) 42 *Common Market Law Review* 367

Konstadinides, T., *Division of Powers in European Union Law. The Delimitation of Internal Competence between the EU and the Member States* (Austin: Wolters Kluwer Law & Business, and Alphen aan den Rijn: Kluwer Law International, 2009)

Koskenniemi, M., 'Global Legal Pluralism: Multiple Regimes and Multiple Modes of Thought', available at: <http://www.helsinki.fi/eci/Publications/Koskenniemi/MKPluralism-Harvard-05d[1].pdf>

Kosta, V., 'European Court of Justice Case C-213/07, Michaniki AE v. Ethniko Simvoulio Radiotileorasis Ipourgos Epikratias' (2009) 5 *European Constitutional Law Review* 501

Kovacs, K. and Toth, G.A., 'Hungary's Constitutional Transformation' (2011) 7 *European Constitutional Law Review* 183

Krisch, N., *Beyond Constitutionalism: The Pluralist Structure of Postnational Law* (Oxford: Oxford University Press, 2010)

Kumm, M., 'Who is the Final Arbiter of Constitutionality in Europe? Three Conceptions of the Relationship between the German Federal Constitutional Court and the European Court of Justice' (1999) 36 *Common Market Law Review* 351

——, 'Who is Afraid of Total Constitution? Constitutional Rights as Principles and the Constitutionalisation of Private Law' (2004) 7 *German Law Journal* 341

——, 'The Jurisprudence of Constitutional Conflict: Constitutional Supremacy in Europe before and after the Constitutional Treaty' (2005) 11 *European Law Journal* 262

——, 'The Cosmopolitan Turn in Constitutionalism: On the Relationship between Constitutionalism in and beyond the State', in J.L. Dunoff and J.P. Trachtman (eds.), *Ruling the World: Constitutionalism, International Law and Global Governance* (Cambridge and New York: Cambridge University Press, 2009), 258

Kymlicka, W., *Multicultural Citizenship* (Oxford: Clarendon Press, and New York: Oxford University Press, 1997)

Lande, R.H., 'Why Antitrust Damage Levels Should Be Raised' (2004) 16 *Loyola Consumer Law Review* 329

Larik, J., *Wordly Ambitions. Foreign policy objectives in European constitutional law*, PhD thesis (EUI, Florence, 2013), 201

Lauvaux, P., *Les grandes démocraties occidentales contemporaines*, 3rd edn (Paris: Presses Universitaires Françaises, 2004)

Lawson, G. and Granger, P.B., 'The "Proper" Scope of Federal Power: A Jurisdictional Interpretation of the Sweeping Clause' (1993-94) 43 *Duke Law Journal* 267

Le Fur, L., *Etat fédéral et confédération d'Etats* (Paris: Editions Panthéon-Assas, 2000)

Leleux, P., 'Le rapprochement des législations dans la communauté economique européenne' (1968) 4 *Cahiers De Droit Européen* 129

Lenaerts, K., *Le juge et la Constitution aux États-Unis d'Amérique et dans l'ordre juridique européen* (Brussels: Bruylant, 1988)

——, 'Constitutionalism and the Many Faces of Federalism' (1990) 38 *American Journal of Comparative Law* 205

——, 'The Principle of Subsidiarity and the Environment in the European Union: Keeping the Balance of Federalism' (1993) 17 *Fordham International Law Journal* 846

——, 'Fundamental Rights in the European Union' (2000) 25 *European Law Review* 575

——, 'L'encadrement par le droit de l'Union européenne des compétences des Etats membres', in G. Cohen-Jonathan and J-P. Jacqué, *Chemins d'Europe. Mélanges en l'honneur de Jean-Paul Jacqué* (Paris: Dalloz, 2010), 421

——, 'The European Court of Justice and Process-oriented Review' (2013) 32 *Yearbook of European Law* 3

—— and Corthaut, T., 'Of Birds and Hedges: the Role of Primacy in Invoking Norms of EU Law' (2006) 31 *European Law Review* 287

—— and Gutiérrez-Fons, J-A, 'The Constitutional Allocation of Powers and General Principles of EU Law' (2010) 47 *Common Market Law Review* 1629

—— and Nuffel, P. van, *European Union Law*, 3rd edn (London: Sweet & Maxwell, 2011)

Lewalle, H., 'Systèmes de santé et intégration européenne', in P. Nihoul and A-C. Simon (eds.), *L'Europe et les soins de santé. Marché intérieur, sécurité sociale, concurrence* (Brussels: Larcier, 2005) 27

Louis, J-V., 'The Lisbon Treaty: The Irish "No": National Parliaments and the Principle of Subsidiarity—Legal Options and Practical Limits' (2008) 4 *European Constitutional Law Review* 429

——, *L'Union européenne et sa monnaie* (Brussels: Éditions de l'Université de Bruxelles, IEE Institut d'études européennes, 2009)

MacCormick, N., 'Powers and Power-Conferring Norms', in S.L. Paulson and B. Litschewski Paulson (eds.), *Normativity and Norms. Critical Perspectives on Kelsenian Themes* (Oxford: Clarendon Press, 1998)

——, 'Juridical Pluralism and the Risk of Constitutional Conflict', in *Questioning Sovereignty. Law, State and Nation in the European Commonwealth* (Oxford: Oxford University Press, 1999), 97

Mak, V., 'Full Harmonization in European Private Law: A Two-Track Concept' (2012) 20 *European Review of Private Law* 213

Malberg, C. de, *Contribution à la théorie générale de l'Etat* (Paris: CNRS, 1920)

Martinico, G., 'Dating Cinderella: On Subsidiarity as a Political Safeguard of Federalism in the European Union' (2011) 17 *European Public Law* 649

Marx, F., *Funktion und Grenzen der Rechtsangleichung nach Art. 100 EWG-Vertrag* (Cologne, Berlin, Bonn, and Munich: Heymanns, 1976)

Mayer, F., 'Competences—Reloaded? The vertical division of powers in the EU and the new European constitution' (2005) 3 *ICON* 512

——, 'Rashomon à Karlsruhe' (2010) 46 *Revue Trimestrielle de Droit Européen* 77

McGowan, L. and Wilks, S., 'The First Supranational Policy in the European Union: Competition Policy' (1995) 28 *European Journal of Political Research* 141

Mei, A.P. van der, *Free movement of persons within the Community: cross-border access to public benefits* (Oxford and Portland, Or.: Hart, 2003)

Menon, A. and Schain, M. (eds.), *Comparative Federalism: The European Union and the United States in Comparative Perspective* (Oxford: Oxford University Press, 2006)

Merkl, A.J., 'Prolegomena einer Theorie des rechtlichen Stufenbaues', in A. Verdross (ed.), *Gesellschaft, Staat und Recht. Untersuchungen zur reinen Rechtslehre. Festschrift Hans Kelsen zum 50. Geburtstag gewidmet* (Vienna: Springer, 1931), 252

Mestmäcker, E.-J., *Wirtschaft und Verfassung in der Europäischen Union, Beiträge zu Recht, Theorie und Politik der Europäischen Integration* (Baden-Baden: Nomos, 2003)

Meuwese, A. and Popelier, P., 'Legal Implications of Better Regulation: A Special Issue' (2011) 17 *European Public Law* 455

Michaels, R., 'Of Islands and the Ocean: The Two Rationalities of European Private Law', in R. Brownsword and others (eds.), *The Foundations of European Private Law* (Oxford: Hart, 2011), 139

Michel, V., *Recherches sur les compétences de la Communauté européenne* (Paris: L'Harmattan, 2003)

Michelman, F., 'Morality, Identity and "Constitutional Patriotism"' (2001) 14 *Ratio Juris* 253

Micklitz, H.-W., 'The Maastricht Treaty, the Principle of Subsidiarity and the Theory of Integration' (1993) 4 *LAKIMIES Special Issue on European Integration* (periodical of the Association of Finnish lawyers) 508
——, 'The Visible Hand of European Private Law' (2009) 28 *Yearbook of European Law* 3
——, 'Failure or Ideological Preconceptions? Thoughts on Two Grand Projects: the European Constitution and the European Civil Code', in K. Tuori and S. Sankari (eds.), *The Many Constitutions of Europe* (Farnham: Ashgate, 2010), 109
——, *The Many Concepts of Social Justice in European Private Law* (Cheltenham: Edward Elgar, 2011)
——, 'German Constitutional Court (Bundesverfassungsgericht BVerfG) 2 BvE 2/08, 30.6.2009—Organstreit proceedings between members of the German Parliament and the Federal Government' (2011) 7 *European Review of Contract Law* 528
—— (ed.), *Constitutionalisation of European Private Law* (Oxford University Press, forthcoming)
—— and Patterson, D., 'From the Nation State to the Market: The Evolution of EU Private Law', *EUI Working Paper* 2012/15, also published in B. van Vooren, St. Blockmans, and J. Wouters (eds.), *The EU's Role in Global Governance: The Legal Dimension* (Oxford: Oxford University Press, 2013), 59
—— and Reich, N., 'The Commission Proposal for a "Regulation on a Common European Sales Law (CESL)"—Too Broad or Not Broad Enough', *EUI Working Paper* 2012/4
—— and Svetiev, Y. (eds.), 'A Self-sufficient European Private Law—A Viable Concept?', *EUI Working Paper* 2012
Middelaar, L. van, *The Passage to Europe. How a Continent became a Union* (Yale University Press, 2013)
Millet, F-X., 'L'ordre juridique international et les doctrines constitutionnalistes: au-delà du monisme et du dualisme', in A. Hamann, E. Lagrange, and J-M. Sorel (eds.), *Si proche, si loin: la pratique du droit international en France et en Allemagne. Perspectives de jeunes chercheurs* (Paris: Société de Législation Comparée, 2012), 27
——, *L'Union européenne et l'identité constitutionnelle des Etats membres* (Paris: LGDJ-Lextenso, 2013)
Millon-Delsol, C., *L'Etat subsidiaire. Ingérence et non-ingérence de l'Etat: le principe de subsidiarité aux fondements de l'histoire européenne* (Paris: Presses Universitaires de France, 1992)
Möllers, C., 'Pouvoir constituant—Constitution—Constitutionnalisation', in A. Von Bogdandy and J. Bast (ed.), *Principles of European Constitutional Law* (Oxford: Hart, 2005) 183
Montgomery, J., 'Impact of European Union law on English healthcare law', in E. Spaventa and M. Dougan (eds.), *Social Welfare and EU Law* (Oxford: Hart, 2005), 145
Monti, G., 'New Directions in EC Competition Law', in T. Tridimas and P. Nebbia (eds.), *European Union Law for the Twenty-First Century* (Oxford: Hart, 2004), 135
——, *EC Competition Law* (Cambridge: Cambridge University Press, 2007)
Monti, M., *A New Strategy for the Single Market–Report to the President of the European Commission* (9 May 2010)
Moravcsik, A., *The Choice For Europe* (Ithaca, NY: Cornell University Press, 1998)
Müller, J.-W., 'A European Constitutional Patriotism? The Case Restated' (2008) 14 *European Law Journal* 542
——, 'A General Theory of Constitutional Patriotism' (2008) 6 *International Journal of Constitutional Law* 72
Neuwhal, N.A., 'Shared Powers of Combined Incompetence? More on Mixity' (1996) 33 *Common Market Law Review* 667

Neves, M., *Transconstitucionalismo* (São Paulo: WMF Martins Fontes, 2009)
Newdick, C., 'Citizenship, free movement and health care: Cementing individual rights by corroding social solidarity' (2006) 43 *Common Market Law Review* 1645
——, 'The ECJ, transnational health care, and social citizenship. Accidental death of a concept?' (2009) 26 *Wisconsin International Law Journal* 845
Nicolaidis, K., 'Constitutionalizing the Federal Vision?', in A. Menon and M. Schain (eds.), *Comparative Federalism: The European Union and the United States in Comparative Perspective* (Oxford: Oxford University Press, 2006), 59
Nicolaidis, K., 'The Federal Vision, Levels of Governance and Legitimacy', in K. Nicolaidis and R. Howse, *The Federal Vision: Legitimacy and Levels of Governance in the United States and the European Union* (Oxford and New York: Oxford University Press, 2001), 1
Nourry, A. and Jung, N., 'EU State Measures against Foreign Takeovers: "Economic Patriotism" in All But Name' (2006) 2 *Competition Policy International* 99
Padoa Schioppa, T., 'Economic Federalism and the European Union', in K. Knop and others (eds.), *Rethinking Federalism: citizens, markets and governments in a changing world* (Vancouver: UBC Press, 1995), 154
Patterson, D. and Afilalio, A. (eds.), *The New Global Trading Order* (Cambridge and New York: Cambridge University Press, 2008)
Pernice, I., 'Bestandssicherung der Verfassungen: Verfassungsrechtliche Mechanismen zur Wahrung der Verfassungsordnung', in R. Bieber and P. Widmer (eds.), *L'espace constitutionnel européen—Der europäische Verfassungsraum—The European Constitutional Area* (Zürich: Schulthess, coll. 'Publications de l'Institut suisse de droit compare', 1995), 21
——, 'Multilevel Constitutionalism and the Treaty of Amsterdam: European Constitution-Making Revisited?' (1999) 36 *Common Market Law Review* 703
——, 'Multilevel Constitutionalism in the European Union', *WHI Paper* 5/2002, available at: <www.whi-berlin.de/documents/whi-paper0502.pdf>
Pescatore, P., 'Fundamental rights and freedoms in the system of European Communities' (1970) 18 *American Journal of Comparative Law* 343
——, *The Law of Integration. Emergence of a new phenomenon in international relations, based on the experience of the European Communities* (Leiden: Sijthoof, 1974)
——, 'Foreword' in T. Sandalow and Eric Stein (eds.), *Courts and Free Markets. Perspectives from the United States and Europe* (Oxford: Clarendon Press, and New York: Oxford University Press, 1982)
Peters, A., 'Compensatory Constitutionalism: The Function and Potential of Fundamental International Norms and Structures' (2006) 19 *Leiden Journal of International Law* 579
Piris, J-C., *The Lisbon Treaty: a legal and political analysis* (Cambridge and New York: Cambridge University Press, 2010)
Poiares Maduro, M., 'Contrapunctual Law: Europe's Constitutional Pluralism in Action', in N. Walker (ed.), *Sovereignty in Transition* (Oxford and Portland, Or.: Hart, 2003), 501
——, 'The Importance of Being Called Constitution. Constitutional authority and authority of constitutionalism' (2005) 3 *I.CON* 332
——, 'Interpreting European Law: Judicial Adjudication in a Context of Constitutional Pluralism' (2007) 1 *European Journal of Legal Studies* 2 (available online at <http://www.ejls.eu>)
Pollack, M.A., 'Creeping Competence: The Expanding Agenda of the European Community' (1994) 14 *Journal of Public Policy* 95
Pontier, J.-M., 'L'Etat et les collectivités locales. La répartition des compétences', D.Phil thesis (Paris: Librairie générale de droit et de jurisprudence, 1978)

Post, R., 'Constructing the European Polity: ERTA and the Open Skies Judgments', in M. Poiares Maduro and L. Azoulai (eds.), *The Past and Future of EU Law* (Oxford and Portland: Hart Publishing, 2010), 234

Powell, T.R., 'Some Aspects of Constitutionalism and Federalism' (1935-36) 14 *North Carolina Law Review* 1

Prechal, S., 'Competence Creep and General Principles of Law' (2010) 3 *European Administrative Law* 5

——, de Vries, S., and van Eijken, H., 'The principle of attributed powers and the "scope of EU law"' in L.F.M. Besselink, F. Pennings, and S. Prechal (eds.), *The eclipse of the legality principle in the European Union* (Aalphen an den Rijn: Kluwer Law International, 2011), 213

Quine, W.V.O., *Ontological Relativity, and Other Essays* (New York: Columbia University Press, 1969)

Rapaczynski, A., 'From Sovereignty to Process: The Jurisprudence of Federalism after Garcia' (1985) *Supreme Court Review* 341

Reich, N., 'Competition, Competition between Legal Orders: A New Paradigm of EC Law?' (1992) 28 *Common Market Law Review* 861

——, 'Der Common Frame of Reference und Sonderprivatrechte im Europäischen Vertragsrecht' (1997) *Zeitschrift für Europäisches Privatrecht* 161

——, 'A European Contract Law or a European Contract Law Regulation for Consumers?' (2005) 28 *Journal of Consumer Policy* 383

Rhinow, R., Schmid, G., and Biaggini, G., *Öffentliches Wirtschaftsrecht* (Basel: Helbing Lichtenhahn Verlag, 1998)

Riker, W.H., *The Development of American Federalism* (Boston, Dordrecht, Lancaster: Kluwer Academic Publishers, 1987)

Ritleng, D., 'De l'utilité du principe de primauté du droit de l'Union' (2009) 45 *Revue Trimestrielle de Droit Européen Revue Trimestrielle de Droit Européen* 677

——, 'Le droit au respect de l'identité constitutionnelle nationale', in J-C. Barbato and J-D. Mouton (eds.), *Vers la reconnaissance de droits fondamentaux aux Etats membres de l'Union européenne?* (Brussels: Bruylant, 2010), 22

Rodi, M., 'Artikel III–194', in C. Vedder and W. Heintschel von Heinegg (eds.), *Europäischer Verfassungsvertrag, Kommentar* (Baden-Baden: Nomos, 2007), 558

Rosenfeld, M., 'The European Treaty-Constitution and Constitutional Identity: A View from America' (2005) 3 *International Journal of Constitutional Law* 316

Rossi, L.S. 'Does the Lisbon Treaty Provide a Clearer Separation of Competences between EU and Member States?', in A. Biondi, P. Eeckhout, and S. Ripley (eds.), *EU Law after Lisbon* (Oxford: Oxford University Press, 2012), 85

Rossi, P., *Per la Patria Comune—Rapporto de la commissione della Dieta ai ventidue Cantoni sul progetto d'Atto federale da essa deliberato a Lucerna, il 15 dicembre 1832* (Manduria: P. Lacaita, 1997)

Roth, W-H., 'Rechtsetzungskompetenz für das Privatrecht in der Europäischen Union' (2008) *Zeitschrift für Europäisches Wirtschafts- und Steuerrecht* 401

Ruggeri, A., *Gerarchia, competenza e qualità nel sistema costituzionale delle fonti normative* (Milan: Giuffrè, coll. 'Pubblicazioni dell'Istituto di scienze giuridiche, economiche, politiche e sociali della Università di Messina', 1977)

Ruiter, D.W.P., *Institutional Legal Facts. Legal Powers and their Effects* (Dordrecht, Boston and London: Kluwer Academic Publishers, coll. 'Law and Philosophy Library', 1993)

——, 'Legal Powers', in S.L. Paulson and B. Litschewski Paulson (eds.), *Normativity and Norms. Critical Perspectives on Kelsenian Themes* (Oxford: Clarendon Press, 1998), 471

Sabel, C.F. and Zeitlin, J., 'Experimentalist Governance', in D. Levi-Faur (ed.), *The Oxford Handbook of Governance* (Oxford: Oxford University Press, 2011), 169
Sadurski, W., 'European Constitutional Identity?', *EUI Working Paper Law* 2006/33
Sagar, A., 'Les relations fédérales-fédérées. Etude comparative des rapports juridiques fondamentaux dans le contentieux des compétences', PhD thesis in Public Law (University of Rouen, 2013)
Sassen, S., *Territory, Authority, Rights: From Medieval to Global Assemblages* (Princeton, N.J.: Princetown University Press, 2006)
Sawer, G., *Modern Federalism* (Melbourne: Watts, 1969)
Scelle, G., *Précis du droit des gens. Principes et systématiques* (Paris: Libr. De Recueil Sirey, 1932-34)
Schermers, H.G. and O'Keeffe, D. (eds.), *Mixed Agreements* (Deventer and Boston: Kluwer Law and Taxation, 1983)
Schmid, C., *Die Instrumentalisierung des Europäischen Privatrechts durch die Europäische Union* (Baden-Baden: Nomos, 2010)
Schmitt, C., *Constitutional Theory* (Durham: Duke University Press, 2008)
Schulze, R. and Zimmermann, R. (eds.), *Basistexte zum Europäischen Privatrecht: Textsammlung* (Baden-Baden: Nomos, 2000)
Schütze, R., 'Supremacy without pre-emption? The very slowly emergent doctrine of Community pre-emption' (2006) 43 *Common Market Law Review* 1023
——, 'Dual federalism constitutionalized: the emergence of exclusive competences in the EC legal order' (2007) 32 *European Law Review* 3
——, *From Dual to Cooperative Federalism: The Changing Structure of European Law* (Oxford and New York: Oxford University Press, 2009)
——, 'The European Community's Federal Order of Competences: A Retrospective Analysis', in M. Dougan and S. Currie (eds.), *Fifty Years of the European Treaties—Looking back and Thinking Forward* (Oxford and Portland, Or.: Hart, 2009), 63
——, 'Subsidiarity after Lisbon: Reinforcing the Safeguards of Federalism' (2009) 68 *Cambridge Law Journal* 525
——, *European Constitutional Law* (Cambridge and New York: Cambridge University Press, 2012)
Sefton-Green, R., 'How far can we go when using the English language for private law in the EU?' (2012) 8 *European Review of Contract Law* 30
Seidel, M., 'Präventive Rechtsangleichung im Bereich des Gemeinsamen Marktes' (2006) 41 *Europarecht* 26
Shapiro, S., *Federalism: a Dialogue* (Evanston, Ill.: Nortwestern University Press, 1995)
——, 'The Evolution of Cost-Benefit Analysis in US Regulatory Decision-making', *Jerusalem Papers in Regulation and Governance*, Working Paper No 5, May 2010
Shaw, J., 'The Emergence of Postnational Constitutionalism in the European Union', *Archive of European Integration*, available at: <http://aei.pitt.edu/2385/1/002528_1.pdf>
Shuibhne, N.N., 'The Outer Limits of EU Citizenship: Displacing Economic Free Movement Rights?', in C. Barnard and O. Odudu (eds.), *The Outer Limits of European Union Law* (Oxford and Portland, Or.: Hart Publishing, 2009), 167
——, 'Margins of Appreciation: National Values, Fundamental Rights and EC Free Movement Law' (2009) 34 *European Law Review* 230
——, 'The Constitutional Uncertainty of EU Law' (2010) 29 *Yearbook of European Law* 496
Simon, D., *La directive européenne* (Paris: Dalloz, 1997)
Snell, J., 'Economic aims as justification of restrictions on free movement', in A. Schrauwen (ed.), *The Rule of Reason: rethinking another classic of European legal doctrine* (Groningen: Europa Law, 2005), 37

Somek, A., *Individualism. An Essay on the Authority of EU law* (Oxford University Press, 2008)
Spaak, T., *The Concept of Legal Competence. An Essay in Conceptual Analysis*, engl. trans. by R. Carroll (Aldershot: Dartmouth, 1994)
——, 'Explicating the Concept of Legal Competence', in J.C. Hage and D. von der Pfordten (eds.), *Concepts in Law* (Dordrecht, Heidelberg, London and New York: Springer, coll. 'Law and Philosophy Library', Vol. 88, 2009), 67
Spaventa, E., 'Seeing the wood despite the trees? On the scope of Union citizenship and its constitutional effects' (2008) 45 *Common Market Law Review* 13
Stein, E., 'Lawyers, Judges and the Making of a Transnational Constitution' (1981) 75 *American Journal of International Law* 1
——, 'On Divided-Power Systems: Adventures in Comparative Law' (1983) 10 *Legal Issues of Economic Integration* 27
Steindorff, E., *EG-Vertrag und Privatrecht* (Baden-Baden: Nomos, 1996)
Stern, R.L., 'The Commerce Clause and the National Economy, 1933–1946' (1945-46) 59 *Harvard Law Review* 645
Sunstein, C., 'Cost-Benefit Default Principles' (2000-01) 99 *Michigan Law Review* 1651
Supiot, A., *Homo Juridicus. Essai sur la fonction anthropologique du droit* (Paris: Editions du Seuil, 2005; English translation: *Homo Juridicus. On the Anthropological Function of the Law* (London, New York: Verso, 2007)
Svetiev, Y., 'Networked Competition Governance in the EU: Delegation, Decentralisation or Experimentalist Architecture?', in C.F. Sabel and J. Zeitlin (eds.), *Experimentalist Governance in the European Union* (Oxford: Oxford University Press, 2010), 79
Syrpis, P., 'In Defence of Subsidiarity' (2004) 24 *Oxford Journal of Legal Studies* 323
Temple Lang, J., 'European Community Constitutional Law: The Division of Powers between the Community and the Member States' (1988) 39(3) *Northern Ireland Legal Quarterly* 209
Thatcher, M., 'The Commission and national governments as partners: EC regulatory expansion in telecommunications 1979-2000' (2001) 8 *Journal of European Public Policy* 558
Timmermans, C.W.A., 'Division Of External Powers between Community And Member States In The Field Of Harmonization Of National Law—A Case Study' in C.W.A. Timmermans and E.L.M. Völker (eds.), *Division of powers between the European Communities and their Member States in the field of external relations* (Deventer: Kluwer, 1981), 15
——, 'Multilevel Judicial Co-operation' in P. Cardonnel, A. Rosas, and N. Wahl (eds.), *Constitutionalising the EU Judicial System: Essays in Honour of Pernilla Lindh* (Oxford and Portland, Or.: Hart, 2012)
Tizzano, A., 'Quelques observations sur le développement des compétences communautaires' (1989) 48 *Pouvoirs* 81
Tremblay, A., *Le droit constitutionnel. Principes*, 2nd edn (Montréal: Thémis, 2000)
Tribe, L., *American Constitutional Law*, Vol. 1 (New York: Foundation Press, 2000)
Tridimas, T., *The General Principles of EU Law*, 2nd edn (Oxford and New York: Oxford University Press, 2006), 363
Tushnet, M., 'Rethinking the Dormant Commerce Clause' (1979) *Wisconsin Law Review* 125
Tusseau, G., *Les normes d'habilitation*, pref. by M. Troper (Paris: Dalloz, coll. 'Nouvelle bibliothèque de thèses', Vol. 60, 2006)
——, 'Classificazioni', in L. Pegoraro (ed.), *Glossario di Diritto pubblico comparator* (Rome: Carocci, 2009)

——, *Jeremy Bentham. La guerre des mots* (Paris: Dalloz, coll. 'Les sens du droit. Essai', 2011)
Unger, R.M., *What Should Legal Analysis Become?* (London: Verso, 1996)
Usher, J., 'Harmonisation of Legislation', in D. Lasok and others (eds.), *Les Communautés Européennes en Fonctionnement* (Brussels: Bruylant, 1981) 171
Uyttendale, M., *Le fédéralisme inachevé, Réflexions sur le système institutionnel belge issu des réformes de 1988-1989* (Brussels: Bruylant, 1991)
Vedder, H., 'Spontaneous Harmonisation of National Competition Laws in the Wake of the Modernization of EC competition law' (2004) 1 *Competition Law Review* 5
Vignes, D., 'The Harmonisation of National Legislation and the EEC' (1990) 15 *European Law Review* 358
Visser, P.R.S. and Bench-Capon,T.J.M., 'A Comparison of Four Ontologies for the Design of Legal Knowledge Systems' (1998) 6 *Artificial Intelligence and Law* 27
Vogelaar, T., 'The Approximation of the Laws of the Member States under the Treaty of Rome' (1975) 12 *Common Market Law Review* 211
Vogenauer, S. and Weatherill, S., *The Harmonisation of European Contract Law: Implications for European Private Laws, Business and Legal Practice* (Oxford and Portland, Or.: Hart, 2006)
Waelbroeck, M., 'The Emergent Doctrine of Community Pre-emption-Consent and Re-delegation', in T. Sandalow and E. Stein (eds.), *Courts and Free Markets, Perspectives From The United States And Europe*, Vol. II (Oxford: Clarendon Press, and New York: Oxford University Press, 1982), 548
Wagner von Papp, F. 'What if all bid riggers went to prison and nobody noticed? Criminal antitrust law enforcement in Germany', in C. Beaton-Wells and A. Ezrachi (eds.), *Criminalising Cartels: A critical interdisciplinary study of an international regulatory movement* (Oxford: Hart, 2011) 157
Walker, N., 'The Idea of Constitutional Pluralism' (2002) 65 *Modern Law Review* 317
Wang, S., *De la Répartition des compétences dans les constitutions fédérale*, D.Phil thesis (Paris: Jouve, 1920)
Watts, R., 'Comparative Conclusions', in A. Majeed, R. Watts, and D. Brown (eds.), *Dialogues on Distribution of Powers and Responsibilities in Federal Countries* (Montréal: McGill-Queen's University Press, 2006), 322
Weatherill, S., 'Shaping Responsibilities in the Legal Order of the European Community', in H.-W. Micklitz, T. Roethe, and S. Weatherill, *Federalism and Responsibility: a Study on Product Safety and Practice in the European Community* (London and Boston: Graham & Trotman/M. Nijhoff, and Norwel, MA, USA: Kluwer Academic Publishers Group, 1994), 153
——, 'Competence Creep and Competence Control' (2004) 23 *Yearbook of European Law* 1
——, 'European Private Law and the Constitutional Dimension', in F. Cafaggi (ed.), *The Institutional Framework of European Private Law* (Oxford and New York: Oxford University Press, 2006), 81
——, 'The "principles of civil law" as a basis for interpreting the legislative acquis' (2010) *European Review of Contract Law* 74
——, 'The Limits of Legislative Harmonization Ten Years after Tobacco Advertising: How the Court's Case Law has become a "Drafting Guide"' (2011) 12 *German Law Journal* 827
——, 'The Consumer Rights Directive: how and why a quest for "coherence" has (largely) failed' (2012) 49 *Common Market Law Review* 1279
——, 'The Constitutional Context of (Ever-Wider) Policy-Making', in E. Jones, A. Menon, and S. Weatherill (eds.), *The Oxford Handbook of the European Union* (Oxford: Oxford University Press, 2012), 572

Wechsler, H., 'The Political Safeguards of Federalism: the Role of the States in the Composition and Selection of the National Government' (1954) 54 *Columbia Law Review* 543

Weinberger, O., 'Der Erlaubnisbegriff und der Aufbau der Normenlogik' (1973) 5 *Etudes de logique juridique* 113

——, *Normentheorie als Grundlage der Jurisprudenz und Ethik. Eine Auseinandersetzung mit Hans Kelsens Theorie der normen* (Berlin: Duncker & Humblot, 1981)

——, 'The Theory of Legal Dynamics Reconsidered' (1991) 4 *Ratio Juris* 18

——, 'Normological Inferences and the Generation of Legal Norms' (1995) 8 *Ratio Juris* 261

Weiler, J.H.H., 'The Transformation of Europe' (1991) 100 *Yale Law Journal* 403

—— *The Constitution of Europe. 'Do the new clothes have an emperor?' and other essays on European integration* (Cambridge: Cambridge University Press, 1999)

——, 'In Defence of the Status Quo: Europe's Sonderweg', in M. Wind and J.H.H. Weiler, *European Constitutionalism Beyond the State* (Cambridge: Cambridge University Press, 2003), 7

—— and Fries, S.C., 'Une politique des droits de l'homme pour la Communauté et l'Union européenne: la question des compétences', in P. Alston and others (eds.), *L'Union européenne et les droits de l'homme* (Brussels: Bruylant, 2001)

Whittaker, S., 'The Relationship of the Unfair Commercial Practices Directive to European and National Contract Law', in S. Weatherill and U. Bernitz (eds.), *The Regulation of Unfair Commercial Practices under EC Directive 2005/29/EC—New Rules and New Techniques* (Oxford: Hart, 2007), 139

Wilks, S., 'Agency Escape: Decentralization or Dominance of the European Commission in the Modernization of Competition Policy?' (2005) 1 *Governance* 431

——, 'Agencies, Networks, Discourse and the Trajectory of European Competition Enforcement' (2007) 3 *European Competition Journal* 437

Willoughby, W.W., *Principles of the Constitutional Law of the United States*, 2nd edn (New York: Baker, Voorhis & Co., 1930)

Witte, B. de, 'Droit communautaire et valeurs constitutionnelles nationales' (1991) 14 *Droits* 87

——, 'A Competence to Protect: The Pursuit of Non-Market Aims through Internal Market Legislation', in P. Syrpis (ed.), *The Judiciary, the Legislature and the EU Internal Market* (Cambridge, UK and New York: Cambridge University Press, 2011), 25

Wyatt, D., 'Could a "Yellow Card" for National Parliaments Strengthen the Judicial as well as the Political Policing of Subsidiarity?' (2006) 2 *Croatian Yearbook of European Law & Policy* 1

——, 'Community Competence to Regulate the Internal Market' (2007) 9 *Oxford Faculty of Law Research Paper*

——, 'Is the European Union an Organisation of Limited Powers?', in A. Arnull and others (eds.), *A Constitutional Order of States? Essays in EU Law in Honour of Alan Dashwood* (Oxford: Hart Publishing, 2011), 3

——, and Dashwood, A., *Wyatt and Dashwood's European Union Law* (Oxford: Hart, 2011)

Ziller, J., 'Le dialogue judiciaire et la Cour de Karlsruhe—Quelques réflexions à propos du jugement de la Cour constitutionnelle fédérale allemande concernant le Traité de Lisbonne' (2010) 46 *Revue Trimestrielle de Droit Européen* 93

Zimmermann, R., 'Savigny's Legacy: Legal History, Comparative Law, and the Emergence of a European Science' (1996) 112 *Law Quarterly Review* 576

Index